# 21st-Century British Gothic

# 21st-Century British Gothic

*The Monstrous, Spectral, and Uncanny in Contemporary Fiction*

Emily Horton

BLOOMSBURY ACADEMIC
LONDON • NEW YORK • OXFORD • NEW DELHI • SYDNEY

BLOOMSBURY ACADEMIC
Bloomsbury Publishing Plc, 50 Bedford Square, London, WC1B 3DP, UK
Bloomsbury Publishing Inc, 1385 Broadway, New York, NY 10018, USA
Bloomsbury Publishing Ireland, 29 Earlsfort Terrace, Dublin 2, D02 AY28, Ireland

BLOOMSBURY, BLOOMSBURY ACADEMIC and the Diana logo are trademarks
of Bloomsbury Publishing Plc

First published in Great Britain 2024
Paperback edition published in 2025

Copyright © Emily Horton, 2024

Emily Horton has asserted her right under the Copyright, Designs and Patents Act, 1988,
to be identified as Author of this work.

For legal purposes the Acknowledgements on p. ix constitute an extension
of this copyright page.

Cover image by Xochitl Ines Horton Smith

All rights reserved. No part of this publication may be: i) reproduced or transmitted in any form, electronic or mechanical, including photocopying, recording or by means of any information storage or retrieval system without prior permission in writing from the publishers; or ii) used or reproduced in any way for the training, development or operation of artificial intelligence (AI) technologies, including generative AI technologies. The rights holders expressly reserve this publication from the text and data mining exception as per Article 4(3) of the Digital Single Market Directive (EU) 2019/790.

Bloomsbury Publishing Plc does not have any control over, or responsibility for,
any third-party websites referred to or in this book. All internet addresses given
in this book were correct at the time of going to press. The author and publisher
regret any inconvenience caused if addresses have changed or sites have
ceased to exist, but can accept no responsibility for any such changes.

A catalogue record for this book is available from the British Library.

A catalog record for this book is available from the Library of Congress.

Library of Congress Cataloging-in-Publication Data

Names: Horton, Emily, author.
Title: 21st-century British gothic : the monstrous, spectral, and uncanny
in contemporary fiction / Emily Horton.
Description: London ; New York : Bloomsbury Academic, 2024. |
Includes bibliographical references and index.
Identifiers: LCCN 2023040345 (print) | LCCN 2023040346 (ebook) |
ISBN 9781350286566 (hardback) | ISBN 9781350286573 (pdf) | ISBN 9781350286580 (epub)
Subjects: LCSH: Gothic fiction (Literary genre), English–21st century–History and criticism.
Classification: LCC PR830.T3 H68 2024 (print) |
LCC PR830.T3 (ebook) | DDC 813.0872909--dc23/eng/20231205
LC record available at https://lccn.loc.gov/2023040345
LC ebook record available at https://lccn.loc.gov/2023040346

ISBN: HB: 978-1-3502-8656-6
PB: 978-1-3502-8660-3
ePDF: 978-1-3502-8657-3
eBook: 978-1-3502-8658-0

Typeset by RefineCatch Limited, Bungay, Suffolk

For product safety related questions contact productsafety@bloomsbury.com.

To find out more about our authors and books visit www.bloomsbury.com
and sign up for our newsletters.

*For Andrew, Solomon, and Xochitl – with love to my little monsters*

# Contents

Acknowledgements ix

Introduction: 21st-Century British Gothic: The Monstrous, Spectral, and Uncanny in Contemporary Fiction  1

1  Post-9/11 Gothic: The Uncanny and Contemporary Trauma in Pat Barker's *Double Vision* and Patrick McGrath's *Ghost Town*  33

2  Decolonial Gothic: Tropical Terrors and Subterranean Ghosts in Tash Aw's *The Harmony Silk Factory* and Nadeem Aslam's *The Wasted Vigil*  51

3  Gothic Inheritance: Imperial Witchcraft and Haunted Houses in Helen Oyeyemi's *White is for Witching* and Sarah Waters' *The Little Stranger*  69

4  Digital Gothic: Digital Technology, Migration, and the Gothic in Hari Kunzru's *Transmission* and Mohsin Hamid's *Exit West*  93

5  Gothic Homelessness: Spectral Inhabitants and Uncanny Spaces in Ali Smith's *Hotel World*, Trezza Azzopardi's *Remember Me*, and Brian Chikwava's *Harare North*  115

6  The Gothic City: Uncanny Spaces, Historical Spectres, and Monstrous Urbanity in Louise Welsh's *The Cutting Room* and Chloe Aridjis' *Book of Clouds*  139

7  Brexit Gothic: Spectral Illusions and Affect Memories in Sarah Moss' *Ghost Wall* and Niall Griffiths' *Broken Ghost*  161

8  Pandemic Gothic: Childhood Terror and Monstrous Illness in the Fiction of Kazuo Ishiguro and M. R. Carey  177

9  Wet Gothic: Ecofeminism and Horror in Julia Armfield's *Our Wives Under the Sea*, Daisy Johnson's *Fen*, and Zoe Gilbert's *Folk*  197

Bibliography 217
Index 251

# Acknowledgements

I would like to thank a number of people for their advice, inspiration, and encouragement in writing this book. First, thanks to Bloomsbury, and especially Lucy Brown, Aanchal Vij, and Ben Doyle, for their forbearance and consideration in seeing me through what has turned out to be a longer venture than expected. I am also hugely grateful to Merv Honeywood at RefineCatch for his enormous patience and hard work in helping me to edit this.

I can date my interest in the Gothic back to 2008, when I applied to work at the University of Derby, UK, teaching on a module entitled 'Mad, Bad and Dangerous', which turned out to focus on contemporary fiction and film, rather than Byron. It was there that I met Monica Germaná, the module coordinator, whose friendship and conversation ignited my interest in the subject and has sustained it ever since. Thanks Monica, for all that you've done to make the Gothic come alive for me!

This book has had a long gestation, dating back more or less to the end of the above module. Correspondingly, various sections have been published previously in different forms. I would like to thank Sian Adiseshiah, Rupert Hildyard, Katy Shaw, Daniel Weston, Sara Upstone, Peter Ely, and Magali Cornier Michael for their help and support with these publications. I list specific chapters and articles below which I have been granted permission from the publishers to republish here.

The revisions made to these earlier published chapters, as well as the writing of other, new chapters, were made possible largely through my receipt of an Athena Swan Award from Brunel University, without which this book would not have happened. I am so lucky to work in such a supportive institution and to have had the backing of an award designed to celebrate and provide valuable research time to new mothers. What a truly wonderful initiative.

Thanks also to my friends and colleagues at Brunel, who have offered constant insight, reassurance, and guidance in my writing. My boss, Jessica Cox, in particular, is a true gift, not only in her expert knowledge of the subject, but also in her friendship, understanding and patience, as I've balanced my work on this book against other departmental and personal responsibilities. Conversations with and support from my colleagues, and especially Katrina O'Loughlin, Emma

*Acknowledgements*

Filtness, and Janice Guthrie, have also directly shaped my writing in this monograph. Many thanks to all of you.

Some crucial changes to my argument took place following my attendance at the International Gothic Association Conference of 2022, where the excellent presentations offered and the conversations that I had with fellow attendees allowed me to critically rethink my understanding of the genre. Key to this were Michael Gamer, Gina Wisker, Emma McEvoy, Rebecca Duncan, Rune Graulund, and Johan Höglund, all of whom deserve many thanks. I am also endlessly grateful to my friends at the Instituto Español Vicente Cañada Blanch, who have encouraged and supported me on a day-to-day basis – your conversations are my sustenance; thank you so much for keeping me sane!

Lastly, I would like to thank Andrew, Solomon, Xochitl, Grapefruit, Ona, Russell, Mom, Meghan, Stephanie, Amy, Queen Elizabeth (the cat), Louise, James, Chloe, Patricia, and Tom. So much love, both human and feline, is more than anyone deserves; I am truly grateful. Thanks especially to Andrew for being the love of my life and for offering such endless patience and kindness throughout this project – and for always 'trusting but verifying'.

I acknowledge that I have received permission to republish the following in altered forms in this book:
(2009), 'Gothic, Global Berlin: Urban Gothic in Chloe Aridjis' *Book of Clouds*', University of Nottingham Landscape, Space, Place Research Group Website, 9 June. Available at: https://www.nottingham.ac.uk/cas/documents/landscapes/emilyhortonfinal.pdf (accessed 24 August 2023).
(2018), 'A Voice without a Name: Gothic Homelessness in Ali Smith's *Hotel World* and Trezza Azzopardi's *Remember Me*', in S. Adieseshiah and R. Hildyard (eds), *Twenty-First-Century Fiction: What Happens Now*, 132–46, London: Palgrave Macmillan.
(2018), 'The Queer Gothic Spaces of Contemporary Glasgow: Louise Welsh's *The Cutting Room*', in M. C. Michael (ed.), *Twenty-First-Century British Fiction and the City*, 181–204, London: Palgrave Macmillan.
(2019), '21st Century Trauma and the Uncanny: A Gothic Reading of Trauma in Pat Barker's *Double Vision*', *C21 Literature: A Journal of 21st-Century Writings*, 7 (1): 1–22.

# Introduction

# 21st-Century British Gothic

## The Monstrous, Spectral, and Uncanny in Contemporary Fiction

Monstrous and contaminating, spectral and hidden, defined by apocalyptic moments of extreme and excessive emotion, by damaged and infested landscapes, and by uncanny and abject encounters with illness and death, the twenty-first-century embodies the Gothic from its very beginnings with the YK2 'bug' to the more viscerally diseased and horrific COVID-19 pandemic, from the terror of 9/11, to the separation of families at the US–Mexico border, to the brutal murder of George Floyd in police hands and the ongoing wars in Syria, Sudan, Gaza, and the Ukraine. The heavily militarized 'War on Terror' initiated by US President George W. Bush and UK Prime Minister Tony Blair's administrations; the equally demonizing 'Migrant Crisis' and its Islamophobic and Latinophobic rhetoric; the destructive invisibility of environmental 'slow violence' brought about by Western industrial relocations (Nixon 2011), as well as the more visible and heavily mediated catastrophes represented by recent tsunamis, earthquakes, and wildfires; and the wide-ranging shift to far-right politics across the globe: all speak to a Gothic experience of twenty-first-century life.

In Britain, this Gothic scenario is also readily visible across the previous two decades, connected, for example, to a boding territorial and social fracture accompanying several national referendums, ongoing tensions in Northern Ireland, as well as the UK's actual exit from the European Union in 2020. Equally if not more horrific are the local minority experiences of fear and discrimination provoked by right-wing rhetoric surrounding this latter event, as well as by Teresa May's 2012 'hostile environment' policy and the 2018 Windrush scandal. Colin Yeo, in examining Home Office immigration statistics since 2009, notes that Britain 'is detaining around 25,000 people per year', with this figure rising above 32,000 in 2015, in connection with the Syrian refugee crisis (Yeo 2020, 234). These disturbing figures are accompanied economically by the shocking losses and inequalities resulting from the 2008 financial crisis, only further heightened by Britain's ongoing austerity government and its policy of protecting the banking sector at the cost of 'the poorest and most vulnerable' (Blake and Monnet 2017, 5). Within this context, events such as the Grenfell Tower fire represent governmental irresponsibility in extreme, where this was caused by corporate mismanagement itself tied to hostile austerity measures (see Walker 2017; Bulman 2019). More generally, as Kerry-Anne Mendoza reflects, Britain now negotiates what might be considered a 'zombie economy', characterized by increasing financialization of public services, and by their unthinking dismantling, or 'defecating', when these are deemed unprofitable (2015, 21–7).

On the one hand, these events and policies in their media representation often specifically draw on conservative discourses of violence and hatred, in this way figuring the Gothic negatively, in reactionary terms. As the chapter in this book on 'Brexit Gothic' indexes, Conservative, Leave-voting politicians in the build-up to Britain's Brexit referendum in 2016 negotiated monster narratives reminiscent of *Dracula* to stigmatize migrants, while Chapter 5 records how scare-mongering UK broadsheets, seeking to promote increased surveillance and policing, categorize the homeless as drug-addicted 'zombies' invading British cities.[1] As Linnie Blake and Agnieszka Soltysik Monnet summarize, 'the gothic is no stranger to regressive attitudes to gender, ethnicity and class, after all. And gothic texts can reveal the hidden tensions of the societies that produced them without proffering any attempt at formulating a solution' (2017, 3). Indeed, Blake and Monnet's study on the *Neoliberal Gothic* attests to both the radical critical potential of this long-enduring creative modality and to the multiple instances of complacency and co-optation rife within its contemporary deployment, as some recent Gothic films and novels proffer 'no way out of the political uncertainty and economic instability of the present beyond the promotion of a "kinder" form of capitalism that is capitalism nonetheless' (2017, 8). Here, Gothic art, literature, and culture betrays a certain investment in global capitalist world-systems, seeking out strategies, sometimes notably dubious, to consolidate 'its position as the material of mainstream entertainment' (Spooner 2006, 25).

Nevertheless, as these critics also recognize, various innovative national cultural productions, both popular and 'high cultural' in status, can also be seen to oppose this hegemonic investment, appropriating Gothic themes, modalities, and narratives precisely to contest these discriminatory outlooks, reaffirming the ignored humanity of oppressed minority lives. More centrally, the Gothic, as it appears in *some* significant twenty-first-century British literary enactments emerges as a challenge to received conservative and market-driven thinking, countering the dominant networks of neocolonial and neoliberal power in favour of more decolonial, feminist, queer, and planetary perspectives. In this book, I seek to explore this latter outlook, more specifically in the context of twenty-first-century British Gothic fiction, a category which, as this study attests, has widely expanded beyond its previous national, cultural, and generic contours, reconceiving the meaning both of 'the British' and 'the Gothic' in new, unorthodox ways.

More centrally, the idea of 'Britishness' for these writers is shown to be intertwined with transnational and migratory movements, as these texts explore 'globalgothic' insecurity, paranoia, and abjection connected to 'the unnerving, unpredictable and uncontrollable scale of world changes' (Botting and Edwards 2013, 13), but also as they interrogate ongoing and still violent legacies of (neo) colonial governance, and as they position Britain politically in relation to this history. The Gothic as conceived by these novels moves critically across a range of colonial and neocolonial histories, disturbing received narratives of imperial, metropolitan, and patriarchal valour, and navigating the monstrous, spectral, and uncanny facets of twenty-first-century life. Following this reading, contemporary British Gothic stands out, in particular, for its refusal of uncritical utopianism and empty sentiment, instead favouring a materialist ideological engagement with sociopolitical critique.

The changing ethnic and cultural make-up of Britain itself is significant within this development, as the Gothic is generally thought to have begun in an eighteenth-century already deeply entangled in the colonial project, 'born out of the immediate reaction to Enlightenment rationalism' and its humanist and Eurocentric ideals (Heise-von der Lippe 2017, 3). As Fred Botting writes, 'Gothic signified an over-abundance of imaginative frenzy, untamed by reason and unrestrained by conventional eighteenth-century demands for simplicity, realism or probability'; its uncertainties 'linked to wider threats of disintegration manifested most forcefully in political revolution' (Botting 1996, 3, 5). More precisely, as Lucy Armitt explains, the origins of the Gothic are commonly located in a 'specific, but small, group of writers, thinkers and painters (Horace Walpole (1717–97), Edmund Burke (1729–97), Clara Reeve (1729–1807), Henry Fuseli (1741–1825), (Mrs) Ann Radcliffe (1764–1823), and Matthew Lewis (1775–1818), all engaging with similar cultural and literary questions in work spanning broadly the years 1750–1820' (2011, 2). As critics such as Michael Gamer, Jim Watts, Rob Miles, and Emma Cleary have made clear, this early Gothic artistry was received by British readers as both titillating and threatening, representing a visible challenge to received social and political mores and cultural biases, even as its sublime and terror-inspiring aesthetics mirrored the extreme emotions of a revolutionary era. As Gamer explains, in a genre widely understood as 'culturally invasive, morally corrupting, and politically jacobin', Romantic writers faced the dilemma of 'how to tap gothic's exploding popular readership while neither corrupting that readership, nor exciting the ire of reviewers' (Gamer 2000, 144–5, 102). They crafted their writing precisely in response to the Gothic's scandalous and equivocal reception, feeding on a conflicted cultural zeitgeist that whispered for more.

Watts indexes the early Gothic's evocation of panic amongst mainstream readers and audiences, as it 'betrayed the fears and the anxieties of the middle classes about the nature of their ascendency, returning to the issues of ancestry, inheritance and the transmission of property' (1999, 2). Within this incipient industrial capitalist context, as David Punter also reflects, 'it is hardly surprising to find the emergence of a literature whose key motifs are paranoia, manipulation, and injustice, and whose central project is understanding the inexplicable, the taboo, the irrational' (1996, 127; Watts 1999, 2). In effect, all of these concerns replicate the pervasive contradictions of late eighteenth-century Europe, mirroring its ambivalent entrance into an inchoate capitalist world system.

This ground-breaking influence and simultaneous uncertain cultural status set the stage for a highly contested national literary oeuvre, situating the Gothic as a transgressive mode of literary and artistic expression, especially attentive to modernity's incongruities and paradoxes. This is visible across Romantic, Victorian, and twentieth-century literary periods: in the villainous family histories of Radcliffe and Lewis; the uncanny and labyrinthine cities of Dickens and Collins; Stoker and Wilde's 'degenerate' monsters; and Carter and Tennant's postmodern Gothic retellings. Indeed, as Kelly Hurley writes, the Gothic is 'a cyclical genre that re-emerges in times of cultural stress in order to negotiate anxieties for its readership by working through them in displaced (sometimes supernaturalized) form' (2002, 194). Registering this cyclicality, and the recurring importance of a Gothic past, this study indexes significant intertextual voices and shared creative strategies from across these earlier periods relevant to the twenty-first-century Gothic, as well as ongoing influences of older themes and forms. In particular, the Victorian period stands out as a favoured source of inspiration in many of these works, where, as Catherine Spooner writes, this age's perceived taboos and insecurities make it representative of 'the repressed material of modernity' and of the modes that modernity finds 'to discipline and control us' (2007, 44).

Before going on to explore these influences, however, I would underline how 'postmillennial Gothic' studies, such as Glennis Byron's *Globalgothic* and Maisha Wester and Xavier Aldana Reyes' *Twenty-First-Century Gothic*, note how different, *non-European* inceptions of the genre are also conceivable apart from these European-based studies, where 'responses to modernity similar to what the West has named Gothic have emerged elsewhere, even if differently modulated by other historical and cultural conditions' (Byron 2015a, 370) and where 'postcolonial and Ethnogothic authors utilise tropes of monstrosity, decay and contamination to cast the West as an alien' (Wester and Aldana Reyes 2021, 12). Indeed, Wai Chee Dimock suggests that such comparative genre-oriented readings more largely, as opposed to 'traditional historical and geographical compartmentalisations of literary studies', allow for a broader understanding of literary origins and innovations, where texts can be 'understood to be prenational in their evolutionary past and transnational in their geographic spread', thus challenging nation-centred approaches to the discipline (Dimock 2007, 1382–3). While this study focuses specifically on the British Gothic, in this way seemingly reaffirming older nation-oriented perspectives, nevertheless, this appreciation of the Gothic's pre- and transnational longevity informs my analysis at a critical level, where decolonial, intersectional, and planetary viewpoints familiar to world literary thinking shape my Gothic reading, and where likewise, traditional nation-centred understandings of both Britain and the Gothic are therein contested.

Against Sarah Brouillette's well known dismissal of world literature as a 'niche category serving relatively elite consumers' desires to be exposed to [the] exotic' (Brouillette 2017, n.p.), my point in reading the twenty-first-century British Gothic within this world-literary framework is precisely to underline its largescale political urgency, as a modality equipped to challenge both nationalist biases and transnational oppressions. In a contemporary context of widespread migration, in which British identity and belonging take on sometimes radical new meanings, and in which British-born writers and artists often choose to live elsewhere or to situate their stories in opposition to British colonial and neocolonial histories, these supposedly peripheral and anti-hegemonic responses to the genre can be seen to filter into twenty-first-century British writing, reconfiguring its established tropes and narratives in poignant and complex ways. Put differently, twenty-first-century British Gothic, as it again appears in some significant texts, responds not only to the gaps in traditional (secular, rationalist) accounts of the genre, but also to subsequent, more transgressive, but still largely European-centred readings, reaffirming instead the wealth of contestatory perspectives arising out of Britain and of British-based Gothic fiction today, especially as connected to decolonial, feminist, queer, and ecocritical thinking. As Nira Yuval-Davis notes, Britain itself can no longer be understood in terms of a pre-designated '"essence" of Britishness', but instead reflects how 'global and territorial spaces coexist and interrelate in complex fashions', prompting 'an increasing blurring of the line for "insiders – [vs] outsiders"' (2011, 25, 28, 39). In a similar way, twenty-first-century British Gothic expressly navigates this changing national and international landscape, reinterpreting its resistance to borders and boundaries in terms of Gothic shifts and disruptions, which reveal the supposedly uncanny and monstrous 'Other' as a part of the national self.

This recognition of the Gothic's multiple, transnational lineages and migratory outlooks, positioning the modality across a range of cultural contexts and geopolitical anxieties – and also recognizing how such diverse genealogies and perspectives often directly contradict Enlightenment positivism – underpins one central strand of this analysis, where writers such as Nadeem Aslam, Hari Kunzru, Tash Aw, Helen Oyeyemi, Brian Chikwava, Mohsin Hamid, Chloe Aridjis, and Kazuo Ishiguro can all be read to navigate anti-Eurocentric approaches, resituating this supposedly 'British' modality in complex, unexpected ways. These writers not only challenge traditional, white supremacist, and nationalist understandings of British identity through their own personal backgrounds as (first- and second-generation) migrant British residents and citizens, but also bring this challenge to Gothic narratives directly opposing ongoing Western (neo)colonialism, and in many cases, presenting empowered, empathic, and resistant 'Otherness' through sympathetic monsters and resilient ghosts: figures who stand in for an altered conception of contemporary belonging. This can be seen, for example, in Nadeem Aslam's haunting genies in *The Wasted Vigil* (2008), who invoke a deep time approach to Afghanistan's precolonial past, as well as in the disappearing phantoms of Tash Aw's Gothic Malaysia in *The Harmony Silk Factory* (2005), the uncontainable digital virus of Hari Kunzru's *Transmission* (2004), and the uncanny clones and robots of Kazuo Ishiguro's *Never Let Me Go* (2005) and *Klara and the Sun* (2021). In each case, these unwanted, 'strange' Gothic creatures present an alternative outlook on colonialist and xenophobic practices, reinforcing the value of the monstrous in uncovering and unsettling empire.

Moreover, the decentring of the colonial metropole emerges not only in fictions informed by diasporic backgrounds and alternative readings of the Gothic, but also through devolutionary perspectives and peripheral localities within Britain itself, as in the northern English settings of Pat Barker and Sarah Moss, the rural Norfolk of Trezza Azzopardi and Daisy Johnson, Niall Griffiths' Welsh countryside, Helen Oyeyemi's Dover, Louise Welsh's Glasgow, and Zoe Gilbert's folk horror rereading of the Isle of Man as 'Neverness'. Across these outlying and circumferential settings, the Gothic at once mediates local fears and anxieties tied to an increasingly globalized and marketized world, and also responds to and contests received global capitalist outlooks and preconceptions, reaffirming more critical perspectives on twenty-first-century life, and on the haunting and monstrosity of contemporary inequality and violence. This Gothic mixture of scales and perspectives sees the modality recognizing and responding to British contemporary history in unexpected ways, and to Britain's changing position within a transnational arena, reinforcing both 'the power of the centre to comprehend and contain that which it perceives and constructs as Other', but also 'the uncanniness of the periphery' in finding ways to evade this (Hughes 2018, 6).

Wester and Aldana Reyes explain how this British or British-based engagement with the Gothic can be witnessed in a widespread institutional investment throughout the UK, stretching through a range of cultural forms and modalities which repeatedly see the Gothic as 'linked to important notions of national identity' (2021, 2), whilst also questioning and reframing these in innovative ways. This is visible, for example, in Britain's central role in founding world-leading Gothic research centres, including the international Gothic research network Haunted Shores, 'Manchester Centre for Gothic Studies, the Centre for the History of the Gothic at Sheffield University and the International Centre for Gothic Studies at Stirling' (ibid., 2), as well as in numerous international Gothic critical series based in national presses. Events such as the British Film Institute's influential 2013–14 film season, *Gothic: The Dark Heart of Film*; the British Library's ground-breaking 2014–15 exhibition *Terror and Wonder: The Gothic Imagination*; and the V&A's current, extensive collection *The Rise of the Gothic*, all speak to a national embrace of the Gothic as a vehicle for exploring British history, identity, and culture and for remapping the darker elements of the national psyche (Wester and Aldana Reyes 2021, 2). Add to these Leeds' *Goth City* event in 2016, the annual *Whitby Goth Weekend*, the *Infest* music festival in Bradford, Swansea's regular *Dead of Night* event, as well as iconic Gothic venues such as Slimelight in London, Satan's Hollow in Manchester, the Jekyll & Hyde Pub in Edinburgh (1998–2016), and the pervasive centrality of this contemporary cultural modality is unmistakable.[2]

On the one hand, this (sub)cultural explosion of the Gothic across the UK may in itself be perceived as reason to pursue this study of recent fiction: a ready invitation to explore the modality's literary-critical pertinence to contemporary British life, and to question how this speaks to a specifically twenty-first-century era. As Wester and Aldana Reyes write, 'the Gothic has moved beyond initial debates about its respectability, anachronistic nature and staying power and is now firmly rooted in the imaginations of readers and those responsible for marketing campaigns and educational programmes', thus requiring scrutiny as means to 'demarcating [its] limits' within the contemporary (Wester and Aldana Reyes 2021, 2). Similarly, Lorna Piatti-Farnell and Donna Lee Brien draw attention to the Gothic's ability 'to adapt and remould itself' across contemporary forms and media, seeing this flexibility as offering a 'compass' on post-millennial life, especially where these genre 're-elaborations' register 'interdependent connections between the literary, cultural, and transnational' (2015, 1, 6). In both accounts, these critics celebrate the Gothic's now institutionally recognized and cross-disciplinary integration within contemporary culture, suggesting perhaps a nominative solution to earlier (now defunct) concerns about the genre as disreputable, reactionary, or simply 'not worth reading' (Sedgwick 1980, 1).

Even so, as Alexandra Warwick argues, the much-lauded ubiquity of the Gothic within the contemporary can also be seen to warrant scepticism in evading precise definition, registering 'not necessarily' the text, but more properly the contemporary critics' wont to 'feel gothicky' (Warwick 2007, 9, 7). As Warwick explains, 'the dominance of Gothic as a critical category is an effect of the aftershock of deconstruction, of the move to an apparently anti-scientific criticism that circulates around the problem of subject/object relations' (Warwick 2007, 9). She continues:

> The problem for Gothic studies, or the reason for the remorseless expansion of the field, is that the subject/object confusion still remains. Gothic criticism pretends that Gothic is inherent in its object and thus the relation between criticism and literature returns to being one of transparency and objectivity in which the texts themselves are coerced into becoming allegories of Gothic critical practice. (Ibid., 9)

In other words, following deconstruction's negotiation of a Gothic, and specifically spectral, vocabulary to navigate poststructuralist ideas of textual subversion and linguistic free-play, the modality becomes suddenly ubiquitous, defined by ghostly 'traces' of textual meaning that nevertheless can be found virtually anywhere and that fail to register specifically Gothic denotations. As Warwick summarizes, 'simultaneously that which haunts and that which is haunted, it is both meaning and text', and therefore potentially 'useless as an interpretive framework, simply because it is so large as to be meaningless' (Warwick 2007, 8). Such a viewpoint threatens to challenge the value of *yet another* contemporary Gothic critical monograph, or at least to suggest limits on what this can or should include: rejecting, in particular, additional deconstructive readings of the genre.

On a related note, Fred Botting writes of how a widespread *domestication* of the Gothic within contemporary postmodern culture also contributes to undermining its critical importance, as its modalities 'collude with the norms they once negatively defined', in such a way as to render '[i]dentity and difference [...] indistinguishable in a proliferation of differentiations and hybrids' (Botting 2011, 10, 11). Within this context, transgression becomes inculcated into the norm and in this way inoculated of its disruptive power: 'Difference and otherness, too, are absorbed in the serial circulations of the same, a flat plane of indifference, the monstrosity of norms' (ibid., 10). In other words, the 'Disneyfication' of Gothic tropes within the contemporary potentially upsets the genre's countercultural exertions, as the Gothic becomes, in Maria Beville's words, 'a buzz-word in literature and culture': its trendiness raising questions regarding its critical and creative heft (Beville 2009, 7).

This preoccupation can indeed be taken further to encompass not simply deconstructive vagaries or the Gothic's modishness in recent literary-critical readings, but also an anxiety regarding the Gothic's engagement with postcolonial thinking more specifically, keeping in mind a late-twentieth-century interconnection between genre writing, postmodernism, and postcolonialism. Rebecca Duncan introduces this concern when she writes that 'postcolonial Gothic does not only interrogate colonial narratives. Rather, it drives at the deeper possibility that narrative in all its forms – and by extension representation – is unavoidably doomed to fail' (2022, 308). Here, the radical relativity of truth under a postmodern critical framework threatens to undermine the postcolonial Gothic's truth claims, instituting ambiguity at the heart of all textual representation. Duncan quotes Neil Lazarus in his ironic summary of postmodern incredulity, where: '[t]he desire to speak for, of, or even *about* others, is always shadowed – or perhaps overdetermined – by a secretly or latently authoritarian aspiration', this making it impossible to speak definitively regarding material relations (Duncan 2022, 309; Lazarus 2011, 146). Andrew Smith likewise reiterates this concern when he draws attention a postcolonial fascination with 'the idea that cultural facts and values are mutable', reinforcing a perceived 'relativity' underpinning critical thinking (2004, 248). From this perspective, he explains, 'political action becomes awkward [...] partly because it would be hard to find the basis on which to judge the validity of any particular stance': protest loses its command due to truth's supposed provisionality (ibid., 248).

In order to avoid this critical pitfall, while also evading a reverse tendency to over-define and mechanize the Gothic, this study seeks to prioritize the modality's relevance to contemporary life and politics *over* oblique textual 'traces' or critical ambiguities, rejecting a deconstructive proclivity to highlight lost or covert meanings ahead of lived experiences. Borrowing John Fletcher's words, I seek not to over-valorize 'haunting in the act of linguistic expression' (2013, 8). Moreover, if a resurgence of scholarly interest in the Gothic is often situated in the 1980s and 1990s, largely in connection with a postmodern and post-structuralist mode of critical thinking – as in the ground-breaking work of Punter (1980); Baldick (1992); Sage and Smith (1996); Botting (1996); and Hogle (1997) – this analysis aims to move beyond this theoretical imperative to engage with the Gothic as a materialist and decolonial mode of social and political analysis, especially attentive to the lived and felt experience of twenty-first-century life (and to colonialism's *still ongoing* violent legacy within this). As Duncan emphasizes, 'concepts drawn from decolonial thinking offer a different entry point to Gothic's engagement with enduring colonial power' (Duncan 2022, 305). In particular, they exchange a focus on representational scepticism with materialist critique and historical specificity. By accentuating this outlook, weaving it into my textual readings, I hope to underline the twenty-first-century Gothic's ideological repositioning: moving away from postmodern scepticism towards material awareness.

Two connected methodological anxieties inform this analysis: firstly, in agreement with a burgeoning (materialist) affect theory gradually being woven into contemporary Gothic and Horror studies (see, for example, Hogle 2010; Davis 2013; Aldana Reyes 2015, 2018), I am interested in the bodily and affective dimensions of the Gothic *as much as* the more conceptual and cognitive aspects of its representation, seeing these as the emotional and physiological basis upon which the Gothic *makes its impact felt*. As Aldana Reyes writes,

> the affective approach takes into account [...] how a novel or a film creates a sense of dread but also how, at a more complex level, the images on screen or the words on the page may be transmuted into specific corporeal and emotive reactions by those who engage with them. [... It] is not predominantly preoccupied with whether something is actually scary but rather with the conventions followed by a genre or mode in the hope that it will be. (2015, 16)

Put differently, an affective reading celebrates creative tactics that disturb and unsettle readers' feelings – generating unease in the hope of provoking critique and/or action.

The importance of this platform for my analysis lies centrally in its acknowledgement of readerly sentiment, and correspondingly, in this writing's strategic potential not only to upset, but also, intervene. As Pheng Cheah writes, one defining aspect of world literature concerns its status as an 'active process in the world', as a form of writing that 'seeks to be disseminated, read, and received around the world so as to change that world and the life of a given people within it' (2016, 36). Accordingly, in paying attention to affect, my contention is that the twenty-first-century British Gothic becomes world literature precisely by attending to readers' feelings and fears: playing on repressed anxieties and desires, as well as worries about collusion and complicity, which may in turn spark shock, horror, and reassessment. As Jerrold Hogle writes, 'the Gothic [...] *is about* the conflicted "social unconscious" of modernity even when it reappears within what many critics now regard as post-modernity' (2014a, 9, my italics). In what can be considered a post-postmodern period, the Gothic continues to toy with readers' thoughts and feelings to *impact* and to catalyze reassessment.

Equally important to this reading is my second aim: to highlight this writing's politicized, anti-capitalist critical orientation, which moves beyond postmodern textual politics to (again) take into consideration key material factors shaping contemporary inequality. Drawing further attention (alongside Duncan) to the critical, decolonial writing of Neil Lazarus, Andrew Smith, Jason Moore, and Simon During, I underline a fundamental concern elaborated by these theorists that the era in which we live is not simply transnational, but also neocolonial and, as Moore (2016) puts it, 'Capitalocene': organized by an ongoing global capitalist imperialism that is at once exploitative and dehumanizing, affecting as much the non-or extra-human and planetary as it is the human in its structural violence. Alongside these theorists and their recent Gothic readers, including Duncan (2018; 2022); Timothy Morton (2016); Pramod Nayar (2019); and Justin D. Edwards, Rune Graulund, and Johan Höglund (2022), I suggest that this understanding itself requires a critical re-reading of contemporary British Gothic literature: not simply as conceptually dystopian, terrifying or paralysing in its reflection of Capitalocene destruction, but also, and equally centrally, *potentially revelatory*, allowing for a timely reconceptualization of present cultural modalities and practices.

In its (unusual) hopefulness and in its critical specificity, this argument demands some elaboration, specifically to identify key theoretical anxieties driving its politicized reading. On the one hand, regarding the affective and physical violence of the present neocolonial predicament, Moore comments on twenty-first-century politics' embattled and predatory expression, where 'the tendency towards militarized accumulation, and its gravitational influence in world accumulation, has accelerated in recent decades' (2022, n.p.), moving global society more rapidly towards radical inequality and planetary destruction. 'Since the 1970s,' he affirms, 'the expansion of a permanent war economy – including America's Forever Wars [in the Middle East and South Asia] – has gone hand-in-hand with a pathological and predatory financialization', in this way bringing about the 'epochal crisis' in which we now live (ibid.). This mode of armed and mobilized profiteering within former colonial nations, and more widely, within a global South aligned to both cheap labour and 'Cheap Nature', situates the supposed progressivism of global capitalist modes of governance (as declared, for example, by Frances Fukuyama) as distinctly unfounded. As Moore explains, 'Capital's real basis – even and especially [for] highly abstract forms of wealth, like crypto-currencies – depends upon very material worlds. They are claims upon anticipated wealth flowing from what Marx called "the soil and the worker"' (Moore 2022, n.p.).

Said differently, contemporary neocolonial oppression cannot be understood as merely ideological nor either post-industrial, but instead encompasses distinctly material processes and uneven modes of development, which impact most forcefully on minority, migrant, and global Southern communities and geographies. These include, amongst other events, the seemingly never-ending conflicts across Iraq, Syria, and Afghanistan; militarized border policing and aggressive deportation across the West; torture; an ongoing proliferation of global Southern sweatshops; black-market organ donation; unethical pharmaceutical testing; trafficked and slave labour; oceanic pollution and exploitation; deforestation; and the displacement of indigenous communities, many of which concerns are explored either directly or indirectly in the fictions examined here. This horrific situation is further amplified in a world in which, according to a recent UNICEF estimate, '52 million children under the age of five will die by 2030, largely of preventable causes,' and in which, as Adam Trexler writes, 'inadequate water supplies, malnutrition, diarrheal diseases, and infectious diseases will become more common' (2015, 2). Accordingly, these Gothic texts' attention to ongoing and neocolonial subjugation, and to the *normalization* of such under the guise of neoliberal individualism, underlies their prescient artistic and critical value, as they viscerally contemplate global capital's flexible and decentred movement within the contemporary and its participation in what

Sayak Valencia describes as 'gore capitalism', defined by 'incredibly brutal kinds of violence' apprehended 'as tools of *necroempowerment*' (Valencia 2018, 20).

For Simon During, as for Moore and Valencia, this exploitative programme carries forward a distinctly colonial political-economic system and ideology, wherein 'the politics of subalternity [are] largely absorbed into the machinery of emergent neoliberal state capitalism', in this way at once continuing and refiguring colonialism's violence within a contemporary transnational context (During 2015, 19). As During explains, this uneven experience results from 'new, more extensive and less visible patterns of global dispossession [...] currently] gaining ground', wherein 'relatively geographically and culturally stable relations of dominance and subordination are being replaced by relatively unstable and dispersed conditions of deprivation and insecurity' (ibid.): in other words, where conditions of socioeconomic precarity are coming to replace stable working environments and climatic relations. Within this flexiblized and unpredictable conjecture, 'intimations of imperilment are extended more widely across various societies in a situation where global social insecurity is backed by planetary ecological insecurity' (ibid., 19). More basically, both human and extra-human life is exposed to extreme vulnerability and threat, creating a dark shadow over questions of mental and bodily health, social welfare, and community solidarity, as well as planetary well-being and sustainability.

Reflecting this combination of abstract and material socioeconomic processes, of both perceived and tangibly lived planetary conditions, a dialectic between the material and immaterial is visible across these world-attentive Gothic fictions, in their diverse confrontations with twenty-first-century life as uneven and precarious. The immaterial dimensions of this textual conjecture emerge in part from attention to technological virtuality and corporate business – for example, in the spectral and viral networks that Hari Kunzru charts in *Transmission*, as well as in the unseen (but very real) migratory movements of Mohsin Hamid's *Exit West* (2017). The privatized and marketed urban centres of Ali Smith's *Hotel World* (2001), Louise Welsh's *The Cutting Room* (2002), and Chloe Ardjis' *Book of Clouds* (2009) also register invisible processes of global capitalist exploitation and cruelty, though equally important is a recognition of neoliberalism's now widely accepted and *taken-for-granted* regulation of daily life, which further extends the violent but usually disguised mechanisms of Western neocolonial power. As Rosemary Hennessy writes, 'intimacy, sexuality, the personal – that is the realm of "private" – are being used in the formation of a new bourgeois hegemonic block that is the outcome of late capitalism's structural changes', and this situation leads to a systematic state-regimenting of social behaviours (2017, 225). Within this predicament, what Justin D. Edwards, Rune Graulund, and Johan Höglund write about climate change is also poignantly true of global capitalism more largely, namely, that 'it cannot always be seen, but it is always there in a liminal and uncanny presence', even as its oppressive effects are also 'frighteningly literal' and darkly monstrous (Edwards, Graulund, and Höglund 2022, xii–xiv). Fred Botting also comments on how 'what was unseen, unthought, or unrecognized now tests the limits and thresholds of visibility, thinking, and knowing', as global capitalism's uncanny violence erupts in unpredicted disturbances and environmental catastrophes (2022, 316).

This said, it should be stressed that the fiction examined in this book is often equally concerned with mundane experiences situated in the global North, such that these above studies' emphasis on global Southern inequality and neocolonial governance is also extended to acknowledge the 'developed' world's own simultaneous labour and planetary oppression and exploitation, as well as that of migrant identities and communities established in the global North (see also Scully 2016). Reflecting on neoliberal deregulation of the global job market, Moore notes how 'white collar' workers, previously having been '[bought] off' by capitalist leaders, are 'progressively rendered surplus to requirements, in process discovering their real class position, if not always their class interests' (2022, 3). The fear implied by this subordinate clause is that workers will be (and have been) swayed by populist rhetoric to 'align with the ethno-nationalist right' against transnational elites, in this way undercutting collective organization and class solidarity across racial and gender divides (ibid., 3–4). Put differently, the rise in far-right politics, as manifested in the election of Trump in America and the event of Brexit in Britain, overtly reinforces a Gothic global capitalist capacity to undermine opposition, as also witnessed in the 'Brexit Gothic' writing of Sarah Moss' *Ghost Wall* (2018) and Niall Griffiths' *Broken Ghost* (2019), and in the 'Pandemic Gothic' of M. R. Carey's *The Girl with All the Gifts* (2014) and Ishiguro's *Klara and the Sun*. In each case, the increasingly reactionary direction of contemporary Western government and society is overtly and Gothically construed, with stark implications both for minority communities and the earth itself.

Moreover, as the above studies attest, the planet's role in this experience is often overtly misconceived and misconstrued, as governments and businesses eager to escape responsibility for the systematic destruction of human and extra-human life strategically position this guilt in the hands of a supposedly predatory ecosystem. As Johan Höglund explains, 'the climate crisis is not merely folded into precarity as yet another stimulant of vulnerability. [Rather,] a growing body of humanities and social sciences scholarship claims that the climate crisis and precarity share material histories, so that the climate emergency arises from the same capitalist record as precarity' (2020). Rob Nixon's now widely recognized notion of global capitalist 'slow violence' (2011) helps to encapsulate this interconnected experience, as systematically aggressive, but often invisible destruction is seen to incorporate both human and non-human communities, situating the planet, and populations living in an exploited developing world, as confronting ever greater insecurity and peril. Theorists such as Moore (2016; 2017), Andreas Malm and Alf Hornborg (2014), and Chakrabarty (2009) all echo this materialist ecocritical standpoint, underlining the central role of global capitalism in driving planetary destruction, in this way (implicitly or explicitly) exchanging the concept of the Anthropocene for that of the Capitalocene.

The fictions I explore in this book confront this Gothic experience directly and candidly, as they highlight overlapping planetary disasters, neocolonial erasures and patriarchal subjugations still continuing within the present day, and as they negotiate a Gothic perception of twenty-first-century life bound up with increasing precarity, fear, and horror. Three central modalities in which this confrontation occurs, as indicated by the subtitle of this monograph, include the monstrous, the spectral, and the uncanny. In what follows, I consider each of these categories in more detail and examine their particular relevance to twenty-first-century life, in this way elaborating the aesthetic and critical framework underpinning my readings.

## The Monstrous

Starting with the first of these categories: the monstrous manifests in numerous British cultural and literary engagements across the twenty-first-century, encompassing mainstream *and* 'gore' capitalism's excess brutality and exploitation; horrific and terrifying deformations enacted on the planet; physical and affective distortions authorized in the name of security and freedom; and abject bodies, both human and extra-human, offering testament to contemporary cruelty, destruction, and viciousness. Within this context, monsters become what Wester and Aldana Reyes identify as 'one of [the Gothic's] most important markers' of our times, representing contrasting meanings, both 'discriminatory' and 'sympathetic', both inviting and repellent (Wester and Aldana Reyes 2021, 5–6). As Ana María Mutis writes, the word 'monster' itself 'derives from the Latin *monere*, meaning "to warn," and from *monstrare*, meaning "to show." The monster is a construction designed to reveal and warn, and its marginal, transgressive, and anomalous nature has been used to interrogate and perturb the status quo' (2020, 45). It is a figure of presage, as well as of counsel and demonstration.

On a similar note, Jeffrey Cohen also positions monsters as a defining *'problem'* for contemporary academia: 'a code or a pattern or a presence [...] that unsettles what has been constructed to be received as natural, as human' (1996, ix). More generally, the monster is a locus of difference and amalgamation, of 'hybridity perceived to be unnatural' (Weinstock 2020, 9), and as Yasmine Musharbash reflects, 'over the last decade or so, monster studies has mushroomed [as a field of analysis,] as a cornucopia of recent articles, edited volumes, journals, and books about monsters attests (including two new compendia, see Mittman and Dendle 2012; Picart and Browning 2012b; and an encyclopedia, see Weinstock 2014)' (2014, 1).

Focusing on the British twenty-first-century Gothic more specifically, the monstrous, as it appears in these recent fictions, manifests in plural and sometimes contradictory ways: as a critical register of hatred, identifying nationalist, misogynist, and racist cultural associations attached to the Other (as in Helen Oyeyemi's *White is for Witching* (2009) and Louise Welsh's *The Cutting Room*), but also, in other cases, as a figure of empathy and compassion: a transgressive, confused, and/or defenceless outsider demanding respect and critical understanding (as in Brian Chikwava's *Harare North* (2009) and Ishiguro's *Never Let Me Go*).[3] Indeed, the monstrous becomes at times more properly a transcultural model of proactive social intervention, a celebration of Otherness as a challenge to conventional and xenophobic thinking. This is visible, for example, in the disruptive transnationalism of Kunzru's 'Leela virus' in *Transmission*, which infests and upends the global-corporate system, as well as in the eco-critical mindset of M. R. Carey's 'hungries' in *The Girl with All the Gifts* and *The Boy on the Bridge* (2017), who ultimately agree to the destruction of humanity in favour of saving the planet. Similarly, the female vampires, changelings, and sea creatures of Daisy Johnson's *Fen* (2016), Zoe Gilbert's *Folk* (2018), and Julia Armfield's *Our Wives Under the Sea* (2022) all speak to Gothic ecofeminist engagements with sympathetic monsters, specifically in ways that foreground dark watery settings. In all cases, these texts offer monsters as progressive infiltrators of Capitalocene systems and infrastructures, unabashedly disrupting established patriarchal, (neo)colonial, and global capitalist practices. Likewise, what is often initially a horror-inspiring threat to Western social and cultural norms in these texts in the end embodies potential redemption, as it proffers an alternative, anti-institutional understanding of contemporary life.

Donna Haraway, while imagining herself in the 'womb of a pregnant monster', suggests that such a vantage point might illuminate 'another relationship to nature besides reification and possession'; more generally arguing that the 'promises of monsters' relate to their role in 'changing maps of the world', including 'building new collectives out of what is not quite a plethora of human and inhuman actors' (1992, 295–6; 2020, 506). Developing this reading, my claim for several works examined in this book (including the texts mentioned immediately above) is that these fictions move toward achieving this transformative communitarian vision precisely through their engagements with monstrous entities, spaces, and experiences, underlining a crucial opportunity opened up by monsters to rethink neoliberal individualism and to move beyond the bigoted, patriarchal, heteronormative, and classist tenants upheld within. Borrowing Neel Ahuja's words, these figures 'offer a methodological generosity toward life and matter without romancing bodies, animals, microbes, cyborgs, and things, disavowing their assimilation into international divisions of labour and life' (Ahuja 2016, xvi). Put differently, these texts conjure lived and bodily experiences of complex interrelation between humanity and planetary life, while also drawing attention to global injustice and systematic inequality.

## The Spectral

The centrality of spectres, ghosts, phantoms, and revenants to the twenty-first-century is mirrored in the sheer abundance of fiction titles directly referencing one or another of these phenomenon, including (alongside Patrick McGrath's *Ghost Town* (2005), Sarah Moss' *Ghost Wall* and Niall Griffiths' *Broken Ghost*, examined here): A. N. Wilson's *A Jealous Ghost* (2005), Robert Harris' *The Ghost* (2007), Michele Forbes' *Ghost Moth* (2013), Jenny McCartney's *The Ghost Factory* (2019), Jenn Ashworth's *Ghosted: A Love Story* (2021), C. J. Cooke's *The Ghost Woods* (2022), Damian Lanigan's *The Ghost Variations* (2022), and Isabella Hammad's *Enter Ghost* (2023), amongst many others. While sometimes less overtly frightening than the monstrous or weird, the spectral is nevertheless centrally bound up with contemporary Gothic disquietude: namely, in these fictions' repeated engagement with ghosts and phantoms, as well as ghostly objects and artifacts, as figures for Capitalocene, (neo)colonial, and patriarchal violence, understood in terms of invisibility, precarity, and disinheritance. As María del Pilar Blanco and Esther Peeren affirm, the spectre stands in for 'categories of social differentiation [...] based on retrospectively naturalized, performatively ingrained distinctions that require constant rematerialization', in such a way that they refocus 'specific past, present, and future struggles for recognition, respect, and justice' (2013, 20). The ghost is, in other words, 'a social figure', as Avery Gordon writes, whose freighted hauntings (both human and non-human) reflect 'modern forms of dispossession, exploitation, repression, and their concrete impacts' both on people and on the planet itself (2008, 8, xvii). Contemporary fiction responds to this ghostly situation by inviting institutional scrutiny, as well as historical reflection and memorial revision at a critical level.[4]

This is, it should be stressed, a reading somewhat at odds with the general direction of twenty-first-century Gothic studies, where a focus on monsters, monstrosity, and body horror, as above, has in some ways come to overshadow an interest in spectres and haunting, or at least to reframe this in notably different terms.[5] Bronwen Calvert, for example, compares the '"restrained, suggestive ghost story"' of an earlier era to the 'more graphic presentation' of contemporary horror in such postmillennial television dramas as *Dexter*, *Being Human*, *The Walking Dead*, *American Horror Story*, and *Fringe*, 'including spectacular scenes of violence and gore' concerned with 'motifs of violation' (2014, 186–7). Likewise, Alison Landsburg, while analysing the American television series *Mr Robot*, identifies a 'corporalisation of spectres on screen', wherein 'the appearance of the ghost in a material form not only destabilises but furthermore compels us to action', again moving away from an emphasis on the ghost story *per se* to the shock and gore of body horror (Lee 2017, 12).[6]

For Duncan, in connection with her above critique of the postcolonial Gothic as a genre problematically resistant to materialist politics – as a postmodern mode 'not only ill-suited to analyses of capitalism, but in fact designed to frustrate efforts in this vein' (Duncan 2022, 311) – the figure of the spectre results not only as *aesthetically* antiquated, but, more worryingly, *ideologically* so, reflecting a Derridean resistance to narrative truth-telling at odds with decolonial thinking. She avers, 'Gothic as haunting becomes a means for hollowing out the narrative of modernity, revealing this to be precisely *only a narrative*, spectral and imperfect' (ibid., 308). In this way, horror becomes (supposedly) reflective of 'a deeper shift that pertains to basic postcolonial assumptions about imperial formations of power' (ibid., 305). As Duncan summarizes, 'what is not dead, after all, cannot come back as a ghost' (ibid.).

Interestingly, while differing from this above analysis in identifying the still ongoing centrality of the spectre to contemporary culture and literature – emphasizing how 'ghosts are everywhere these days', increasingly part of 'globalized everyday life and its popular cultural products' (Blanco and Peeren

2010, ix, xi) – nevertheless, del Pilar Blanco and Peeren agree with Duncan in challenging a postmodern and/or deconstructive reading of the ghost, questioning Derrida's emphasis on 'deferred meaning and absence-presence as other' as problematically abstract and ahistorical (2010, xv). As they reflect,

> As an apposite approach to a variety of political, economical, and ethical problems, care needs to be taken not to turn the ghost into an abstract universal figure or catch-all, as Derrida's hauntology risks doing. A more careful spectral turn teases out the differences between various ghostly phenomena, bearing witness to their status as concrete, culturally specific, and historically and socially situated events. (Ibid., xix)

Put differently, rather than seeing the ghost in terms of textual 'traces' or as otherwise indicative of a failure of representational meaning, these theorists prioritize material signifiers and localized associations, reading the spectre as 'simply *there* as part of everyday life' (Peeren 2010, 109). On a similar note, Jeffrey Weinstock identifies a notable 'twenty-first-century twist to the spectral turn':

> one that shifts the spectral turn away from psychoanalysis and deconstruction and instills it instead at the heart of our interactions with objects: in our twenty-first-century narrativization of the Anthropocene, we move from uncanny ghosts to weird spectrality. (2023, 23)

Agreeing with this outlook in part, while nevertheless continuing to recognize the uncanny's central importance to much contemporary fiction, my argument in flagging the twenty-first-century British Gothic spectre likewise sees this figure in pointedly everyday, materialist, and often object-oriented terms: as shaped by biopolitical practices directly reflective of global capitalist oppression, as well as by planetary anxieties connected to Capitalocene 'hyperobjects', including chemical pollution, military mining practices, deforestation, and the overuse of antibiotics and pesticides in farming (Morton 2013, 1).[7] Judith Butler and Gayatri Chakravorty Spivak offer a clue to the human dimensions of this reading when they write of 'spectral humans' constructed within late capitalism, whom, they suggest, are 'produced as the stateless at the same time that they are jettisoned from juridical modes of belonging' (Butler and Spivak 2010, 15–16). As Butler elaborates:

> It is not just that some humans are treated as humans, and others are dehumanized; it is rather that dehumanization becomes the condition for the production of the human to the extent that a "Western" civilization defines itself over and against a population understood as, by definition, illegitimate, if not

dubiously human.... [In this sense,] the spectrally human, the deconstituted, are maintained and detained, made to live and die within that extra-human and extra-juridical sphere of life. (2004, 91)

Incorporating a Foucauldian critical register to contemplate the specific dehumanizing practice of indefinite detention – but in a way that easily extends to encompass other spectral populations explored in twenty-first-century fiction – Butler develops Giorgio Agamben's thinking on the figure of the *homo sacer* – a person whose 'entire existence is reduced to a bare life stripped of every right by virtue of the fact that anyone can kill him without committing homicide' (Agamben 1998, 183). Butler and Spivak, and more explicitly Gordon, add to this an appreciation of the popular cultural and literary imagination, invoking the ubiquity of the ghost as a figure for the contemporary dehumanized. Under this framework, spectrality stands in as a dominant form by which practices of exclusion and exploitation, happening at a systematic level, are popularly represented within contemporary life, seen not as infractions to a larger democratic norm, but more crucially, defining aspects of minority and subaltern existence.

Again here, this reading informs my chosen fictions, especially as these incorporate a twenty-first-century preoccupation with contemporary 'bioviolence', understood as the 'aggression of exclusion and neglect' against those whom the State is 'duty-bound to protect' (Watkin 2021, 8). In Smith's *Hotel World*, this emerges in a ghostly vision of contemporary homelessness made inevitable under the remit of privatization and leisure, while in Trezza Azzopardi's *Remember Me* (2004), a homeless woman's social differentiation excludes her from institutional empathy and casts her as Other within her provincial surroundings. Sarah Waters' *The Little Stranger* (2009) also works with neo-Victorian ghost tales, navigating materialist facets of this historically minded genre to register conservative and nationalistic practices still powerfully present in the twenty-first-century.

Somewhat differently, in Sarah Moss' *Ghost Wall* and Niall Griffiths' *Broken Ghost*, more specific socioeconomic and political concerns arise, connected to Brexit and austerity, wherein the 'increasing precariousness [of] social and industrial relations' means that 'employment conditions [themselves] can even become spectral' (Murnane 2017, 60). In this situation, anxieties regarding unemployment and poverty see characters not only converted into spectral non-entities, but also importuning ghostly rituals and auguries, often connected to a local landscape, as a response to desperation. Borrowing Peter Hitchcock's words, the spectral here invokes 'a counter-narrative to the automaton that is capital and the organs it is compelled to proletarianize' (2010, 43); it beseeches alternative outlooks and perspectives, resistant to capitalism's supposed victory. More largely, across these works, marketization and widespread social conservatism see these characters entrapped in spectral alter-worlds, even as they grapple with local community support programmes and social media platforms in an attempt to survive beyond the scraps of a dissolving welfare system.

The non- or extra-human dimensions to this Capitalocene experience are also registered across these texts, in ghostly visions of planetary suffering and ecological destruction often indexed through disturbing 'hyperobjects' or assemblages of systemic eco-wreckage, as in the complex infrastructures of military and technological pollution and land degradation of Carey's *The Girl with All the Gifts* and Ishiguro's *Klara and the Sun*. On a more positive note, these fictions also contemplate Benjaminian 'profane illuminations', or 'chance occurrences [with objects and artifacts] that modify our daily perception' (Metzidakis 1995, 173), as well as what Jane Bennett refers to as 'vibrant matter': the 'strangely vital things' exhibiting a '*resistant force*' against capitalist violence (Bennett 2010, 3, 1). Peripheral settings, both within and outside the UK, are especially significant in this respect, in so far as they offer witness to capitalist 'slow violence' – that which happens on the fringes of transnational society, 'outside our flickering attention space – and outside the purview of a spectacle-driven corporate media' (Nixon 2011, 6). By engaging with these spaces, and with the buried objects and concealed affects that inhabit them – for example, in Aslam's subterranean Afghanistan and Tash Aw's tropical Malaysia, as well as in the hidden English backwaters of Johnson's *Fen* and Gilbert's *Folk* – these fictions grant witness to Capitalocene aggression 'after the end of the world' (Morton 2013, 3), that is, after the familiar concept of a knowable world is no longer available.

## The Uncanny

The third element of these fictions I seek to highlight is an ongoing engagement with the Gothic uncanny, not simply as a psychological commentary (though it is this too), but also a sociopolitical insight connected to decolonial, feminist, queer, and anti-capitalist thinking. Two concerns in particular drive this reading: firstly, echoing Anthony Vidler's description of the uncanny as a 'metaphor for a fundamentally unliveable modern condition' (Vidler 1992, x), I read this trope as navigating a distinctly material and *spatialized* contemporary situation: an experience of 'warped space' especially relevant to global capitalist living (Vidler 2000, 1, 2). Here, neocolonial and neoliberal power are understood jointly to encompass everyday inequalities uncannily visible within urban spaces, as reflected in highly deregulated, privatized, and deterritorialized forms of living. As Aris Mousoutzanis writes, within this situation, 'interplay and conflict between global flows and local cultures' constitute the 'defining feature' of the 'global unhomely', especially as minority cultures and communities become strategically entrenched within neoliberal practices (Mousoutzanis 2016, 3). Again, 'the politics of subalternity [are here] largely absorbed into the machinery of emergent neo-liberal state capitalism' (During 2015, 19), even as contemporary governments disguise precarity under a banner of progressive individualism and flexible working conditions. In this context, what appears as a 'democratic' twenty-first-century social norm, or even as a promise of agency and work-time balance, is felt and lived as 'cruel optimism': a condition wherein 'something you desire is actually an obstacle to your flourishing' (Berlant 2011, 1). A normative embrace of neoliberal aspiration becomes, in other words, the ironic foundation for hopelessness and despair, experienced not simply as misery but more complexly, as ongoing, unwarranted optimism *and* unexplained worry – a feeling itself so ambiguous as to stand in the way of active, self-conscious protest. As Sianne Ngai writes, 'the unsuitability of these weakly intentional feelings for forceful or unambiguous action is precisely what amplifies their power to diagnosis situations, and situations marked by blocked or thwarted action in particular' (2007, 27).

Accordingly, these fictions negotiate these uncanny sentiments precisely as a tactical approach to materialist and affective critique, wherein what is presented as liberating and/or aspirational is ultimately revealed as imprisoning – as for example, in the uncanny visions of American superpower put forward by Pat Barker's *Double Vision* (2003) and Patrick McGrath's *Ghost Town*. Indeed, Mark Fisher's now well-known distinction between the uncanny and the eerie further cements this appreciation, as he notes how the uncanny 'always process[es] the outside through the gaps and impasses of the inside', whereas the eerie 'allow[s] us to see the inside from the perspective of the outside' (2016, 10). Within this definition, the strength of the uncanny for sociopolitical critique emerges precisely in its unique insight on human psychology and affect, such that 'outside' encounters and landscapes are seen to reflect and project this interior situation. While I will return to the eerie in my final chapter, where I explore recent folk horror-inspired explorations of watery landscapes, I nevertheless underline this uncanny aesthetic as a defining feature of the genre, offering a mirror on widespread social anxieties, and on the way that these act as underlining filters through which the world is assessed and comprehended.

This brings me to the second feature of the uncanny I also hope to emphasize in this reading, which is its investment in uncovering not only personal, but also (again) *planetary* distortions, including landscapes and ecosystems wrecked by global capitalist violence and institutional indifference. Quoting Amitav Ghosh, 'ours [is] a time when most forms of art and literature [are] drawn into the modes of concealment that [prevent] people from recognizing the realities of their plight' (Ghosh 2016, 11). What should perhaps be understood as straightforward or 'realist' cannot be presented as such: 'the irony of the "realist" novel [is that] the very gestures with which it conjures up reality are actually a concealment of the real', such that it is left to popular genres, including the Gothic, to confront the truth (ibid., 23–4).

On a similar note, Mark Bould notes how speculative and weird fiction, specifically in its recent crossovers with Gothic-Horror, offers a unique insight on 'climate upheaval', charting the complex and distorted 'destabilisations' of the 'Anthropocene unconscious' (2021, 148n5). As he puts it, 'whatever else they might mean, in this current conjecture, any depiction of a massive, mobile and unwanted population' – such, for example, as depicted in recent zombie fiction and film – 'cannot not be about climate refugees' (Bould 2021, 29), just as other 'Envoys of the Weird [...] have come from the future to infect us with their language so that we begin to perceive time differently,' challenging our conventional linear, human-oriented perspective (Bould 2021, 113). Developing these readings, twenty-first-century British Gothic participates in eco-critical thinking precisely by foregrounding uncanny violence imposed by capitalism on both humans and the planet: uncovering identities, spaces, and landscapes deformed by market-oriented enterprise. While this is not necessary to the genre – as discussed, the Gothic has a long history of conservatism, which continues – nevertheless, its concern with repressed truths and disguised realities, including those propagated by Capitalocene practices, makes it critically amenable.

More principally, if as Carole Davison writes, 'death serves as the quintessential emblem of the Freudian uncanny', in so far as 'while being [...] familiar, it also remains secret, concealed, and unfamiliar, a reality that has become, like mourning, "obscene and awkward"' (Davison 2017, 2), then the prevalence of death and death-ridden landscapes in these fictions underlines the centrality of the uncanny in this milieu, as a means of confronting readers with misshapen sceneries, psychologies and relationships, as well as personal experiences of loss and grief. In other words, throughout these Gothic texts, descriptions of brutality and horror enacted on others and on the planet are accompanied by a Gothic anxiety that *this is now the norm*, and that unequal and discriminatory systems regulate 'everyday' behaviours and interactions. By making this explicit in their mode of writing, through Gothic tropes and styles formally attentive to this silenced reality, these authors and texts give voice to the (not so) hidden truth of global capitalist oppression.

In what follows, I outline the order and focus of my subsequent chapters, where in each case I prioritize a particular Gothic theme and a comparative analysis. By making apparent how these texts incorporate monsters, spectres, and the uncanny to illuminate twenty-first-century violence and inequality, and by situating this against a largely present-day landscape of fear and horror, these readings highlight Gothic fiction's central importance as a contemporary mode of sociopolitical critique, underlining its vital significance in negotiating a deeply uneven and precarious transnational present.

## Chapter Summaries

In Chapter 1, this emerges through an early postmillennial investigation of terror and trauma, as I read Pat Barker's *Double Vision* and Patrick McGrath's *Ghost Town* as prominent examples of 'Post-9/11 Gothic'. The intertwining of traumatic and uncanny aesthetics in these texts, attentive to the ghosts and hauntings of wartime history, underpin a damning critique of contemporary British and American military violence authorized in the name of 'freedom'. In so doing, they prioritize uneasy connections available between trauma, violence, and libidinal fantasy in wartime practices, suggesting dark and cruel pleasures taken both in patriarchal dominance and military brutality, especially as these are enacted on (neo)colonial 'Others'. The ambivalent ethics of these characters' traumatic memories, and of the wartime histories retold in these narratives, act as a source of hermeneutic excess in the texts and of political insight for the reader, animating anger at what has been done in pursuit of 'democracy'. In other words, both works offer glimpses into practices of torture, rape, and murder, even more horrific as sites of (post-9/11) imperial fantasy, in this way underlining the psychological and political cruelty buttressing (neo)colonial Western 'interventions'.

Extending this post-9/11 outlook more broadly to consider two recent representations of terroristic and counter-terroristic violence, Chapter 2 navigates the layered 'Decolonial Gothic' of Nadeem Aslam and Tash Aw. Focusing on Aw's *The Harmony Silk Factory* and Aslam's *The Wasted Vigil* as twenty-first-century instances of 'tropical' and 'subterranean' Gothic writing respectively, I see these novels as navigating these topographies precisely to contest Western (neo)colonialism presented in the form of political or economic 'assistance', registering hidden and buried consequences of an ongoing imperial violence. Concerned especially with dismantling discourses of 'terror' connected to colonial ventures, both novels tie this focus to lingering historical ghosts and monsters who return to disturb the post-9/11 present. The resurrectionary spirits, uncanny temporalities, and abject military landscapes which haunt these narratives emphasize at once decolonial resistance and ongoing violence with multiple casualties, visible both in the battered terrains of these battlefields and in the exploitation of natural resources and local populations. Hence, this chapter speaks to British Gothic reassessments of a dominant Capitalocene norm, as it exposes established military and market-driven practices as harbouring layered destruction.

In Chapter 3, turning to 'Gothic Inheritance' in Helen Oyeyemi's *White is for Witching* and Sarah Waters' *The Little Stranger*, I consider further how this decolonial Gothic perspective animates materialist critique in fiction otherwise shaped by neo-Victorian anxieties and aesthetics. Foregrounding a simultaneously Gothic and materialist approach to contemporary discourses of inheritance – as described in the writing of Sara Ahmed and bell hooks – I explore how these twenty-first-century novels develop earlier Gothic narratives to attend to the violence of family legacies: the routine aggression, exclusion, and dehumanization justified in the name of maintaining a national 'household'. Starting with Ahmed's concept of the (neo)colonial 'body-at-home', which obliges minority individuals to 'inhabit' a disenfranchising whiteness, I consider how this thinking underpins Oyeyemi's politically topical re-writing of Bram Stoker and Edgar Allan Poe. Similarly, for Waters, I consider how ideas of respectability and tradition, again tied to a programme of national inheritance, underwrite her intertextual engagements with Poe, Charlotte Perkins Gilman, and Henry James. While these writers appropriate and reframe nineteenth-century Gothic narratives to challenge and upend contemporary prejudices, they also interweave folklore and spiritualism to decentre enlightenment narratives, introducing non-European genre modalities that upset long-established critical orientations.

Also concerned with contemporary practices of exclusion, both material and virtual, and with an increased demonization of migrants following 9/11, Chapter 4 takes this anxiety in a new direction to explore new technology and digital innovation, interrogating corporate networks and platforms, and false promises of opportunity in Hari Kunzru's *Transmission* and Mohsin Hamid's *Exit West*. More centrally, in these 'Digital Gothic' fictions, global capital's much lauded mutability and flux ultimately underpins a Gothic critique of present-day violations of migrant lives enabled through technology. In so doing, the novels offer, on the one hand, a critical indictment of corporate power and surveillance, but also (more positively) a Gothic celebration of viral anti-capitalist movements, attending to digitally enabled possibilities for resistance and solidarity. In working with the tropes of the virus and portal in particular, these novels navigate alternate worlds and deviant potentials made alive through the Gothic. In this way, in coordination with fantasy and sci-fi tropes resistant to realist modalities, the narratives reveal technology's ultimately *adaptable* critical unconscious.

Turning to yet another oppressed community in Chapter 5, this section investigates contemporary 'Gothic Homelessness' in three twenty-first-century texts: Ali Smith's *Hotel World*, Trezza Azzopardi's *Remember Me*, and Brian Chikwava's *Harare North*. As with Aslam's *The Wasted Vigil* and Tash Aw's *The Harmony Silk Factory*, all three novels can be seen to develop combined spectral and uncanny aesthetics to explore a shared sociopolitical anxiety: in this case, rough sleeping and the neo-liberal norms underpinning this contemporary experience. In Smith's novel this emerges in relation to a global corporate hotel, where an underpaid chambermaid's death provokes Gothic inquiry into capitalist anonymity and exploitation. By contrast, Azzopardi's novel unfolds within a small Norfolk town, where a local street-woman's robbery uncovers provincial mistreatment connected to her traveller background, and Chikwava's Brixton reveals monstrous unsettlement within new African migrant communities. The contrasting local and transnational dynamics of these settings reflect diverging perspectives of rough sleeping, tied to corporate alienation, provincial small-mindedness, and migratory displacement, respectively. Nevertheless, a common Gothic aesthetic of paranoia and spectrality suggests a conjoint literary preoccupation regarding contemporary homelessness, especially in the context of Britain's uneven neoliberal economy and its social fallout.

Moving from homelessness to metropolitan life more broadly, Chapter 6 explores 'The Gothic City', emphasizing the uncanny and monstrous European urbanities of Louise Welsh's *The Cutting Room* and Chloe Aridjis' *Book of Clouds*. Drawing on older Gothic texts, such as *Jekyll and Hyde* and *Dracula*, in some ways comparably to Oyeyemi and Waters in Chapter 3, both authors can be seen to update these texts to contemplate neoliberal hypocrisies and aggressions, especially as these connect to global marketing platforms and the lived and felt dimensions of urban planning. In *The Cutting Room*, this encompasses a crime-ridden Glasgow monstrously enmeshed in global sex trafficking, where stockbrokers and pornographers alike take part in vampiric neoliberal practices. By contrast, in *Book of Clouds*, Berlin's monstrosity lies in its refusal to attend to the city's still present Second World War spectres, promoting 'the new' at the risk of 'disappearing' a still violent, encroaching history, including that represented by anti-Semitic factions. In either case, Marxist and feminist critical agendas underline these novels' Gothic critique of neoliberal governance, as earlier urban theorists such as Walter Benjamin and George Simmel also emerge as Gothic perspectives on these spaces and their hauntings.

Turning from the city to the country, and from Europe back to Britain, Chapter 7 examines two key literary instances of 'Brexit Gothic': Sarah Moss' *Ghost Wall* and Niall Griffiths' *Broken Ghost*. As the titles of these fictions reflect, their narratives engage the illusory figure of the spectre as a means of examining prominent Brexit-era mythologies, offering the contemporary ghost as a register of popular disquiet within a volatile neoliberal order. Recognizing a tendency within the Gothic to revive past histories of unrest, not simply as haunting registers of cultural anxieties, but also as indexes of the past's return within a crisis-ridden modernity, this chapter seeks to recognize how these texts' uncanny and spectral aesthetics function to disassemble a supposedly intact present, exposing the Gothic instability underpinning austerity 'progress' and its isolationist politics. Working with Michael Gardiner's 'aesthetics of anachronism' (2018, 105) and with Robert Eaglestone's 'affect memory' (2018, 96), as cultural and political indexes for the haunting violence of conservative politics, this analysis adds to these theoretical lenses an attention to the Gothic cruelty underpinning austerity governance, seen here as a basis for Leave voting sentiment and its nostalgic tendencies.

Chapter 8 shifts focus to the world-shattering experience of the global COVID-19 pandemic, which I explore in relation to the monstrous 'posthuman' in Kazuo Ishiguro's *Never Let Me Go* and *Klara and the Sun* and M. R. Carey's *The Girl with All the Gifts* and *The Boy on the Bridge*. Developing the writing of Roberto Esposito regarding the contemporary biopolitical paradigm of *immunitas* – an idea of self-defence based on 'exclusionary inclusion or exclusion by inclusion' (2019, 8) – I read these texts as Gothic representations of two dominant instances of this thinking: in the form of technological exploitation and military aggression respectively. Even so, I also explore how the sympathetic representation of monsters in these novels grants room to alternative forms of political and medical thinking: based not on defence, but on cross-cultural and cross-species community. Challenging a viropolitical outlook on the 'Other' as intruder and registering how *immunitas* itself represents a far more monstrous entity, these texts contemplate the value of living *alongside* the supposed outsider or threat, creating a home based not on security, but rather planetary entanglement and inter-species 'chimerism'.

In Chapter 9, I further extend this reading to investigate recent 'Wet Gothic' engagements with dark and ambivalent waters, particularly as these emerge in new British women's writing in the second and third decades of the twenty-first-century. This includes disturbing deep-sea narratives of oceanic violence in Julia Armfield's *Our Wives Under the Sea*; folk horror stories of island ritual and oppression in Zoe Gilbert's *Folk*; and tales of Norfolk vampirism, mud creatures, and metamorphosis in Daisy Johnson's *Fen*. These narratives participate in larger ecofeminist, decolonial, and folkloric turns in twenty-first-century Gothic writing notably connected to representations of water: underlining the central role that wetlands, oceans, rivers, lakes, and shorelines play in Capitalocene violence, and in the nationalist endeavour to uphold coastal and maritime borders as spaces of exclusion. Against such reactionary contemporary political projects, these novels proffer a chimeristic vision of hybrid coexistence, of immersive intermixture between the human and extra-human, the land and water.

## Conclusion

In summary, these fictions register a range of thematic, aesthetic, and ideological anxieties alive within the twenty-first-century British Gothic, extending across a rich and diverse contemporary national opus and its critical readings. My choice of texts and concerns is by no means exhaustive, instead offering a focused and selective critical intervention into the field, concentrated specifically on Gothic decolonial, feminist, queer, and ecocritical anxieties and their *fictional* representation. Notably, I choose not to address other cultural and aesthetic mediums in any detail, not because these are not integral to the genre – as clearly, they are – but rather because Gothic investments in other contemporary disciplines (and in particular, TV, film, and games) have now been widely indexed by other critics, leaving a visible gap with respect to contemporary fiction as a unique creative modality, with its own particular strengths and strategies – not least, pertaining to the narrativization of political oppression and resistance.

Connectedly, I have also chosen not to address the more light-hearted, sentimental, and comedic elements of the twenty-first-century Gothic, as visible, for example, in what Spooner (2017) describes as 'Happy Gothic', and what Fred Botting refers to as 'Candy Gothic' (2001, 133). As Spooner reflects, much twenty-first-century Gothic is *not* so obviously political, concerned instead with more personal, psychological, and often more celebratory themes, 'to do with sex, desire, and romance', as, for example, in recent mainstream Gothic TV series such as *Buffy the Vampire Slayer*, *True Blood* and *Being Human* (2010, xi). Likewise, Spooner affirms, '[f]ear might not be the primary mood or concern of contemporary Gothic narratives – rather comedy, or romance, or macabre quirkiness, or melancholia, or desire, or mourning' (ibid.). This perception is further amplified by new mergers and mixtures across contemporary genre categories, where the Gothic 'has been so thoroughly hybridised with so many different kinds of other texts that it is difficult to securely pin down any longer' (ibid.).[8] Unmistakably, such aesthetic border crossings make it difficult even to identify predominant trends or anxieties in the modality, much less to make all-encompassing claims about any one particular canon or mode of reading.

Even so, as I see it, there *is* something important to be said about these above texts and about this materialist approach to them, as this proffers a new critical insight on contemporary culture and its Capitalocene politics and practices. Thus, by positioning this complex and bodily oriented outlook within the remit of twenty-first-century British Gothic writing, as a subsection of modern Gothic world literature and as a space in which modern fears and violence are made textually central, this study highlights the British Gothic's critical importance as a platform for exploring twenty-first-century precarity, oppression, and inequality, particularly as connected to radically uneven networks of global affinity and power. The twenty-first-century British Gothic navigates modernity's often dislocating, exilic, and unhomely dimensions, as well as its more parochial and folkloric components, connected to periphery settings and marginalized populations – and with this, it also illuminates repressed and hidden involvements in transnational and planetary violence. Borrowing Zygmunt Bauman's words, the Gothic makes apparent 'the production of [...] wasted humans [and I would add, non-humans] (the "excessive" and "redundant", that is the population of those who either could not or were not wished to be recognized or allowed to stay)' as 'an inevitable outcome of modernization, and an inseparable accompaniment of modernity' (Bauman 2004, 5). In short, this fiction illuminates through a Gothic register and imaginary, global capitalism's continuing systematic abuse, asking readers to investigate the real causes for horror and anxiety within the twenty-first-century.

# Notes

1. In highlighting these associations, I reference Neil McRobert's writing on Brexit and Liviu Alexandrescu's research on British news media representations of the homeless: see McRobert (2019) and Alexandrescu (2020).
2. Emma McEvoy's *Gothic Tourism* (2016), located specifically in Britain, navigates this national counter-cultural investment in detail, as does Catherine Spooner's *Post-Millennial Gothic* (2017), which also situates this cultural investment more transnationally.
3. For compelling discussions of the sympathetic monster, see also de Bruin-Molé (2021), 163–4; Wester and Aldana Reyes (2021), 6; Erman (2021), 5–6; and Zanger (1997), 19–20.
4. I would underline in particular the importance of spectres, spirts, and haunting to contemporary Northern Irish fiction, which unfortunately, I have not had the space to explore in sufficient detail here. This trend is visible in fictional negotiations of The Troubles, as well as of a longer legacy of British colonialism in Ireland. A handful of key titles include Seamus Deane's *Reading in the Dark* (1996), Anna Burns' *No Bones* (2001), Bernie McGill's *The Butterfly Cabinet* (2011), Carolyn Jess-Cooke's *The Boy Who Could See Demons* (2012), Michele Forbes' *Ghost Moth* (2013), Jenny McCartney's *The Ghost Factory* (2019) and Jan Carson's *The Raptures* (2022). Declan Long's *Ghost-Haunted Land: Contemporary Art and Post-Troubles Northern Ireland* (2017) also foregrounds this spectral panorama directly. For other fascinating discussions on the Northern Irish Gothic, see Davey (2008), Schultz (2014), Coulter (2021), and Magennis (2021).
5. One notable exception to this trend is offered in the work of María del Pilar Blanco and Esther Peeren, whose edited collections, explored below – including *The Spectralities Reader* (2013) and *Popular Ghosts* (2010) – vocally emphasize the spectre's centrality to contemporary literature and culture. Likewise, Botting and Spooner's *Monstrous Media/Spectral Subjects* (2015) examines the ongoing intermingling of monsters and ghosts in Gothic cultural productions, moving across history from the nineteenth-century to the present day.
6. China Mieville's twenty-first-century reading of M. R. James – discussed in Chapter 9 of this book – as a purveyor of the Weird, as opposed to 'ghost stories', is also reflective of this trend. Here, Mieville seeks not only to extend but also reconceive and revalidate James' critical importance to the contemporary in line with a bodily focused and Horror-intoned reading, reinforcing the importance of 'touch and touchability' and 'strangeness' to James' writing, ahead of the 'hauntological'. See Mieville (2011).
7. Morton defines hyperobjects as 'things that are massively distributed in time and space relative to humans', whose existence 'end[s] the possibility of transcendental

leaps "outside" physical reality' (Morton 2013, 1–2). In other words, these objects and assemblages require us to recognize a material experience desperately in need of critical attention, but which cannot be understood in full, only in 'phases' or 'pieces' (Morton 2013, 70).

8  Piatti-Farnell and Lee Brien also note how the 'fascination with the legacies of the Gothic, and its connections to cultural practices' in the contemporary 'testifies to the mutating nature of Gothic scholarship and the way in which Gothic concerns bleed into areas of both academic and popular interest that have not been historically associated with the literature of terror' (2015, 3).

# 1

# Post-9/11 Gothic

## The Uncanny and Contemporary Trauma in Pat Barker's *Double Vision* and Patrick McGrath's *Ghost Town*

'The Gothic' writes Jerrold E. Hogle, 'is about the conflicted "social unconscious" of modernity even when it appears within what many critics [perhaps erroneously] now regard as *post*-modernity' (2014, 9, original italics). This critical reflection on the 'modern Gothic' – implicitly challenging the dominance of the '*post*' – offers a helpful starting point for introducing the simultaneously psychological and material components of this opening chapter, as it investigates the troubled and 'socially unconscious' dimensions of twenty-first-century 'post-9/11 Gothic'. Now, many years on from the events of September 11, these occurrences remain poignant symbols of US political and military vulnerability, even as, at a discursive level, their meaning is often masked behind postmodern cultural references to American superpower, impenetrable 'justice', and sociopolitical invincibility. More generally, disrupting long-held assumptions about US neocolonial strength within the realm of Western popular culture and ushering in a moment of profound shock and insecurity, the events of September 11, 2001 are now widely recognized as associated with trauma, but also and more largely, with a Gothically violent and *ongoing* Western response of reprisal and retribution.

Those who frame the trauma of that date often call to attention the horror of these events for those who experienced them: the shock, but also a subsequent entrancing and disturbing fascination comparable to hypnosis. Judith Greenberg, for example, writes of how, 'no matter how many times one repeats the scene of watching, ultimately it confronts us with an absence, an empty skyline, ground zero – the stare of trauma' (2003, 30). On a similar note, Jenny Edkins writes of 'the sudden, totally unanticipated and spectacular appearance of a new type of indiscriminate, instrumental violence in the centre of major cities in the United States. [...] Something that until that moment had been totally inconceivable happened' (Edkins 2003, 245). Britain's own subsequent experiences of terror, in the bombings that took place on the London underground and bus transport system on 7 July 2005 and later in the Manchester Arena bombings of 22 May 2017, unsurprisingly prompted similar trauma-centred responses from the media, as well as from some of Britain's most prominent authors. For example, responding to 7/7, Ian McEwan writes of how 'once we have counted up our dead, and the numbness turns to anger and grief, we will see that our lives here will be difficult. We have been savagely woken from a pleasant dream' (McEwan 2005). Likewise, Howard Jacobson writes of the Manchester bombing in terms of 'the eruption of indiscriminate violence in a peaceful place [...], the horrible intrusion of menace where we had no reason to expect it' (Jacobson 2017). In both of these reactions, an emphasis on terror's unassimilable shock and horror underpins a privileging of trauma as a critical response, seeing these events as representing 'a kind of historical and experiential abyss, a yawning and unbridgeable gap between before and after' (Gray 2009, 130).

While this acknowledgement of trauma is important at the level of clinical diagnosis and recovery, in that it permits a widespread recognition of national disbelief, horror, and loss, nevertheless, it remains to question to what extent trauma discourse actually aids this agenda, instead often further abetting military aggression and violent 'securitization'. As Edkins comments in relation to the War on Terror, here trauma has become a convenient excuse for a state-sanctioned restriction of civil liberties and the authorization of radically undemocratic interventions abroad: 'the state has, arguably, attempted to take control of trauma time, to operate through or in a permanent state of exception' (Edkins 2014, 127). Likewise, Linnie Blake and Agnieszka Soltysik Monnet note how this widespread emphasis on trauma and crisis within public discourse functions to serve 'the corporate agenda', fuelling neoliberal politics precisely by exploiting public vulnerability to justify economically lucrative policies and conflicts. 'Sold to the public as a justifiable response not only to the events of 9/11 but to the ongoing terrorist threat,' they write, 'the "War on Terror" became the militarised face of neoliberalism' (Blake and Monnet 2017, 6).

Keeping in mind these critical anxieties, this chapter turns to two early twenty-first-century British Gothic novels: Pat Barker's *Double Vision* (2003) and Patrick McGrath's *Ghost Town* (2005), exploring how each responds to this post-9/11 trauma-centred perspective both critically and ideologically. Both authors' work repeatedly prioritizes trauma-related questions across a range of histories, often in connection with a Gothic aesthetic, where uncanny wartime settings and disturbed psychologies overtly reference larger national and transnational traumatological experiences. For Barker, whose writing balances 'corporeal vulnerability' with 'recurrent images of ghosts and spectres' (Brannigan 2005, 10), this emerges first in her early fictional explorations of Northern working-class poverty in such works as *Union Street* (1982), *Blow Your House Down* (1984), and *Liza's England* (1986), where gritty realism slips into scenes of gory violence, connecting trauma to domestic abuse within a disenfranchised community. In the *Regeneration Trilogy* (1991, 1993, 1995), Barker then moves back in history to consider the ghosts of World War I, questioning in particular how this conflict's trauma was overlooked and misinterpreted by the medical establishment (Rawlinson 2010, 68). More recently, *Another World* (1998) and *Border Crossing* (2001) again incorporate spectres and the uncanny to explore traumatic violence enacted against and by children, taking into account the perspective of victims, onlookers, psychologists, and child perpetrators themselves. Her work thus repeatedly engages in Gothic ways with the occurrence and interpretation of trauma, often making apparent where this is misread and distorted, or where more nuanced perspectives are necessary to convey its fuller meaning.

A similar understanding also applies to Patrick McGrath's lengthy oeuvre, where, as Sue Zlosnik notes, his writing plays 'a significant part in the evolution of the term "gothic" that lifted it out of its categorization as a historically based genre' (Zlosnik 2020, ix). Dedicated engagements across McGrath's writing to probing scenes of sexual, political, war-based violence, whether in relation to mid-century Britain, contemporary America, or elsewhere, mean that McGrath's investment in the Gothic prioritizes both psychological and political anxieties, often leaving his ghosts hovering between the supernatural, pathological, and memorial. In early works, such as *Spider* (1990), *Dr Haggard's Disease* (1993) and *Asylum* (1996), this concerns the post-war British medical establishment, where understandings of 'therapy' take on a distinctly macabre tone, often betraying unreliable doctors and cruel methods. Similarly, later works, such as *Port Mungo* (2004), *Trauma* (2008), and *Constance* (2013), while shifting the setting to post-war and contemporary America, continue to prioritize trauma-related anxieties, in relation to the 1950s New York art world, the 1970s medical establishment, and the contemporary publishing industry. In all cases, McGrath's self-conscious appropriation of Gothic tropes and forms can be understood, as Rebecca Duncan and Matt Foley write, 'as taking shape within the context of [major geopolitical] upheavals', building figurative connections between private and public registers and in this way demonstrating the haunted dimensions of wider transnational events and debates (Duncan and Foley 2020, 1). In other words, they negotiate personal and (trans)cultural afflictions and disturbances, moving between registers in order to calibrate multiple levels of horror.

As I explore here, this strategy also informs both *Double Vision* and *Ghost Town*, their respective uncanny engagements with post-9/11 trauma likewise incorporating psychological, sociological, and political elements and exposing received understandings of trauma as limited and deceiving. My argument regarding these novels' Gothic depictions sees them overtly challenging culturally assimilated trauma discourses, instead turning these on their head to expose trauma's libidinal dimensions. Registering the violence of Western 'trauma'-based politics, and the neocolonial brutality of the War on Terror, these texts make apparent the Gothic face of Western 'trauma', registering against this the need for critical humility and reflection.

## Trauma and the Uncanny

In an era in which the American Psychiatric Association only officially acknowledged post-traumatic stress disorder (PTSD) in 1980 (Caruth 1995a, 3), and in which new developments in Holocaust Studies pushed its academic importance across the 1990s, the above-mentioned critical responses to 9/11 marry with an understanding of trauma as defined by theorists such as Dori Laub, Shoshana Felman, Geoffrey Hartman, and Cathy Caruth, in so far as they relate an idea of experiential belatedness.[1] 'It is not simply the scale of violence that qualifies September 11 as traumatic but the way that the events surprised us,' Michael Rothberg writes. '[They] took us unawares, and broke with our previous horizon of expectations, thus disallowing our defences against anxiety, our *Angstbeitschaft*' (Rothberg 2003, 149). In describing trauma in this way, Rothberg negotiates Caruth's interpretation of the concept, which sees this in terms of its 'structure of reception':

> The pathology [of trauma] cannot be defined either by the event itself – which may or may not be catastrophic, and may or may not traumatize everyone equally – nor can it be defined in terms of a distortion of the event, achieving its haunting power as a result of distorting personal significances attached to it. The pathology consists, rather, solely in the structure of its experience or reception: the event is not assimilated or experienced fully at the time, but only belatedly, in its repeated possession of the one who experiences it. (1995a, 4)

Caruth here conceives of trauma in notably Gothic terms, as a structural failure to assimilate certain events, not because of their innate catastrophic nature but rather on account of how they are experienced at the time: belatedly and without full comprehension. The traumatized are, as it were, temporally undermined, unable to 'possess' the historical moment they have experienced, even as psychologically this moment appears to possess them (Caruth 1995a, 5).

The strength of this argument as a form of cultural interpretation lies in its appreciation of the temporal elusiveness of 9/11, 7/7, and subsequent terrorist attacks, even as it also conjures the shared experience of those watching.² Trauma is understood as communal, 'shared because it is composed of structural features', which likewise facilitate new avenues for cross-cultural connection, invoking 'the types of sharing that emerge in the belated space of traumatic reception' (Rothberg 2003, 149). As James Berger argues, trauma constitutes 'a sort of poetics': 'It is about making, about the creative acts – combining conscious and unconscious motives and powers – that arise out of horror and confusion' (ibid., 52). For some, such as Rothberg and Peter Brooks, this articulates a paradoxical opportunity opened up by 9/11, suggesting a possible forging of new forms of international connection, allowing Americans to understand the trauma experienced regularly in other parts of the world, often as a result of America's own foreign policy. As Brooks writes, 'It's not that one wants to find anything positive in terrorism and mass destruction but that precisely our new vulnerability to them might alert us to how much they are part of the daily experience of much of the world' (Brooks 2003, 48).³

Despite this optimism, however, the dominant political and cultural response that the American government and media adopted to 9/11 decidedly did *not* invoke a larger appreciation of global trauma, but to the contrary promoted an increasing retribution and dogmatic patriotism, such that, as David Simpson suggests, 'in less than two years we went from the fall of the Twin Towers and the attack on the Pentagon to the invasion of Iraq, a process marked by propagandist compression and manufactured consent so audacious to seem unbelievable' (Simpson 2006, 4). The aftermath of 9/11 throws into question in this way just how critical this traumatological designation is, challenging the presumed ethical value it is so often granted by the above theorists. The 'inassimilable' quality of trauma may provide a metaphor for emotional horror, but as several critics have noted, such figurative depictions often fail to attend to the discursive and symbolic dimensions of the catastrophe of 9/11, in particular with respect to its pre-imagined and mediated conditions. Žižek writes that '[t]he unthinkable which happened was thus the object of fantasy [...] America got what it fantasized about, and this was the greatest surprise' (Žižek 2002, 16). Likewise, Claire Kahane comments on the 'uncanniness' of 9/11, which was not only 'hyper-real' but also 'surreal' in its occurrence: 'We saw death that day in the only way that we could see it and live, as a dark hole in the side of a superstructure, the site of disappearance of the object, which nevertheless left the trace of its impact in space' (Kahane 2003, 114). In thus drawing attention to the libidinal allure of 9/11 – its eroticism and spectacle – in ways that complicate any notion of a straightforward shock, both thinkers offer symbolic readings of 9/11 that challenge prominent trauma theory designations, reaffirming the discursive and imaginary dimensions of catastrophic experience as opposed to emphasizing their inassimilable horror.

These theorists draw on Freud's Gothic concept of the uncanny or *unheimlich*, the idea of something strange that is nevertheless familiar in an unnerving way, having previously 'remained secret and hidden but [having] come to light' (Freud 1919, 225). For Freud, this classification, explained in terms of 'repressed infantile complexes' or 'primitive beliefs' (ibid., 249), helps to account for certain aesthetic experiences not easily made comprehensible: those which cannot be put down simply to rational fears, surprising moments, or gruesome encounters. Instead, these involvements, including instances of doubling and repetition – hence their immediate relevance to descriptions of 9/11 – are here understood in terms of the unconscious: an encounter which reveals hidden and disguised fantasies and primal fears. For Nicholas Royle this concerns 'the ghostly effects of delay and deferral', but also 'the return of something repressed [...] the strange insistence, repression and disavowal of the "death drive"', as well as other fears and fantasies associated with shame and guilt (Royle 2003, 60, 84–5). These belated but often self-destructive fantasies are seen to unexpectedly re-emerge in deeply discomposing ways, throwing into question accepted identifications and norms, as well as cultural institutions.

Respecting contemporary Gothic fiction, this suggests a new way of reading trauma within the twenty-first-century, which calls to attention both memorial and libidinal concerns often explored within the Gothic. Questioning the temporally focused reading of trauma pronounced by such prominent theorists as Hartman and Caruth and asserting instead the continued importance of fantasy and double meaning in trauma, many post-9/11 Gothic novels self-consciously manipulate ironic and fantastic signifiers as a way of recognizing trauma's heterogeneity and possible duplicity as a cultural designator. From within the UK, examples include Iain Banks' *Dead Air* (2002), J. G. Ballard's *Millennium People* (2003), Chris Cleave's *Incendiary* (2005), and Nadeem Aslam's *The Wasted Vigil* (2008), the latter also explored in the following chapter. In all of these works, as Kirby Farrell warns, 'trauma is both a clinical syndrome and a trope something like the Renaissance figure of the world as a stage: a strategic fiction that a complex, stressful society is using to account for a world that seems threateningly out of control' (Farrell 1998, 2).

The susceptibility of trauma to narrative manipulation must therefore be taken into account in reading these texts, assessed alongside its more prominent interpretation as inassimilable horror. As Roger Luckhurst reminds us, 'trauma psychology frequently resorts to the Gothic or supernatural to articulate post-traumatic effects', both in sensational and critical ways (Luckhurst 2008, 98). Developing this suggestion, I argue that some recent British Gothic fictions, including Barker's *Double Vision* and McGrath's *Ghost Town* (2005), navigate the layered experience of contemporary trauma precisely to complicate simplistic readings that focus solely on delayed memory or alternatively, depth psychology. The twenty-first-century British Gothic, in this way, offers access to a highly politicized and culturally attentive reading of trauma post-9/11, recognizing how deeply embedded Western neoliberal fantasies of violence structure its reception.

## Traumatic Abjection and Libidinal Allure in *Double Vision*

Two aspects of Barker's Gothic aesthetic are clear from the opening pages of *Double Vision*, through the novel's concern with uncanny spectrality and its fragmented structure. Opening with a pointedly uncanny and abject imagery, the initial scene of a car accident leaves the reader with an overtly Gothic sense of physical and psychic wounding:

> There was no time to think. Trees loomed up, leapt towards her, branches shattered the windscreen, clawed at her eyes and throat. A crash and tearing of metal, then silence, except for the tinny beat of the music that kept on playing. [...] Saliva dribbled from the corner of her mouth, blood settled in one eye. (Barker 2003, 3)

Capturing the immediacy and confusion of the event, as well as its bodily pain for the protagonist, this description offers trauma as an abject form of corporeal suffering, setting the tone for the rest of the novel. Summoning the connotation of a 'rupture of the skin or protective envelope of the body', resulting in 'a catastrophic global reaction of the entire organism' (Leys 2000, 19), Kate's helplessness as victim figures her simultaneous physical and emotional displacement, as she struggles both to describe this event and to position herself within it. Searching her memory, she reflects, 'There was something else, something she needed to get clear, a memory that bulged above the surface, showed its back and then [...] turned and sank again [...]. She had a sense of missing time' (Barker 2003, 13). This reflection echoes Caruth's idea of trauma as a sort of *'possession'* (Caruth 1995a, 4), haunting the sufferer, with an event that exists outside of conscience perception, on the fringes of memory.

Reading this scene in light of J. G. Ballard's *Crash* (1973), where trauma emerges as a form of technological pornography (ibid., 1975, 49), a high-tech atrocity converted into trauma spectacle, narrative references to the 'tearing of metal' and 'shifting parallelograms of light and shade' (Barker 2003, 3) introduce a new public forum of traumatic witnessing for the contemporary. As Mark Seltzer explains, 'this coalescence, or collapse, of private and public registers [...] makes possible the emergence of something like a pathological public space' (Seltzer 1997, 4). In this case, Kate's abject body – dribbling saliva and clotting blood, on exhibit for the reader as well as passing drivers – speaks to this new spatiality, her exhibition of pain reinforcing trauma's violence but also its alluring quality. The unnamed presence standing by Kate's car, 'breathing, watching, not calling for help' (Barker 2003, 14), introduces voyeurism in no uncertain terms.

Stephen Sharkey, a former colleague of Kate's husband Ben, offers yet another instance of trauma in the novel, wherein he is also disturbed by recent public disasters that overwhelm him. Having worked with Ben in Afghanistan, where he acted as a foreign correspondent, Stephen feels the tragedy of Ben's loss, if also the foolishness of its occurrence. 'Your life – *for that?*' (Barker 2003, 305), he remarks on seeing the photograph that led to Ben's death. As Brannigan comments, Stephen seems unable in this passage to understand or credit Ben's photographic commitment, outraged by the suggestion of a 'sacrifice [of life] for art' (Barker 2003, 155). Nevertheless, what traumatizes Stephen is not only Ben's death but also his own ambivalent position towards his demise and the numerous atrocities he has witnessed on assignment, including the falling bodies on September 11, the war in Afghanistan and the violated corpse of a young woman in Bosnia. Connecting personal experiences to prominent global political events, these memories, unbidden, return to Stephen and haunt him in the form of nightmares, tying his life in direct ways to public wartime and post-9/11 discourses. Lying in bed at night, he imagines '[the girl's] head beside his on the pillow, and when he rolled over on to his stomach, trying to get away from her, he found her body underneath him, as dry and insatiable as sand' (ibid., 55). Reoccurring without apparent impulse or meaning, these dreams echo Caruth's idea of trauma as 'the literal return of the event against the will of the one it inhabits' (Caruth 1995a, 4), also suggesting that such recurrences emerge repeatedly in the public psyche in its negotiation of national and transnational aggression. The memory 'possesses' Stephen despite himself, just as memories of neocolonial violence emerge in the post-9/11 consciousness, haunting Western culture in ways that it does not fully comprehend, or perhaps does not wish to.

Indeed, it is not only the memory of the girl which haunts Stephen but also Ben's photograph of her, which leaves Stephen unsettled in an unexpected way: 'shocked on her behalf to see her exposed like this, though, ethically, Ben had done nothing wrong' (Barker 2003, 121). In this scene, Ulrich Baer's description of the photograph as capable of 'captur[ing] the shrapnel of traumatic time' (Baer 2002, 7) – 'confront[ing] the viewer with a moment that had the potential to be experienced but perhaps was not' (ibid., 8) – seems fitting, offering an apt account of Ben's photograph's likeness to, and therefore participation within, Stephen's traumatic encounter. As Baer explains, 'Because trauma blocks routine mental processes from converting an experience into memory or forgetting, it parallels the defining structure of photography, which also traps an event during its occurrence while blocking its transformation into memory' (ibid., 9). Stephen's inability to process the photo's affective impact – which, 'simply restored the corpse to its original state' (Barker 2003, 121) – buttresses this reading, authorizing a Gothic, trauma-centred approach to photographic temporality.

Nevertheless, this scene also complicates Caruth and Baer's readings of trauma by adding to these an interest in its libidinal dimensions and in their political and cultural resonance. While Stephen has no trouble confronting and integrating the impact of his experiences both in Bosnia and after 9/11, the struggle and shock he experiences following these events reveal his own erotic and violent impulses, which encompass a more visceral horror than might be expected from a Caruthian diagnosis. What overwhelms Stephen in this scene, as revealed by his vision of the girl 'underneath him […] dry and insatiable' (Barker 2003, 55), is his own sexualized attitude towards her violation and murder, which makes him complicit in her atrocity. Stephen is stunned by how he remembers this young woman in the context of libidinal arousal: seeing the photograph, he expresses shock 'on her behalf to see her exposed like this'; it is as if, in the process of being photographed, '[she] had been violated twice' (ibid., 121).

This emphasis on the uncanny and libidinal, and their ability to inculpate the sufferer (and the nation) despite presupposed victimhood, echoes the perspective of Susannah Radstone, who likewise emphasizes the psychic participation of the West within 9/11's trauma. Trauma may, according to Radstone, entail not only an 'anomalous' or unnameable event, but also a crucial 'puncturing' or achieving of libidinal fantasy, which returns unbidden:

> An event may prove traumatic, indeed, not because of its inherently shocking nature but due to the unbearable or forbidden fantasies it prompts. Or, conversely, an event's traumatic impact may be linked to its puncturing of a fantasy that has previously sustained a sense of identity – national as well as individual. (2003, 120)

Radstone, drawing explicitly on Freud, signals a wider understanding of traumatic paralysis, which recognizes the 'ungovernability of the unconscious' both for the individual and the collective. 'What is lost [with trauma theory]', she suggests, 'is that fundamental psychoanalytic assumption concerning the challenge to the subject's sovereignty posed by the unconscious and its wayward processes – processes which might include, but should not be limited to, an identification with the aggressor' (Radstone 2007, 16). Reinforcing trauma's potential to encompass not only victimhood but also an active libido, this reading complicates Stephen's ethical position, inferring at once guilt and unacknowledged attraction to the violated girl.

Horrified and indeed traumatized by how he feels, Stephen shuts down to the world around him, even as he develops strategies to consciously repress his awareness of complicity. Responding to the falling and 'thudding' bodies on 9/11, he recalls fantasizing sexually as a means of forgetting these occurrences: 'To shut the sound out, he focused on [his wife's] breasts and was rewarded by a stir of lust. Sometimes when you're so saturated in death that you can't soak up any more, only sex helps' (Barker 2003, 97). What traumatizes Stephen in this moment is precisely the allure of 9/11's violence, which allows him to translate trauma into fantasy in order to exploit this. Here, trauma mediates 'in the formation of neuroses, even where what appears to be at stake is the relation between a neurosis and memory of the past' (Radstone 2007, 16): Stephen is entranced by his own ungovernable conscious, affected not only by memory, but also libido.

Two other narratives in the novel further develop this reading: Kate's relationship with Peter and Stephen's with Justine. The first, which begins with an assistantship when Kate takes on Peter following her crash, quickly transforms into something more disturbing and suggestive. Kate's discovery of Peter dressed in her clothes and pretending to sculpt the Christ figure disarms her, as Kate expresses terror at seeing Peter so transformed: 'she felt a spasm of revulsion, not from him, but from herself, as if he had indeed succeeded in stealing her identity'

(Barker 2003, 179). The scene, ending with Kate backing slowly away from the studio and running to the house, conforms neatly to a familiar Gothic topology: of the pursuant stalker or double, who creates fear through their likeness to oneself. As Catherine Spooner explains, often in Gothic texts, 'one character "steals" the identity of another or, alternatively, becomes trapped in an alien identity by wearing (or recreating) their clothes' (Spooner 2004, 130). In this novel, what stands out is that it is Kate's own persona, rather than Peter's that disturbs her: 'the truth about her' is what frightens and provokes a traumatic response. Locating trauma in repressed insecurity, the novel questions not only Kate's, but also the *West's* larger inward-looking response to traumatic violence, as anxiety over what has been unearthed about Western culture and politics, as much as what has been done to it, prompts its trauma.

Stephen's relationship with Justine also draws on the trope of unconscious involvement, again making evident an internal, libidinal dimension to this (public) experience. Stephen recognizes how he is drawn to Justine despite his own reservations: reflecting on his 'paternal' feelings for her (Barker 2003, 139), he later reconsiders this verdict, as he 'grind[s] her pelvis into his, throwing his head back and baring his teeth as he came': 'Nope, paternal wasn't the right word either' (ibid.). The sexual aggressiveness of this passage underlines his libidinal attachment to Justine, but also implicitly, the West's own libidinal involvement in its paternalist foreign policy. Through a negotiation of excess and the uncanny, Barker discloses Stephen and Kate's uneasy relationship with their own desires and fears, but also a larger political anxiety regarding trauma's contemporary importance and psychosomatic resonance. Implicit in the novel's attention to post-9/11 media spectacle is an awareness of how trauma might be *and has been* manipulated within the Western media to disguise repressed fantasies and to promote authoritarian and paternalist power.

## Multiple Histories of Uncanny Violence in *Ghost Town*

McGrath's *Ghost Town* can also be read as a critique of post-9/11 Western trauma, again drawing attention to this experience's libidinal content and its representation's questionable ethics. Here, the text is split into three separate narratives or short stories, set respectively around the events of the American War of Independence, the Civil War, and 9/11, each represented in Gothic terms as a period of national violence. Trauma emerges here both in the dark and spectral plotlines driving each of these stories, and in the larger palimpsestic structure informing the wider text, where uncanny repetitions implicitly echo a traumatological 'structure of reception'. Despite this clear recognition of American historical crisis, however – in each case drawing poignantly on references to 9/11 – the emphasis across these texts is on secrets and lies underpinning familial histories, fantasies undergirding domestic tales of lust and betrayal, in this way drawing attention to the role of the unconscious within the American psyche. This representation functions, as in Barker's novel, to reassess American post-9/11 trauma discourse, looking beyond established national mythologies to a darker, more disturbing past and present.

Told from the perspective of a traumatized son, haunted by the abject vision of his murdered mother, who now returns to bring him with her into the realm of death, the first story of McGrath's *Ghost Town*, 'The Year of the Gibbet', unambiguously parades its Gothic view of history, foregrounding both gory violence and the spectral uncanny in its retelling of the American War of Independence. In a narrative unmistakably relevant to post-9/11 times, this narrator tells of how New York had 'become a place not so much of death as of the *terror* of death' (McGrath 2005, 1), in this way underlining affective anxieties expressly aligned to terrorism. Nevertheless, what is perhaps most notable about this tale is the way it self-consciously plays on established military-historical narratives, seeing this period *not* as an era of heroic nation-building, but instead, precisely, deception and trauma. As Todd McEwen writes, the text 'remind[s] us that America was born in violence, in terrorist actions that were deemed to be in a just cause' (2005), thus challenging the established post-9/11 view of perpetrator and victim. Indeed, not only does America here appear as a yet *unrecognized* nation – the geopolitical superpower as the oppressed and angry pawn – in addition, the psycho-sexual dynamics of this power relation are explicitly reversed: America's mother revolution disrobed and paraded as a figure of shame, while a bemused empire casually denies her citizenship.

The loss of innocence implicit in this representation is central to the Gothic vision McGrath here establishes, wherein the narrator recalls 'an innocent time when Manhattan was a place of farms and tranquil orchards and it was said that visitors smelled the island even as their vessels came beating up through the Narrows' (2005, 2). This pristine countryside contrasts sharply with the ruinous and death-ridden state of the occupied city, described as a 'wasteland' in which 'there was no glory, no victory, only suffering' (ibid., 14). Indeed, both the landscape and the narrative voice participate in constructing this vision, as the text returns in traumatic cycles to masochistic tropes of abjection and self-punishment, figuring life itself as a 'state of wretched solitude' awaiting death (ibid., 57). Here, this allegory of filial guilt – seeing the narrator plagued by visions of his revenant mother – underlines a Gothic portrayal of a nascent America, wherein the complicity felt by subsequent generations manifests in abject fantasies of urban destruction and obsessive paranoia: 'a burden', as Sue Zlosnik aptly puts it, 'generated in the compromises and betrayals attendant on the making of a new nation' (Zlosnik 2011, 112).

The second tale in the tryptic, 'Julius', moves this traumatic depiction into a later stage of American history: the mid-nineteenth-century, in the years preceding the Civil War. In this story, the narrator emerges as the granddaughter of the protagonist's art teacher, this relationship again reaffirming McGrath's self-avowed interest in a Gothic inheritance: 'the sins of the father being visited upon the child – the past working its particular power in a negative sense upon the lives of individuals of later generations' (McGrath and Welsh 2006). While in the previous story this encompasses the guilt and collusion produced by post-revolutionary compromises, linking originary trauma to the oppressed condition of America's current 'enemies', in this case it instead invokes the paternal oppression tied to an increasingly market-driven nation, a history tainted by the legacy of the trans-Atlantic slave trade and racist violence.

The narrative's protagonist, Julius, is again an unmistakeably traumatized figure, having been abused by his father and subsequently sectioned for madness during his adulthood. The reason for his abuse, it becomes clear, concerns his father's resentment: his son is an ill-fit within the family enterprise, and he tries to mould him through repeated and bloody beatings. Despite this violence, the text records how Julius precariously manages his oppressed condition, burying his pain 'so deep that nobody saw it, not even himself' (McGrath 2005, 83). While Noah van Horn thus showcases authoritarian and patriarchal practices as the necessary components of an American success story – also encompassing 'a powerful commitment to aggressive enterprise and the getting of money' (McGrath 2005, 64) – his son navigates a growing trauma notably specific to nineteenth-century American paternalism, incorporating suppression and denial as the hidden counterpart to market prosperity.

By contrast to his father, Julius' preferred calling in fine arts locates him within an aesthete milieu specifically associated with American wilderness, this figured in direct opposition to the 'ferocity, speed, and cunning' of the mid-century urban landscape (McGrath 2005, 117). Within this 'sentimental education' (ibid., 85) – a direct reference to Gustave Flaubert's 1869 novel, an important intertext here – Julius meets Jerome Brook Franklin, his teacher, and Annie Kelly, an Irish immigrant who models for the class, but whom his father rejects due to 'the taint of her race upon her' (McGrath 2005, 113). As Noah reflects, 'he must thwart this upstart girl, despite the fact that she aroused him – or *because* she did, perhaps – or the family would begin to look like a way-station for every aspiring nobody in New York' (ibid., 116–17). In this confession of paternal lust – figuring Annie as the exotified, dangerous 'Other' of the neoimperial imagination – the text reveals the jealousy implicit in Noah's reaction: his claim to protect his son inadvertently revealing his underlying competition. When Noah then carelessly agrees to Max Rinder's offer to dispense with Annie, the reader easily identifies his hidden motives: alongside racism stands the elder man's guilt in betraying paternal duty.

Contextualized against the events of 9/11, this depiction again resonates with contemporary cultural politics, as violence employed in the name of State paternalism, in particular in relation to war and migrancy, reveals at once radical prejudice and market-based opportunism of extreme dimensions: the unabashed acquisitiveness of the neoimperial father in his protectionary outlook. What follows in the novel is the fallout of this politics as this emerges within the domestic arena: defined by the insanity of the son (the proverbial nation), alongside the deterioration of the father (the State), the latter replaced by an even more 'ruthless' (neoliberal) successor, who plays on his weaknesses. The fact that Rinder himself is also eventually brought down and the demonic culprit of the break-up revealed as Booth only further emphasizes the underlying precariousness of this domestic situation, where unexpected interlopers and carefully guarded secrets situate the polis in a state of radical crisis. Indeed, it seems especially fitting that Booth represents a leading figure of the wilderness tradition, in this way effectively reinforcing the text's dismissal of American pastoral innocence, as it turns out that Julius was right all along to suspect him. Within this framework, the story's final demand that 'love must never be denied' underlines both the danger implicit in America's paternalist prejudice *and* the lie inherent in the idea of an 'unspoiled' national spirit, as the painted 'ghosts' of the narrator's forefathers continue to haunt her (McGrath 2005, 173, 75).

The novel's final story, 'Ground Zero', takes these lessons explicitly into a contemporary context, wherein 9/11's recent occurrence in the narrative again serves to highlight both national trauma and state violence, underlining the complex psychological, cultural and political conditions shaping America's response to this event. The narrator of this story, a New York therapist, mirrors McGrath's long-standing (and deeply Gothic) distrust of medical psychiatry, as her claims to objectivity and ethical open-mindedness, much like those of McGrath's past narrators in *Dr Haggard's Disease* and *Trauma*, gradually unravel to demonstrate her underlying instability and moral prejudice. As John Sheng Kuo relates, 'Her calmness and detachment are merely a façade. As the sessions continue, we recognize that she is in fact self-deceived, and that she is as much altered by 9/11 as Dan is' (Kuo 2007, 68). A textual focus on psychiatric unreliability, then, situates trauma as both a condition and diagnosis, negotiating the mode of Gothic thriller to question how the latter becomes culturally and politically problematic.

The narrator's patient, Daniel Silver, confronts issues, as the narrator describes them, 'largely sexual in nature, and which originated in a suffocating maternal relationship [...], becoming visible only when he tried to sustain intimacy with another woman' (McGrath 2005, 175). Given the narrator's own view of Daniel as 'like a son' (ibid., 175), with whom she employs a notably condescending register – referring to him as her 'big bear' (242) and chastising his 'suicidal infantilism, a primary unthinking embrace of the death instinct' (214) – the psycho-sexual pitfalls of this relationship become evident from the start of the narrative, as her attempts to diagnose her patient's trauma re-enact and impose these self-same 'suffocating' conditions, figuring Daniel (and America with him) as morbidly death-bound and in need of salvation. The result, as the narrative imagines it, is a sordid love triangle disturbingly reflective of post-9/11 relations, wherein a conflict is wrought between Daniel (the American people), the narrator (the monitoring State), and Daniel's Asian-American lover, Kim Lee (the projected 'enemy'). The story's overt attention to new post-9/11 policing policies, including 'ethnic profiling' and 'the suspension of due process' (ibid., 212), reinforce this political allegory, as the text at once confronts and contests the dubious methods employed by the post-9/11 US state.

The specific reason Daniel returns to visit the narrator concerns Kim's particular response to 9/11's terror, which includes Gothic visions of the ghost of her former lover, Jay, following his death in one of the towers. Indeed, the situation is more complex than this, compounded by Kim's guilt at having cheated on Jay with his father, 'a prominent New York banker and philanthropist' (ibid., 216), who hires her as a prostitute, later arranging for Jay to catch them in the act. The sadistic father–son power-play exhibited in this scene thus reinforces the story's concern with patriarchal fantasy, wherein post-9/11 conflicts themselves can be read in terms of a 'continuing battle between competing versions of masculinity' (Radstone 2003, 121), the aberrant liberal-minded son coming up against the acquisitive dominance of his neoliberal father.

The fact that the narrator here effectively sides with the father, seeing Kim as the seductive perpetrator willing to entertain 'the possibility of having sex with the father' (McGrath 2005, 227), only further reiterates the critical danger of this fantasy, whereby racial signifiers attached to an exotified and demonized East become the easily normalized register by which State violence is permitted to happen, passed off as mere acquisitional fetishism, or worse, victimization. Jay's willingness to make amends with Kim following this incident in this way decidedly rejects the pathological diagnosis the narrator assigns to it – as a refusal 'to absorb the pain his father attempted to cause him' (McGrath 2005, 240) – instead registering a healthy instance of constructive forgiveness and reconciliation: an attempt, in Peter Brooks' words, 'to look up from the wound, and to see what's happening in the world' (Brooks 2003, 51). While Daniel, in his love for Kim, is able to recognize and condone this outlook – his commitment to her enshrining his own confident embrace of political progressivism – the narrator's contrasting refusal of sympathy instead figures the other side of post-9/11 politics, where anger and prejudice are granted privilege ahead of recovery. Her final insistence that 'John Ashcroft is right' in his 'wholesale pullback of traditional American freedoms', and likewise in allowing the Patriot Act's radical curtailment of human rights law (McGrath 2005, 212, 240), stands as the Gothic underside of this contemporary politics, favouring war over reconstruction, and justifying the imposition of biopolitical surveillance in the name of 'security'.

In summary, all three of *Ghost Town*'s narratives, however indirectly, register the violence of post-9/11 America, asking the nation to reassess its traumatological diagnosis and to reinterpret this in light of where it is heading. In 'The Year of the Gibbet', this pertains to originary mythologies figuring revolutionary America as a sight of heroic martyrdom, a narrative often repeated following 9/11 with problematic consequences. In 'Julius', by contrast, it invokes the betrayals and deceptions of the industrial mid-century, yet again linking these to post-9/11 discourse invoking both American protectionism and an 'innocent spirit'. Finally, in 'Ground Zero', the text incorporates the more immediate post-9/11 moment, registering two contrasting responses to the trauma of 9/11 and the pain this causes: one reactionary, the other open-minded and recovery oriented. Brought together, these distanced narratives thus construct a critical Gothic overview of post-9/11 relations, asking, as Barker does, for more sympathy and compassion, in place of ongoing hatred.

## Conclusion

More generally, the force of these two twenty-first-century Gothic texts lies in their awareness of both trauma's material reality *and* its complex and layered psychological significance for post-9/11 Western culture. If trauma is 'real' and viscerally experienced, these fictions illustrate, it is also symptomatic of hidden fears and fantasies, including fears of impotence and fantasies of dominance on a geopolitical scale. Put differently, what commends these disturbing and often horrifying works is their uncanny awareness of the West's repressed desires, and with this also the problematic 'morality' put forward under the banner of unanticipated trauma. While for Barker this comes through in a novel of personal histories intersecting within a post-9/11 context, for McGrath, it instead encompasses multiple historical generations, but in each case registers multifaceted dynamics of power and oppression. More centrally, integral to this Gothic post-9/11 artistry is a picture of trauma misused and misrepresented: offered in defence of Western pride and retribution, in place of recovery.

## Notes

1   In the subtitle to *Testimony* (1992), Felman and Laub refer to a 'crisis in witnessing' provoked by the trauma of the Holocaust. Laub explains how this is 'an event without witness' in so far as 'it is only now, *belatedly*, that the event begins to be historically grasped and seen' (1992, 84). On a similar note, Hartman writes that:

    [t]he knowledge of trauma [...] is composed of two contradictory elements. One is the traumatic event, registered rather than experienced. It seems to have bypassed perception and consciousness and falls directly into the psyche. The other is a kind of memory of the event, in the form of a perpetual troping of it by the bypassed or severely split (dissociated) psyche. (1995, 537)

2   It is notable, with respect to what follows, that both Hartman and Laub have also written on the traumatic character of 9/11's experience, in each case invoking this temporally centred reading: see Hartman (2003) and Laub (2003).

3   Similarly, Rothberg considers how

    [t]he attacks on New York and Washington [...] have awakened some people in the United States – at least momentarily – to a vista of global suffering. They have put Americans in touch with parts of the world, such as Afghanistan, that had previously occupied the most restricted possible zone of public consciousness for the majority of citizens. [...] the recognition that 'we' are not alone in the world may be the first step to any productive engagement with histories of political and personal violence. (2003, 148).

# 2

# Decolonial Gothic

## Tropical Terrors and Subterranean Ghosts in Tash Aw's *The Harmony Silk Factory* and Nadeem Aslam's *The Wasted Vigil*

While the Gothic has from its beginnings been concerned with the meaning and representation of terror, conventionally seeing this 'as happening "out there" [...] elsewhere, outside the self, [as] something that takes place away from the security of the homely' (Botting and Edwards 2013, 21), the distinctly domestic and unhomely import this concept acquired following the events of 9/11 means that this connection must now be rethought, especially in relation to oppressed South Asian, Middle Eastern, Arab, and Muslim communities living as the focal point of Western threat narratives. In the previous chapter, I explored this anxiety with respect to post-9/11 Western 'trauma', considering in particular how this discourse was strategically appropriated to defend aggressive Western military interventions abroad and to expel and demonize supposedly foreign 'intruders' on the so-called 'home-front'. Fictions such as *Double Vision* and *Ghost Town*, I argued, incorporate the Gothic to underline trauma's ambivalent (and often libidinally inflected) psychological and discursive value, showing how Western governments and media negotiate this concept tactically to facilitate political and military violence, justifying a perpetual biopolitical 'war' whose political and economic advantages for the West are conspicuously evident. In Jenny Edkin's words, the Western state conspires 'to take control of trauma time, to operate through or in a permanent state of exception', such that practices of remembrance, memorialization, and witnessing are co-opted to exonerate ongoing imperial violence (Edkins 2014, 127). Yet, if trauma, as a discourse and experience, plays a vital role in maintaining contemporary neocolonial practices, so too does terror itself, in similar guises.

One anxiety that arises, then, in contemporary scholarship examining terror's present meaning and representation concerns its relevance not only *outside* the

West, but also *within* and *in connection to* this. As Simon Dalby notes, 'the point that some of the hijackers were legally resident in the United States and that the weapons, training and skills needed to carry out the attacks were gained within the boundaries of the United States stretched arguments about "keeping the bad guys out" as the most appropriate mode of dealing with the possibility of further attacks' (Dalby 2003, 68). Fred Botting and Justin D. Edwards comment on how terrorism 'forces us to recognise that "elsewhere" is here, not only because the formulation of the distinction was always located in the privileged site of power but also because we can no longer refuse to see the shadows we have cast' (Botting and Edwards 2013, 21). In other words, Western imperialism's history of foreign-based wars necessarily implicates the West itself in the disasters it identifies abroad, invoking the deception implicit in a view of terror as supposedly alien.

Indeed, recognizing the West's complicity in abetting terrorism both financially and technologically, 'not just in the fluid transfer of funds for acts of resistance but also in the communication technologies that enable networks to develop across distance, time and space' (ibid., 21), Botting and Edwards make clear how terrorism escapes national and regional delimitations set out by a self-exonerating West, instead actively dismantling these categories and crossing over the supposedly impermeable borders they represent. As Tabish Khair extrapolates, terror arises not only from a desire to wreak violence and havoc in the name of a particular principle, but also from a Western imperial 'refusal to recognize all that can exceed our beautified (beatified) and domesticated limits' in creating the conditions for non-Western war, poverty, and insecurity (2015, 70).[1] The West's refusal to recognize its own responsibility in creating the historical and material conditions for terrorist activities in this way further contributes to the continued generation of extremist sympathies.

Such an awareness, with its emphasis on the permeable boundaries between self and Other, colony and postcolony, and global North and South, underpins this chapter's exploration of two twenty-first-century postcolonial Gothic texts: Tash Aw's *The Harmony Silk Factory* (2005) and Nadeem Aslam's *The Wasted Vigil* (2008). While set in very different global geographies and time periods – the latter in 1930s and 1940s Malaysia, the former in contemporary Afghanistan during the 'War on Terror' – both novels register how imperial practices play a role in shaping terrorist violence, histories of invasion and impunity themselves constituting a normalized form of terrorism. Central to this understanding, to borrow Derek Gregory's words, is an appreciation of terror's proverbial 'vanishing point', where law becomes 'a site of political struggle not only in its suspension but also in its *formulation, interpretation and application*' and where unjust but supposedly democratic policies are legitimated through proscribed legal discourses (Gregory 2010, 63–4). As Edward Said likewise asserts, terror's discourse spawns 'uses of language, rhetoric and argument that are frightening in their capacity for mobilizing opinion, gaining legitimacy and provoking various sorts of murderous action' (Said 2006). In effect, in confronting terror through a decolonial Gothic lens, these texts bear witness to the West's own terroristic violence both in 'states of exception' and *in the law itself*, simultaneously criminalizing global Southern and minority identities and seeking to police and punish these.

As Sarah Ilott comments, this critical understanding is visible across the Gothic's literary history, where repeated engagements with imperial terror function to destabilize social and political hierarchies, revealing 'the Helegian dialectic on which such binary oppositions of good/evil, white/black, centre/margin and self/Other rest' (2021, 20). Moreover, as Rebecca Duncan avers, this history can be comprehended not only in terms of a 'destabilising strategy' or an ambiguous aesthetic, but also through a Gothic rendering of more 'accretive' forms of identity out of line with the colonial or neocolonial status quo. 'On this view,' she explains, 'hybrid gothic figures are constructed through a dynamic and indiscriminate agglomerative process, standing as a mode of being that is realised in the unpremeditated and disorganised forging of temporary connections with elements of the organic and inorganic world' (Duncan 2017, 129). In other words, the Gothic's investment in hybrid and monstrous identities and landscapes makes visible new transhuman, cross-species, and planetary forms of interaction not always accessible in other more realist modes of writing.

In the fictions I examine here, Aw's *The Harmony Silk Factory* and Aslam's *The Wasted Vigil*, this latter appreciation becomes visible through complex engagements with indigenous landscapes, which haunt the narratives in various monstrous and uncanny ways. In Aw's novel, this encompasses both British and Japanese imperial histories in modern-day Malaysia, here gradually uncovered as a Gothic equatorial space of ghostly presences enshrouded amongst dense vegetation and uncertain borders. By contrast, Aslam's novel confronts the palimpsestic terrain of modern-day Afghanistan, where layered geological excavations and uncanny returns of past battles again encode a laminous spectral history of ongoing warfare. In either case, terror emerges as a practice registered not only on or by the characters but also *the land*, which itself bears witness to and participates within hidden cartographies of Western-authorized violence.

While these texts in this way abound with Gothic descriptions of Eastern individuals and communities terrorized under Western imperialism, they also offer testimony to how terror operates more subtly, on the planet itself, concealing and erasing its exploitative strategies, even as it inflicts indelible violence. As Esthie Hugo writes, the cost of war in such texts can be read in 'urgent allegories for the unevenness of capitalist development, where foreign investors prepare to feast on the profits of new ventures, while locals must endure the horrors of a dying planet shaped by centuries of social and ecological violence' (Hugo 2022, 96). Similarly, in these fictions' Gothic chronicles both military violence and a 'dark ecology' (Morton 2016) become apparent, registering layered eras of (neo) colonial brutality and in this way chronicling the pressing need for anti-capitalist critique and reassessment.

## Tropical Gothic and Imperial Deception in *The Harmony Silk Factory*

Negotiating a lyrical language, as well as a multivocal narrative structure established around a central mystery plot, Aw's *The Harmony Silk Factory* garnered enormous attention upon its 2005 release, longlisted for the Booker and winning the Whitbread first novel award. Set in the verdant equatorial landscape of twentieth-century Malaysia and moving between the 1990s and the 1930s and 1940s, the novel offers a prime example of what Justin D. Edwards and Sandra Guardini Vasconcelos refer to as the 'tropical Gothic', deftly negotiating uncanny and spectral signifiers to 'return the colonial Other to the center of Empire' (Edwards and Guardini Vasconcelos, 2016, 2). Within this politically complex and self-conscious genre, Gothic questions regarding 'notions of (un) belonging, racialised identity, [...] and the burden of the clandestine past on the uncertain, crumbling present' are brought forth through representations of colonial oppression, as well as 'racism and resistance against the practices of imperialism – all of which are shared by many tropical and sub-tropical regions' (Lundberg, Ancuta, and Stasiewicz-Bieńkowska 2019, 4). In positioning this novel within this critical framework, then, this reading seeks to underline its decolonial Gothic concerns, seeing these as central to its twenty-first-century relevance and cultural-political timeliness.

In a feature common to both novels and reflective of their transnational outlooks, Aw's text negotiates an array of international characters, including Malay, Straits Chinese, Japanese, and English voices, underlining migratory movements and contrasting global perspectives attached to Malaysia's Second World War conflicts. This focus on a haunting past and multiple readings of

Malaysian history explicitly underlines historiographical anxieties, foregrounding 'the emplotment of history in terms of structures of literary genres' (Saxena 2020, 2), moving between multiple narrative viewpoints and aesthetic registers. While postmodern textualist questions of 'selection, exclusion, and interpretation' (Saxena 2020, 2) clearly shape the direction of this narrative, however, equally vital within a contemporary context is the novel's concern with discourses and practices of terrorism, wherein the central (unspeaking) character, Johnny Lim, is repeatedly presumed a terrorist, though the meaning, truth, and force of this categorization changes depending on the narrator. Based on the real-life 'triple agent' Lai Tek, known for his terrorist engagements in connection with the Malayan Communist Party (MCP), British Empire, *and* Japanese Empire, this particular choice of central character thus prioritizes tropical Gothic questions of presumed racial monstrosity, positioning this specifically within the context of twentieth-century Southeast Asia.

Following Anita Lundberg, Katarzyna Ancuta, and Agnieszka Stasiewicz-Bieńkowska's description of the tropical Gothic as balancing 'a paradisiacal terrain of sensuality and opulent beauty' with 'a hellish space of hidden terrors and masked monstrosities' (2019, 2), the main events of *The Harmony Silk Factory* take place at a distance from urban Kuala Lumpur, in the jungle landscape of the Kinta Valley and the mysterious oceanic topography of the fictional Seven Maiden Islands. Here, in a terrain defined by its dense vegetation, ghostly inhabitants and uncanny sea-faring encounters, Johnny changes his fate from that of imperial 'coolie' to local Communist leader and wealthy owner of a successful textile company, thus throwing into question his hidden tactics in achieving such power. Beginning with the account of his son Jasper, who describes him as a 'monster' (Aw 2005, 35), willing to betray family and friends to improve himself, the narrative then shifts to his wife Snow's more sympathetic perspective and finally to that of his English companion and confidant (but also betrayer), Peter Wormwood. Over the course of this multivocal chronical, then, three different perspectives emerge for the reader's inspection: proffering Johnny as a duplicitous traitor, a struggling outsider, and an (ultimately abandoned) friend. In each case, the landscape surrounding the account shapes and complicates its Gothic narrative outlook, enshrouding Johnny in an aura of exoticism and mystery, but also undercutting such Orientalist registers through self-consciousness critical overtones.

One way of approaching this narrative structure, then, consistent with what Gina Wisker describes as a postcolonial Gothic attention to forms of '"becoming" [...], moving constructively beyond indictment and guilt to new unities' (Wisker

2007, 155), is by recognizing how these contrasting tropical narratives together invoke an entirely different wartime biography, reaching beyond a defined or static viewpoint in favour of fluidity. In this case, an attention to notable gaps running throughout the three narratives in connection to their distinct representations of Johnny sees the novel hinting at repressed colonial horrors and abjections, challenging established personal and political truth claims. In this way, Jasper's supposedly official account of Johnny's 'monstrous' persona in fact makes clear his own unreliability, underlining that the authoritative 'truths' framing archival history include ghost stories as well as facts. The much darker reality of systematic oppression, as Johnny is exploited and tortured under his British imperial employers, and later laughed at and scorned by his Malay in-laws and betrayed by Peter, also comes through in this layered narrative, which seeks to situate his 'terroristic' behaviours, positioning these contextually under a retrospective awareness of imperial deception.

Three narrative scenes in particular elucidate the decolonizing focus of the novel's Gothic agenda: first, Jasper's Gothically laden and unreliable account of Johnny's supposed monstrosity; second, Snow's likewise Gothic recollections of his attraction and her desire; and third, Peter's depiction of both Johnny and the country itself as untameable Gothic wilderness. The first of these stories, Jasper's, begins by directly positioning Johnny in the guise of a haunting 'spirit', invoking the local legend of the pirate Mat Hitam as a site for comparison. As the latter 'for nearly twenty years [...] terrorised the stately ships filled with valuable cargo', upsetting the local community with his 'ruthlessness' and 'fury' (Aw 2005, 16–17), so Johnny too is accused of wreaking terror through carefully organized acts of pillage, smuggling, and murder, appearing in local folktales as 'no flesh and blood at all but a phantom' (ibid., 92).

In so far as this story draws on a distinctly Orientalist register, where Mat Hitam is described as 'the rarest of all people: a black Chinese' (ibid., 16), the novel seeks to investigate this traitorous history within a distinctly decolonial agenda, combining historical detail with critical awareness of the narrator's untrustworthiness and violence. While Jasper thus authorizes stereotyped archival accounts of his father's brutality, seeing him as innately criminal, 'born with an illness [...] erasing all that was good in him' (Aw 2005, 35, 51), other details of the narrative upset this demonizing account, instead engaging the reader's sympathy and critical scepticism. In particular, Jasper's own disturbing record of his father's abuse under his colonial employers clearly complicates the son's allegations of his father's ruthless self-interest, contextualizing Johnny's behaviour within an equally Gothic chronical of colonial terror. More than a monster, what Johnny appears here is battered spirit worn down by constant brutality and driven by the need to survive to strategize resistance.

By contrast to Jasper, Snow's narrative is more sympathetic and emotionally nuanced, expressly registering Johnny's outsider status within the Malay community and seeking to expose his mistreatment on the part of elite society. As Vandana Saxena writes, 'In Snow's account, one catches the glimpse of Johnny Lim in the liminal time and space in-between the public archival records. The fact that Jasper misses reading Snow's diary [...] hints at his neglect of alternate narratives or memories that might disturb his preconceived notions about his father's past' (Saxena 2020, 5). Indeed, where Chinese settler communities play a key role in catalysing Malaysian independence, and where the novel's focus on the occupation period functions to accentuate this (Sim 2011, 302), this ghostly narrative also registers Johnny's critical importance in strategically playing imperial governments against each other and in incentivizing collectivist sentiment and anti-imperial activism. As he insists, 'The Chinese people believe communism is the only thing that will save them from oppression, and they are right' (Aw 2005, 172). In this determined protest against oppression, even while Snow's narrative allows for Johnny's betrayal of the party under the weight of Japanese imperial threats, her letters self-consciously bear witness to his faith in local solidarity, contrasting the easy complicity of her own parents and friends within Japanese Empire.

Such a reading thus underlines Snow's general sympathy for Johnny's cause, as it emerges that it is *she*, rather than he, that initiates their relations, again contesting Jasper's bitter claims that Johnny seduced her in pursuit of his own ambitions. It becomes clear, indeed, throughout this section that *she* desires *him* and is drawn by his perceived authority and supposed otherworldliness, a position which reinforces her naivety and inexperience. Despite Snow's ostensibly congenial reading of Johnny and his politics, however, other aspects of her narrative complicate her position, again incorporating Gothic signifiers to situate her desire and his attraction. Repeatedly throughout her chronical, Snow positions her feelings for Johnny specifically in relation to his perceived difference, describing him as 'alien' and like 'some strange, sinuous animal, [...] almost as if we were a different race' (Aw 2005, 159, 146). This could be read as reflecting Snow's resistance to her parents' racism and snobbery, in that she contests their unashamed disdain for Johnny's Chinese heritage and autochthonous background and embraces his assumed difference. On the other hand, in a novel repeatedly attentive to colonial discourse's violence, this exoticizing language clearly alerts the reader's suspicion: despite her evident attraction to Johnny, her idiom reduces him to an exotic animal, casting both her desire and his identity in fetishizing terms. Echoing Eddie Tay's description, 'Malaya here becomes the "inscrutable East" that is familiar in the discourse of Orientalism', especially as Johnny is rendered 'unfamiliar' and 'unknowable' and in this way made to stand in for the 'unhomely' nation more largely (Tay 2011, 138). Accordingly, a call for critical scepticism underpins the text's decolonial Gothic politics, urging caution regarding this discourse's own terroristic facets.

One other key aspect of this representation, specifically important to the tropical Gothic, concerns its idea of the jungle itself as supposedly violent, where both Johnny *and* his surroundings are read to represent a kind of alluring, forbidden danger, an exotic alter-world the British and Japanese have mistakenly intruded upon. As Christopher Menadue writes, this understanding reads the jungle precisely in terms of a boundary between civilization and savagery, where those who cross the line are said to 'exhibit carnal desires and violent behaviours in response to the opportunities and threats they encounter' (Menadue 2017, 125). In *The Harmony Silk Factory*, this exoticizing outlook becomes especially relevant to apprehending Peter's narrative, where the latter's aesthete viewpoint likewise understands this space as a kind of paradise lost: a 'tropical Eden' revealed as 'the high capital of Satan and his peers' (Aw 2005, 319). The sense of deception contained in this account of the jungle sees Peter reduced to a problematic desperation, his fantasy of tropical perfection pushing him to betray his friend and to seduce Snow as a route to utopia. In effect, Peter seeks to impose a European colonial perspective on both the land and its inhabitants, incorporating both discourse and physical violence (in the form of rape) in this project – achieving his 'vision' regardless of its consequences on those around him.

Throughout the course of the novel this disturbing conclusion is prefaced by Peter's repeated advances on Snow, as well as, metaphorically, by his attempts to penetrate, hold back and contain the jungle, constructing miniature garden sites which curate and preserve its paradisiacal qualities. As Pauline Newton summarizes, 'Peter seems to play the role of the imperialist who wishes to tailor the colonised land to his or her own taste, but as Aw slowly reveals, Peter simultaneously and self-consciously recognises the inevitability and futility of this accomplishment' (Newton 2008, 175). In this frustrated awareness of imperial futility, then, the novel emphasizes Peter's blindness in enacting his treachery, where it is bitterness, rather than hope, that drives his behaviour. The condemnatory implications of this ending see colonialism's violence again shaping and structuring Johnny's identity, acting as the terroristic cause for his anger and struggle, rather than vice versa.

In the final account, then, all three narratives bear witness to the Gothic destructiveness of colonialism's methods, tactics which simultaneously exoticize the colonial subject and selectively accuse him of terroristic behaviours. In Boehmer and Morton's words, such discourses and practices exemplify 'the terroristic violence through which modern states randomly assert their authority' (Boehmer and Morton 2015, 9), playing on the imposed voicelessness of the colonial subject to make this Law. In the self-conscious contours of this historically reflexive novel, Johnny Lim's ghost is re-encountered and revived, granted a voice through the contradictions and gaps between the unreliable accounts of these three narrators. More than terror what here becomes explicit is Johnny's resistance to control and subjugation, as he defies and challenges the multiple conflicting powers that seek to contain him.

## Subterranean Gothic and Afghanistan's Ghosts in *The Wasted Vigil*

By contrast to the flourishing tropical landscape of *The Harmony Silk Factory*, the setting of *The Wasted Vigil* is much less verdant, representing instead the war-torn and desolate terrain of modern-day Afghanistan, a geography which war photographer Lynsey Addario describes as looking 'bombed out when it hasn't been bombed' (Addario 2015, 103). On a contrasting note, journalist Emma Graham-Harrison notes how 'Afghanistan's spectacular beauty stuns most foreigners who visit primed to expect violence, suffering and terrible poverty, because that is mostly what gets on televisions and makes headlines' (Graham-Harrison 2014). For Aslam, combining these divergent viewpoints, the reality represented by Afghanistan is something more complex, encompassing radical violence, but also hidden beauty and artistry of incredible proportions: a recognition that he offers as 'a way of mourning the dead' in a form that 'in no way takes away from the deaths' (qtd in Jaggi 2013). Put differently, *The Wasted Vigil*'s rubble-strewn and Gothic topography also houses numerous buried treasures and concealed wonders: a subterranean Gothic, which incorporates both horror and revelatory spectres.

Described by Joan Passey as a genre concerned 'with the buried and disinterred, the repressed and re-emergent' (Passey 2020), the subterranean Gothic is present from the first line of this text, in the ghostly description enshrouding the figure of Lara. 'Her mind is a haunted house' (Aslam 2008, 5), the novel begins, commenting on her disturbed, trauma-laden psychology, as she comes to Afghanistan in search of her missing brother Benedikt, a former

Soviet soldier. The house she visits, that of Marcus Caldwell, mirrors this spectral, haunted consciousness, embodying in its location and decoration its occupants' bruised and fractured sensibilities, as well as the buried detritus of multiple decades of wartime destruction. Lara reflects:

> the area around the lake is said to contain the djinn. Lake wind, mountain wind, orchard wind collide in the vicinity, but to the Muslims the air is also lastingly alive with the good and bad invisible tribes of the universe. (Aslam 2008, 15)

While Marcus himself rejects these ghostly associations, seeing the djinn as the product of political scheming – the convenient 'myth' of a local cleric needing to cover up the murder of his wives, whose bodies he has buried here (Aslam 2008, 25) – in another sense, the text reveals how the house and the country itself are indeed haunted by 'the invisible tribes of the universe', damaged and distorted by an ongoing war whose violence has reconfigured it. As one passage puts it, '[t]his country was one of the greatest tragedies of the age. Torn to pieces by the many hands of war, by the various hatreds and failings of the world. Two million deaths over the past quarter-century' (ibid., 12–13). Through the language of destruction and spectrality, then, the novel underlines Afghanistan's damaged contemporary situation, as it remains haunted by a seemingly ever-returning cycle of wartime violence.

This Gothic understanding is evident both in the novel's setting – with its palimpsest landscape of wars and disasters – and in its characterization, where the shared and intertwining traumas of these five individuals make up a transnational 'kinship of wounds', as the novel describes this (ibid., 10). Prior to its destruction in the event of war, the house was characterized by its display of Afghan art, artefacts and education, symbolic in exhibiting the cultural backlog of Afghan history. Not only does it pageant the ornate paintings of a nineteenth-century artist and calligrapher, representative of Afghanistan's long artistic investment, it also houses a perfume factory on its grounds, and within this, an enormous head of a Buddha, the latter reflecting a previous cultural and religious heritage now facing destruction.[2]

Both Marcus' house and the Buddha have recently come under the violence of the Taliban, a ban on representations of living things forcing Marcus to cover over room after room of artwork with mud. As Lara reflects, 'Even an ant on a pebble had been daubed. It was as though all life had been returned to dust' (ibid., 13). Despite this project of systematic erasure however, the novel suggests how this buried terrain continues to re-emerge in ghostly emissions, reminding the house's inhabitants of its still-living presence and cultural authority.

This is evident, for example, in Marcus' discovery of the Buddha, where the endeavour to excavate this ancient Gandharan artifact sees him confronting 'a face from another time', which then makes him wonder 'if the rest of the body was buried nearby, whole or fragmented' (ibid., 22–3). Marcus later continues, 'he now seemed to be opening fully his almost shut eyes, the lids chiselled in the stone beginning to rise without sound in what felt like an endless moment' (ibid., 43). This description of a waking ghost, lifting itself out of the land: 'a stone stillness' and a perfume 'like the soul vacating the body after death' (ibid., 23, 7), invokes a reinstatement of cultural signifiers comparable to what Walter Benjamin refers to as 'profane illumination', a notion offered to explain the encounter with cultural artifacts as a form of ghostly 'materialist, anthropological inspiration' (Benjamin 1978, 179).

As Margaret Cohen elaborates, this concept invokes 'the valorization of the realm of a culture's ghosts and phantasms as a significant and rich field of social production,' and likewise as a 'dehierarchization of the epistemological privilege accorded the visual in the direction of integration of the senses' (Cohen 1995, 11). By repeated emphasis on cultural spectres and sensuous forms of historical recall, then, the novel elucidates an alternate spirit-world still alive despite ongoing annihilation, a world in which 'a different kind of materialism, neither idealistic nor alienated, but [rather …] receptive, close, perceptual' (Gordon 2008, 205) counters the relentless violence of state sanctioned terror. Borrowing Pheng Cheah's words, this is the 'non-utopian promise' conjured by Aslam's Gothic vision, where 'quivering beneath the surface of the existing world are other worlds to come' (Cheah 2016, 308).

This understanding also emerges in more explicitly politicized passages, where spectral images and abject objects, uncovered and excavated from the land, conjure larger collective experiences of hidden violence and trauma, as well as potential restoration. Marcus wife Qatrina's endeavour to rescue the family's books from demolition sees her unearthing and nailing these to the ceiling in terror: 'A spike driven through the pages of history, a spike through the pages of love, a spike through the sacred' (Aslam 2008, 5). While on the one hand, this act of destruction itself indexes Qatrina's trauma in surviving the Taliban, where she 'repeats the violence she has had to inflict on her husband' under this government, conjuring 'an assault on love, the sacred, and history that is the tally of the quarter century of war in Afghanistan' (Abbas 2014, 204), on the other hand, it also positions these levitating volumes as spectral reminders of a haunting national past, ghostly remnants of what was once a thriving culture. As Alla Ivanchikova writes, such artifacts instance 'the layer of deposits associated with Taliban rule […] audiotapes, books, paintings, family photographs', all here recovered and placed on display as ghostly 'fossils' (Ivanchikova 2019, 186).

In one notably disturbing excerpt, the novel describes Afghanistan itself as a site of collective burial, wherein 'everyone's life now lies broken at different levels within the rubble' (Aslam 2009, 29). The text continues:

> Some are trapped near the surface, while others find themselves entombed deeper down, pinned under tons of smashed masonry and shattered beams from where their cries cannot be heard by anyone on the surface, only – and inconsequentially – by those around them. (Ibid., 39)

In this Gothic passage, reinforcing, again, a 'deep-time' approach to Afghan history (Ivanchikova 2019, 177), this depiction registers the nation's continuous exploitation and entombment on the part of imperial powers, but also the idea that this violence is recorded in the land's own history, carved in ghostly substrata which might, however tenuously, be excavated and recovered. The fragments of broken paintings that Lara slowly pieces together also clearly register this *long-durée* history, summoning up 'an army of ghostly lovers' in the process of restoration in such a way as to record a promise of societal healing (Aslam 2009, 39).

The novel's engagement with the Gothic in this way emerges as equivocal but also hopeful, inviting confidence in history's capacity to heal and recover, as the text moves fluidly between scenes of anguish and poetic fascination. As Peter Morey remarks, 'Aslam's novel identifies with those, however imperfect, who are able to respond to the beauty of human cultural activities, seeing in them a shared instinct for self-expression that transcends time and place' (Morey 2018, 192). In other words, the text counters its 'kinship of wounds' with 'a citizenship of the realm of the mind' (Aslam 2008, 10 and 87), conjuring a common intellectual investment providing wartime solace.[3] Indeed, more than horror (despite its 'documented savagery' (Adams 2008)), this novel offers a subterranean Gothic focused on critique of (neo)colonialism, unearthing alongside Afghanistan's dark history a ghostly symbol of strength and resistance. In this respect, by incorporating motifs of burial and excavation, as well as uncanny returns of submerged histories, the novel strategically identifies the Gothic factors shaping contemporary War on Terror conflicts, but also the still glimmering hope of national recovery and post-war affirmation.

## Uncanny Returns and Reprisals

This message is also reaffirmed in both novels at the level of narrative events and storyline, in what emerge as deeply fractured and cyclical plots. In Aw's novel, this comes through in a structure of repeated returns, as the novel breaks off after each individual narrator's chronicle, only then to return to previous events from a new perspective, which then casts new insight on the gaps and errors in what came before. In accordance with a long Gothic tradition of blurring fact and fiction through use of the trope of the found document, as well as through multiple narrative perspectives and styles, the novel endeavours to 'convey the truth about events of the past in a more adequate way than a potential unitary perspective would, although this mode of presentation lacks the compelling explanatory power of a unified narrative' (Kucała 2022, 157). In these circular returns to pre-narrated events, the reader is thus prompted to reread and reinterpret established truth claims to recognize hidden realities and misconstruals, thus garnering more perspective on what has ensued and how this is best deciphered.

Indeed, to borrow Michael Rothberg's terminology, the reader here becomes an 'implicated subject' within these events, required through rereading and re-interpreting to re-define her own complex relationship to the historical events related, and to understand participation beyond the simple categories of 'victims' and perpetrators' (Rothberg 2019, 1).[4] As Rothberg writes, 'Modes of implication – entanglement in historical and present-day injustices – are complex, multifaceted, and sometimes contradictory, but are nonetheless essential to confront in the pursuit of justice' (ibid., 2). Through them, we can begin to distinguish 'collective responsibility among those positioned as implicated subjects – that is, those who occupy the histories and structures of racial privilege and white supremacy' (ibid.). In this way, through repeated challenges to the reader to rediscover and reanalyse these events, and to consider again and again, with whom she empathizes or commiserates, a larger structure of complex violence underpinning these incidents becomes evident, incorporating questions of sympathy and beneficence alongside guilt and innocence. As Snow reflects, 'the pages of this diary, clear and indelible' reflect new 'burning light' on these events – their words 'throw open the shutters and let the light in' (Aw 2005, 131, 130).

Comparably, Aslam's novel also incorporates a complex chronology to complement its sedimented topography, this requiring some exploration to understand its Gothic meanings. Starting with an epigraphic citation of former National Security Advisor, Zbigniew Brzezinski, which encodes an *unheimlich* return of repressed American violence in the Cold War, this passage immediately foregrounds uncanny temporalities. Having been asked whether 'he regretted "having supported Islamic fundamentalism, having given arms and advice to future terrorists,"' Brzezinski answers by dismissing the question, disavowing any hint of political responsibility (Aslam 2008, Epigraph). In this unbending political confidence, dismissing 'a few agitated Muslims' (Aslam 2008, Epigraph), the passage highlights the Cold War's haunting return within the present, as it reconfigures existing wartime relations in ways that explicitly recall the West's past complicity in Islamic fundamentalism, what Mahmood Mamdani refers to as the 'monster of modernity' instanced by American jihadi politics (Mamdani 2005).[5]

In representing multiple layers of Afghanistan history, *The Wasted Vigil* thus investigates such eerie 'return' moments, in this way situating its excavations overtly within a larger purview of untimely encounters.[6] This emerges through complex relations between individual characters, but also through the historical-political battles and environmental destructions surrounding these, all played out on Afghanistan's palimpsestic landscape. Indeed, it is not simply that British imperialism (represented in the person of Marcus) predicates future (neo) colonial projects in the region. Rather, uncanny similarities between past and present position Cold War and War on Terror brutalities as ghostly repetitions of not-quite-forgotten imperial brutalities: British, Soviet, and American 'interventions' all summoning up similar tactics and consequences.

The younger characters, Casa and Dunia, also tie this history to Afghanistan's current situation, the former's terrorist connections seeing him as part of a radicalized youth movement, while the latter's devout but non-fundamentalist viewpoint positions her as an oft-overlooked victim of contemporary extremist power.[7] Visiting Marcus for medical help after accidentally exploding a local landmine, Casa is forced to stay to escape retributions after being spotted in the company of Westerns, thus compromising himself through a moment of radical vulnerability (Aslam 2008, 191). By contrast, Dunia seeks refuge knowing Marcus' liberal viewpoint, having herself become the target of post-Taliban extremism on account of her progressive values, as well as her refusal to marry a local warlord, Gul Rasool. Disgusted by the violence and pettiness of this warlord's position, she commits to her faith and remains at odds with the other characters' secularism, seeing Islam as encompassing a defence of liberal tolerance and respect for difference (ibid., 319–20).[8] While both characters thus emerge as notably exposed to fundamentalist violence, what becomes clear across the course of the narrative is just how equally defenceless Afghani lives are against American brutalities, where, as it transpires, the CIA works directly alongside Rasool to gain intelligence information.

The fact that by the time David attempts to rescue Casa, the latter has already decided to martyr himself as a suicide bomber, also killing David in the process, emerges merely as the tragic irony of this too-late acknowledgement on David's part: where had he only admitted his own responsibility for Casa in anticipation of this event, he might well have saved both himself and the boy from this gruesome fate. In this way, the 'wasted vigil' of the novel's title crucially references America's failure of ethical accountability, calling for an urgent confrontation with exceptionalist politics and ethical and political infractions. While this does not deny the violence of local Afghan warlords, it sees this as bound up in a larger (neo)colonial venture, in this way repositioning Afghan 'civil war' as part of a much larger transnational conflict.[9]

## Conclusion

In both novels explored in this chapter, then, multiple local, national, and international considerations register a layered colonial history, as diverse actors and institutions each play a part in shaping these conflicts and characters. To some extent, the reader is left to decide for herself how to interpret the (notably complex) battleground, balancing a sense of ambivalent hope against ongoing destruction and devastation. Nevertheless, what is clear in both cases is how these fictions confront terrorism as a modern *Western* institution, negotiating decolonial Gothic techniques to demonstrate its state-based and material violence and misapplication. In this way, while set in radically different locations and invested in contrasting geopolitical histories – taking into consideration both tropical or subterranean Gothic landscapes – these texts nevertheless conjointly bear witness to colonialism's own terror and to the need for continuing resistance, as a means to dismantling ongoing power structures and to bolstering a decolonial critical agenda.

## Notes

1 Khair's writing on the postcolonial Gothic is significant in underlining the surfeit of emotion produced by Gothic writing and how this functions to rupture established norms of Western conformity and compliance. He reflects, 'If the displaced become instruments of terror, it is as much because we, who have decided to stay at home or who have the privileged option of making the entire globe our home, have for too long averted our eyes from those who are "elsewhere" or who come from "elsewhere"' (2015, 70). His suggestion, as I read it, is that the postcolonial Gothic may help to

amend this blindsightedness, making readers more aware of the West's own investments in terroristic violence.

2   The specific reference here is to the decision on the part of the Taliban to destroy the Buddhas of Bamiyan, huge statues carved into the sandstone cliffs of the Bamiyan Valley. As David Cook explains, this decision was key to establishing stronger relations between the Taliban and their foreign supporters by supposedly demonstrating 'the complete fidelity of the Taliban regime to the literal implementation of the shari'a in its totality' (2005, 175).

3   Eoin Flannery's reading of the novel likewise underlines this recuperative focus, noting how *The Wasted Vigil* 'cleaves to the notion that hope and redemption are possible, even in the most acutely violent crucibles of warfare: Afghanistan' (2013, 298).

4   Lisa Lampert-Weissig also incorporates Rothberg's terminology in her excellent reading of Sarah Perry's *Melmoth* (2018), which navigates found documents to examine the Gothic history of Second World War Prague. See Lampert-Weissig (2022).

5   Mamdani's writing is critical to understanding this repressed American Cold War investment in jihad. He explains,

> In the 1980s, the Reagan administration declared the Soviet Union an 'evil empire' and set aside the then-common secular model of national liberation in favor of an international Islamic jihad. Thanks to that approach the Afghan rebels used charities to recruit tens of thousands of volunteers and created the militarized madrassas (Islamic schools) that turned these volunteers into cadres. Without the rallying cause of the jihad, the Afghan mujahideen would have had neither the numbers, the training, the organization, nor the coherence or sense of mission that has since turned jihadist Islam into a global political force. (2005)

Aslam repeatedly draws on this 'monstrous' historical-political understanding throughout the novel.

6   Pei-chen Liao identifies such uncanny returns as instances of political 'blowback' occasioned by the fallout of US Cold War policy, wherein 'the former familiar (homely) friend becomes the present unfamiliar (unhomely) enemy' (2013, 4). Again, this reading reaffirms *The Wasted Vigil*'s politicized Gothic aesthetic.

7   While noting Casa's positioning in the novel as a radicalized youth that is being manipulated by local warlords, as Amit Chaudhuri notes, it is important to recognize that the novel never directly refers to Casa as a terrorist, thus evading the demonizing implications that this categorization carries (2009, 5).

8   Countering what Ruzy Suliza Hashim and Noraini Md Yusof explain as a common Western myth of Muslim women deprived of 'voice and agency' (2014, 132), Dunia emerges as a strong female character, outspoken in asserting her beliefs and

challenging patriarchal oppression within the country. Likewise, while Aslam's earlier novel, *Maps for Lost Lovers*, can be seen to in some ways sustain Orientalist stereotypes, authorizing a view of Islamic religious intolerance and ideological short-sightedness, as Sara Upstone comments, Dunia's composed and humble devotion, entirely at odds with Taliban fanaticism, invokes an alternative, more celebratory perspective on Islamic piety (2010, 106).

9  Oona Frawley's reading of the novel also emphasizes this transnational reading of Afghan civil war in the novel. She reflects,

> the novel demonstrates [...] what scholars have increasingly argued: that the term 'civil war' glosses over many situations to which it cannot (and arguably should not) apply. [...] When we consider the current Afghani 'civil war' in this light what becomes immediately apparent is the absurdity of deeming it to be an internal conflict deriving from an identity crisis of local or even regional proportions. (2013, 445–7)

3

# Gothic Inheritance

## Imperial Witchcraft and Haunted Houses in Helen Oyeyemi's *White is for Witching* and Sarah Waters' *The Little Stranger*

Retaining the previous chapter's concern with a decolonized contemporary Gothic, attentive to oppressive material relations and socioeconomic practices underpinning (neo)colonialism – and visible as much *now*, in our Capitalocene present, as in the industrial past – this chapter continues and extends this analysis by exploring the theme of inheritance within twenty-first-century British Gothic, most specifically in the neo-Victorian Gothic writing of Helen Oyeyemi's *White is for Witching* and Sarah Waters' *The Little Stranger*. Set respectively in the postmillennial present and in the post-war 1940s, neither novel invokes this neo-Victorian classification immediately, instead more readily signalling postcolonial and historiographical anxieties tied to other eras. As Emma Parker registers, Waters' novel can be read as a non-traditional 'country house novel', comparable to Evelyn Waugh's *Brideshead Revisited* (1945) and Josephine Tey's *The Franchise Affair* (1948), though consciously upending these earlier texts' conservative values in favour of critique (Parker 2013, 99–101). Likewise, Oyeyemi's novel, while widely read as Gothic, is also often critically situated outside the genre, set alongside other contemporary (often non-Gothic) texts and praised for being 'at the vanguard of innovation in contemporary Black British women's literature' (Bekers and Cousins 2021, 205) or as part of a larger African literary diaspora (Leetsch 2021; Wester 2019; Durán-Almarza and Álverez López 2013). In each case, other concerns apart from a nineteenth-century Gothic sociopolitical or intertextual inheritance take priority over this neo-Victorian Gothic reading, positioning it as secondary to understanding the novel's contemporary importance.

Nevertheless, in themselves, neither of these approaches necessarily obstructs a neo-Victorian Gothic analysis, as indeed, various critics of these works have already recognized (see Heilmann 2012; Cousins 2012). As Andrew Smith notes, 'in order to understand our culture's engagement with the past, it is necessary to rethink any narrowly defined view of the neo-Victorian that simply depends on the model of a contemporary novel set in the nineteenth-century' (Smith 2012, 53). Likewise, Louisa Hadley notes how 'rather than merely being another manifestation of that cultural fascination [with the Victorians in the present...], neo-Victorian fictions seek to both reinsert the Victorians into their particular historical context and engage with contemporary uses of the Victorians which efface that historical context' (2010, 6). With this in mind, and with a simultaneous concern that neo-Victorian texts need not be read under a solely postmodern or metafictional agenda – given the 're-entry of "feeling and the affective" into both literary re-visions and "critical discourse on this period"' (Kohlke and Gutleben 2012, 16) – this chapter looks to recognize how these texts' respective engagements with the Victorian Gothic provide invaluable insights on twenty-first-century British society, including in its darker aspects and engagements with abjection, fear, and horror.

More specifically, I explore how both Victorian *and* contemporary representations of inheritance in these novels feed into a Gothic materialist politics, for example in relation to post-2000 UK immigration law (in *White is for Witching*) and New Labour economics (in *The Little Stranger*). While in each case these concerns invoke expressly twenty-first-century anxieties, seemingly disconnected from the nineteenth-century past, nevertheless, as I emphasize, they engage Victorian Gothic intertexts and idioms in direct and compelling ways, demonstrating how, in Robert Miles' words, the nineteenth-century emerges 'as the site of struggle between incipient modernity and an unenlightened past' – the 'Gothic cusp' against which we now understand modern identity (Spooner 2007, 44).

As Sophie Gilmartin reflects, the inheritance theme is crucial to the nineteenth-century novel, where 'younger brothers, arranged marriages, adoption, illegitimacy, misalliance, the need for an heir [...] become the driving force of plot, and [narratives] are centred in the family tree and the will to keep the family line going' (Gilmartin 1998, 12). Put differently, inheritance structures the nineteenth-century novel in its engagement with a rapidly fading past, as well as in its negotiation of changing familial, national, and imperial traditions. On a similar note, Jessica Cox, looking at the Victorian sensation novel and considering its overlap with the Victorian Gothic, identifies how this modality 'persistently exhibits a concern with the inheritance of wealth, property, title, and names, as well as physical and mental health and characteristics' – for example through 'concealed marriages, forged documents, secret wills, and hereditary maladies' (Cox 2019, 196, 199). In each case, violence in the act of bequeathment at once directs and in other ways complicates the plot and narrative, proclaiming as 'natural' an order which nevertheless overtly upends depicted social relations. As Cox continues, 'just as the focus on the past in the neo-sensation novel conceals the genre's concern with contemporary issues [...], so too does the Victorian genre's engagement with the present obscure its interest in the influence of the past' (ibid., 199). Put differently, inheritance comes to be understood in many Victorian Gothic texts as *given*, rather than constructed – a site of scandal, but also a (deeply problematic) destiny that remains at once mystified and triumphant.

Such textual anxieties are visible across a range of celebrated Gothic fictions, such as Charlotte Brontë's *Jane Eyre* (1847), Emily Brontë's *Wuthering Heights* (1847), Wilkie Collins' *The Woman in White* (1860), and Mary Elizabeth Braddon's *Lady Audley's Secret* (1862), all of which figure the theme of inheritance centrally. Such texts reflect prominent changes happening in connection to a number of nineteenth-century political and legal reforms, including working-class male voting rights; a rapidly growing women's movement and accompanying shifts in marriage and property law; the abolition of fee tails and changes to the law of primogeniture; as well as a prominent evolutionary discourse increasingly seen to define biological inheritance (Cox 2019, 198). Such radical shifts and disruptions to the established social order produced widespread fears of degeneration and decline, which were then often reflected and channelled in Gothic fiction's dark and titillating hereditary narratives. As David Punter reflects, such ancestral and materially oriented fictions are central to the genre's late-eighteenth-century emergence, where this arose 'when the bourgeois, having to all intents and purposes gained social power, began to try to understand the conditions and history of their own ascent' (Punter 1980, 112). Confronting unreliable parentages and monstrous family secrets, the middle class found themselves enthralled by Gothic inheritance narratives, at once compelling and terrifying in their disclosure of unknown histories.

That such fictions should also reflect imperial anxieties regarding the nation's possible 'contamination' or usurpation by the colonial 'Other' further mirrors the genre's penchant for tying inheritance to threatened white European lineages, and more largely to an endangered imperial project increasingly offset by resistance and rebellion. As Gillian Beer reflects regarding Darwin's *The Origin of Species* (1859), 'one crucial and recurrent metaphor' in this ground-breaking publication 'is the heraldic record of great families [...]. Succession and inheritance form the "hidden bond" which knits all nature past and present together' (Beer 1983, 196). Within this pervasive evolutionary discourse (morphed by Francis Galton into the widely popular and horrifically racist philosophy of eugenics), fears concerning 'tainted' familial parentages became a staple Gothic preoccupation, touching a visible nerve within the Victorian mainstream understanding of identity and culture. Gilmartin extrapolates,

> After the publication of Darwin's *On the Origin of Species* in 1859, consideration of the family tree inevitably brought one face to face with very early ancestors; the proverbial monkey, or even earlier, the trilobite. For many this was a confrontation to be avoided. [...] Gone is the Romantic adulation of the 'noble savage'; these primitive men are threatening and dangerous. (Gilmartin 1998, 17–18)

Indeed, Gilmartin identifies sociopolitical anxieties regarding not only *genealogical* pedigree, but also *geographical* derivation, as evolution suggested much wider, transnational components to the British family tree. Here, in the same way that terror emerges regarding a possible non-human or ostensibly less 'civilized' component to the family lineage, there surfaced 'a sense of alarm at the possible spatial infinitude of pedigree' (ibid., 19). Indeed, recognizing how established Victorian understandings of familial inheritance – whether 'based on primogeniture, or upon the patrilineal rather than matrilineal' pedigree – were being exposed as essentially 'arbitrary' and in no way defined by laws of 'nature', Gilmartin argues that Victorian society confronted radical doubt regarding the normative 'representation of genealogy' – in effect, any nation, race, or ethnicity could now be included amongst one's relations; the possibilities for a world-spanning ancestry were 'boundless' (ibid., 20).

Turning to the neo-Victorian Gothic novel, this anxiety surfaces as a focus of exploration in the present day, in this case doubled by a simultaneous concern regarding nineteenth-century literature's own influence and bearing on contemporary heritage discourses, which also look to the past as a site of authorization. As Marie-Luise Kohlke and Christian Gutleben explain, this often results in a self-consciously constructed opposition between past and present:

> the Victorians often become 'the damned', whom we must confront in the underworld of the re-imagined nineteenth-century, a purgatory to burn away their unexpiated sins so as to allow present-day subjects to re-emerge from the text, if not purified of historical guilt and association, at least reconfirmed in our own comparatively more liberal-ethical subjecthood. (Kohlke and Gutleben 2012, 11)

Put differently, the neo-Victorian Gothic returns to 'typical Gothic intergenerational plot[s] surrounding genealogy, inheritance, contested legacies and family secrets' (ibid., 10) only to challenge these narratives and to question their (often enduring) bigotry. Contemporary texts both draw on and re-work these Victorian intertexts, often from a putatively more 'liberal and "liberated" ideal' of identity, while also recognizing how this past 'gothically extends, disseminates, and transmutes into the very fabric of subsequent *being*' (ibid., 11).

Previous chapters in this book already reflect on this inheritance thematic, for example in the domestic narratives of Patrick McGrath's *Ghost Town* and Tash Aw's *The Harmony Silk Factory*, both of which pointedly include nineteenth-century Gothic components in their respective critiques of neocolonialism. Other notable twenty-first-century examples include James Wilson's *The Dark Clue* (2001), Diane Setterfield's *The Thirteenth Tale* (2006), Graeme Macrae Burnet's *His Bloody Project* (2015) and Laura Purcell's *The Silent Companions* (2017), all distinctly attentive to the disasters provoked by hereditary mythologies. As Ann Heilmann and Mark Llewellyn write, one prevalent trope by which all such family narratives are mediated is the haunted 'ancestral home: [...] that maternal testimonial to the family's past, its idiosyncrasies, sorrows, and secrets' (Heilmann and Llewellyn 2010, 35–6). 'A house haunted by past tragedy,' they elaborate, 'constitutes itself as dangerous and disputed territory for the protagonist: a site of alienation, betrayal, [...] ferocious sibling rivalry, harrowing family collapse, even mortal combat' (ibid.) Disinheritance and disillusionment with inheritance in this way repeatedly surface through ghostly and monstrous interactions within the haunted house, which often conspires to exclude the rejected familial 'Other' or to defend established mores and traditions against potentially progressive change. While domestic familiarity *seems* in these texts at first to promise refuge and security, then, it is later revealed as standing at the foundation of uncanny horror. As Rosario Arias and Patricia Pulham write, in the neo-Victorian 'return "home"', the 'ghost story [...] functions as a form of revenant, a ghostly visitor from the past that infiltrates our present' (Arias and Pulham 2009, xiv, xv), often in ways that make us deeply uncomfortable.

In Oyeyemi's *White is for Witching* and Waters' *The Little Stranger*, this 'unhomely' metaphor is at the centre of the texts' decolonial politics, underpinning the critique of xenophobia, patriarchy, and classism in their inheritance narratives. On the one hand, this is achieved via reference to nineteenth-century Gothic intertexts, including Stoker's *Dracula* (1897), Edgar Allan Poe's 'The Fall of the House of Usher' (1839), Charlotte Perkins Gilman's 'The Yellow Wallpaper' (1892), and Henry James' *The Turn of the Screw* (1898), all of which in different ways inform these novels' engagement with nineteenth-century 'tradition'. Borrowing Louise Hadley's words, such involvements reaffirm 'the bi-directionality of neo-Victorian fiction, pointing both to the Victorian past and the contemporary present' and recognizing 'the political and cultural uses of the Victorians in the present', not least in contemporary nostalgia and heritage industry rhetoric (Hadley 2010, 15).

Even so, unhomely affects are also visible in contrasting *non-European* and *anti-Enlightenment* narratives in these novels, which also borrow from the Gothic, only to subvert these established reference points and turn them on their heads. For Oyeyemi, this comes through in spiritual and folkloric allusions to the African *soucouyant* and the practice of *juju*, while for Waters, it emerges in the supernatural or paranormal 'poltergeist' and in the accompanying hermeneutic of psychokinesis. In either case, spiritualist understandings of haunting and spectrality make way for alternative readings of the home and inheritance, suggesting a possible way out of contemporary nostalgic entrapments in an imperial past. By recognizing and engaging with these references, this chapter seeks to give credit to these fictions' transgressive politics, underlining the significant ways in which the Gothic functions here to reread and counter twenty-first-century British misreadings of history and its cultural and sociopolitical value.

## Monstrous Whiteness in Oyeyemi's *White is for Witching*

Winner of the 2010 Somerset Maugham Award, and written by one of Granta's 2013 'Best Young British Novelists', Oyeyemi's *White is for Witching* represents the third of her at once popular and critically acclaimed Gothic novels. (There are seven in total, all written between 2005 and 2021.) Central to this importance, as I read it here, is Oyeyemi's complex engagement with both historical and literary inheritance, particularly as this encompasses imperial ancestries and texts. More specifically, developing what Sara Ahmed refers to as a 'phenomenology of whiteness' dominant within twenty-first-century culture, wherein (neo)colonial histories 'surface on the body or even shape how bodies surface' (Ahmed 2007, 153), here minority inheritance is likewise cast in material and bodily felt terms, as a form of unhomeliness experienced by Black British and immigrant characters. Set in the British coastal town of Dover, known for its historic legacy of national border policing, a history here conjured through textual references to immigrant detention, as well as to xenophobic Second World War patriotism in the form of Vera Lynn's 'The White Cliffs of Dover' (Oyeyemi 2009, 194), this geography is envisioned politically as a locus of uncanny horror, a space of radical violence directed against black and diasporic communities, who are conceived as 'Other' to British ancestry. If historically Dover's white cliffs represent what Paul Gilroy describes as 'nation-defining ramparts', which, symbolically preserve 'an anxious melancholic mood [which] has become part of the cultural infrastructure of [Britain]' (Gilroy 2005, 14), here the aggression of these connotations is registered in distinctly Gothic terms, the town reeling from a series of vampiric/soucouyant murders of its refugee population.

As a now well-known interview with Oyeyemi highlights, the novel approaches this Gothic scenario, in part, through an intertextual engagement with Bram Stoker's *Dracula*, negotiating the latter's central 'reverse colonization' discourse creatively and subversively (see also Ilott 2021, 23; Wester 2019, 297). Inspired during a period of illness in South Africa, wherein the author recalls having 'spent a lot of time in bed with *Dracula* in the dark wing of this big house', and where she 'started thinking that vampire stories were a lot to do with the fear of the outsider' (Machell 2009), the text brings to bear the figure of the vampire *not* as a foreign 'Other', but rather an *internal* threat, precisely tied to a discourse of ancestral whiteness monstrously imposed on minorities and migrants. In this way, the arrival of the non-white 'stranger' initiates a decolonial critique of British immigration politics which circles back to the imperial home, especially as this manifests in xenophobic haunting and nationalistic violence.

The narrative framework for this representation is established through the trope of the inherited Gothic mansion, now converted into a (haunted) guesthouse, and through the Gothic figure of the vampire-soucouyant, here represented in the person of Miranda. The latter's family takes up residence in the house and starts a business following the death of Miranda's mother, Lily, and it is here where a host of strange happenings begin to take shape. While Miranda's father Luc, a Frenchman, invests visibly in this hotel project, eager to convince his children of its financial worthiness, Miranda's matriarchal ancestors have other plans that do not include Luc: 'We are on the inside,' these predecessors affirm, 'and we have to stay together, and we absolutely cannot have anyone else' (Oyeyemi 2009, 118). The house, possessed by these women, agrees: 'They shouldn't be allowed in [. . .] those others, so eventually I make them leave' (ibid.). Here, Ahmed's idea of whiteness functioning simultaneously as a kind of 'residence' and 'inheritance' – a united 'we' oriented against a 'them' in defence of 'a form of family resemblance' (2007, 154) – is textually apposite, echoed in the novel's domestic and familial metaphors, and in its recourse to uncanny and monstrous Gothic signifiers as a means of recontouring this sinister heritage.

The notion of a prized bloodline, here transformed into an ancestral bloodlust, buttresses the text's Gothic negotiation of contemporary xenophobic signifiers, as the figure of the vampire-soucouyant functions as a creative metaphor for racist monstrosity employed in defence of a white heritage, as well as conjuring the horror attendant upon this ideological position. Suffering from rare eating disorder known as 'pica', passed down from her maternal forebearers, which sees Miranda hungry 'for non-food items, things that don't nourish' (Oyeyemi 2009, 22), her perverse appetite for non-edible substances is here seen as the source of her own destruction, even as it also figures a monstrous strategy for national housekeeping, attacking and expelling the proclaimed foreigner under the banner of the familial bloodline. As the text puts it, Miranda agrees to 'eat for' her ancestors by feasting on an immigrant classmate, a boy named Jalil, as well as by enacting her forebearer's hatred on various houseguests (ibid., 128). The house itself recounts how this history can be dated back to even before the onset of pica, to 'another woman ... thought an animal,' whose way 'was to drink off her blood then bite and suck at the bobbled stubs of her meat ... her appetite only for herself' (ibid., 24). In this way, vampirism is positioned by the text as both predatory and masochistic, a form of violence against the self as well as the Other. Miranda's grandmother – ironically called the 'Good Lady', on the basis of her enactment of Victorian moral ideals – demonstrates an obsession with her own and her nation's bloodline to the point of self-destruction, passing this down to the following generations in her interactions with Miranda and her mother.

Echoing Oyeyemi's comments regarding vampire stories reflecting 'the fear of the outsider', such xenophobic sentiments are familiar to a larger European Gothic tradition, including but also extending beyond Stoker's *Dracula* to other *fin de siècle* writing, including Robert Louis Stevenson's *The Strange Case of Dr Jekyll and Mr Hyde* (1886), H. G. Wells' *The War of the Worlds* (1898), and Rider Haggard's *She* (1886), all of which negotiate 'imperial Gothic' anxieties regarding the threatening foreign 'Other' (Brantlinger 1988, 227–53; Arata 1990). As Stephen Arata explains, in such 'reverse colonization' narratives, in connection with the anxieties of colonial decline and devolution, 'the "civilized" world is on the point of being colonized by "primitive" forces', such that 'the colonizer finds himself in the position of the colonized' – 'vulnerable to attack from a more vigorous, "primitive" peoples' (Arata 1990, 623). Maisha L. Wester elucidates:

> The racism inherent in much Gothic literature of the late nineteenth-century is rooted in an imperialist fantasy of the colonial other coming to 'our land.' Racially colored stories of vampirism became particularly popular in Britain during the

last third of the nineteenth-century 'when issues of "unfair" economic competition, immigration of "the unfit," and race degeneration featured prominently' in the publications of popular and political culture. (Wester 2014, 159)

Stoker's *Dracula* in particular is significant in demonstrating the Gothic inflections within this tradition, mirroring 'British cultural angst over the racial other's successful infiltration of society, as well as the late Victorian era's "obsession with racial degeneration and imperial decline"' (Wester 2014, 159). By contrast, in Oyeyemi's novel, this imperial Gothic is upended to comment on the *colonizer's* violence, recognizing the vampire's extreme monstrosity but situating this oppositionally, in critique of European colonial power. Notably, this differs from much late twentieth and early twenty-first-century vampire writing, wherein, as Jules Zanger reflects, the vampire 'becomes more human' and more sympathetic to the reader, seen as capable of good as well as evil, in connection with changing ideas about Otherness and difference (Zanger 1997, 20). By contrast, in *White is for Witching*, the vampire's evil, expressly tied to ongoing (neo)colonial violence in the contemporary, invokes the limitations and contradictions of twenty-first-century multiculturalism under New Labour government, as the supposed 'outsider' continues to experience racial persecution in explicit and routine ways.

The novel's adaptation of Stoker in this sense is central both to its critique of New Labour politics (with its false banner of cross-cultural harmony and understanding; see Yuval-Davis 2011; Parekh 2000; Hall 1998b) and its decolonial political message, as Oyememi's inversion of the Dracula motif functions to expose continued racist violence and hatred within a contemporary globalized Britain, understood in both discursive and material terms. Interestingly, black feminist scholar bell hooks also negotiates this vampire metaphor in in her 1992 essay 'Eating the Other', likewise challenging a widespread racist practice connected to white supremacism and cultural appropriation within a dominant white culture, seeing this as a form of vampiric consumption. She writes that:

> from the standpoint of white supremacist capitalist patriarchy, the hope is that desires for the 'primitive' or fantasies about the Other can be continually exploited, and that such exploitation will occur in a manner that reinscribes and maintains the *status quo*. (hooks 1992, 22)

Speaking of a 'current wave of "imperialist nostalgia,"' which seeks 'not to mourn but to celebrate the sense of a continuum of "primitivism" [...] reenacting and reritualizing in different ways the imperialist, colonizing journey as narrative fantasy of power and desire,' she writes, 'White racism, imperialism, and sexist domination prevail by courageous consumption. It is by eating the Other [...] that one asserts power and privilege' (ibid., 36)

By connecting Miranda's vampirism, like Dracula's, not only to her ancestor's monstrous legacy, but also to her avid and often sexualized desire for the racial Other, Ore – wherein 'Miranda had needed Ore open. Her head had spun with the desire to taste' (Oyeyemi 2009, 191) – *White is for Witching* echoes this critical, anti-appropriative ideological message, likewise declaiming contemporary culture's vampiric ingestion of the racial 'Other'. Miranda sees Ore not only as an onus of queer desire, but also and more primarily, as '*food*' (ibid., 192). As Aspasia Stephanou comments, 'The focus on consumption as a primary trope encompasses consumptive activities that take place within or in association with the house,' as this,

> manifests hatred against all foreign visitors, black, Kurdish, refugees, and immigrants, expelling difference and non-white bodies [... and continuing] to insist on white supremacist ideology, feeding off and given life by old hatreds. (Stephanou 2014, 1248, 1247)

In other words, Miranda's own and her ancestors' consuming behaviours are here an indication of *ongoing neo*colonial aggression, furthering the reach of consumer capitalist patriarchy to encompass the black female body.

Such critical associations reinforce the importance of the nineteenth-century Gothic and the vampire figure to Oyeyemi's writing, underlining her intellectual and creative links to a longer Euro-American canon, which she at once draws on, rewrites, and subverts. Indeed, the text invokes not only Stoker, but also the earlier Gothic of Edgar Allan Poe, as the tropes of the haunted house, the family curse, the emaciated damsel and the melancholic brother all explicitly reference key elements of 'The Fall of the House of Usher'. In this way, Oyeyemi moves between transatlantic Gothic traditions, crossing intertextual waters to draw on a range of established conventions in her exploration of imperial inheritance. Even so, Oyeyemi's novel also reaches outside Europe to identify Miranda more primarily with the soucouyant figure of African and Afro-Caribbean folklore, in this way bringing into play a contrasting, non-Western spiritual ontology. More generally, African and Afro-Caribbean oral narrative here overturns the Gothic's traditional Eurocentrism, instead incorporating an alternative, spiritualist reading of vampiric aesthetics.

Described by Giselle Lisa Anatol, this 'diabolical' soucouyant 'appears as an old, wrinkled woman by day but then at night sheds her skin, flies about the community in the form of a ball of fire and invades houses through open windows and keyholes to drain the blood of her unsuspecting neighbours' (Anatol 2004, 33). In *White is for Witching*, it is the new Nigerian housekeeper, Sade, who first identifies Miranda with this figure, asking her in response to her illness if her 'old ones' are 'calling [her]' (Oyeyemi 2009, 96). In reply, Miranda finds herself caught out by her inherited monstrosity, unexpectedly mirrored on the floor: 'Her eyes were small wild globes. The skull was temporary, the skull collected the badness together and taught it discipline, that was all. Miranda wanted to say, *That is not my face* [...], she had to get away from it, peel it back' (ibid., 97). In keeping with a traditional African understanding of the soucouyant, Miranda's countenance is here encased in her elders' skin, barely concealing her optic 'globes' of fire, while Sade, 'alarmed', employs *juju* to protect herself: as Miranda reflects, 'Sade's talisman was a thing worked against her' (ibid., 98).

African spiritualism functions in this way as a counter to Miranda's personal evil, but also and more largely, as a defence against the racist and xenophobic national mentality promoted by her ancestors and visible contemporaneously in the British government's continued oppressive treatment of migrant communities, for example, in the passage of the 2006 Immigration, Asylum and Nationality Act, just three years before this novel's publication. As Nisha Kapoor explains, this legislation made 'possible the removal of citizenship from someone if it was deemed that to do so would be "conducive to the public good"', in this way revoking the 'right to have rights' from migrant identity (Kapoor 2015, 105). This tightening of border control at the cost of civil liberties is made explicit in the novel through news of detention centre inmates who have 'hung themselves' (Oyeyemi 2009, 114), as well as through a radio report of a group of fifty-eight Chinese migrants found dead, suffocated in the back of a truck (ibid., 107).

In response to this necropolitical landscape – a *'generalized instrumentalization of human existence and the material destruction of human bodies and populations'* (Mbembe 2019, 14) – Sade performs juju regularly, also actively establishing connections to the larger migrant community, regularly visiting the local Immigration Removal Centre and cooking food for those detained before deportation. This investment in migrant wellbeing in the context of state-authorized anti-immigrant sentiment and policy constructs what hooks refers to as a symbolic 'homeplace' within the larger context of institutional oppression. As she explains,

> The task of making homeplace [is] not simply a matter of black women providing service: it [is] about the construction of a safe place where black people [can]

affirm one another and by doing so heal many of the wounds inflicted by racist domination. [...] Historically, black women have resisted white supremacist domination by working to establish homeplace. (hooks 1990, 42–3)

Miranda, while initially helpful in supporting this project, later responds in her soucouyant state by setting fire to the kitchen, while her ancestors haunt Sade with voices that urge her to commit suicide by jumping out of the window (Oyeyemi 2009, 211). Despite this ongoing persecution, Sade's continuation within the house seems motivated by a desire to help Miranda and her girlfriend, Ore, to fight the soucouyant inside Miranda and thus to provide succour, even in the face of personal vulnerability and oppression (ibid., 212). As Ore remarks, 'Why do this job? You've got choices. Get a job that pays better. Go somewhere else,' to which Sade replies, 'Normally you would be right, [...] but the other one says, "Wait."' (ibid.).

This positive, community-oriented portrayal of Sade's juju can be seen to reaffirm with what Andrea Shaw Nevins refers to as African spirituality's legacy of collective 'power and resistance,' which 'operates outside the bounds of Western empirical knowledge and therefore cannot be explained or controlled by Western systems of belief' (Nevins 2019, 2). She continues,

[African and Afro-Caribbean people] believe in their capacity to transform their experience through their own agency and in the midst of oppressive circumstances. [...] [T]hese belief systems [...] survived the transatlantic voyage, that is, as part of the cultural heritage of captured Africans. (Ibid.)

Diane Paton further adds that while European colonizers read juju, voodoo, and Obeah as 'witchcraft,' in this way criminalizing and stigmatizing these practices as malicious and demonic elements of supposedly outdated cultures, they are in fact 'a sign of resistance rather than evil,' systems developed as a 'spiritual means to protect, to heal, and to attack others' in the name of safeguarding community and strengthening social 'solidarity' (Paton 2015, 21, 8, 23).

It is worth reinforcing the central importance of this reading to Oyeyemi's novel, where, in juxtaposition to this positive portrayal of African spiritualism, the text specifically identifies whiteness with witching and oppression. As Eugenia O'Neal writes, 'Africans, like Europeans, considered witches to be quite distinct from priests. Witches were evil, and all their works were considered evil' (O'Neal 2020, 2). By contrast, '[p]riests oversaw your acceptance into society as a baby and presided over your rites of passage. They helped you to navigate the pitfalls of life by consulting the ancestors and the gods and protecting you from harm' (O'Neal 2020, 3). While witches were violent, then, priests were enabling and conducive to change and empowerment. Like Oyeyemi's Sade, they were concerned with building 'homeplace'.

Oyeyemi makes subtle reference to this spiritualist terminology via Miranda's discussion with Eliot regarding Edgar Allan Poe. Commenting on Poe's interest in the fear of death, Miranda responds by reflecting on how she would 'rather [his characters] talked to someone about this fear', as opposed to keeping it to themselves, recommending recourse to a priest over a psychiatrist: 'A psychiatrist would sedate you and act as if it wasn't normal to be so scared. In a situation of Poe's kind, I would always, always go to a priest before I went to a psychiatrist' (Oyeyemi 2009, 93, 94). In this passage, the celebration of religion and ritual over psychiatry, while cast through an implicitly Christian discourse, nevertheless reinforces the importance of Sade's spiritualism to the ethics and politics of the text, as Miranda's rejection of psychiatry in favour of priestly guidance relates an explicitly anti-Enlightenment set of values: she prescribes faith and communication ahead of science. While Miranda fails to comprehend this perspective's relevance to her own life, repeatedly denying her ancestry's spiritual malevolence and even seeking to abet this, nevertheless the novel itself, through its affirmation of juju, reaffirms this non-Western hermeneutic expressly, underling the danger of white European witching and its cultural prevalence.

It is not only Sade who celebrates African spirituality in the novel, but also Miranda's girlfriend, Ore, whose own Nigerian background and interest in Nigerian folklore likewise grant her cultural access to this tradition. For Ore, increasingly wary of Miranda's self- and Other- destructive behaviour, 'the soucouyant [...] is not content with herself. She is a double danger – there is the danger of meeting her, and the danger of becoming her' (Oyeyemi 2009, 155). Ore confronts the first of these threats personally in her relationship with Miranda, as her time with her girlfriend causes her to lose weight in alarming proportions: 'I had never eaten so much, I had never wanted to eat so much. But my clothes kept getting looser' (ibid., 185). The climax of this persecution occurs when Ore visits the family guesthouse, where following a shower, the bathroom's white towels strip the colour from her skin: 'Where it had touched me it was striped with black liquid, [...] there were shreds of hard skin in it' (ibid., 214). The overt xenophobic violence rendered in this depiction, where racism's horror takes the form of an actual stripping away of female black skin – this physical violence further accompanied by a verbal invocation of 'Rule, Britannia' (ibid., 214) – again reinforces the novel's Gothic materialist approach to decolonial thinking, tying this to subjective fragmentation, as well as visceral corporeal harm. As Jessica Porter writes, 'the "gross violence" of physical *and* psychological dissolution is disturbingly near the surface throughout the novel' (Porter 2013, 25), in this way reinforcing the material and affective aspects of the house's racist persecution.

Indeed, as Lucy Mayblin, Mustafa Wake, and Mohsen Kazemi remark, this embodied approach to racism emerges as disturbingly appropriate to twenty-first-century Britain, where the treatment of migrants, and asylum seekers in particular, can be likened to what Mbembe describes as 'the creation of *death-worlds*, new and unique forms of social existence in which vast populations are subjected to conditions of life conferring upon them the status of *living dead*' (2020, 111; Mbembe 2019, 40). In figuring Ore in this way – her life actively *sucked out of her* by her white soucouyant companion; her skin stripped by a white-dominated 'guest house' allocation – the novel captures the brunt material ferocity that white supremacy imposes on UK minority populations, again reaffirming Ahmed's reading of minority experience as not 'at home' (2007, 162). In Sade's words, this outlook turns Britain's supposedly open borders into a 'locked gate' (Oyeyemi 2009, 107) for all potential newcomers, capturing the UK's increasingly tenuous link to democratic values.

Ore's response, like Sade's, also calls on juju, rubbing salt into the soucouyant's eyes and later drawing back layers of skin from Miranda in order to try to extract her from her ancestors' curse. As the text recounts, 'She split, and cleanly, from head to toe. There was another girl inside her, the girl from the photograph' (Oyeyemi 2009, 230) – this alternate identity suggesting another, earlier and more amendable presence. While Ore herself manages to escape the house alive, however – enshrouded in a protective white cotton net, which Sade wraps around her (ibid., 231) – by contrast, Miranda fails to evade her ancestral curse, ultimately buried alive beneath the house, 'her arms outstretched, her fists clenched, her black dress clinging to her like mud' (ibid., 1). In this Poean ending, circling back to the novel's opening and registering the difficulty of escaping ancestral bonds, the reader confronts a dark warning regarding white supremacy's recurring and vicious nature, which here returns across generations to destroy those who obstruct it. Miranda, now trapped beneath the floorboards, is brought down by her forebearers in their search for ethnic and racial 'purity', entangled in a state of living death, while her gentleman brother continues to walk above her.

## Imperial Nostalgia and the Haunted Manor House in Sarah Waters' *The Little Stranger*

Waters' *The Little Stranger* also negotiates this imperial inheritance directly, likewise drawing on earlier Gothic texts to comment on present violence. In this case, as Ann Heilmann comments, these texts are at once nineteenth and twentieth-century in origin (and I would add, also eighteenth-century), reflecting 'a patchwork of literary references' to all three periods and creating a neo-Romantic / neo-Victorian Gothic take on 'the postwar imagination' (Heilmann 2012, 39–40). Set in the 1940s, in the country estate of the upper-class Ayres family – known as Hundreds Hall, thus referencing centuries of familial ownership – the novel immediately identifies sociopolitical anxieties tied to both post-war and contemporary 'heritage' discourse, especially as this is conceived in terms of class, gender, and nation. While not yet fallen, like Poe's House of Usher, Hundreds Hall is notably in decline, and also seemingly haunted by an unknown spectre or poltergeist intent on causing havoc. In this way, the novel references a Gothic tradition notably defined by inheritance thematics, while at the same time complicating this: tying it to destructive post-war nostalgia and contemporary conservatism. As Matthew Whittle reflects, 'In today's post-recession world of austerity, anti-immigration, imperial nostalgia, welfare reform [...], our contemporary moment more closely resembles the immediate postwar years' than any other recent period (Whittle 2020). Working with this familiarity, Waters brings to bear the ghosts of this earlier 'transition' moment and its intertexts, reflecting on *ongoing* socioeconomic inequality and recurrent nostalgia.

The premise for this transgressive, transhistorical ghost narrative, much like those of Poe, Stoker, and Oyeyemi, is the arrival of a stranger into this domestic space: in this case, one defined predominantly by class difference, rather than race or ethnicity. Faraday, the first-person narrator, is a grammar-school educated doctor and a new member of the post-war middle class: an aspiring bourgeois professional, who nevertheless conceals hidden jealousy and resentment, in this way situating himself both as (supposed) friend and aggressor. Arriving at Hundreds Hall as an adult, he recalls having visited as a child, for an Empire day celebration, wherein 'we sat to tea with our parents' on the south lawn, and where 'I was allowed to take my pick of the jellies and "shapes"' (Waters 2009, 1). This nostalgic and *consuming* image of imperial tradition (shared with Oyeyemi's novel) – complete with a private trip into the house to meet the kitchen girls and the cook, and to eat from a silver spoon 'almost bigger than my mouth' (Waters 2009, 2) – is further reinforced by Faraday's coveting view of the estate, as something 'he had suddenly and blindingly become enamoured of' (Waters 2009, 3). In this scene, while later disapproving of the Ayres' elitism, indignant of their disregard for their servants' lives, Faraday nevertheless betrays a desire to enter into their position, celebrating imperial heritage, even as he bemoans his exclusion from this.

The ghost arrives with Faraday's first visit, or in fact, shortly before this, announced by the protests of the new housemaid, Betty, who complains of nightmares and visions, and worries that she 'shall *die* of fright sometimes!' (Waters 2009, 13). Here, in a Gothic reminiscent of Ann Radcliffe's *The Mysteries of Udolpho* (1794), complete with supernatural apparitions and a persecuted maiden swooning in distress, Betty insists, 'It's just, this house! [...] It's too big! [...] All me friends say I'm mad to have gone into service' (Waters 2009, 12–13). In this passage, the haunted house (whose basement has 'the feel of a castle dungeon' (ibid., 2)), is introduced directly alongside changing post-war class relations: Betty is a figure for a new, more economically enabled and independent (female) working class, where domestic service has lost its kudos following the war and with the rise of urban factory work (Summerfield 1994, 60–1; Langhamer 2005, 359; Willis 2018, 94). As she remarks, 'Me cousins've all got factory jobs. And I could've had one too – only, me dad won't let me! [...] He says I must stop here for a year first, and learn housework and nice ways' (Waters 2009, 13). In this scene, patriarchal reprobation over changing gender norms coincides with a call for conventional class structures, reaffirming the intersectional and reactionary nature of post-war social discipline, encompassing 'a long history of complicity with imperial, capitalist, and White hegemony' (Coddington 2015, 214). In reclaiming elitist divisions, Betty comes up against the further obstacle of paternal censure, only finally escaping at the novel's close with the Ayres' demise.

In accordance with this oppressive heteropatriarchal viewpoint, also offered in Poe's 'The Fall of the House of Usher' and Charlotte Perkins Gilman's 'The Yellow Wallpaper', and likewise through the figure of the middle-class family doctor, Faraday quickly dismisses Betty's fear as feminine melodrama: 'If I want play-acting,' he retorts, 'I'll go to the theatre' (Waters 2009, 15, 11). Indeed, throughout, Faraday repeatedly casts blame on Betty, precisely in accordance with her deferral to the Gothic, seeing her as untrustworthy and suspicious, potentially liable for the house's difficulties. As he reflects at one point, 'You don't think she might have been responsible for it somehow, then been too frightened to own up?' (ibid., 144) – this question framing her as a kind of Catherine Morland figure, undone by her Gothic imagination. Nevertheless, despite (or perhaps precisely *in conjunction with*) Faraday's incriminations, Betty is not the most obvious suspect, and continued hauntings reinforce the house's own seemingly class directed animus.

The second victim of attack in the novel reaffirms this sociopolitical reading, further consolidating a connection between traditional class structures and market economics, as the former model is cast out and the latter made to replace this with its own elitism. This victim is the Aryes' parvenu neighbours, the Baker-Hydes, whose daughter Gillian is set on by the Ayres' family dog, Gyp, leaving 'her cheek and lip [...] turned into drooping lobes of flesh – [...] practically severed' (Waters 2009, 98). Apart from the Gothic garishness of this episode, conjuring Julia Kristeva's description of corporeal abjection – the mutilated corpse representing 'the most sickening of wastes' (Kristeva 1982, 3) – what is compelling about its presentation is how visibly it pin-points the nouveau riche as the house's apparent target, reasserting the clash between the Ayres and Baker-Hydes as critically pertinent. As Peter Baker-Hyde reflects, from their perspective, the Ayres 'swan it over everyone around here like lords of the manor' (Waters 2009, 107). By contrast, the Ayres see the Baker-Hydes as interlopers, arrogantly disrupting established class conventions in the name of heritage tourism. Caroline mocks that they'll 'probably knock Standish down and build a roller-skating rink' (ibid., 71). In this context, the violence of Gyp's attack would seem at first to reassert the Ayres' weight as lords of the manor, only then to see them demoted as the Baker-Hydes force the Ayres to put Gyp down. As Gina Wisker reflects, 'the old house comes alive falsely in a time warp, a liminal moment when it seems to be reminding and repeating the past glory of a decadent and dead age', only then to give way as 'the fabric refuses and attacks' (Wisker 2016, 107). Put differently, nostalgia cast through manor house ideals here falls victim to market-oriented economics: the house symbolizes the past, but this history is waning and replaced by 'heritage industry' consumerism – what Jerome de Groot describes as 'a creation of history as leisure activity' (de Groot 2016, 165).

The house's attacking 'fabric', notably, is represented by the drooping yellow wallpaper which Caroline struggles to re-pin on the living room walls, thus signalling an anxiety regarding oppressive gender relations reintroduced by imperial nostalgia and echoing Gilman's classic domestic Gothic text. As Caroline affirms, 'this house doesn't want me. I don't want it' (Waters 2009, 448) – its opposition underlining Faraday's consuming atavism in attempting to revive the manor and its traditions, in part by marrying Caroline. As Heilmann reflects, 'any resistance to the new order, even the attempt to fit into it, appears foredoomed'; however eagerly he may struggle to join the Ayres' tribe, the house openly rejects this (Heilmann 2012, 43). Even so, there is a clear sense in which Faraday *does* manage to displace the family patriarch, and later even to do away with the need for marriage, as Caroline unexpectedly falls to her death from the house's upper landing. In this way, Faraday's drive to possess the house comes through as a reflection of post-war changes and contradictions, as he negotiates both to preserve the manor *and* redirect its upper-class inheritance. Recalling the haunting legacy of imperial conservatism, at once both nostalgic and repressed, the house can be read simultaneously to try to expel Faraday and to applaud his parochial investment, allowing 'heritage' tradition finally to continue, but in new, middle-class hands.

Connecting this to the context of a contemporary, post-financial crisis UK affected simultaneously by widespread poverty and ongoing 'heritage tourism', and by a will to reinstate the past under increasingly right-wing ideals, this narrative's focus on the dangers both of nostalgia and acquisitiveness is distinctly significant and topical, reinforcing the double-sidedness of New Labour rhetoric in its approach to the past. As Parker relates, New Labour's discourse of change and equality, while putatively opposed to Thatcherite traditionalism – concerned to level class divisions and make Britain 'all middle class now' – nevertheless continued to espouse heteropatriarchy and class hegemony in various ways (Parker 2013, 112). This was especially visible, as Roger Luckhurst further clarifies, through New Labour's deference to global capitalist norms and to ideals of 'cultural governance' as a means to power (Luckhurst 2003, 421). As Luckhurst reflects, New Labour's 'central government might adopt a rhetoric of devolution and the dispersal of power to localized agencies, but this model of governance *enforces* conformity to the market' (2003, 422). Socioeconomic divisions remain intact, as capitalism is endorsed and strategically promoted (ibid., 421). More generally, New Labour's façade of social progressivism in the shape of 'asset-based welfare' (Watson 2009, 44) gives way to elitism and austerity, as a basic disinterest in welfare ideals allows for an easy move to further public sector cuts, including an ongoing dismantling of the NHS and public housing, and the privatization of higher education (Mason 2017, 94).

The novel's engagement with post-war welfare initiatives further reinforces this contemporary connection, underlining the violence implicit in the family's championing of imperial order. Confronting the construction of new affordable post-war housing alongside Hundred's Hall, Caroline is appalled to have to sell off inherited land, seeing this as an attack on family tradition and social order. She complains of how 'of course people must have homes, and all that. But it's as if they're chewing Hundreds up – just so they can spit it all out again in nasty little lumps' (Waters 2009, 246). Indeed, her own and her family's preference for consuming Hundred's *whole*, at the cost of dismissing social welfare – overlooking all the 'people coming out there, wanting to know how to get their names down for a house' (ibid., 247) – discloses a Gothic vampirism flagrantly disinterested in redistributive initiatives, keeping these *outside* a putatively respectable social vision. As it surfaces, even Faraday's poorest patients, who live in 'an abandoned hut, with holes in the roof and gaps in the window' (ibid., 469), fail to inspire in the family a recognition of this fantasy's distortion. As Caroline comments, 'I would as soon want to move into a little brick box like that, with a lounge and a fitted kitchen, as live in our old cowshed' (ibid., 249). Borrowing from Karl Marx, in this instance, 'capital is dead labour which, vampire-like, lives only by sucking living labour' (Marx 1867, 342) – the Ayres' economic parasitism ultimately defines this 'dead' family's ongoing livelihood.

For Faraday himself, importantly, the situation is more complex. As his parents were themselves staff of the Ayres' manor, the Ayres' snobbery inspires in him feelings of bitterness and offense. He reflects,

> Hundreds had been made and maintained [...] by the very people they were laughing at now. After two hundred years, those people had begun to withdraw their labour, [...] and the house was collapsing, like a pyramid of cards. (Waters 2009, 27)

In this passage, what Hillary Mantel describes as 'the corrosive power of class resentment' (2009), eating away at Faraday's calm, comes through in no uncertain terms. Even so, in his eagerness to escape the working class, Faraday also reveals a sense of shame regarding his own upbringing – as Caroline reflects, 'it sounds almost as though [...] you hate yourself' (Waters 2009, 250). This self-loathing, the text suggests, propels him to embrace and even possess the manor, eventually coming to displace the Ayres, exerting a monstrous energy to dislodge their ownership and make Hundreds his.

The closing sentence of the novel would appear to reaffirm this accusatory reading, seemingly revealing Faraday as the ghost that haunts Hundreds all along. Looking in the estate's 'cracked window-pane', he realizes how 'the face gazing distortedly from it, baffled and longing, is my own', this passage recalling the monstrous reflection ending Henry James' *The Turn of the Screw*, where likewise, a spectral presence lurks 'at the window – straight before us' (Waters 2009, 499; James 1986, 261), seemingly betraying the narrator as ghost. Even so, as with Shoshana Felman's well-known reading of James' novel, *The Little Stranger*'s putative 'solution' to this anxiety goes beyond traditional Freudian psychoanalysis, instead here invoking a discourse of 'psychokinesis' to situate and politicize Faraday's aggression: connecting this to unconscious psychic and environmental forces which at once drive and obstruct his and the family's behaviours (Felman 1977, 97–8). Moving the narrative into a dialogue with

Victorian spiritualism that in many ways approaches contemporary affect theory – working with bodily felt and enacted emotions, which nevertheless evade the subject's direct perception (Grossman 2013, 81; Massumi 2002, 25) – this hermeneutic complicates the text's neo-Victorian Gothic, invoking a materialist conception of agency and vitality, which (as with Oyeyemi's novel) both draws on and challenges nineteenth-century conventions.

Central to this 'psychokinetic' reading is an understanding of Hundred's 'ghosts' as defying the (supposed) laws of nature, intruding on a 1940s social realism in favour of the Gothic supernatural. As Heilmann notes, the novel does not 'rely on any sudden revelations arising from shifts in perspective or temporality', as with Waters' earlier novels, but rather plays on a post-war 'country house' narrative only to imbue this with 'the Victorian trope of the Gothic mansion engulfed by the past' (Heilmann 2012, 38). More radically, not only does it disrupt its own apparent naturalism, it does so in a way that directly defies Enlightenment thinking, presenting the ghost or 'poltergeist' not as a recurrent memory or psychological disturbance, but rather as a 'bundle of bad energy' at odds with the house's natural dynamism (Waters, qtd in Allardice 2018). Invoking what Jane Bennett refers to as 'vibrant matter' – 'the active powers issuing from nonsubjects' (2010, ix) – what comes to the fore in this narrative is the house's own insurgent physicality. As Waters writes, 'I tried to anchor the novel's creepiness in the materiality of a house like that' (Kummer 2019).

It is worth taking a minute to examine this understanding more closely in order to better appreciate Waters' meaning – the idea is not simply to scare the reader or to identify a still haunting past. Rather, more complexly, it seeks to provoke political critique regarding the Ayres' ongoing conservative mindset by engaging critically with an 'ecology of things' – a concept grounded in the 'vitality' of nonhuman bodies and/or 'nonsubjects' (Bennett 2010, viii–ix). As Bennett explains,

> By 'vitality' I mean the capacity of things – edibles, commodities, storms, metals – not only to impede or block the will and designs of humans but also to act as quasi agents or forces with trajectories, propensities, or tendencies of their own. My aspiration is to articulate a vibrant materiality that runs alongside and inside humans to see how analyses of political events might change if we gave the force of things more due. (Bennett 2010, viii)

More generally, the focus of this object-centred critical investment is to explore how 'these material powers, which can aid or destroy, enrich or disable, ennoble or degrade us, in any case call for our attentiveness, or even "respect", as operative agents functioning alongside human actants, shaping our intentions and behaviours (Bennett 2010, ix).

With this focus in mind, the principal effect of *The Little Stranger*'s alter-world is not simply to identify psychological hauntings, but more centrally, to pinpoint lived experiences of paranormal discord with specific political relevance: the manor's spirits become 'vibrant matter' set loose by Faraday's class resentment – intent on creating havoc in order to disrupt established house relations. For example, Hundred's material depletion upon losing its domestic staff and upkeep would seem (perhaps unsurprisingly) to re-energize otherwise defunct domestic objects: candles, oil lamps, washing stands, speaking tubes, gramophones, and sheet music – all artifacts of an earlier age (Waters 2009, 234, 161, 331, 295). These objects become loaded with supernatural vibrance, which then works against the family's exertions, obstructing the regular machinery of the household and undermining the Ayres' endeavours to revive Hundred's 'grander days' (ibid., 79). As the text relates, the house plays 'parlour games' with the Ayres, trying to 'tease' them and 'catch [them] out'; these objects are its 'conductors', which challenge their pretensions of grandeur (ibiid., 304, 309, 353, 381).[1]

One passage in particular makes this reading explicit. Examining the house's speaking tube, which Betty and Mrs Bazeley report, has been making 'a queer sort of noise', and which seems to suggest a listening operator, Faraday becomes disturbed by 'a disconcertingly palpable air' (ibid., 332–3) produced by this object, which throws into doubt his former cynicism regarding the Gothic:

> A less sinister-looking thing it would have been hard to imagine – and yet, [. . .] the very quaintness of the object before me began to seem slightly grotesque. [. . .] I remembered those 'ordinary things' [. . .] which had seemed, in [Rodrick's] delusion, to come to crafty, malevolent life. [. . .] I had the sudden irrational idea that, in putting my ear to the cup, I would hear my mother's voice. (ibid., 334)

Unequivocally here, these 'ordinary things' take on a dark agency of their own, and furthermore, one that directly conjures Hundred's divisive economic history. It is Faraday's realization that what he is holding is the nursery servant's speaking-tube and that his own 'mother had been a nursery maid here' (ibid.) that prompts his unrest, suggesting that his repressed awareness of labour exploitation plays a central part in this haunting.

That Faraday himself fails to understand how this happens, stubbornly unconscious of his own role in these events, is not in itself at odds with this materialist hermeneutic. His ignorance regarding his complicity in the hauntings – his subliminal desire to evict the Ayres – merely underlines these objects' capacity to act independently from him, channelling insurgent energies which he and the Ayres only vaguely distinguish, and which surface in 'queer' disturbances to everyday residence (ibid., 334). To quote Sianne Ngai, these hauntings are the 'negative affects' or 'ugly feelings' which remain largely undetected in their emergence – feelings which are 'perceived rather than felt and whose very *nonfeltness* is perceived' (Ngai 2007, 76). Put differently, they are secondary order or 'dysphoric' emotions, whose cognitive importance has yet to be clarified or fully processed (Ngai 2007, 83); they appear as 'intensities' (Massumi 2002, 25), invading the manor and finally overturning this.

In the end, this 'psychokinetic' violence leaves Faraday himself in informal ownership of the manor, possessing the keys with which to reopen it and 'air' it out. Now emptied of its former possessions, without sinister objects capable of evicting him too, Hundreds becomes new again: 'its plaster detail fresh and unchipped' (Waters 2009, 498). Returned to its pristine, unowned state, it no longer harbours the same malevolent energies; class resentment is not an issue and therefore neither are the spectres. Nevertheless, security is not guaranteed in this context, as Faraday continues to occupy and covet the house, and glimpses of movement jolt him into 'fear and expectation' (ibid., 498–9). The suggestion with this ending is not simply that Faraday is responsible for the haunting, but more centrally that his designs on Hundreds keep it from exorcism. As long as he remains dedicated to traditional class ideals, the ghosts will return.

## Conclusion

Looking back over these two inheritance-themed texts, this focus on *the material* is especially significant. The Gothic here encompasses not simply the past or haunting intertexts, but also disturbing imperialist practices still alive in the present day, continuing across centuries and driven by violence alarmingly normalized within contemporary society and politics. That Oyeyemi and Waters should tie this anxiety to a Victorian (and twentieth-century) legacy at once both sociopolitical and literary is essential, as is the fact that they should work with neo-Victorian allusions to accomplish this. Nevertheless, equally important to these contemporary narratives is their overt departure from these Victorian antecedents and from a Gothic often more associated with psychology than with spirits, affects, or objects. In this way, what Maria del Pilar Blanco describes as a routine 'haunting of the everyday' and as an interest in *contemporary* 'strangeness' and the 'paranormal' (Blanco 2010, 253), here becomes explicit through lively witches, soucouyants, and poltergeists, who inhabit these haunted houses and imbue them with ongoing neocolonial horror. Rather than prioritizing the past and its haunting memories, these fictions highlight this legacy's demonic continuance, as it animates twentieth and twenty-first-century 'ordinary things' and bodily presences in monstrous ways.

## Notes

1 Katharina Boehm (2011) also draws attention to the importance of these objects for the novel's materialist politics, as she challenges the predominant historiographical reading of the text. While her analysis is not strictly focused on the Gothic, it nevertheless serves as an inspiration for my reading here, indicatively highlighting the object-oriented outlook implicit in Waters' engagement with psychokinesis.

4

# Digital Gothic

Digital Technology, Migration, and the Gothic in Hari Kunzru's *Transmission* and Mohsin Hamid's *Exit West*

While the previous chapter concentrated on Gothic encounters with the past and inherited intertexts, this chapter focuses on more futuristic technologies and geographies informed both by the Gothic and speculative modalities. In fact, anxieties regarding global capital's spectral mutability, flux, and transformation are at the heart of many twenty-first-century British Gothic fictions, including China Mieville's *Perdido Street Station* (2000) and *Embassytown* (2011a), Ian McDonald's *Necroville* (1994) and *Brasyl* (2007), Nick Harkaway's *The Gone Away World* (2008), Adam Roberts' *New Model Army* (2010), Christopher Priest's *The Islanders* (2011), Tim Maughan's *Infinite Detail* (2019), and Kate Dylan's *Mindwalker* (2022), all of which balance Gothic and sci-fi/fantasy tropes to explore the violent intertwinement of corporate business and new technologies, generally as forms of surveillance, control, and exploitation.[1] As Justin D. Edwards reflects, such works continue a longer Gothic tradition of dark and transgressive engagements with technology linking back to *Frankenstein* (1818), *The Strange Case of Dr Jekyll and Mr Hyde* (1886), and *The Island of Dr Moreau* (1896), and encompassing also twentieth-century 'cybergothic monsters' responding to AI, biotechnology, neuropharmacology, and genetic engineering (2015a, 8). As Edwards elaborates, 'since the eighteenth-century, Gothic has been at the centre of the anxieties provoked by each new media technology, and [...] such fears have perpetuated moral panics over penny dreadfuls, horror comics, horror films, "video nasties" and, most recently, horror-themed computer games' (ibid., 9). These various innovations on the genre play on ongoing cultural uncertainties regarding technology's progressive promises, which in turn also create unease around the genre's own moral and political leanings.[2] Nevertheless, as Fred Botting suggests, 'monsters, ghosts and vampires' emerge not only as agents of moral panic and enervation within contemporary global culture, but also more optimistically, as 'figures of transitional states representing the positive potential of posthuman transformation' (2011, 14). In this way, Digital Gothic narratives of fear and horror also serve as registers of more transgressive technological possibilities, invoking significant 'developments in genetic and information science, cyborgs, mutants, clones' (ibid.), as explored, for example, in Chapter 8's reading of Ishiguro.

Indeed, twenty-first-century critical writing on generic crossovers between the Gothic, Horror, and speculative writing often explicitly foreground this technological anxiety, connecting it to 'weird' non-human entities, viral systems, and networks, biomedical monsters and eerie capitalist landscapes 'partially emptied of the human' (Fisher 2016, 11). Mieville contributes to this critical discussion by commenting on the more-than-ghostly dimensions of M. R. James' 'Weird grammar', this consisting not only in 'weird, inhuman, Cthulhoid figure[s]', but also 'mass commodification [...] in the age of mechanical reproduction', the combination of which speaks to a 'crisis blasted modernity showing its contradictory face, utterly new and traced with remnants, chaotic and nihilist and stained with human rebukes' (Mieville 2011b). On a related note, Robert Macfarlane underlines the eerie dimensions of English rural landscapes, which far from being devoid of surveillance technology, reveal this to be ever-present but invisible: 'its sources and effects – like all eerie phenomena – glimpsed but never confronted' (Macfarlane 2015).

This chapter builds on this discussion to examine similarly double-sided (haunting and eerie) understandings of contemporary technology in relation to two expressly diasporic Gothic sci-fi texts: Hari Kunzru's *Transmission* (2004) and Mohsin Hamid's *Exit West* (2017). Both novels investigate contemporary migration with a focus on transnational electronic communications, making evident the migrant's vulnerability within emergent digital technologies. In so doing, these fictions offer, on the one hand, a critical attack on corporate ethical bankruptcy, and on the other, a Gothically inflected vision of migratory suffering and loss, repeatedly underlining uncanny, eerie, monstrous, and morbid reflections on contemporary technologies. In each case, speculative and Gothic devices in the novels call to attention global technology's violence and translocation, stepping outside social realism's restrictive boundaries to envision digital aggressions and to identify eerie landscapes and digital monsters in the form of viruses, portals, and ubiquitous security systems. Even so, these texts also recognize transgressive possibilities opened up by such digital innovations, negotiating generic frameworks within and outside the Gothic to navigate digital transgression and protest.

## Banal Technology and the Gothic

One central topic in contemporary discussion of digital media concerns the perception of this as moving beyond a postmodern cultural context defined by unquestioning celebrations of interconnectedness and fluidity. Within this latter framework, digital media's impact on identity and community is seen largely in terms of the compression both of space and time, wherein 'speed is accelerated, people are ever more mobile, communication is person-to-person, rather than place-to-place, identities are multiple, and communication media are ubiquitous' (Baym 2010, 5). By contrast, under a post-postmodern reading, what is instead stressed are the day to day material realities connected to digital encounters: realities wherein, precisely on account of such globalized transitions, 'digital media are made mundane, boring, and routine as they are increasingly embedded in everyday lives and social norms coalesce around their use' (ibid.). More recent publications on digital technology often favour this critical reading, stressing the increasingly everyday and humdrum quality of digital interactions (see for example, Graham, 2004; Ling, 2004; Humphreys, 2005).

Zara Dinnen's *The Digital Banal* offers a literary critical expansion on this latter trend, confronting contemporary literary representations of digital culture and technology through a combined lens of digital media scholarship and affect theory, in this way questioning the emotional resonance of everyday technologies. Her argument, put briefly, is that technology often presents itself as a banal dimension of everyday life – something that we can take for granted, because it is easily accessible, or seemingly straightforward, often masking its novelty as a unique and distinctive form of mediation. As Dinnen puts it, 'Just as the "platformativity" of Facebook is both a means for knowledge and connection and at the same time a radical rewriting of what those terms mean, so are digital media, in general, complex meditational entanglements that are too often presented as inevitably progressive' (Dinnen 2018, 1). Building on the premise that such technologies are often 'written off as just another detail of contemporary life' (ibid., 2), or indeed, as a necessary improvement upon this, Dinnen's analysis explores how recent fictions, in different ways, reflect, expose, and problematize this tendency, often highlighting the effacement of 'radical, disturbing affective novelty', and with this the 'commodification of "new" as a driver of the free-market logic of late capitalism' (ibid., 9).

Focusing on the twenty-first-century Gothic in the texts mentioned above, I hope to develop Dinnen's argument, not by revisiting or challenging her readings, – which are excellent throughout – but by considering how such an approach sits in relation to migrant lives, specifically as represented within this Gothic modality, and to literary responses to the hatred and violence witnessed in recent media representations of the same. Eve Sedgwick defines the Gothic as a genre that explores feeling in its excess, an excess which furthermore 'becomes charged with potent excess meanings' as it is taken up by reactionary cultural prognosticators, as well as by literature (Sedgwick 1980, 1; ibid. 1990, 102). What is interesting about this understanding for the purpose this reading is that for migrants and refugees, far from the banal understanding of the digital outlined above, such excess emotions often come to define everyday digital engagements, as new developments in communications and social media technology, enabling new forms of communication and connection across vast distances, can mean the difference between intimacy and separation, hope and despair, and life and death. Carleen Maitland emphasizes this latter awareness when she writes of how deterritorialization places refugees within an 'information no-man's land' ('Migrants with Mobiles' 2017), in the sense that travel and the corresponding loss of communication can make it difficult to map one's route or to know where to find help or accommodation. One recent article in *The Economist* (ibid.), which quotes Maitland, describes how in this context:

> Phones become a lifeline. Their importance goes well beyond staying in touch with people back home. They bring news and pictures of friends and family who have reached their destination, thereby motivating more migrants to set out. They are used for researching journeys and contacting people-smugglers. Any rumour of a new, or easier, route spreads like wildfire. (Ibid.)

The article also quotes Maurice Stierl, a spokesperson for Watch the Med, 'an NGO that tracks the deaths and hardships of migrants who cross the Mediterranean', noting how migrant travel is 'like the underground railroad, only that it's digital' (ibid.). Under this reading, both the personal and historical importance of new technologies is magnified by migrant and refugee experiences fundamentally dependent on recent digital innovations, in ways that are not so apparent either for more geographically established communities or for more elite cosmopolitan travellers.

The other, more expressly Gothic, side of this predicament is that new technology may also of course pose a source of fear and horror for migrant communities, threatening to revoke rights of entry into potential new homelands, to enable deportation, or to curtail claims to repatriation, healthcare, education, or accommodation. A 2018 Wired article reviewing contemporaneous EU discussions regarding the construction of new migrant detention centres, notes how, 'immigration agencies across Europe are showing new enthusiasm for laws and software that enable phone data to be used in deportation cases' (Meaker 2018). While tracking technologies and biometric data stored in governmental and NGO databases may offer a crucial means of identifying migrant peril and of directing aid appropriately, it can also be used to retract basic human rights, especially when privacy, security, and even bodily safety are themselves often considered a condition of national citizenship, a situation whose violence is witnessed in the numerous mass drownings punctuating the media across the 2010s (see, for example, Walawalker, Rose and Townsend 2023). As Maitland again reflects, 'Will a refugee, who does not enjoy the protections of citizenship, be granted privacy rights to data stored in a cloud service? As a function of their protection mission, will UNHCR offer cloud storage to refugees to house their digital selves?' (Maitland 2018b, 243). Such questions highlight the legal risks and ambiguities accompanying migrant uses of technology, where (often non-consensual) state monitoring becomes readily apparent as a foundation for threat and violence.

Keeping this in mind, I want to argue that these contemporary Gothic representations of migration and technology often work with another set of affects than those which Dinnen categorizes under the 'digital banal', affects more appropriate to the ambiguities and excesses of Gothic writing, but also to the overtly threatening technologies surrounding migrant and refugee lives. Looking at Kunzru's *Transmission* and Hamid's *Exit West*, what is compelling about these diasporic fictions is precisely the energy and urgency that they themselves, and their characters, invest in digital technologies, as these latter become inscribed as crucial means of survival and resistance, but also as modes of Gothic intimidation and menace proffered by the state. What is perhaps more appropriate to this representation, then, are the polarized affects of hope and anticipation, *alongside* fear, horror, and desperation, such that, more dramatic emotional dynamics circulate around what are otherwise seen as ordinary digital technologies, reflecting the unique situation of these precarious communities.

## Corporate Business, Migrant Exploitation, and the Virus in Kunzru's *Transmission*

*Transmission* offers a perhaps surprising instance of this tendency in that, in some ways, it would seem to reflect the digital banal. The protagonist, Arjun Mehta, a computer programmer from New Delhi, subscribes to the progressive rhetoric of new media culture to such an extent that he takes it as given that his programming skills will equip him with elite cosmopolitan privilege, allowing him to escape the local 'upheaval' of his global Southern hometown and to relocate to a virtual paradise, epitomized for him by Silicon Valley (Kunzru 2004, 5). As he puts it, '*The Valley*: so exciting that, like Lara Croft, you had to rappel down a cliff-face to get in' (ibid., 23). As this recourse to the simulated reality of gaming reflects, Arjun has little clear understanding of what life in America entails for many migrant communities, envisioning instead a fantastic consumer paradise of new media culture. Employed and relocated to California on an HP1-visa provided by an international IT consultancy corporation aptly named Databodies, his unquestioning faith in the company's exaggerated professional promises ultimately parallels his naïve and conventional view of new media technology, as a form of pure mathematical thinking fundamentally capable of transcending both human error and geographical borders. As he puts it, philosophically, 'reality ought to be transparent, logical. You should be able to unscrew the fascia and view the circuitry inside' (ibid., 103). He is, in other words, won over by the popular discourse of digital transparency, failing to recognize how this masks serious social and economic inequalities, including those pertaining to his own migrant situation.

Matthew G. Kirschenbaum, commenting on this pretention towards abstraction common within new media discourse, sees this as central to the cultural allure of the digital. 'A digital environment is an abstract projection supported and sustained by its capacity to propagate the illusion [...] of *immaterial* behaviour', he reflects, 'identification without ambiguity, transmission without loss, repetition without originality' (Kirschenbaum 2012, 11). Within this world, reality seems accessible, if complex, sustaining an illusion of never erring coherency precisely by incorporating 'hyper-redundant error-checking routines', which appear infallible (ibid., 12). Nevertheless, whatever the obvious attraction of this ideal, 'computers are not flawless. Errors typically occur at the juncture between analog and digital states' (ibid.), that is, at the point where the material world's infinite sensorial data is reduced to the discrete register of digital programming. The digital's insistence on finite terms in this way harbours the capacity to obscure reality's more complex dimensions, a tendency likewise visible in Arjun's own reductive mathematical thinking.

Arjun is compelled not only by digital technology's supposedly abstract mathematical purity but also by a popular vision of such technology as geographically transcendent – existing outside local infrastructural problems and national (or indeed, international) governmental control, and instead in a theoretically conceived 'cyberspace' that remains 'in the future ... a hope, an expectation, for future fulfilment' (Coyne 1995, 154). Within this context, technology is seen in quasi-spiritual terms as 'shining above everyday concerns' (Haythornthwaite and Wellman 2002, 4), at a distance from present mundane realities and geopolitical tensions. Jane Fountain's celebration of technological revolution in *Building the Virtual State* exemplifies this fantasized outlook expressly, noting how 'when information is digitized and shared, geographical distance becomes less relevant – in most cases irrelevant – to information flow, making possible geographically distributed partnerships, collaborative problem-solving, and highly coherent organization' (Fountain 2001, 33). Arjun's view of the digital as facilitating a 'properly organized daydream', involving 'a world which appreciated the importance of the principles of prediction and control' (Kunzru 2004, 15, 14), echoes this reading, seeing new technology as a means of broaching an imagined future, a utopian dream of immediate contact and unfettered communication.

As Christopher Pollitt summarizes, the digital, under this redemptive umbrella, 'can lead to changes in the jurisdictional boundaries, accountabilities, and collaborative arrangements of organizations', as well as 'reach[ing] out to citizens who either live in remote locations or are immobilized for some reason' (Pollitt 2012, 26). Nevertheless, this new media view of geography also problematically overlooks the pressing spatial politics surrounding digital developments, where indeed, 'even the virtual has its roots in particular places' (ibid., 28). As Stephen Graham reflects, 'against the widespread assumption between the 1960s and late 1990s that electronic communication would necessarily work to *undermine* the large metropolitan region, all the evidence suggests that the two are actually supporting each other' (Graham 2004, 18). In this way, the virtual era takes on distinct special and material dimensions, which as Miguel Castells also affirms, tend to take root 'in the periphery of large metropolitan areas' (Castells 1996, 213), in this way reinstating a transnational hierarchy of metropolitan power.[3] 'The profile of America's informational city is', Castells affirms, 'represented by [...] the relationship between fast ex-urban development, inner-city decay, and obsolescence of the suburban built environment', in ways that reinforce existing metropolitan inequalities and leave 'the lower social classes and ethnic minorities trapped in their ruins' (Castells 1996, 431).

Arjun's relocation to Silicon Valley, alongside his new media-inspired infatuation with American consumer culture, confirms this metropolitan mapping precisely, identifying elite, urban America as the source and generator of contemporary IT's radical influence, an understanding which raises questions regarding the digital's popular anti-establishment claims. Offered employment at an anti-viral software company, Virugenix, Arjun's encounter with its 'meticulously landscaped' campus reminds him of the 'perfect, glossily pleasing' scenery in the video-game SimCity, his first reference point in attempting to spatially situate himself within corporate America (Kunzru 2004, 52–3). As he imagines it, 'he [...] took the bus downtown, past the Sim marina and the Sim park and the mall full of Sims shopping at the drugstore and drinking tea at the British Pantry. Redmond was a town with nice graphics and an intuitive user interface. His kind of town' (Kunzru 2004, 52). This computer-simulated version of the San Francisco Bay area, featuring the US at the heart of emergent technology, offers a Gothic critique of high-tech corporate city scaping and its deceptive simulacra, which David Bell describes as 'a silicon-induced *illusion* of community' (Bell 2001, 102). More generally, it mirrors the idealized libertarian outlook of the so-called 'Californian Ideology' – as Richard Barbrook and Andy Cameron explain:

> During the '70s and '80s, many of the fundamental advances in personal computing and networking were made by people influenced by the technological optimism of the new left and the counter-culture. By the '90s, some of these ex-hippies had even become owners and managers of high-tech corporations in their own right and the pioneering work of the community media activists has been largely recuperated by hi-tech commerce. (Barbrook and Cameron 1996)

Under this description, the 1960s McLuhanite project of embracing media and communications technology as a route towards a more legitimate, uncensored democracy is revealed as another offshoot of that 1990s market ethos itself, incorporated into neoliberalism through a direct conflation of information and capital. 'By naturalizing and giving a technological proof to a libertarian political philosophy,' Barbrook and Cameron continue, 'and therefore foreclosing on alternative futures, the Californian Ideologues are able to assert that social and political debates about the future have now becomes meaningless' (1996). In other words, for such ideologues, innovation becomes a tool of neoliberal dogma and free-market competition: 'in place of the collective freedom sought by the hippie radicals, [this ideology has] championed the liberty of individuals within the marketplace' (Barbrook and Cameron 1995). What started as a dream of open access to information became a politicized means of strategically managing access to capital.

Arjun's romanticized and deterritorialized view of the digital thus functions to efface the vampiric neoliberal politics behind the information age's supposed translucence, facilitating a reification of established social hierarchies and market values. As Alexander Galloway elucidates, '[t]he promise [of information technology] is not one of revealing something as it is, but in simulating a thing so effectively that "what it is" becomes less and less necessary to speak about, not because it is gone for good, but because we have perfected a language *for it*' (Galloway 2012, 13). Arjun's easy acceptance of technology's supposedly revelatory and progressive social capacities obscures his basic awareness even of his own oppressed situation, as he ignores his temporary contract, his sub-minimum wage salary and his ghettoized inner-city neighbourhood, and instead imagines himself rising up the ranks of programming culture to acquire the much-desired status of what Castells calls the 'techno-managerial elite' (Castells 1996, 415–16). In Fredric Jameson's terminology, Arjun appears deluded by the 'free-floating' claims of global finance capital, which emerge as spectrally detached 'from the concrete context of [their] productive geography' (Jameson 1997, 259).

This naïve and fantastical outlook clearly affirms the premise of the digital banal, in so far as Arjun's institutionalization occludes and enables his socioeconomic exploitation. By establishing a direct textual opposition between Arjun and his elite cosmopolitan counterpart, Guy Swift, a British advertising executive, 'paper millionaire and proud holder of a platinum card on three different frequent flyer programmes' (Kunzru 2004, 12), the novel underlines the radical geographical unevenness implicit in Arjun's migrant situation, where far from benefiting from any superior intelligence or ability, Guy succeeds professionally as a result of his strategic, consumer-oriented engagements with global wealth, as well as his cynical manipulation of new media advertising discourse in the pursuit of profit. Thus, 'his future lay in the science of "deep branding", the great quest to harness what [. . .] he termed the "emotional magma that wells from the core of planet brand"' (ibid., 21). This hallow rhetoric and the unmistakable arrogance that accompanies it plainly displays Guy's moral vacuity, as he negotiates utopian affective registers as a means of promoting crass consumer values.

In the course of the novel's diasporic travels, the Gothic dimensions of this consumer thinking are clearly revealed through Guy's involvement with the EU border agency, where his new media enthusiasm combines with his elite conception of Europe to facilitate a reactionary tightening of border surveillance across the whole continent. 'Citizenship is about being one of the gang,' he affirms, 'or as we like to say at *Tomorrow\**, "in with the in crowd"' (Kunzru 2004, 253),[4] this language parading a shameless social exclusionism which nevertheless authorizes an unprecedented sweep of undocumented populations, a raid 'aimed at taking 5,000 *sans papiers* off the streets by tomorrow morning' (ibid., 255). The EU director's unfeeling summation of this operation's aims makes the authoritarian politics at stake in this project explicit: 'Identify them, process them, and return as high a percentage as possible to their countries of origin within seventy-two hours. All based on common information handling' (ibid.). The novel underlines in this way the Gothic foundations of corporate business in its complicity in transnational border policing, maintaining the established uneven boundaries between global North and South precisely via means of popular consumer advertising rhetoric and related technologies.

Such disciplinary uses of digital technology are, of course, not uncommon within the post-9/11 West, where immigration has increasingly become a central focus of political and cultural debate, not least in Britain.[5] Thus, following 9/11, Western political rhetoric embraces invasive surveillance technology as a means of supposedly securing public wellbeing and safety, often in relation to 'suspect' global movements and tightened national borders, as also explored in Oyeyemi's *White is for Witching*. As Matthew Sparke likewise explains, such risk-based 'smart border' technologies promise 'a solution to the competing geopolitical and geoeconomic concerns: delivering economic liberty and homeland security with a high-tech fix' (Sparke 2006, 13). Recent political discourse in the UK echoes this sentiment, clamping down on borders in connection with Brexit and more generally in accordance with a larger 'hostile environment' policy, which posits migrants as supposed parasites on the UK economy and potential criminals (see Goodfellow 2019; Yeo 2020) As Raymond Pun reflects, the prejudicial associations attached to such technologies are also visible in the racialized language of popular media culture across the West, where terms such as 'cyber jihad' and 'E-jihad' demonstrate 'the complicit role(s) of technology in perpetuating Islam in Orientalist stereotypes that underscore the dominant discourse of the "clash [of civilizations]" in the digital era' (Pun 2013). Central to the violence of the so-called 'War on Terror', then, is the systematic demonization of Eastern and Islamic cultures, characterized as pre-modern and anti-Western, and Gothically linked to participation in violent technologies, including cyber-terrorism.

Arjun's own South Asian migrant identity, combined with his involvement in viral technology, ultimately situates him under this demonizing rubric, his release of the Leela virus seeing him branded an international terrorist and hunted by the US government. As Pei-chen Liao writes, 'through the moving figure of the computer virus [...] Kunzru relates the discourse of terrorism to anti-immigration'; drawing links between the virus and right-wing border-control rhetoric, he 'highlights the implication of biopolitics in anti-immigration bias and post-9/11 paranoia' (Liao 2013, 54). The broader political import of this representation is a deep-seated critique of post-9/11 security rhetoric, where repeatedly throughout the novel Arjun's technological involvements are falsely and hyperbolically conflated with terrorist activities, his decisions seen as monstrous precisely as a result of his Asian heritage and migrant status. 'This was it,' broadcasters in the novel affirm, 'the enemy within, a technological fifth column in the homes of everyday Americans [. . .,] a consensus had emerged that the attack should be avenged in blood' (Kunzru 2004, 154). The text here captures the War on Terror's inflated and misdirected register, which unabashedly ignores the migrant's increasingly desperate socioeconomic situation and the impact this might have on his behaviour. While Arjun continues to lie to his family back home to maintain his reputation as a successful IT professional, he betrays an increasingly altered view of programming from that which he upheld upon leaving India, seeing this *not* as a tool for virtual connectedness or progress, but rather, mere survival.

As Caren Irr comments, this panic underlies the novel's critique of the pernicious 'interface of digital and cultural codes', where Arjun's engagement with corporate America sees him confront a 'new, even more aggressive culture of capitalism in formation', this in turn, 'laying the groundwork for a new kind of corporate satire for the wired age' (2014, 59). Indeed, as Liam Connell likewise avers, the novel 'suggests a context for Mehta's actions which implicates the systems of contemporary capitalism' (Connell 2010, 283), especially with respect to corporate technology. Nevertheless, and this is also perhaps where the Gothic emerges most visibly in the novel, such technologies take on not only *comic*, but also *monstrous* dimensions in the text, unexpectedly appearing in forms of spectral noise, ghostly transmission, and viral contagion, which haunt the characters and undermine their personal and professional intentions. Where Arjun ultimately fails to either apprehend or contain the virus, as it spreads across the internet, the excitement surrounding this process of mutation incorporates an incredible affective energy, this underlining technology's disruptive potential both negatively and positively.

This can be seen, for example, in the text's descriptions of the virus as at once a form of technology and an 'organism', a 'cluster of digital cells', which blurs 'the borderline between life and not-life' (Kunzru 2004, 157, 107, 109). This uncategorizable Gothic entity, spectrally 'invisible' until the point at which 'she took over', is also 'a swarm' or 'horde [. . .] her organs rearranged, mutated, [and] hidden', in order to allow her to successfully infect and contaminate the system, 'flar[ing] up like a rash on the computing body of the world' (ibid., 113–14, 109). The fact that the novel begins with the virus *in the act* of invasion – creeping into the reader's own (imagined) computer – underlines this Gothic framing explicitly, as Leela strategically imitates the internet user's own banal language to gain access to his system. Employing such emotive clichés as, 'Hi! I saw this and thought of you!'; 'check it out!'; and 'just for you' (ibid., 3), her programme systematically attracts and deceives its target, mimicking human correspondence in order precisely to disrupt this.

In one sense, this mirrors what Guy himself attempts in his corporate branding practices, as he likewise strategically negotiates consumer rhetoric to generate profit. He, too, invades and reshapes his clients' businesses in viral-like capacities, reaffirming Michael Hardt and Antonio Negri's well-known claim that 'the age of globalization is the age of universal contamination' (Hardt and Negri 2000, 136). It is no wonder that Arjun's employers are similarly engaged in the business of corporate body-shopping: they too see profit-making in viral terms, as a project of testing and exchanging migrant 'databodies' in a laboratory-like 'petri dish' of low-paid labour (Kunzru 2004, 7, 54). As Connell writes, this practice reduces 'workers to components in the production cycle with little regard for their welfare' (Connell 2010, 283). Arjun and his housemates become the human mechanisms exchanged and exploited in pursuit of ever greater market success.

This said, the fact that the opening chapter only indirectly introduces Arjun or Guy, instead leaving this task for subsequent sections, pointedly complicates this understanding, shifting the reader's attention away from programming itself and onto the programme – the anthropoid, or perhaps better, feminoid, agency of the virus and her rhizomatic movement as she extends across the system. Correspondingly, only one page after introducing this virus, the text conflates this 'data body' with the actual person of Leela Zahir, the Bollywood actress whose image has been used to circulate the virus behind a video clip. As the novel puts it, her dancing 'made her famous, beyond even her mother's wildest imaginings' (Kunzru 2004, 2), though of course it is the digitalized image's dancing, copied from Leela, which explains this fame. In establishing this connection, the novel emphasizes the real-world effects that viral technology has on individual lives, impacting on Leela's reputation and financial situation, just as it later does on countless local and transnational businesses alluded to across the narrative: 'the effect was cumulative, an accretion of frustration, a furring of the global arteries' (ibid., 176). This conflation between girl and virus also constructs a symbolic link between technology and oppressed female agency, situating Leela herself as at once a form of 'surface effect', manipulated by corporate film companies, and an active mediator: someone who conspires with 'the machinery at work under her skin' (ibid., 2). The Leela virus is, in other words, representative of digital culture's simultaneously monstrosity and liberating potential: her structurally destructive energies enable violence, but also subaltern empowerment within a global capitalist world system.

In the context of the novel's diasporic politics, this invokes a distinct ambivalence regarding technology's sociopolitical value, where what comes through most prominently in these scenes are the digital's simultaneous connections to *and* independence from corporate neoliberalism, in this way allowing for the possibility that contemporary security and surveillance programmes will *not* maintain disciplinary power over migratory movements. As the text explains, the virus exists as 'noise': a form of aberration and interference, which impedes the smooth operation of the system and its pretension to certainty and closure. 'Perfect information is sometimes defined without loss, without the introduction of the smallest uncertainty or confusion', the novel affirms. 'In the real world, however, there is always noise' (Kunzru 2004, 271). As Jussi Parikka elucidates, such an understanding counters the conventional biopolitical reading of technology affirmed by the surveillance state, instead upholding a construction of the digital as imminent, open and unfolding (see also Leonard 2014, 278–80). Thus, while on the one hand, 'Digital capitalist culture [...] seems to be the first system that has succeeded in converting its own accidents into profit,' 'reterritorizaliz[ing]' noise 'into its circuits' and in this way containing it (Parikka 2007, 100), on the other hand, 'noise [...] can also be cultivated' (ibid., 286) in order to 'multiply events and accidents and create heterogeneous assemblages that endure and sustain a new understanding of practices and discourses' (ibid., 285). The virus's centrality to the system suggests an important threat to established information monitoring processes, illuminating how the digital might, in its networking capacity, outstrip the punitive control of border authorities.

This ambiguous potential is made evident in the novel's expressly fantastical ending, where Arjun is, on the one hand, branded a cyberterrorist and pursued by the state, but also seemingly able to disappear beyond the radar of the system. Arjun's criminal status is at once secured and complicated by the release of the virus, such that his identity itself becomes radically subject to diverse interpretations. As the text reflects, 'Arjun Mehta, Gap loyalty-card holder and habitué of Seattle Niketown, is rapidly changing shape' (Kunzru 2004, 287–8), taking on the form of a notorious lawbreaker but also a paraded countercultural icon. Indeed, his engagement with the digital finally situates him beyond his material body, within a virtual realm wherein his meaning escapes fixed designation. At once innocent and a crafty leftist hacktivist, an anti-establishment invader and protector of the people, his shapeless heterogeneity both evades and upends informational control, in this way conjuring a reading of subaltern power as poignantly viral: in Emily Johansen's words, the novel 'privileges a persistent instability, modelled by the constantly moving and mutating computer virus' (Johansen 2013, 419). In the final reckoning, this mutability, while refusing to offer any particular comment on the threatened migrant body, nevertheless reaffirms and celebrates the far-reaching spectral capacity of contemporary technology, which, like the migrant, depends on a distinctly deterritorialized logic.

## War, Portals, and Death in Hamid's *Exit West*

Hamid's novel works differently, even while it also draws overt connections between migratory movements, technology and the Gothic, in particular in relation to wartime violence and related human displacements. In this case, beginning a few months before the actual event of migration, the arrival of war to an unnamed city brings with it a quick shift in everyday digital engagements, such that individuals, cut-off from their work emails and constrained to their houses by a freshly established curfew, become newly dependent upon their only recently acquired mobile phones in order to maintain contact. As the novel relates:

> Nadia and Saeed were, back then, always in possession of their phones. In their phones were antennas, and these antennas sniffed out an invisible world, as if by magic, a world that was all around them, and also nowhere, transporting them to places distant and near, and to places that had never been and would never be. (Hamid 2017, 35)

This opening creates a fantastic aura around the digital, situating new innovations, on the one hand, against the experience of global Southern poverty and violence, but also, new opportunities made available through the switch from wire-based to wireless technologies. As Sukhdev Sandhu reflects, the novel is 'about migration and mutation, full of wormholes and rips in reality', encompassing 'the almost contradictory nature of Saeed and Nadia's digital life

[…] whose broadband freedoms contrast with the roadblocks, barbed wire and camps they face in what passes for reality' (Sandhu 2017). Much as in *Transmission*, there is a pointed clash between the digital's much lauded liberating capacity and its disturbing complicity in biopolitical surveillance systems.

The protagonists' phones are also, importantly, the necessary condition for their budding romance, as despite the obstacles put in place by the war, they equip Nadia and Saeed with a ready means of communication, allowing them to '[touch] each other, but without bodily adjacency […] to be penetrated', even when 'they had not yet kissed' (Hamid 2017, 37). Intimacy is in this way aligned to digital communication, in a manner which far outstrips the banal 'friending' of Facebook, instead allowing for sexualized forms of contact comparable to the physical. Immediately, the emotions at play in the narrative are more potent and intensive than those admitted under the 'digital banal', partly on account of how these are formulated in fantastic terms and, again, in relation to arduous and Gothically inflected migrant and refugee experiences.

Equally apparent in this first section, in a way that it is not for Arjun in *Transmission*, is the digital disjunction between global North and South, where the former's wealth is seen to radically contrast, and depend upon, the latter's poverty. As the text reflects:

> even now the city's freewheeling virtual world stood in stark contrast to the day-to-day lives of most people, […] who went to sleep unfed but could see on some small screen people in foreign lands preparing and consuming and even conducting food fights with feasts of such opulence that the very fact of their existence boggled the mind. (Hamid 2017, 39)

The digital is here understood as a Gothic testament to socioeconomic inequality and destitution, witnessed through the eyes of newly connected subaltern populations made abruptly aware of their own socioeconomic disenfranchisement. As a 2016 report from the World Bank elucidates, '[d]igital technologies [are] spreading rapidly, but digital dividends – growth, jobs and services – [have] lagged behind'; 'in many developing countries, more families own a mobile phone than have access to electricity or clean water' (Elliott 2016). Recognizing, then, the uneven personal, emotional, and social importance of the digital for the global Southern communities represented in the novel, especially given the context of wartime insecurity and an increasingly pressing need to stay at home for extended periods, this recognition underlines a Gothic confrontation with destitution and radical precarity.

When an escalation of the fighting in the city disrupts this connectivity, abruptly short-circuiting all digital signals, the sense of crisis this creates is thus pointedly urgent. What becomes visible in this section of the novel, even before the event of the protagonists' migration, is precisely the 'no-man's-land' arena referred to by Maitland ('Migrants with Mobiles'), wherein the result of disconnection is decidedly *not* tech-free autonomy, but profound isolation and emotional distress, augmented by failed communication. As the novel relates:

> Deprived of the portals to each other and to the world provided by their mobile phones, and confined to their apartments by the night-time curfew, Nadia and Saeed, and countless others, felt marooned and alone and much more afraid. (Hamid 2017, 57)

Saeed's struggle to reconnect with Nadia following this experience involves daily calls to a city operator in panic and frustration, and when they finally meet, following a dangerous trip across the city, Nadia too is beside herself, so 'glad to see him, [she] felt she might start yelling at him at any moment' (ibid., 60). The affective burden engendered by digital disconnection is in this sense immense, almost unsustainable, and again, this brings into play fantastic and Gothic registers as a means of capturing related emotions.

Writing on similar experiences as felt by migrant and refugee communities in the context of war and displacement, Maitland notes how, '[t]he displaced have pressing needs to stay in touch with those back home, as well as to keep updated on the status of the general situation that drove them to leave' (2018a, 8). The concern is that, 'for the displaced, accessing assistance requires entering what is often a labyrinth of information systems, receiving and providing critical information all while attempting to recover from trauma and loss' (ibid.). In this context, she suggests that digital communications charities offer little relief to these communities, where they are themselves often closely monitored by the state, and where 'currently, access to networks and computing facilities tends to favor organizations, with the displaced often left to their own devices' (ibid.). Moreover, she relates, 'where cellular network connectivity is available, refugees and the displaced may be able to maintain access, but mostly through their own means' (ibid., 10). In this way, Maitland underlines the absence of structural support provided by governments and NGOs to these communities, which stands at the heart of the affectively laden depiction of Saeed and Nadia's situation.

This anxiety is further reflected in *Exit West* through repeated references to sporadic digital encounters, which punctuate extended periods of disconnection and non-communication between these characters. During such moments, the protagonists 'caught up on the news, [...] the various routes and destinations migrants were taking and recommending to each other, the tricks one could gainfully employ, the dangers one needed at all costs to avoid' (Hamid 2017, 103). Such passages offer a form of documentary reminder of both the difficulty and importance of digital media for migrant populations more largely, and for discrete individuals affected by such now widespread crisis situations. Moreover, the emphasis here on complex feelings of joy, frustration, fear, and unrest, spurred by encounters with digital media, bears witness to what Rebecca Rotter identifies as the affective nature of migratory 'waiting', wherein 'heightened anticipation of the future and reflection on desired and dreaded outcomes', balances a more widely recognized conception of waiting as 'passive, stagnant time spent "doing nothing"' (2016, 80). Within such passages, waiting becomes 'a dynamic, engaged process in terms of its intentional structure and the cognitive and emotional resources it requires'; it conjures dread, anxiety and unease, as well as hope and expectation, offering 'a powerful trope through which people can critique political, economic and social systems of oppression which usurp their time' (ibid., 93, 97; see also Lagji 2019, 221).

This insight resonates with the more fantastic and Gothic dimensions of the text, which in addition to recording daily mundane encounters negotiated in the act of 'waiting', add to this a weighted appreciation of affective battles endured in such liminal moments. As Beatriz Pérez Zapata reflects, the novel is replete not only with decisions, but also with violence and death, such that time itself often results as notably precarious, failing to match up with realist chronologies otherwise implicit in the novel's more documentary moments. As she reflects, '[w]hile it is the finitude of life that unites all human beings, *Exit West* also reminds us that life, and thus the experience of time, is more precarious for those whose lives are ungrievable' (2021, 771). Indeed, such Gothic engagements with the digital also offer a means navigating technology's own precariousness in the text, as for example with the central sci-fi Gothic trope: the door. Thus, as Nadia and Saeed begin to consider migration while confronting escalating conflict and bloodshed, what is arguably the principal aesthetic focus of the novel becomes evident, namely, an emphasis on doors or portals as sci-fi Gothic metaphors for routes of transit and digital connection.[6] It becomes evident (retrospectively) at this point in this text that this trope has in fact been implicit from the start of the novel, in brief snippets of other migratory narratives interspersed throughout. Such passages themselves negotiate a hypertextual digital logic, reflecting a relatively immediate migratory movement between places, and in this way, a spectral compression of time as decisions are made and lives suddenly propelled across the globe. As the text explains, 'the effect doors had on people altered':

> Rumours had begun to circulate of doors that could take you elsewhere, often to places far away, well removed from this death trap of a country. [...] A normal door, they said, could become a special door, and it could happen without warning, to any door at all. (Hamid 2017, 69–70)

Here, the popular generic motif of thresholds or portals emerges as crucially relevant to the novel's Gothic diasporic politics, as doors take on a spectral quality of invisibly summoning or aiding migratory transportations otherwise obstructed by the state. What is interesting about this trope as it appears here is not only how it elucidates invisible transnational movements and dispensations, but also, in the process, how it engages new media enthrallment with hypertexts and interfaces that might take part in this experience. As Alexander Galloway affirms, '[p]refatory evocations of the form "once upon a time" are common across media formats', often digitally situating narratives of travel and new beginnings:

> The French author François Dagognet describes it thus, 'The interface [...] consists essentially of an area of choice. It both separates and mixes the two worlds that meet together there, that run into it. It becomes a fertile nexus'. (Galloway, 2012, 32; Dagognet 1982, 49)

This 'fertile nexus' is essentially what Hamid negotiates in the novel, as Nadia and Saeed's travels likewise repeatedly involve 'two worlds that meet together'. His use of sci-fi Gothic thus becomes a way of narratively taping into digitally enabled migratory cultural interfaces: the choices that Nadia and Saeed make as they pass through fantastical hidden doorways are also implicitly the choices made possible through available digital resources.

This again is a way in which this novel escapes the so-called 'digital banal': by making new media discourse itself an aesthetic foundation for migratory understandings – a modal resource, clearly informing and extending the novel's sci-fi Gothic landscape, – the text synthesizes these central aspects of globalization into one, capitalizing on contemporary enthusiasm for the digital to draw the reader into a difficult refugee narrative. Put differently, the innovative excitement the Western reader often feels in relation to the emergence of new digital technology is here used to engage a topic equally politically weighty and emotionally daunting within current sociopolitical discourses. Rather than simply questioning reified social hierarchies through recourse to exulted digital novelties, the text instead reframes and defamiliarizes these social relations rhetorically so as to alert a global audience to alternate, more obscured, ghostly, and precarious elements of contemporary transnational life, in particular those relevant to migrant and refugee populations.

The affective and ideological effects of this portal aesthetic are powerful. On the one hand, it captures the experience of global shrinkage produced by digital communications, while also alerting the reader to enormous life-changing decisions reduced to mere seconds. Travel becomes Gothically irrevocable: 'passage [...] both like dying and being born, [...] experienced [as] a kind of extinguishing as [Nadia] entered the blackness and a gasping struggle as she fought to exit it' (Hamid 2017, 98). The alacrity with which such movements are made amplifies their emotional weight and personal importance in these dark scenes, in such a way as to reverse the reifying effect that digital culture so often has on socioeconomic relations. Indeed, Galloway's understanding of the 'intraface' is especially relevant here, for in calling to attention what he refers to alternately both as an 'area of choice' and 'non-choice' – a critical mode of thinking which accommodates necessary connections between seemingly detached spaces, – he effectively modulates existing discussions of digital technology to integrate diasporic thinking, looking beyond the centre-periphery model to celebrate movement. As he writes, '[t]he intraface [...] is not a window or a doorway separating the space that spans from here to there':

> It is no longer a question of choice [...]. It is now a question of nonchoice. The intraface is *indecisive* for it must always juggle two things (the edge and the center) at the same time. [...] It is a type of aesthetic that implicitly brings together the edge and the center. (Galloway 2012, 40)

In other words, the notion of the intraface moves the discussion beyond the appearance of binary oppositions so often associated with digital interfaces, instead apprehending the difficult, multidimensional experience involved in migratory 'flows, transformations, [...] and lines of flight' (ibid., 39). At the heart of such moments is not a simple exchange of one world for another, but instead a more complex, multi-layered communication between seemingly detached spaces.

As the text then returns to quotidian migrant life and to the various encounters with technology and the digital that Nadia and Saeed face in their travels, this sense of emotional weightiness and situational complexity is again renewed and ideologically reinvested in nuanced representations of deterritorialized thinking. For example, we see Saeed trying to call his father but failing to get through, this further amplifying his sense of guilt and bereavement following his mother's death, but also making apparent how central transnational communication is to his personal identity and belonging. As Nadia reflects, 'she had never seen bitterness in him before, [...and] it struck her that a bitter Saeed would not be Saeed at all' (Hamid 2017, 102–3). By contrast, Nadia connects 'with people via chat applications and social media' and receives immediate replies, including from 'an acquaintance who had made it to Auckland and another who had reached Madrid' (ibid., 103). Such quick and easy communications reinforce her confidence in transnational connections, making her more readily comfortable with distance and heterogeneity, appreciative of 'all these people of all these different colours in all these different attires' (ibid., 156). Her friends, it becomes clear, also unmistakably benefit from access to social media communications proffered by their privileged points of arrival, this again making clear the digital's geographical unevenness and the critical impact this has on displaced individuals and communities (see, for example, ibid., 103). These passages in this way reaffirm a clear awareness of the digital's transnational necessity, even as they register complex and varying personal experiences of digital innovations.

The fantastical and often Gothic interspersion of other migrant narratives in the novel, briefly interrupting Nadia and Saeed's story, again draws on this interface aesthetic, highlighting the infinitely diverse experiences of this community, as well as a common dependence upon and vulnerability within the realm of the digital. One family, who find themselves having arrived on a beach in Dubai, are captured on phones by 'selfie-taking' tourists, while surveillance cameras make their presence known precisely in the way these migrants' story is focalized (ibid., 88). In this scene, a distinctly Gothic depiction of digital technology emerges as the lens that captures their unexpected arrival is also responsible for actively 'intercept[ing]' them and leading them away, 'apparently bewildered, or overawed, for they held hands and did not resist or scatter or run' (ibid.). Similarly, another man, who comes through a door in Australia, finds himself evading the security alarm in a woman's apartment, eking out his way only by means of 'the glow of her computer charger and wireless router' (ibid., 6). Here again, an individual emerging through a hidden door contemplates a new and unexpected form of danger introduced by technology, subject to various intersecting, malicious, and potentially fatal data flows. Indeed, even death itself in the novel is compared to 'a phone screen shutting off' (ibid., 163), thus tying human mortality expressly to digital erasure.

## Conclusion

In short, while the digital banal is very much relevant to the Western world, and more broadly to geographically established populations and cosmopolitan elites, for the migrants and refugees in these novels, the culture of new media conjures a very different set of emotional, aesthetic, and political coordinates, often more dramatic and more appropriate to genre modalities and devices. This is distinctly visible within these texts' varying engagements with Gothic and speculative structures, where their representations of migration and technology position the digital in unique affective lights: as fundamentally necessary to and intertwined within the fears and horrors of dislocation, as well as within the hopes and opportunities of diasporic life. Within this framework, what is often experienced as commonplace or mundane is not necessarily banal, but rather subject to the affective extremes of precarious existence.

# Notes

1. McFarlane (2024, forthcoming) offers a compelling speculative reading of some of these texts, specifically in relation to 2010s British society and politics. It is also worth noting how this digital concern factors into a number of other UK Gothic media productions, including film, TV, gaming, and visual arts, as explored for example in van Elfren (2014) and Gronlund (2014). Likewise, Sara Wasson's writing is integral to understanding the Gothic's role in recent biomedical technologies, as for example in Wasson (2015a) and Wasson (2020).
2. See Lázaro (2017) for a compelling study of the role of the taboo in Gothic Horror and of instances of state censorship that have resulted from this.
3. Castells' larger argument on the digital's geographical placement is also worth quoting. He explains how,

    > [t]he Internet Age has been hailed as the end of geography. In fact, the Internet has a geography of its own, made of networks and nodes that process information flows generated and managed from places. [. . .] The resulting space of flows is a new form of space, characteristic of the Information Age, but it is not placeless: it links places by telecommunicated computer networks and computerized transportation systems. It redefines distance but does not cancel geography. (Castells 2001, 207)

    This again reaffirms the digital's interconnection with contemporary global capitalist systems, including their spatial and geographical infrastructure.
4. The asterisk in this passage is in the original text. 'Tomorrow' is the name of Guy's company, a marketing agency concerned, in Guy's words, with 'the science of "deep branding"' (Kunzru 2004, 21). The formatting used here – italics followed by an asterisk – is meant to underline Guy's own conception of the agency as a brand in itself, a marketed label whose graphics complement and reinforce the company's popularity.

5  Lisa Nelson also comments on the US's politicized negotiation of surveillance and information technology following 9/11:

> Because of the events of September 11, new technology, including such innovations as *FaceIt* and *Carnivore* software […], has been subsumed by a new rhetoric. No longer is new technology necessarily viewed as a threat to individual privacy; rather, it is perceived as serving the common good and protecting freedom as represented in legislation such as the US PATRIOT ACT. (2002, 69)

In other words, such technology aids in the proliferation of often invasive and morally dubious Western 'security' systems.

6  Jeffrey Weinstock also highlights the importance of portals to the object-oriented politics of contemporary Gothic. He notes how portals 'open to other dimensions, and in many cases something from the outside, from that other dimension, is allowed access to our world' (2023, 53). This is also clearly true for the portals of Hamid's novel, which underline how neocolonial conduits into the global South also open the way for reverse migrations.

5

# Gothic Homelessness

## Spectral Inhabitants and Uncanny Spaces in Ali Smith's *Hotel World*, Trezza Azzopardi's *Remember Me*, and Brian Chikwava's *Harare North*

Commenting on the counter-establishment focus of contemporary British Gothic fiction, Dani Cavallaro highlights its special interest in marginal social identities: 'The taboos confronting both twentieth-century and post-millennial audiences revolve around the awareness of a radical disjuncture between the self's aspirations and the dehumanizing requirements of its environment. Not surprisingly, perhaps, a major manifestation of Gothicity in recent history comes from disaffected subcultures' (Cavallaro 2002, 12). Previous chapters in this book consider this statement's truth in relation to various oppressed minority subcultures, including global Islamic communities post-9/11, as well as Asian, African, and other migrant and refugee populations subjugated by ongoing (neo)colonialism. Developing this analysis further, this chapter foregrounds twenty-first-century Gothic depictions of another marginalized demographic: the homeless, in this case in Ali Smith's *Hotel World* (2001), Trezza Azzopardi's *Remember Me* (2004), and Brian Chikwava's *Harare North* (2009). As Loïc Wacquant notes, recent analysis on the subject of homelessness 'reveals a close link between the ascendency of neoliberalism [...] and the deployment of punitive and pro-active law enforcement policies targeting street delinquency', in this way evidencing a strong and systematic causality between the law and destitution (Wacquant 2009, 1). Claiming to 'put an end to an era of leniency' (ibid.) via means of surveillance, policing, and criminalization, this policy landscape targets 'the jobless, homeless, beggars, drug addicts and street prostitutes' (ibid., 2) as supposedly undeserving communities, supplanting 'a therapeutic philosophy of "rehabilitation"' in favour of 'a managerialist approach centered on the cost-driven administration of carcereal stocks and flows'

(Wacquant 2009, 2). Accordingly, neoliberalism's oppressive impact on contemporary society and politics can be witnessed directly in relation to this most vulnerable of populations, a demographic manifestly in need of social support and institutional investment perhaps more than any other.

As the website homeless.org.uk cites, statistics surrounding rough sleeping in Britain reflect a dramatic rise of 38 percent over the course of 2010–1, with a snapshot estimate of 4,266 people sleeping rough on an average autumn night in 2019 (Homeless Link 2021a). This figure dipped slightly between 2020 and 2021, by 9 percent, most probably as a result of 'government interventions undertaken during the COVID-19 pandemic', including emergency accommodation allowing 'many individuals who might otherwise be rough sleeping still' to be temporarily housed (Homeless Link 2021b). Despite this optimistic dip, however, as Arabella Kyprianides, Clifford Stott, and Ben Bradford note, a number of factors within contemporary neoliberal society make homelessness an ongoing concern, including 'upward pressure on housing costs coupled with reduced availability of affordable social housing, reduced funding for supporting vulnerable people with their housing and restrictions on housing benefit for lower-income families' (2021: 673). As Emma Davidson, Briege Nugent, and Sarah Johnsen also reflect, these concerns are amplified in twenty-first-century Britain due to austerity government, which in addition to reducing national 'social security entitlements [and] housing affordability', has also scaled back 'local government functions [...] in response to budgetary pressures, with cuts to funding in homelessness services hitting the media headlines in a number of cities' (2021, 685). Such concerns make clear what Megan Ravenhill titles a modern 'culture of homelessness' endemic within contemporary Britain, wherein even 'the current system for tackling homelessness [...] can itself be a cause of homelessness [...] inadvertently discourage[ing] and prevent[ing] people from leaving homelessness and reintegrating back into society' (Ravenhill 2008, 1). Neoliberalism in this way precipitates increased rough sleeping through its failure to care for the most vulnerable, while also dictating the dubious, market-driven, and censorious measures by which it is confronted and managed.

As Inge van Schipstal and Walter Nicholls argue, neoliberalism as an ideology is directly opposed to homeless identity not only in its promotion of a ruthless monetarism and 'security'-led policing of homeless lives, but also in its view of citizenship and human rights themselves as temporary and retractable. 'Neoliberal citizenship also entails a shift in the moral and normative underpinnings of citizenship', they argue.

Individuals are obligated 'to take on more responsibility for their own welfare requirements' [...]. [R]ights are no longer conferred by birth or residency. Rights must be 'earned' by demonstrating a contribution to the community and conformity with its values, modalities, and norms. (van Schipstal and Nicholls 2014, 176)

The fact that the homeless by definition fail to reflect this required conformity and indeed often stand in direct contention with a host of established social values – including norms regarding behaviour, speech, appearance, consumption, and sociability – reaffirms in the light of this understanding, their necessary exclusion from neoliberal society: cast as 'undeserving' or 'failed citizens', they are systematically stigmatized, punished, and excluded (Anderson 2013, 4). Indeed, Liviu Alexandrescu notes how in recent years (from 2016 onwards), following a 'larger symbolic economy of austerity policies and poverty shaming', UK journalists have begun to categorize rough sleepers as 'zombies', supposedly invading public streets, their 'severe substance-induced fits', brought on by the use of SCRA drugs, seeing them cast as a social 'menace and danger', warranting increased policing (Alexandrescu 2020, 99). As he explains, such stigmatizing labels further service in 'channelling condemnation of the abject and "undeserving" poor and [aid] to legitimise anti-welfare measures as political common sense and cultural consensus' (ibid.). In short, contemporary news media bill the homeless as 'compulsive', 'unpredictable' and contagious: a monstrous threat to the public in need of corralling (Alexandrescu 2020, 101).[1]

As Joseph Anderton notes, this increase in homelessness as a social concern is also accompanied by a rise in twenty-first-century British literature focused on the topic, where at the close of 2020, 'approximately as many full-length novels and autobiographies written by British authors about or largely featuring homelessness were published in the last two decades as in the 50 years between 1950 and 2000' (Anderton 2020). This new literary attention reflects a heightened awareness of homelessness both in academic and popular culture, including television and film, as well as social media (see Yost 2012; Hu and De Choudhury 2019; Marler 2022). In addition to the texts explored here, other prominent literary examples of late twentieth and early twenty-first-century Gothic engagements with homelessness include Neil Gaiman's *Neverwhere* (1996), Charles De Lint's *The Onion Girl* (2001), Jon McGregor's *Even the Dogs* (2010), Max Brooks' *The Extinction Parade* (2014), Lonnie Nadler and Zac Thompson's *The Dregs* (2017), and Peter Morgan's *The Spice Boys* (2017).[2] This highly diverse and variegated panorama – often combining Gothic aesthetics with other genres, ranging from realism, crime, and horror to sci fi and fantasy – speaks to this genre's special pertinence in tackling this topic, where, as Linnie Blake and Agnieszka Soltysik Monnet also write, 'the geopolitical context of the gothic's migration from the periphery to the fast-beating heart of popular culture' encompasses 'specifically the rise to economic and cultural predominance of global neoliberalism' (Blake and Soltysik Monnet 2017, 1). Of course, this has been a repeated focus of attention within this book, wherein neoliberalism's dominance can be connected to a number of prominent Gothic anxieties, encompassing the War on Terror, (neo)imperialism, racist discrimination, and anti-migrant sentiment, increased poverty and crime, climate crisis, as well as homelessness, leading to a wider sense of this ideology's destructive centrality across twenty-first-century culture. While this may be true of the modality more largely however, given the directed attention granted to homelessness across Gothic writing today, it seems worth highlighting this concern more expressly in this chapter, in order to investigate its particular twenty-first-century literary and cultural prominence.

## The Unhomely and Homelessness in Gothic Writing

Significantly, as becomes clear across a range of historic Gothic studies, homelessness and homeless trauma are by no means new to Gothic writing, whose central interest in the uncanny or *unheimlich* prioritizes the individual's uneasy and sometimes paradoxical relationship with the home, as well as the larger unstable domestic space that the home encircles. The experience of, or even the desire for, homelessness is in this sense intrinsic to the Gothic, which again repeatedly features the domestic as a site of uncanny terror. Cavallaro notes how the term 'Gothic' itself, upon entering the Western lexicon in the eighteenth-century, 'came to signify everything which a middle-class residence should disdain: discomfort, coldness, extravagance, unclear boundaries between inside and outside, and, above all, sprawling structures suggestive of lack of control over one's space' (Cavallaro 2002, 85–6). Similarly, Susan Fraiman writes that 'the "gothic" house,' is a 'house that imprisons rather than shelters women; that keeps them in thrall to norms of marital femininity; that hides domestic violence, exploits female labor and thwarts female ambition; that binds some women in domestic service to others at the expense of their own households' (Fraiman 2017, 18). In this way, from its very beginnings, the Gothic invokes an opposition or threat to middle-class domestic norms: the centrality of private property, the division of public and private space, the supposedly inherent truth of the patriarchal family order and the necessity for social constraint, conformity, and cleanliness.

This is reflected in a wealth of historic Gothic literatures, which repeatedly represent the home as a discomforting space, as well as examining the oppressed and disenfranchised lives of homeless characters. From Horace Walpole's *The Castle of Otranto* (1765) and Ann Radcliffe's *The Mysteries of Udolpho* (1794) to Nathaniel Hawthorne's *The House of the Seven Gables* (1851), Edgar Allan Poe's 'The Fall of the House of Usher' (1839), and Daphne du Maurier's *Rebecca* (1938), the Gothic explores what Nicholas Royle refers to as the inextricable connection between the uncanny and 'thoughts of home and dispossession' (Royle 2003, 6), connecting this alternatively to domestic identity, privacy, property, and habitation. 'The uncanny [is] a means of thinking about so-called "real life"', Royle writes, 'the homely and unhomely, property and alienation, [it] becomes, in the words of Anthony Vidler, "a metaphor for a fundamentally unliveable modern condition"' (ibid.). On a similar note, David Ratmoko explains how the original meaning of the verb 'to haunt' is '"[to] provide a home", to "get home" (*Oxford English Dictionary*) – that which in German is still preserved in the word *heimsuchen*. Provided with an agency or a subject, it implies a spirit looking for permanent residence, for a fixed abode' (Ratmoko 2005, 1–2). In short, the Gothic's connection to discourses of dwelling and inhabitancy, but more centrally, dislocation and estrangement, is linguistically constitutional, bound up in the notably slippery etymology underpinning its aesthetic fixtures.

Examining contemporary filmic Gothic depictions of domesticity, Tyson Lewis and Daniel Cho note how 'the home, which is something that should feel most comfortable and familiar, has increasingly in late capitalism become a space where the uncanny is experienced', thus demonstrating 'the repressed truth concerning the alienating results of private ownership' (Lewis and Cho 2006, 69, 72). The comforting domain of familial domesticity in this way becomes 'a nostalgic impossibility, contaminated by the remembrance of "family interests" or rather family disputes, quarrels, and betrayals' (ibid.). Likewise, Monica Michlin notes how, 'contemporary gothic narratives display post-Freudian awareness that the haunted house is the place where trauma occurred, but also, and subsequently, the projection of the traumatized and haunted psyche itself' (2012): a place of ghosts, demons, and terrors. These explanations draw attention to Gothic literature's repeated repudiation and subversion of established domestic structures, making homelessness a central Gothic theme and motif.[3]

Nevertheless, as John Allen also remarks in his study, *Homelessness in American Literature* (2004), the treatment of this subject in literature (both

Gothic and other), as in the media, may often be tainted by 'romanticising' or 'objectifying' discourses which alternatively glorify or demonize the homeless person as outside 'normal' society and exempt from its historical sympathy (ibid., 3–4), treated as a 'form of vicarious adventure' or 'a glimpse of abject poverty' (ibid., 5). Allen comments on how the homeless person is on the one hand 'elevated' to 'homeless wanderer as rebel' and on the other 'objectified' as the focus of observation and education, in either case reducing her psychological and political complexity to what the 'dominant culture' chooses to read in this population (ibid., 3–5). In this way, literature representing homelessness often falls under the criticism of evading or misreading traumatic material histories, seeing these as too morbid or corporeal for its romantic and/or pedagogical purposes.

Indeed, this can be seen not only in literature – Allen's examples include work by Harriet Beecher, Horatio Alger, Jacob Riis, Stephen Crane, and Jack London – but also in contemporary criticism, where writers such as Edward Said, Giles Deleuze, and Félix Guattari use the term 'homelessness' in specifically *figurative* ways to invoke ideals of cultural and political displacement, rather than concrete material conditions relatable to discourses of trauma and violence. Said writes of 'a generalized condition of homelessness' (Said 1979, 18) in modern postcolonial life, where, in an often-positive way, familiar dichotomies between colonizer and colonized, or centre and periphery become blurred. As Denise deCaires Narain summarizes, Said 'embraces homelessness and the condition of exile as an enabling space while acknowledging that texts and other cultural artifacts do not transcend the political, historical, and cultural circumstances of their production and consumption' (deCaires Narain 2010, 122). Likewise, Deleuze and Guattari celebrate homelessness as a revolutionary ideal, where the nomad's 'deterritorialized' cultural outlook offers a necessary escape from capitalism's Oedipal constrictions. As *A Thousand Plateaus* expresses this, '[d]eterritorialization must be thought of as a perfectly positive power that has degrees and thresholds [...]. Every voyage is intensive, and occurs in relation to thresholds of intensity between which it evolves or that which it crosses' (Deleuze and Guattari 2014, 62). The homeless nomad thus becomes a figure for contemporary anti-hegemonic thinking and its affective and artistic power.

These uses are evidently politicized in tone, rejecting Western society's prioritization of domestic or nationalist norms, and invoking a critical reaffirmation of hybrid and marginal experience, as a basis for cross-cultural and collective social engagement. As Samir Dayal explains:

Nomadic homelessness should not be conceived as resituating the post-colonial subject in an imagined, idealized, and hypothetical space, an imaginary homeland, a space where no one has ever lived. One of the chief attractions of the lightness of being implied by the metaphors of nomadism, cosmopolitanism, homelessness, and diaspora, is that they trouble the borders of belonging. (1998, 44)

Nevertheless, this underlying *metaphorical* conception of homelessness, celebrating the homeless person's migratory view with little concern for actual lived experience and material poverty, arguably eludes the historical trauma of homelessness, as a condition of social rejection and stigmatization comparable to many other modern social catastrophes: destitution, rape, drug addiction, murder, all of which might form a part of homeless experience. Indeed, the migrant homeless subject herself also evades this categorization, where, as Aijaz Ahmed writes, '[m]ost migrants tend to be poor and experience displacement not as cultural plenitude but as torment; what they seek is not displacement but, precisely, a place from where they may begin anew, with some sense of a stable future' (Ahmed 1997, 373). In this sense, socioeconomic struggle, much more than nomadic plenitude, shapes the homeless person's consciousness, registering clear materialist anxieties in need of attention.

The novels I analyse in this chapter, Smith's *Hotel World*, Azzopardi's *Remember Me*, and Chikwava's *Harare North*, move beyond this central evasion, updating contemporary literature by exploring homelessness in material terms, as a social and lived phenomenon, and likewise, by manipulating Gothic and fantasy techniques to better appreciate homeless experiences of oppression and trauma. In the case of *Hotel World*, this entails an urban and corporate textual space, specifically tied to the global, where the accidental death of a hotel chambermaid provokes an unsettling inquiry into capitalist anonymity and exploitation: Sara's ghost becomes a figure for twenty-first-century economic invisibility in a world structured by wealth and status. Indeed, all the characters in the novel participate in this experience, either directly – through reference to global capitalism's spatial exclusion (as in the case of Else) – or indirectly – through episodes of death, mourning, and illness which narrativize the traumatological dimensions of capitalist estrangement. The novel evokes, to quote Judith Butler, our 'common corporeal vulnerability' (Butler 2004, 42), even as it makes clear how visible displays of this vulnerability in the form of poverty, homelessness, and illness, egregiously disqualify individuals from consideration as equally human.

While *Hotel World* focuses on an urban setting, reflective of the global corporate venue of its title, Azzopardi's *Remember Me* instead unfolds within small-town Norwich, where a local street-woman's unlikely robbery uncovers a history of provincial mistreatment. Winnie's disturbance, again inflected with spectral and uncanny signifiers, reflects her namelessness within conservative small-town society, where discourses of reform and compassion serve as ironic justifications for social ostracizing. Put differently, Winnie is persecuted precisely under the dictates of a local institutional framework which claims to support her, made ghostly on account of her traveller identity, learning impairments, and speech difficulties. As Louise France writes, referencing the local woman, Nora Bridle, whose life inspired Winnie's character, '[l]et down by everyone she comes across, she finds herself on the streets. [...] *Remember Me* is almost a plea - don't ignore women like Nora or Winifred' (France 2004). Nevertheless, Azzopardi's eye to the transnational is reflected in the text's repeated references to Britain's larger global historical connections and to histories of prejudice and exclusion tied to the Second World War, which position migrants in a similar (at times overlapping) relation to the domestic homeless population.

In Brian Chikwava's *Harare North*, this migratory experience also emerges at the centre of this text's Gothic homelessness, where the violence of displacement is compounded by the search for a safe and stable accommodation. In this novel again, this experience is read through a deeply unstable psychology, here situated against the backdrop of twenty-first-century Brixton, positioned as a settling place for multiple diasporic African populations. As the narrator navigates this new environment, balancing horrifying memories of wartime violence against his current dislocation, the novel's troubled picture of twenty-first-century homelessness comes through. Just as in Smith and Azzopardi's novels, this representation is balanced against a call for greater collective awareness, in this case communicated through a textual engagement with Shona folklore and its community-centred ethics, also recalling Oyeyemi's inspired investments in Nigerian folktales.

The contrasting transnational and local dynamics of these settings reflect diverging preoccupations regarding corporate alienation, provincial close-mindedness, urban poverty, and migratory displacement. Each novel has its own pointedly signposted sociopolitical anxieties. Nevertheless, the common Gothic aesthetic of these novels, invoking motifs of paranoia, ghosts, and doubles in relation to a shared theme of homelessness, suggests a conjoint literary preoccupation, building on a persistent anxiety regarding property, ownership, and dispossession running throughout Gothic writing from Walpole, Radcliffe, and Hawthorne to Jon McGregor and Niall Griffiths. Developing ideas introduced by Henri Lefebvre and Michel Foucault in relation to modern spatial and discursive exclusivity and by Julia Kristeva and Mark Seltzer concerning homeless depression and mental illness, I see these novels as again contributing to a twenty-first-century Gothic critique of neoliberalism and austerity, negotiating spectral and uncanny aesthetics to reflect on growing concerns regarding homeless displacement. Reframing the concept of homelessness in specifically spectral and 'traumatological' vocabularies, these novels offer a concerted reckoning of contemporary homeless distress, moving beyond the false romance of the homeless wanderer.

## Corporate Exclusion and Hotel Ghosts in Smith's *Hotel World*

Beginning with *Hotel World*, a Lefebvrean concern with the anonymity of urban space can be seen from the start of the text, where the ghost of Sara Wilby, estranged from her body and floating invisibly through space, relates the experience of her death by falling in a hotel dumbwaiter:

> Wooooooooo-hooooooo what a fall what a soar what a plummet [...] what a drop what a rush what a swoop what a fright what a mad hushed skirl what a smash mush mash-up broke and gashed what a heart in my mouth what an end. (Smith 2001, 3)

Here the anaphoric repetition of Sara's cry reflects the quickening of her thoughts as she falls, conjuring a pre-death ghostliness: she seems to be swallowed up by this architectural hole, sucked supernaturally into its hidden centre and transformed in the process into a spectre. The unexpected finality of this event, occurring when she is joking around with a fellow employee in the staff quarters, registers the building's latent violence: the shaft betrays a murderous potential conspicuously directed at the working class. Promoted as a space for relaxation and escape for off-hours employees, it emerges as a death-trap, an open grave: situated, as with all abject spaces, 'outside the symbolic order [...] where meaning collapses' (Starr 2014, 7). Thus, as Monica Germanà puts it, 'the dumb-waiter becomes a coffin. The hotel is a crypt' (Germanà 2010b, 163).

Placed within a contemporary Gothic framework of neoliberal precarity, this understanding reflects an urban updating of the traditional 'haunted hotel' motif, drawing on classic horror films such as Alfred Hitchcock's *Psycho* (1960) and

Stanley Kubrick's *The Shining* (1980) and connecting these to a critique of corporate architecture, patriarchy, and the consumer capitalist ethos (as also explored, for example, in Philip Kerr's *Gridiron* (1995) and Louise Tondeur's *The Water's Edge* (2003)). 'Breathing people in and out' of its rotating doors (Smith 2001, 30), the technologized and corporate aesthetic of the building, with floor after floor of identical rooms and well-made beds, 'their mouths open saying *welcome, hurry up, get it*' (ibid., 7), asserts an obsessive consumerist regulation, systematically effacing the possibility of difference and reaffirming Marc Augé's categorization of the corporate hotel as a supermodern 'non-place', where 'people are always, and never, at home' (Augé 2009, 109). Sara's evanescent presence within this structure acts as a window on this consumer fantasy: 'waft[ing] about the restaurant from [...] plate to nouvelle plate', 'seep[ing ...] out the back [to where] five dustbins are stacked against a wall, each full of uneaten things'; 'hang[ing] in reception like muzak' (Smith 2001, 29) – her ghostly presence mimics the superficiality of the hotel's symbolism. Likewise, her unpredicted death functions both as an assertion *and* subversion of hotel control: re-avowing on the one hand the dispensability of the workers – where 'there were always new chambermaids, chambermaids have a high turnover' (ibid., 109) – and on the other, the gaping ontological void at the building's centre, an emptiness which must be carefully covered up. As Sara's sister Clare puts it, 'something about that metal still being there like it would always be there [...] I suppose they will do that change the building' (ibid., 199–200).

In the switch in the second chapter from Sara's narrative to that of the homeless woman, Else, this understanding is both reiterated and complicated, adding to it the notion of an *externalized* privatization. Thus, sitting with her back against the hotel front, Else inhabits a space at once outside and yet also within the remit of hotel regulation, dominated by its threatening architecture and surveillance mechanisms:

> From this side of the road you can't not see the hotel. [...] With its awnings either side of its door, the building has a kind of face. The awnings are the eyelids, the word GLOBAL scarred across them both. [...] Round the ground floor at the front [...] are spike-topped railings painted white. Else remembers a girl at school who had a scar under her chin from falling on to some railings; a railing had gone right through her chin and mouth and tongue. She had had stitches. (Smith 2001, 64–5)

In the references here to the building's visual aggressiveness – its looming obedient 'face', scarred 'eyelids', and foreboding 'spike-topped railings' – this passage depicts a technologized Gothic, connecting postmodern architecture to social control and abjection. Semi-autonomous and automaton-like, the structure intrudes upon Else's imagination, securing her cooperation through its carceral imagery. Foucaudian, or perhaps more Orwellian in nature, its giant eyes monitor her every behaviour, threatening violence should she attempt an illicit entrance. In the words of Mark Wigley, 'the corporate building provides a fixed, visible face for an unfixed, invisible and carnivorous organization' (Wigley 2002, 75): it is the material embodiment of the insidious practices happening inside. Accordingly, Else's own disturbed response makes clear her sense of threat within the neoliberal city: she envisions sadistic images which take on a literal, active presence in her mind, of penetration, 'scarring' and 'stitches'. In other words, she becomes the building's victim, seeing its enormity as an actual peril: it represents for her a monster, its spiky teeth ready to devour her.

The problem goes beyond that of interior–exterior segregation, the maintaining of the homeless outside the hotel's private enclosure. Rather, the dense network of architecture, security cameras, and public rhetoric surrounding the space corral even Else's *outside* presence, systematically asserting an exclusivist discourse which stigmatizes Else's identity and which forces her to seek night-time shelter elsewhere. Else's memories of police encounters register this verbal persecution:

> Is that your stuff? Move it. Or we'll bin it. Move it. Move. (a man) ...
>
> You've got a home. Everybody's got somewhere. Go home now, there's a good girl. (a man) ...
>
> (whispered) Now I'm telling you straight and I'll only tell you once. You want a good raping, and you're for it. You let me see you in here again and you'll get it. I *mean* it. [...] (a man, at the station) (Smith 2001, 43)

Read in relation to contemporary urban space studies, this incident corroborates recognized scholarship regarding architectural and spatial exclusion and its destructive impact on homeless individuals and communities. As Joe Doherty et al. explain, 'access to public space for homeless people is increasingly under threat [in the twenty-first-century metropolis] as city authorities and some national governments impose restrictions on access for certain categories of people' (2008, 292–3). This public policing reflects various so-called 'soft' and 'heavy handed' mechanisms including not only 'panoptic' monitoring through CCTV cameras, gated architecture and guards, but also a media discourse of 'security' and 'safety' (heightened since 9/11) which 'can be influential in acquiring public acquiescence to restrictive practices' (ibid., 293). Correspondingly, in the words of Don Mitchell, 'homeless people are in a double bind. For them, socially legitimated private space does not exist, and they are denied access to public space and public activity by capitalist society which is anchored in private property and privacy' (Mitchell 1995, 118). Seen as intruders or parasites, who at best impose and at worst pollute and contaminate, the homeless become spatial non-entities, forced to float in the margins of community. As Bridget Anderson likewise writes, these so-called 'Benefit Scroungers' or 'Failed Citizens' include those 'who are imagined as incapable of achieving, or failing to live up to, liberal ideals' (2013, 4). 'They [supposedly] have a problem of culture, fecklessness, and ill-discipline leading to them making the wrong choices and also to welfare dependence' – such are the assumptions which see them deemed 'unworthy of membership of the community of value.' (Ibid.).

Following the contemporary economic shift away from the post-war 'managerialist' aims of 'welfare, public services and collective consumption' to those of consumer 'entrepreneurialism' and later, austerity (MacLeod and Ward 2002, 155), the plight of the homeless becomes particularly tragic, shaped by the cruelty not only of corporate business but also public policy. The postmodern 'revanchist' city maintains diversity not 'by protecting and struggling to explain the rights of the most disadvantaged', but rather by 'pushing the disadvantaged out, making it clear that, as broken windows rather than people, they simply have *no* right to the city' (Mitchell 2001, 71). This understanding damages not only the larger social perception of the homeless, as an intolerable presence within the public sphere, but also the homeless communities' perceptions of themselves: they become supposedly unworthy of social assistance, responsible for their poverty and/or illness and meriting the violence practiced upon them.

Else's often distressed self-image reflects this destructive discourse. Describing her interior condition as a 'waste ground round a condemned building whose windows have been broken' (Smith 2001, 50), she internalizes her public exclusion, projecting her depressed surroundings onto her own fragmented identity. Her breath becomes 'broken glass' and her cough 'the whole fucking National Trust ancient fucking property breaking up into nothing but rubble' (ibid., 41). Likewise, her language too is broken down to shorthand fragments, patterns without vowels, which resist the realm of the symbolic in the same way that the symbolic rejects her. She thinks of how 'she doesn't need vowels either. [...] She imagines the pavement littered with the letters that fall out of the half-words she uses' (ibid., 47). Commenting on this 'mutilation' of everyday language, Germanà notes how 'the letters she imagines are the broken form of the only language that remains' (Germanà 2010b, 166): nothing complete is now possible; she must make do with sounds and gestures.

Nevertheless, there is also a clear independence and humour to Else's perspective which complicates this distressing assessment, introducing a subversive critical vision to this Gothic portrayal of homelessness. When Else finally enters the hotel, through the help of the receptionist, her outsider's viewpoint deconstructs the symbolic order of the building, uncovering a hidden history of abuse which effectively re-materializes an invisible working community. Thus, the 'dazzling' taps in the bathroom reflect that 'every day someone has come in here and wiped them back to being new again', while the individually wrapped soaps invoke 'someone in a factory or workshop somewhere [...] wrapping up the soap in paper [...] like it's a gift' (Smith 2001, 70–1), and even the cupid's head over the door conjures a man once 'slicing lumps out of stone as if stone was cake or bread. [...] Else wonders how much the man was paid' (ibid.). Borrowing Foucault's notion of a 'heterotopia', 'a kind of effectively enacted utopia in which the real sites [...] are simultaneously represented, contested, and inverted' (Foucault 1986, 24), Else's homelessness here can be seen as a twenty-first-century example of spatial inversion, overturning global capitalism's spectacle society and invoking against it a phantasmal counter-reality of awareness and directed social consciousness.

## Provincial Abuse and Mental Illness in Azzopardi's *Remember Me*

In *Remember Me*, this dissident understanding is reasserted through the figure of Winnie, an elderly and mentally ill homeless woman whose evident abandonment in the hands of social services relates an implicit social invisibility. Like the workers of the 'Global Hotel', she too exists outside recognized social categories, inhabiting a symbolic spectrality which distorts everyday cultural perceptions. Sleeping in an abandoned shoe shop, where the broken furniture provides insufficient fuel for the winter cold, and where an intruder burglarizes her few possessions, Winnie's discursive non-entity overwhelms her minimal actuality. To borrow from Rosemary Winslow, her trauma places her in 'a *separate* world, because it is outside everyday experience and thus outside ordinary language' (Winslow 2004, 609).

Within this context, Winnie's burglary functions as critical indicator of her social precarity, tacitly referencing her victimized situation in a way which challenges conventional social perceptions. The effort to unravel this crime and indict the criminal re-prioritizes Winnie's forgotten identity and viewpoint, consecrating her displaced legal and social importance via means of her personal narrative. As D. J. Taylor writes, Winnie's story is 'a search for identity, a journey in pursuit of something that is recognisably her own' (Taylor 2004): she seeks to restore to her person the shelter, love, and protection she has been denied. Nevertheless, the unusual nature of the attack, apparently disconnected from expected bigoted motives against the homeless, obscures this understanding, introducing an element of mystery to the narrative which partially implicates Winnie within the crime. In this way, Winnie's story becomes at once a window on abuse and an exploration of homeless mental illness, the final chapters disclosing a criminal history in which Winnie has stolen and shaved another woman's baby, claiming her as her own: an act which dislodges simple binaries of persecutor and persecuted.

Much more than *Hotel World*, the emphasis here is on the psychological causes (and later, consequences) of contemporary homelessness, in this case relating to Winnie's childhood displacement, her mother, Lillian, suffering from a chronic depression which conscribes Winnie's involvement and which later affects her own relations with children. The narrative's explanation for *Lillian's* condition emerges through a network of textual clues, including Winnie's father and grandfather's argument over the rite of christening, her grandfather's claim of custody after Lillian's death, and, ultimately, her red hair, which matches neither of her parents' but does match that of the local cobbler. The additional knowledge that Lillian was formally employed by the cobbler, and latterly, that the cobbler has a history of rape (ultimately including Winnie), completes this narrative, tacitly diagnosing Lillian's depression as a response to institutional violation and unwanted pregnancy.

The traumatic impact of this unspoken history on Winnie herself is underscored in the narrative by a range of Gothic motifs. Encumbered by her mother with the fantastical task of chasing ghosts from the room, Winnie begins to adopt this spectral vocabulary as her own, affirming the authenticity of the apparitions against her father's rationalizations: 'the ghosts are real', she insists, 'they live inside her.... I've got a bird inside me; it flaps if things start to go wrong' (Azzopardi 2004, 26). Additionally, in response to her mother's mirror fixation, centred around the fairytale mantra 'who's the fairest?' (ibid., 34), Winnie develops a mirror-phobia of her own, interpreting her reflected image as a persecuting spectre: 'even at night, even through the dark, I felt her inside it, sitting in the frame, waiting for me to come and look' (ibid., 80). Through these haunted representations, Winnie evades her negative self-image, transferring her personal anxieties and insecurities into a phantasmal imaginary realm: in Freudian language, she at once interjects her mother's trauma and projects this unto a phantastic dream-world.

Winnie's further experiences of loss and trauma, including her mother's suicide, her father's abandonment, her grandfather's death, her own wartime evacuation, a forced abortion and repeated rape at the hands of her (unknowing) biological father, extend this delusional imaginary, pulling Winnie increasingly further from stable social identity. In her present homelessness, sleeping in her rapist's vacant shop, wearing a wig which covers her 'telltale' red hair, and floating from place to place without 'think[ing] about anything' (Azzopardi 2004, 8), Winnie appears numb to reality, existing as a fictional entity, cut off from regular social responsibility and absorbed by anonymity and amnesia: 'I never looked back and I never looked on [...] if a memory came creeping into my head [...] I'd say, That wasn't your life, now, that belonged to someone else. That was just before' (ibid., 9). Indeed, following her break from everyday communication, even speech becomes difficult, where 'talking's like being behind glass, the words can be hard to fathom' (ibid., 123). In this pre-symbolic ethereal realm, identity and meaning lose relevance and are replaced by obsessive denial.

Reading this narrative in the context of contemporary psychoanalysis, a clear link can be discerned between Winnie's disturbing history and her current melancholic state. Describing the illusory quality of melancholia, as something which exists largely outside the symbolic domain, in an 'unnameable narcissistic wound', Julia Kristeva explains how 'the depressed person [...] retreats [from general society], disconsolate and aphasic, alone with the unnamed Thing' (Kristeva 1989, 12–13). Clinging to the lost 'place or preobject', she abandons spatial and linguistic order, 'confining the libido or severing the bonds of desire' (ibid., 13). The ultimate effect of this severing – paralleling Winnie's claim that '*I* felt stolen' (ibid., 73) – is the disintegration of the self: the depressed subject becomes unable 'to transmit psychic energies and inscriptions' (ibid., 13), trapped in a static, inchoate imaginary.

For Winnie, living not only with loss but also violence, including a forced abortion and rape, this condition entails disengagement, but also a traumatic pathology. In her attempt to process the wound of her violation and to achieve some form of stable personhood, Winnie crosses over conventional boundaries between self and Other, interpreting her own identity as that of another person entirely. Holding Alice's baby in her arms, she thinks, 'I was her mother now, and she was our child, mine and Joseph's. She was no mistake' (Azzopardi 2004, 250). The baby thus comes to stand in for her own failed motherhood *and* her unavailing social legitimacy: through it, she attempts to overcome her status as 'unwanted' and to position herself as a valued member of an established family.

When she then steals and shaves the baby, using the cobbler's blades to remove 'every single last hair' (Azzopardi 2004, 259), she takes this fantasy even further, symbolically erasing the signs of her own illegitimacy, extracting the 'telltale' red strands as a means of mimetically 'saving' the baby (herself) from her own fate. 'It was Telltale,' she explains, 'I had been a long time in hiding at Hewitt's; I recognized his stamp. It had to be removed' (ibid.). The delusional character of this reasoning, confusing empathy with identification and ignoring the brutality of her behaviour, reaffirms Mark Seltzer's pathological conception of trauma, as a '*breakdown* in the autonomy of the subject: a fundamental shattering or *breaking-in* of the boundaries between the external and the internal', often with some form of 'hypnotic mimetic identification' as a result (Seltzer 1997, 9–10). In other words, by re-staging her own motherhood and infantile illegitimacy *representationally*, in an act of symbolic removal, Winnie fulfils her fantasy selfhood pathologically, collapsing the distinction between inner and outer, and in this way removing social obstacles to atonement. She performs her own enforced woundedness, enacting this literally as a means to treating the source.

In the context of Winnie's repeated claims to narrative reliability – 'to be straight' (Azzopardi 2004, 3), 'if I'm true' (ibid., 5, 6, 8, 46) – this final twist in the plot overtly complicates her moral authority, introducing conditions on the reader's commiseration which potentially invert the novel's subversive social message. One response to Winnie's revelation, put forward by Janice in the novel, is thus a rejection of concern for the homeless: 'My mother always taught me to feel sorry for people like you. But I don't. I really don't' (ibid., 260). Following this pronouncement, from the perspective of Winnie's victim, her violence emerges as insuperable, overwhelming any sense of sympathy or compassion her narrative inspires and instead asserting censure as the only appropriate response to her aggressive behaviour.

Nevertheless, given what we know of Winnie's past and her losses, Janice's reaction itself seems misjudged, ignoring not only the psychological but also sociological history of Winnie's transgression, including twenty-five years of institutionalization run on principles of silence, discipline, and moral reform. Winnie notes, 'I discovered from reading the rules that we are not patients but

Objects, who through prayer and guidance may be restored. I am a thief. Denying the fact has made me a liar' (ibid., 235). The systematic stigmatization evidenced here, replacing therapy and economic support with accusation, suggests a deeper layer of social prejudice against the mentally ill and homeless which underpins Winnie's transgression. Classed as 'insane' and 'criminal', she appears effectively to have absorbed her designated illness, making *this* (however disturbingly) her social purpose.

The final passages of Winnie's narrative offer an ambiguous reassertion of this message. On the one hand, Winnie appears partially freed by her narrative, her confrontation with her crime offering a sense of relief in which 'the bird in my chest has flown; the words are no longer needed, and I have no more accounting to do' (ibid., 262). Nevertheless, as in *Hotel World*, a continuation of partially delusional experience, as Winnie imagines herself sitting with her lost loved ones, emptied of responsibilities and free to be 'anyone I choose. [...] Anybody, or nobody' (Azzopardi 2004, 262) suggests that the complexities of homelessness are not easily resolved. Like Else, Winnie too inhabits a spectral heterotopia, where life outside conventional institutional boundaries means at once freedom and invisibility.

## Migrancy, Homelessness, and a Haunting Spirit-World in Chikwava's *Harare North*

If homelessness underpins the socially conscious Gothic of Smith and Azzopardi's novels, it also figures centrally in Brain Chikwava's *Harare North*, in this case offering a clue to the narrator's psychological unravelling in the context of transnational displacement. As outlined above, Smith's choice of an unnamed postmodern city as her setting for *Hotel World* echoes that novel's concern with 'non-space' anonymity, while Azzopardi's provincial Norfolk countryside instead infers 'the uncanny space of regionality' (Hughes 2018, 1), especially as this encompasses small-town prejudice and discrimination. By contrast, Brian Chikwava's *Harare North* returns to the imperial centre of metropolitan London, casting this urban topography in equally uncanny terms, through an unreliable narrator and a haunted landscape reminiscent of Robert Louis Stevenson's *The Strange Case of Dr Jekyll and Mr Hyde* (1886).

As context for this depiction, it is significant that 'Harare North' is Zimbabwean slang for London, while 'Harare South' references Johannesburg (Mbiba 2012), in each case invoking the contemporary rise in Zimbabwean migration to these international cities, especially following the political-economic crisis of 2000 (Sachikonye 2012, 163). While on the one hand this reference invokes the stark reality of Zimbabwe's political and economic unrest following Mugabe, leading to increased emigration to London and Johannesburg as recognized spaces of asylum (ibid., 163), on the other hand it also suggests a Gothic doubling between Harare and London, as the narrator's anxieties upon relocation re-establish an unsettling duplicate precarity in his new home. As Dave Gunning writes, 'an African present, or very recent past, is never far from the text' and the tension between the two cities 'is built into not only Chikwava's content, but also at the level of form' (Gunning 2015, 127), where both the text's diasporic language and its often-dreamlike structure create uncanny links between past and present, home and abroad. Here, the narrator's phantasmagorical dream-scenes replay the past and conjure dark and angry spirits connected to his traumatic upbringing, in this way opening up a doubled topography overtly tied to transnational inhabitancy, positioning home and host country as spookily intertwined at the level of subjective reflection.

Set primarily in Brixton, known for its Black British demographic, but whose population has undergone a recent shift towards a greater African migrant residence (Kociejowski 2011, 55), the novel is concerned particularly with a new body of African migrants and asylum seekers looking for refuge in this 'glocal' London neighbourhood and with the complex assortment of memories, dreams, and traumas this community brings with it. To borrow James Procter's language, it is novel about diasporic 'dwelling', conceived not as 'a signifier of closure or resolution', but instead as 'a spatial and temporal process', implying that accommodation into a host country takes time and involves multiple levels of adjustment and adaptation (Procter 2003, 15). Announcing his status as asylum seeker upon arrival, the narrator is not, the novel underlines, a romantic embodiment of diasporic innocence. Rather, he is weighted with a dense memorial luggage, which at once beseeches the reader's sympathy and repels this. Meeting Immigration Control with a pre-set strategy for approval, wherein he 'flash[es the] toothy grin of friendly African native' (Chikwava 2009, 4), he pleads compassion as a persecuted member of Zimbabwe's opposition party, the Movement for Democratic Change (MDC), only then to later confess his membership within the 'Green Bombers', the youth organization for Mugabe's Zimbabwe African National Union Patriotic Front (ZANU PF). Having carried out various brutalities on behalf of the party, the reader soon appreciates the narrator's role in the murder of an MDC member, which explains his emigration, as he seeks to escape imprisonment living abroad until he can raise enough money to pay off the police. In this way, the narrative at first seems to play into a conservative discourse of immigrant deception and false testimony, catering to far-right biases and misrepresentations. Nevertheless, as the text continues, the narrator's oppressed relationship with his country's leadership, as a child soldier also exploited by his commanding officer, brings to bear a larger historical framework of political corruption surrounding his migration, complicating any straightforward categorization of reliability or deception.

This narrative framework thus positions this migratory experience as complex and multisided, as the narrator is at once invested in military brutality and also clearly scarred by his involvement in government warfare and susceptible to exploitation. As Annie Gagiano affirms, there is much to warm the critical reader to this (unnamed) young refugee, who remains a figure of radical vulnerability, 'yearning for an irretrievably lost innocence and [suffering] great pain at his betrayal of his mother's hopes and ideals' (Gagiano 2013). Indeed, the narrator returns throughout the text to his distressed concerns regarding his mother's disapproval and also his filial irresponsibility in failing to perform her burial rites, or '*umbuyiso*' (Chikwava 2009, 16, 74, 146). As Patricia Noxolo clarifies, his false confession of opposition membership at the airport does not impede our commiseration, where 'very young people being initiated, forced or manipulated to commit violence is a recognised and recurrent feature of a range of recent conflicts worldwide and in Africa in particular', such that again, a clear distinction between perpetrator and victim is not straightforward (Noxolo 2014, 301). This knowledge, combined with various unconscious confessions of guilt throughout the narrative, suggests that the narrator is indeed as much a *target of*, as he is a *participant in* violence, abused by a Zimbabwean government unashamed to employ child soldiers and subsequently excluded from mainstream British society and made homeless in the event of his migration.

This critical awareness of the narrator's vulnerability, and of the layered trauma this carries with it, sets into relief the complex circumstances surrounding his increasingly erratic behaviour. We see him, for example, dismissing his close friend, Shingi, in the name of self-promotion: the latter has become a 'big headache for me' and a 'danger to my plan' (Chikwava 2009, 1). In fact, the narrator not only disregards Shingi's fervent protection in providing accommodation and sustenance upon his arrival, he also actively seeks to undermine him, first by competing for his love interest, Tsitsi, and later by gradually stealing his identity. This latter persecution ends in murder, as the narrator recounts stabbing Shingi in the alleyway outside their squat, a chronicle which emerges as extremely Gothic, not only in its goriness, but also in its uncanny and bizarre interweaving of an attack on an injured squirrel:

> I take out my screwdriver, put my boot on squirrel's head to pin him down, position my screwdriver right behind the head; on the spine. One quick jerk of the wrist, and snap. The screwdriver go through the neck right into the grass and wet ground below. [...] Blood squirt everywhere. I put him out of his misery and put back some order into his life. [...] Water run down my face and go inside my mouth. [...] I see Shingi soaked; his trousers heavy with the blood of big mama [...] (Chikwava 2009, 184–5)

In this scene, while the narrator endeavours to separate his attack on the squirrel and his violence against Shingi, carefully disassociating himself from the killing, their gruesome details intertwine in the telling, also bringing to bear his repressed guilt regarding his mother's neglected *umbuyiso*, as 'her' blood runs down his face and leaves Shingi's trousers 'soaked'.[4]

What is compelling about this narrative, apart from its strange layering of dream and reality, is how it draws on a language of 'order' precisely in the moment of describing extreme violence, in this way implicitly connecting the narrator's socioeconomic aspiration and his anti-social tendencies. If the protagonist is erratic in his speech and behaviour, the text suggests, this is in part on account of his obsessive concern to appear invulnerable, where extreme bravado and aggression make up his new, post-traumatic attitude on the streets of London. As Noxolo writes, 'the trauma of violence seeps insidiously into the space of asylum, bringing about the slow disintegration of the narrator's bodily integrity amidst the disappearance of his hopes of return to Zimbabwe to give his mother proper funeral rites' (Noxolo 2014, 303). Mental illness, in this way, is understood not as aberration, as in many Imperial Gothic narratives (see for example Daly 2014), but rather as the unsurprising effect of ongoing material abuse and disenfranchisement in the context of war, migration, and homelessness, countered by a frantic endeavour on the narrator's part to retain control of his life through paranoid behaviours. To borrow Fred Botting's words, 'the horror emanates', in this novel, as in *Dr Jekyll and Mr Hyde*, 'from the revelation of the extent and power of [the protagonist's] buried energies' (Botting 1996, 139), both more extreme and also more brutal than initially suggested.

In Stevenson's novel, this repressed monstrosity can also be read as reflective of a larger sociopolitical anxiety concerning racial contamination, a concern which appears here (ironically) to influence Chikwava's narrator himself, as he distances his London identity from other Zimbabweans. As David Punter writes,

Stevenson's novel poses 'a question appropriate to an age of imperial decline: how much ... can one lose – individually, socially, nationally – and still remain a man?' (Punter 1980, 239–40). Rewriting the novel from a decolonial perspective, Chikwava also integrates this Victorian discourse into his narrative to underline the pressures placed upon his narrator in the context of migration and homelessness, reinforcing his crisis of masculinity and ethnicity as having produced 'buried energies', themselves the product of earlier wartime violence and transnational displacement.

Indeed, in both novels a central motif of doubling underpins the Gothic aesthetic, making it clear that much of what the narrator *feels* is repressed or disavowed. For Stevenson, this involves a *fin de siècle* critique of Victorian bourgeois morality, whose pervasive social taboos and prohibitions, offered in the name or justice and reason, 'produced the divided lifestyles of the middle classes, respectable by day and pleasure-seeking by night' (Botting 1996, 136). By contrast, in *Harare North*, the migrant's ongoing social disenfranchisement erupts in a radical subjective split, the narrator desperate to repair his damaged past, while also unable to assume full control over his behaviour. This manifests in particular in the strange intimacy the narrator shares with Shingi, where a language of doubling, and of ghostly or spiritual possession, underpins his ambiguous identity, positioning Shingi as a possible alter ego to the narrator's disturbed character. This trope can be explained in various ways in the novel, depending upon the reader's critical viewpoint, such that it is worth noting the ambivalence of this representation in the text – as it moves *between* Freudian psychoanalysis and a contrasting spiritualist hermeneutic inspired by Zimbabwean Shona folklore. As Gunning writes, *Harare North* 'occup[ies] the languages of trauma' but also refuses 'the final ascription of a traumatic reality "behind" the text', instead turning to 'spirit possession as a counter-trope' to explain the narrative events differently (Gunning 2015, 130).

Under this latter reading, the narrator is possessed by an angry spirit, or *ngozi*, come to destroy him, in this way chastising him for his unwillingness to repent and to live up to his past crimes. This explanation becomes visible already in the opening description the narrator provides of Shingi's abode, wherein a physiognomic idiom invites us to read this house *as* Shingi:

> It have two top windows that have red brick arch. That make the windows look like big sad eyes. Below them sad eyes there is one large bay window that stick out like nose. When I look at the nose, the eyes and black parapet wall – this is Shingi straight and square. But you don't tell anyone that they head look like

house if you still want to be friends. So, Shingi live inside this head? (Chikwava 2009, 29)

In occupying the house (or squat), the narrator is also occupied by Shingi, the latter playing the role of a ghost, or the Zimbabwean *ngozi*, who comes to avenge past crimes and to restore a larger spiritual order. In his own words, Shingi 'possesses' him (or he, Shingi – the relationship remains unclear), and increasingly puts his 'head out of gear' (ibid., 38 and 11), forcing him to act in ways at once destructive and unpredictable.

Given the centrality of this spiritual cosmology to the novel, it is worth underling its key dimensions, both in order to better appreciate its textual importance and to explain how it distances *Harare North* from Stevenson's *fin-de-siècle* Gothic. As Terrence Musanga explains, 'The core foundational principles of justice, peace, and love constitute the Zimbabwean Shona universe'; when these principles are not respected this 'results in the destabilization of this complex universe, and corrective measures have to be taken to restore balance and stability' (Musanga 2017, 778). Within this context, 'to kill a fellow human being or commit suicide is to commit "ngozi"', which must be 'recompensed in order for restorative justice to occur' (ibid.). Furthermore, a failure to placate or assuage ngozi 'results in inexplicable sicknesses or eventual death or deaths of the person or persons who would have committed the "ngozi"' (ibid., 779), even while 'the spiritual dimension brought about by the manifestation of "ngozi" forces contesting/warring parties to dialogue' (ibid., 780). As Fainos Mangena also expounds, such dialogue 'leads to consensus, which enables the victim of crime to be healed through the payment of restitution and/or compensation', this contrasting with a Western-based understanding of justice as primarily 'retributive' (Mangena 2015, 10). As he concludes, 'wronging an individual is tantamount to wronging the community, which is a clear demonstration that in Africa restorative justice and ubuntu [or ngozi] cannot be looked at in isolation' (ibid., 11).

In the context of Chikwava's transnational Gothic landscape, moving between Harare and London, this 'ngozi' must be understood as both personal and political, invoking the narrator (also Shingi's) own past violence in connection with his/their unburied mother(s), but also the violence of the Zimbabwean and British states in their respective irresponsibility towards young combatants and refugees. As Musanga writes, 'Chikwava [...] uses the trope of "madness" to articulate the need to recompense "ngozi" as a way of gaining favour and blessings from the "living dead." Madness is one of the ways that "ngozi" uses to register its presence' (Musanga 2017, 783). In other words, rather than simply according with a

European account of 'spirit possession' as a sign of psychological illness or distress, Chikwava's instead engages with the Shona 'ngozi' as a critical reminder of personal and state responsibility, recalling the need to restore a forgotten justice in the context of oppression. The narrator's final comments on his own increasing vulnerability serve to critically reinforce this sociopolitical message, as he positions himself as an '*umgodoyi*', a 'homeless dog' wandering its village, and whose 'soul is tear from his body in a rough way' (Chikwava 2009, 226). In this closing description of migrant precarity, the narrator announces his call for renewed social justice in the context of anti-migrant policy and anti-homeless sentiment, this set against a picture of his own unravelling mind within a merciless contemporary London.

## Conclusion

In the uncanny, monstrous, and ghostly aesthetics these fictions negotiate – uncovering corporate violence, provincial stigmatization, and migratory displacement, and in all cases, navigating potent experiences of social abjection and 'wasted lives' (Bauman 2004) – these fictions bring to light the homeless experiences made invisible through the onslaught of contemporary neoliberalism, whether in the form of privatization and profiteering, or systematic reprobation. Working with a range of past and present Gothic modalities, including the haunted house, the corporate monster, the female spectre and the *ngozi*, and in each case, making explicit the structural conditions underpinning the contemporary 'unhomely home', these texts make explicit this modality's centrality in exposing the truth of modern homelessness and in connecting this to the neoliberal and global capitalist structures currently reigning. While much more work is still to be done on this area, which Alexandrescu likewise sees as obscured by a focus on 'personal irresponsibility', rather than 'structural changes and ruthless individualism eroding webs of solidarity' (Alexandrescu 2020, 100), nevertheless, these novels make a start in the right direction, paving the way for a more critical and transgressive understanding of homeless identities, and demonstrating the power of twenty-first-century Gothic fiction in shifting the frame.

## Notes

1  This anxiety is further explored in Peter Morgan's *The Spice Boys* (2017), which recounts the Gothic experience of a group of Manchester-based rough-sleepers

addicted to the SCRA drug 'spice'. Likewise, in Jon McGregor's *Even the Dogs* (2010), a Northern British homeless community negotiates drug and alcohol addiction, their trials recounted through a darkly spectral aesthetic.

2. Recognizing the mix of genres at play in this list, Steve Toase (2020) reads several of these works under the banner of sci fi fantasy, focusing on representations of homeless 'outsiders' and their often-alienated relation to surrounding communities. While I find this reading compelling, it seems to me that awareness of these fictions' engagement with the Gothic positively extends this analysis, registering a host of key tropes which underpin these novels' representations of the homeless, in particular in relation to uncanny, monstrous, and spectral aesthetics, as explored here.

3. On a similar note, Chloé Germaine Buckley also highlights the central (and often surprisingly optimistic) importance of homelessness to recent children's Gothic literature, writing of how 'the nomadism of twenty-first-century Gothic […] offers an affirmative account of subjectivity that undoes the othering often initiated by a discourse that reads Gothic monstrosity through the lens of social and cultural anxiety' (2019, 6). Given the above-said connections between Gothic homelessness and domestic strife, this account is notably encouraging, though questions regarding the possible romanticization of (child) homelessness as nomadic liberation also apply.

4. It is worth underlining the Gothic importance of blood in the passage, which amplifies the distortion of order described therein. As Aspasia Stephanou explains, blood within the Gothic is not simply a 'symbol or metaphor' or either 'part of an organic whole', but rather a 'mechanic materiality flickering at the uncanny limits of figuration' (2019, 2). Its status as at once 'both living and dead, organic and inorganic, material and immaterial' (ibid., 2) situates it as a portal or 'conduit for an unnameable materiality' and a lens onto life beyond the human, gesturing towards a 'totally alienating and inhuman otherness' (ibid., 8).

# 6

# The Gothic City

## Uncanny Spaces, Historical Spectres, and Monstrous Urbanity in Louise Welsh's *The Cutting Room* and Chloe Aridjis' *Book of Clouds*

If the previous chapter examines representations of gothic homelessness within a twenty-first-century context, foregrounding the neoliberal politics in which this is imagined and explored, in this chapter I expand my inquiry to consider the spectral, uncanny, and monstrous aspects of the contemporary city more largely, tying this again to neoliberal government and the consumer capitalist dimensions of modern urban planning. As Monica Germanà writes, 'The city—and, in particular, its monstrously magnified version found in the metropolis—encourages a Gothic reading of its space: its buildings may be suggestive of sublime responses, its dead-ends of claustrophobic fears, its mysterious topography of cryptic uncertainty' (Germanà 2010a). Indeed, the city has occupied a central place within Gothic writing since the late eighteenth-century, wherein, as Richard Lehan affirms, 'the symbiotic relationship between the city and the country turned parasitic' with the advent of industrialism, mirroring a historical shift in power from 'the land to the city' and an influx in urban Gothic fears and anxieties (Lehan 1998, 39).

More basically, the turn to the city within the literature of the Gothic can be read as accompanying a gradual shift in the genre itself from a focus on external to internal threats and from the sublime to the uncanny (Botting 1996, 10–11). In its fascination with the distortions of the imagination, the Gothic, alongside Victorian psychology, opened the way for writers to explore a growing disquiet regarding the dark and labyrinthine settings accommodating these newly uncovered subconscious fantasies. As Fred Botting notes, 'The city, a gloomy forest or dark labyrinth itself, became a site of nocturnal corruption and violence, a locus of real horror' (ibid., 11). Likewise, Lucy Huskinson refers to the 'urban uncanny' as a site that 'imbues the city with power over its citizens' (Huskinson 2016, 6).

One aspect of this uncanny experience particularly relevant to the present analysis, and complementing my chosen texts' preoccupation with metropolitan violence, concerns the often-popularized correlation between urban growth and criminality, an anxiety centrally tied to narratives of doubling and vampirism within the established bourgeoisie. Urban criminality, as a supposed manifestation of mounting social degeneracy in the *fin-de-siècle* period and categorized pseudoscientifically in the writing of Max Nordau, found perhaps its most popular form in chronicles presenting a bourgeois duplicity, in the mode, for example, of the gentleman murderer, the blasphemous scientist, or the domesticated fiend. The scandal of such duplicity is visible in the Victorian press' horrifying accounts of the Whitechapel murders, iconized in the figure of Jack the Ripper, but also in Stevenson's *The Strange Case of Dr Jekyll and Mr Hyde* (1886), Oscar Wilde's *The Picture of Dorian Gray* (1890), H. G. Well's *The Island of Dr Moreau* (1896), and Bram Stoker's *Dracula* (1897) – all fictions in which the respected man of honour, transgressing the social code, becomes connected to monstrosity. As Linda Dryden explains, 'Taking their lead from the urban gothic which emerged in the mid-nineteenth-century, Stevenson, Wilde and Wells, among others, fictionally inscribed on the London landscape monstrous transformations, mutilations and dualities that spoke of urban concerns' (Dryden 2003, 16). These popular narratives furthered the interpretation of urban crime as a manifestation of the city's darker inflections, wherein the limitations of human rationality and ingenuity, so integral to the Victorian imagination, thenceforth were exposed and made available to Gothic scrutiny (Botting 1996, 13). As Glynnis Byron reflects, 'Late Victorian society had become all too aware of the dark side of Victorian progress, all too aware that, as Nordau declared, night was drawing on' (Byron 2015b, 186).

Similarly, as I shall show here, the twenty-first-century British Gothic novel, as instanced in Louise Welsh's *The Cutting Room* (2002) and Chloe Aridjis' *Book of Clouds* (2009), navigates the uncanny, spectral, and monstrous precisely to bring attention to the city's irrational dimensions, offering a wider critique not simply of criminality or dereliction, but more properly of the systematic injustice of neoliberal government, both in its negotiation of contemporary urban society and the ghosts of the past.[1] Set in the contemporary period in Glasgow and Berlin, respectively, with both cities visibly altered through changes brought about by globalization and postmillennial urban planning, these narratives invoke the ongoing relevance of this Victorian fantasy of bourgeois rationality, updating it to the terms of a transnational arena. Responding to Glasgow's transition into a service sector economy and its rebranding as a 'European City of Culture,' Welsh's text makes evident the contradictions alive within this tourist-friendly façade, uncovering the scandal of alienation and criminality persistent within Glasgow's quotidian reality. Likewise, Aridjis' Gothic contemporary Berlin makes clear the imminent danger of neoliberal historical revisionism, underlining the urgent need for memorial confrontation and reflection as a means to obstructing the past's violent return. While these novels thus confront and condemn individual acts of criminality, their focus is on the wider oppression produced by market politics and by the corporate glorification of progress and presentism, which stands in the way of a more constructive urban governance.

## Marketing a Gothic Glasgow in Louise Welsh's *The Cutting Room*

In a 2007 article exploring 'The Glasgow Novel in the Twenty-first-Century,' Alan Bissett describes a new outpouring of Glasgow literature 'by writers who hail from, or have written in or about, the city' since the millennium (2007, 59). Here he includes a host of relatively new figures, such as Des Dillon, Alan Kelly, Laura Marney, and Colette Paul, as well as already well-known authors, such as James Kelman, A. L. Kennedy, Suhayl Saadi, Zoe Strachan, and Louise Welsh. Bissett concludes that '[i]t is hard to imagine any British constituency beyond London with an output to rival contemporary Glasgow's' (2007, 59), thus making a strong claim for the city's postmillennial literary importance. Such creative deluge, Bissett stresses, does not infer a unity of vision; indeed, 'the diversity of [these authors'] material is testament to a place which Moira Burgess has called "Kaleidoscope City"' (Bissett 2007, 59). Nevertheless, in the context of Scotland's contemporary literary history, this shift in creative output is worth underlining, given that for earlier authors of the 'New Scottish Literary Renaissance' of the 1980s (Wallace and Stevenson 1993, 1), the *dearth* of Glasgow-based writing drew critical attention. As the character Duncan Thaw in Alasdair Gray's (1981) novel *Lanark* famously remarks,

> If a city hasn't been used by an artist not even the inhabitants live there imaginatively. What is Glasgow to most of us? A house, the place we work, a football park or a golf course, some pubs connecting streets. [...] Imaginatively Glasgow exists as a music-hall song and a few bad novels. That's all we've given to the world outside. It's all we've given to ourselves. (Ibid., 243)

Both Gray and his narrator are artists concerned with addressing local culture, and this lamentation reflects Gray's call for a new investment in the city on the part of its authors, which retrospectively reveals the zeitgeist-changing significance of Gray's own work, as well as that of other subsequent Glasgow-based writers (see Germanà 2014, 55). The new twenty-first-century milieu advances this trend, demonstrating a concern to explore Glasgow and to inhabit its streets imaginatively, even while also displaying, in often bleak and Gothic portrayals, that the city is by no means necessarily a welcome haven for its diverse working-class and minority communities.

Indeed, what this comparison of historical outlooks between the 1980s and the 2000s perhaps best reflects are the changes that have taken place in Glasgow in terms of its image, politics, and infrastructure since the Thatcher era and since the early, seminal Glasgow-based novels of Gray and Kelman. Fiction in the 1980s was concerned largely with the sense of national discord, fracture, and complacency produced by or in response to sectarian political and religious division at the time and registered in the failed referendum of 1979 (Germanà 2014, 51–5). As both Monica Germanà and Alison McCleery make clear, however, Glaswegian writers of the late twentieth and early twenty-first-centuries confront a different but related set of anxieties, having officially shrugged off the status of imperial outpost with the successful referendum of 1997 and the formation of a Scottish parliament in 1999 but still confronting 'a weakening of social cohesion', 'spatial dislocation' and 'societal regrouping' brought about by the demise of the shipbuilding industry and, more largely, by changes enacted in the name of globalization and consumer capitalism (McCleery 2004, 10). According to Germanà, 'What binds together these "imagined [Scottish] communities", then, rather than the collective knowledge of shared values and traditions, is the spectral web of secrets that may undermine any stable reading of "community spirit"' (Germanà 2016, 238).[2]

Alongside ongoing poverty and class division a noticeable preoccupation emerges within contemporary Glaswegian fiction concerning the continued rebranding and commercialization of the city, where, as Bissett notes, a corporate eye toward inclusion within a global market economy of shopping and tourism often leaves unattended, or further aggravated, the plight of disenfranchised identities and communities (Bissett 2007, 59–60). This concern is visible in texts such as Anne Donovan's *Buddha Da* (2003), Zoe Strachan's *Spin Cycle* (2004), Suhayl Saadi's *Psychoraag* (2004), Colette Paul's *Whoever You Choose to Love* (2004), Alison Miller's *Demo* (2006), and Karen Campbell's *The Twilight Time* (2008).[3] As Ian Spring comments in his 2001 study *Phantom Village*, the 'myth of the New Glasgow' manufactured in the build-up to Glasgow's 1990 designation as European City of Culture did perhaps more damage than benefit to the city in terms of its cultural self-conception, casting it in a cosmopolitan façade of international connections, technology, and wealth, while structural inequality and community discord continued unabated. As Spring indicates, the 'New Glasgow' title, connected to the 'Glasgow's Miles Better' campaign, made no more than 'the most superficial difference to the economic and social reality of the lives of the poor and unemployed in the city [...] — the forty per cent or so of the population of Glasgow who [...] live in the large soulless housing schemes created as modern slums by the great Modernist housing revival of the 60s and 70s' (Spring 1990, 3, 43).

Similarly, Carla Rodríguez González reflects on how 'Glasgow has had to reinvent itself architectonically and symbolically over the last two centuries,' shifting from 'the title of Second City of the British Empire to what Willy Maley defines as a "post-industrial heritage museum"'—the latter an allusion to 'the recurrent nostalgic evocations of the city's past prosperity and their exploitation by economic sectors' (Rodríguez González 2016, 2). In other words, the city's self-promotion has also involved a resurgence of imperial reminiscence, often with marginalizing implications for minority and multicultural ethnic communities. Within this amnesiac globalized context, Glasgow faces a host of recurring doubts about its own local, national, and global significance, often again assuming Gothic proportions with respect to the city's divided sectarian politics, its ongoing class and ethnic tensions, and its high crime rate. Indeed, in a 2013 index published by the UK's Institute for Economics and Peace, the city ranked as the UK's most violent area (BBC News 2013), while a 2021 poll names it among Europe's most dangerous cities (Williams 2021).

Confronting this divided and crime-torn context head-on, Louise Welsh's *The Cutting Room* (2002) was a great success for its newly emerging Glaswegian author, winning the 2002 Saltire First Book Award, the 2002 Crime Writers' Association John Creasey Memorial Dagger Award, and the 2003 BBC Underground Award, as well as receiving extensive praise on the part of reviewers (see, for example, Magrs 2002; McDowell 2002; Taylor 2003; Johnstone 2005). Structured around an investigation into an assemblage of unsettling photographs, wherein a woman appears to have been tortured for sexual gratification, the novel is alive with references to the Gothic from its very first pages, referencing earlier Scottish writers such as James Hogg, Robert Louis Stevenson, and Alasdair Gray, and painting the city in distinctly morbid colours. The snapshots discovered by Rilke, an auctioneer, while clearing a wealthy suburban estate, lead him on a search to determine their veracity as snuff pornography, a project also driven by Rilke's own haunted past and disturbed psychology. As Victor Sage puts it, 'Rilke's vulnerability [...] drives the need to exorcize this ghost, this "other woman", who is associated with many of the women he meets [...] but we know he is disturbed by his own behavior' (Sage 2011, 73). This allusion to Rilke's past functions, then, to emphasize an unreliable narration and an unsettled unconscious, the latter of which in turn comments upon Glasgow's own repressed urban psychology.

Indeed, Rilke's distinctive appeal in the novel lies in his nefarious links to the subterranean city, a connection reinforced by his noir persona and his vampiric appearance: he is referred to as 'the Cadaver, Corpse, Walking Dead' (Welsh 2002, 2). As Leslie McDowell writes, 'Masculine, hard drinking and happy to use his fists when necessary, he could easily have become a caricature – but for his promiscuous homosexuality' (McDowell 2002). McDowell's reading captures something of the generic aptitude of the narrator: like Philip Marlow, Rilke's solitary outlook and his ties to a masculine urban criminal underworld do much to explain his charisma and noir attraction. As Welsh herself puts it, he is a 'night surveillant,' who 'walk[s] alone in [his] society' (García Agustín 2014, 206). Yet, Rilke's queer sexuality also extends beyond mere sexual preference and promiscuity, encompassing a counterhegemonic and *flâneurial* outlook on the city's various spaces and affective and material relations. As Mary Gluck remarks, the importance of the metropolitan *flâneur* relates to his ability to 'render the labyrinthine urban landscape legible,' accomplishing this feat precisely 'through his virtuosity as urban observer' (Gluck 2003, 69). Through Rilke's inquisitorial vision, Welsh navigates Glasgow's underground communities, uncovering their hidden dimensions with an eye toward critical exposure.

The protagonist's name connects him most obviously to the *fin-de-siècle* Austrian poet, Rainer Maria Rilke, who explored in his writings the unease and estrangement produced by an increasingly technologized urban life, and whose semi-autobiographical novel *Malte Laurids Brigge* (1910) also sees the narrator suffering from an acute form of vertigo. As Paul Carter comments, 'The anxiety-ridden landscape of the metropolitan nightmare [in Rilke's writing] resembles a post-earthquake scene along the San Andreas Fault' (Carter 2002, 50–2). Likewise, Welsh's Rilke confronts a host of giddy, dazed, and dizzying urban experiences and complains of a fear of heights, a loss of balance, breathlessness and a trance-like or surreal consciousness of his surroundings (Welsh 2002, 18, 43, 172, 224). Such depictions build intertextual parallels between these writings and their urban landscapes, tying Glasgow to the "new urbanism" of an earlier century. As Jo Collins and John Jervis reflect,

By the late nineteenth-century ... a sense of unease, linked to the loss of continuity with the past and the natural environment, is associated with a range of distinctively modern anxieties which become increasingly codified as neuroses; and some of these, notably disturbances of the spatial sense (claustrophobia, agoraphobia) prove both symptomatically and culturally to have pronounced affiliation with the experience of the uncanny. (Collins and Jervis 2008, 4)

Developing this *fin de siècle* connection through a range of intertextual references that see the narrator precariously navigating a sepulchral city, *The Cutting Room* is awash with allusions to the Romantic and late Victorian periods: not only Hogg and Stevenson, but also Poe, Blake, Keats, Verlaine and Rimbaud – authors who position Welsh's Glasgow within a distinctly decadent European cultural history. Rilke's investigation into the fate of the tortured woman in the photos he finds explicitly plays with these links. Both he and the sexual predator he pursues appear as conjoint participants in this urban milieu: Gothic doubles, each guarding his own carnal secrets. The fact that the villain McKindless' library contains a large collection of the Olympia Press (Welsh 2002, 19), a 1950s Paris-based publisher known for its avant-garde erotic fiction – and indeed, the fact that the photos themselves appear to be taken in mid-century Paris, with '*Soleil et Desole*' written on the back of one to mark its provenance (Welsh 2002, 22) – reinforces this decadent association, thereby connecting contemporary Glasgow to an aesthete Europe of eccentric proclivities.

The novel's broad cartographical engagement with Glasgow's upper, middle, and working-class neighbourhoods – stretching from the wealthy Hyndland, south-eastward past the university and then further south, taking in the Gorbals, the Royal Infirmary, and the Necropolis – registers the far-reaching (and again decidedly Gothic) implications of this landscape, invoking a comprehensive web of metropolitan complicity. The location of McKindless' estate in Hyndland makes this understanding immediately apparent, indexing, as Germanà notes, 'a strong sense of the city's Jekyll and Hyde complex' (Germanà 2016, 242). The suburb's 'green leafy' surroundings and 'petty respectability up front' function as a camouflage, meant to disguise 'intricate cruelties behind closed doors' (Welsh 2002, 2). Rilke's travels through the city further extend this uncanny aura. Repeatedly, the façade of a building or the demeanour of those with whom he is meeting indicates something other, and more reputable, than what is concealed inside. As he puts it at one point, commenting on the generic porn shop and its place within the globalized city, the everyday shopper doesn't see the dreary storefront, the unwashed window that displays nothing, nothing at all. But if you are sympathetic, [...] you can be in any town, any city, in the world, a stranger on your first day, and it will sing to you. (Welsh 2002, 63)

Here, the focus on a shared secrecy common to 'any town, any city in the world' reinforces an uncanny impression of a homogenized global sex market. In keeping with Jacques Derrida's reading of the contemporary city as 'the singular organization of the experience of anywhere' (Derrida and Malabou 2004, 14), this passage makes evident the transnational, anonymous quality of Glasgow's pornography business.

Such an understanding is most obviously relevant to the conclusion of the novel, wherein the 'transcript' contained in the appendix (another *Jekyll and Hyde* motif) exposes Glasgow's part in the global sex-trafficking market, tying it to the horrific experience of one particular trafficked woman. Before getting to this conclusion, however, Welsh traverses a much wider Gothic panorama of uncanny urban experience, reinforced by the text's repeated references to the spectral and vampiric (Welsh 2002, 16, 27, 80, 190, 198, 241). By developing Karl Marx's Gothic reading of capital as 'dead labour which, vampire-like, lives only by sucking living labour, and lives the more, the more labour it sucks' (Marx 1990, 342), *The Cutting Room* becomes not only a *flâneurial* investigation of the city's hidden impunities but also a Gothic indictment of global capitalism's blood-sucking culture, making evident what David McNally refers to as 'the monstrous forms of every-day life in a capitalist world system' (McNally 2012, 2).

This indictment emerges clearly in a chapter entitled 'The Nature of Pornography', wherein the text confronts a Baudrillardian vision of contemporary urban estrangement. Walking along Argyle Street, one of Glasgow's major shopping thoroughfares, Rilke witnesses school children weaving their way between 'cardboard boxes littered with rotting vegetables'; a group of Sikh pensioners being slandered by a passing woman on the basis of their ethnicity; and later an old man creeping amongst abandoned factories 'under demolition near the quay' (Welsh 2002, 64). The portrayals involve a pointed reference to the city's more vulnerable urban communities: the working class, migrants, and the elderly, whose ongoing experience of poverty, exclusion, and disaffection is here plainly evident. As Ulrich Beck remarks, the globalizing transition which promises to envelop such communities – what he calls the shift to a global 'risk society' – involves, inextricably, an unequal distribution of risk between rich and poor: 'a systematic violation of basic rights, a crisis of basic rights whose long-term effect in weakening society can scarcely be underestimated' (Beck 1999, 39). As Welsh's novel indicates, the most economically marginalized suffer 'the dark side of globalization' (Giddens 2002, xvi): its Gothic investment in capitalist profit making and commercial exploitation.

This impression of urban inequality and estrangement becomes stronger as Rilke continues into the heart of the city. Passing Finnieston Fish Emporium, he sees a policeman handling a suspect stumbling 'as if drunk, or too tired to care' and later, newspapers revealing a 'toddler's drowned body and the promise of full details on the slaughtered "vice girl"' (Welsh 2002, 65). By locating the source of the uncanny in the city's historical shift from shipping to service sector economy, the text reveals its materialist politics and makes unambiguous the socioeconomic reasons for urban despair. As Rilke reflects, 'The industrial age had given way to a white-collar revolution and the sons and daughters of the shipyard toilers now tapped keyboards and answered telephones in wipe-clean sweatshops' (Welsh 2002, 65). His description of the blur of automated activity highlights the mechanical quality of this 'white collar' experience:

> They shuffled invisible paper and sped communications through electronic magic. Dark suits trampled along Bath Street, past the storm-blasted spire of Renfield St Stephen's, home to prepare for another day like the last and another after that. [...] And all around me mobile phones. People talk, talk, talking to a distant party while the world marched by. (Welsh 2002, 65)

The passage provides an account of the simulacral disconnection from surrounding realities produced by Glasgow's transition from manufacturing and shipping to services. The so-called sanity of global technology, in the form of keyboards, telephones, 'invisible paper' and 'electronic magic', also results in increased hyper-individualism to the point of social breakdown: a society too absorbed by competitive daily routine to recognize a proximate actuality of poverty and exploitation. Indeed, while Glasgow's marginalized and vulnerable populations emerge as the primary victims of the city's vampiric tendencies – reduced to squalor and hardship as a result of global economic networks – even the black-suited locals appear in this passage as zombified functionaries of a global corporate system, 'disgorged' from their respective office buildings into crowds of strangers. As McNally notes, 'What is most striking about capitalist monstrosity... is its elusive everydayness, its apparent seamless integration into the banal and quotidian rhythms of everyday existence' (McNally 2012, 2). This quotidian quality is further mirrored in the text's focus on anonymity and repetition: the 'dark suits' travel home 'to prepare for another day like the last and another after that'.

A curious temporal estrangement accompanies this everyday monstrosity (what I explored in Chapter 4 in relation to the 'digital banal'; see also, Dinnen 2018), tying it not only to postmodernist simulacra but also, perhaps more centrally, to modernist disillusion. Just as George Simmel defines the modern city as a space of nervous intensification, where 'the rapid crowding of changing images' produces a response of defensive rationalism in the urban subject (Simmel 1903, 2), Welsh's novel frequently plays with the alienating effect of crowds on the solitary narrator, who likewise responds by positioning himself in the role of observer: 'I wear my mirrored aviator's shades. The black of the lenses is like the eyehole gaps in a skull. Instead of my eyes, a mineral reflection of the crowd' (Welsh 2002, 124). In this passage, the text enacts a modernist critique of contemporary urban anonymity: Rilke's skeletal gaze mirrors the soulless indistinctness of the urban masses.

Moreover, this modernist view of the city also connects to the novel's uncanny *sexual* politics, which likewise draw on morbid and vampiric signifiers to characterize the urban sexual underground. As Steve Pile notes, the vampire can be read not only as a threat to his victims but also, simultaneously, as a 'figure of desire: a gendered and sexualized figure, revealing perhaps something of the perversity of sexual desire in city life' (Pile 2005, 112). In this respect, the text's materialist critique, combined with its feminist anxieties, reinforces the consumer dimensions of the urban male gaze. Indeed, while Rilke plays the part of the *flâneur*, who navigates the city's criminal obscurity and reveals the brutal violence hidden beneath a cosmopolitan façade, he also investigates how individuals and communities desire and *see* each other and how this seeing itself can become a form of exploitation.

The novel's depiction of a taxi ride that Rilke and his employer, Rose, take through the city, for example, links the voyeuristic gaze of the driver to the heavily mediated face of the global city center, where a compilation of busy streets, fluorescent lights, urban architecture and commercial advertisements create an impression of speed, innovation and sexiness. As Rilke comments:

> The taxi driver kept sneaking looks at Rose in his rear-view mirror. [...] Sure enough, she had crossed her legs high on the thigh. [...] We slipped through a florescent white tunnel, then climbed high over the city on the curving expressway; the River Clyde oil-black and still beneath us, a backdrop to the reflected lights of the city; [...] scarlet neon sign of the Daily Record offices suspended in the dark sky to our right. (Welsh 2002, 98–9)

As Rilke reflects, the technologized, transnational impression that the city presents functions, like Rose's body language, as a kind of sexual performance. A radio advertisement further makes clear the city's sordid consumer foundations: 'a Marilyn Monroe sound-alike whispered an invitation to an Indian restaurant, where, her voice intimated, she would fuck and then feed you' (Welsh 2002, 99). The tawdriness of the commercial stands in for the artificiality of the city's cosmopolitan panorama, where economic transactions and anonymous encounters between strangers have taken the place of legitimate connections between individuals. In effect, inhabiting the city means negotiating a host of false reflections.

Indeed, this simulacral representation points (as in Ali Smith's *Hotel World*) to what Marc Augé refers to as the 'non-place' of contemporary cities, where urban identity has been reduced to consumer capitalist relations:

> The installations needed for the accelerated circulation of passengers and goods (high-speed roads and railways, interchanges, airports) are just as much non-places as the means of transport themselves, or the great commercial centres, or the extended transit camps where the planet's refugees are parked.[...] The world of supermodernity does not exactly match the one in which we believe we live, for we live in a world that we have not yet learned to look at. (Augé 1995, 34–6)

In other words, the financialization of urban relations also implies a remodelling of the city in terms of consumer simulations: a careful artistry of social cohesion, which masks an underlying emptiness. As Nigel Thrift likewise notes, 'cities are increasingly expected to have "buzz", to be "creative" [...] now affect is more and more likely to be actively engineered' (Thrift 2004, 58). Welsh's novel utilizes a Gothic materialist reading of the dominant metropolitan culture to engage in a critique of such middle-class duplicity in the urban landscape itself; her uncanny portrayal of contemporary Glasgow makes clear its fraudulent dimensions.

At the same time, vampiric consumerism is also visible in Rilke's own *sub*cultural interactions: for example, in his illicit sexual encounter in Kelvingrove Park. As he explains, the 'mantra' accompanying sexual reunions is 'Looking for business?' The ghostly appearance and 'glazed eyes' (Welsh 2002, 27) of the boy who seeks his company in asking this question are a function ultimately of the city's atomizing transactional logic, where a failure to see the *Other* as more than a product for consumption only naturally attends the violence implicit within consumerism. Indeed, as Gavin Miller notes, 'such glazed indifference to others is a recurring motif in Welsh's Glasgow' — repeatedly and explicitly, the text calls attention to the city's 'depersonalized' gaze (Miller 2006, 77).

This concern with the gaze can be read as a primary component of the global city more largely, where, according to David Holmes, two changes in particular define an urban transnational perspective: 'the shift from products to services and the intense use of information and communications technologies' (Holmes 2002, 34). Both of these changes, Holmes elucidates, contribute substantially to determining a city's global representation, including in relation to the increasing convergence of urban and tourist spaces:

> the distracted shoppers' gaze, the surveillant gaze, and the gaze upon the screen are kinds of looking which dovetail with the tourist gaze. [...] Through visual consumption places are transformed into destinations and attractions. Herein lies a powerful convertibility between the image and the tourist's destination. (Holmes 2002, 36)

In other words, the directed gaze of consumer capitalism becomes a way of transforming a city into an image, a 'consumer landscape,' wherein relations become 'privatized and increasingly totalized' in the competition for profit (ibid.).

More basically, then, the focus in the novel on the disenfranchising effect of the processes of consumer capitalism for Glasgow's marginalized communities reveals the violent and disastrous implications of global capitalism: the working class and migrant populations, in particular, feel the brunt of this rebranding project. In this respect, the text negotiates its Gothic and decadent aesthetics to make explicit not only inequality and consumer depersonalization but also corruption and exploitation, drawing attention to a systematic form of exploitation condoned within a global market economy. Such exploitation includes various illegal transactions explored within the novel: for example, Rilke's antique business itself – the dodgy counterpart to Glasgow's 'post-industrial heritage museum'; John's erotic book trade; Leslie's drug trade, which also involves punishing non-paying customers with a baseball bat; and of course, McKindless' sexual murders and Trapp's transnational pornography business (Welsh 2002, 68–75, 111–12, 164, 278, 283). The latter men's Gothic invisibility, explained through their links to a well-disguised corporate crime network, further bolster a materialist critique of this subterranean landscape, highlighting, in Zygmunt Bauman's words, the 'liquid' quality of transnational relations: how in a global context, 'it is the most elusive, those free to move without notice, who rule' (Bauman 2000, 120).

The feminist dimensions of this concern come through most directly in the conclusion of the novel, where, by subverting the conventional terms of the crime genre, the text draws overt attention to the contemporary plight of sexually victimized women and connects this plight specifically to Glasgow's modern-day consumer urbanity. Thus, despite initially reaffirming the crime drama's traditional patriarchal values by drawing attention to the tortured female body – the dead and bloodied corpse of the woman in Rilke's photograph – and seeing this body as a locus of investigative anxiety, the conclusion of the novel instead undermines this fascination by substituting the female victim with a genre-defying instance of successful self-defence. Here, as Gavin Miller adeptly elucidates, 'Welsh plays with our generic expectation that Anne-Marie [a burlesque dancer whom McKindless visits and photographs] requires someone to save her, and that—if Rilke or the police are too late—she will be found butchered, in a suitable combination of sex and gore' (2006, 82). Instead, it is McKindless' body that now lies bleeding on the floor, all the more surprisingly as he has until this point been thought dead:

> The body looked small in death. Head thrown back, pale face raised to the sky [...]. A red sea glazed the rough pile of the carpet. [...] 'Who'd have thought the old man would have so much blood in him,' I whispered. (Welsh 2002, 276)

In toying with reader anticipation in this way, Welsh rejects the crime genre's more usual ideological complicity in patriarchal violence and implicitly highlights the generic objectification of female bodies as a source of urban male pleasure. *The Cutting Room* thus reaffirms Laura Mulvey's anxiety about the sadistic dimension of the male gaze, where 'pleasure lies in ascertaining guilt [...], asserting control, and subjecting the guilty person through punishment or forgiveness' (Mulvey 1998, 590).

Correspondingly, the novel substantiates the danger of the sex market's globalized expansion within Glasgow, highlighting a materialist feminist awareness that 'what turning persons into objects is all about, in our culture, is in the final analysis, killing them' (Cameron and Frazer 1987, 176). The pseudo-realist transcript contained in the novel's appendix, wherein Welsh grants a voice to a particular (fictionalized) Eastern European sex worker, Adia Kovalyova, further strengthens this message, accentuating the Jekyll-like perversion that such a supposedly 'normal' global city is capable of: men 'go home and kiss their wives, cuddle their daughters, with the smell of [the trafficked sex worker's] abuse still on their fingers' (Welsh 2002, 282). In other words, the text reveals Glasgow's contemporary urban public as a duplicitous collectivity in its widespread acceptance of patriarchal exploitation in the sex trade business.

The novel's concern with this urban problem is at once a reflection on materialist feminism's contemporary social urgency and a comment on Glasgow itself as a globalized city, where even here, in a place so apparently removed from cosmopolitan *flâneurie*, the violent implications of the global sex trade are readily apparent. Leslie, Rilke's criminal friend, draws attention to the problem when he underplays the situation by saying, 'Glasgow likes to think it's a hard city but compared to London or New York, fucking Paris probably, we're a peaceful wee haven' (Welsh 2002, 112). Here, his reassurances to Rilke turn out to have misjudged the city's criminal outlay. Adia Kovalyova's testimony against Trapp, which appears as the pseudorealist transcript near the close the novel, exposes the lie of Leslie's verdict, making explicit Glasgow's substantial involvement in 'the trafficking of young men and women into the city for the purposes of prostitution' (Welsh 2002, 283).

## Gothic Global Berlin in Chloe Aridjis' *Book of Clouds*

Much as with Glasgow, as explored above, in contemporary advertising and marketing discourses regarding modern-day Berlin, the city is often represented as a centre for reconstruction, growth, and renewal. 'We have witnessed immense efforts towards the re-capitalization of post-Wall Berlin,' writes Janet Ward, 'a process that has continued regardless of whether this contemporary post-industrial city may have lost its right to represent the nation in the first place' (Ward 2011, 79). In writing in this way, Ward questions the city's continuing, post-Wall importance as a cultural and political capital, instead highlighting its increasing financialization and homogenization under the banner of neoliberal acquisition. On a similar note, Claire Colomb reflects on how from the 1990s forward, 'the entire inner city was "staged" through a series of events which turned construction sites into tourist attractions. New sites and spaces gradually became part of the 2000s place marketing imagery and narrative, as urban leaders sought to promote the "creative city"' (Colomb 2011). While such redevelopment projects work by no means to banish spaces of activism and opposition – in some cases, making these even more visible, as attempts to 're-politicize' the city's tourism (Novy 2016, 55) – nevertheless, as Colomb further explains, this 'new Berlin' project is at heart fundamentally neoliberal, prioritizing 'the search for global competitiveness at all costs and the transformation into a post-Fordist "service metropolis"' (Colomb 2011, 106).

In a city so clearly saturated by its past, including the Weimar, Nazi, and Stasi governments, the problematic character of this project is easily visible, potentially eluding a dark and layered history of authoritarian oppression in favour of competitive presentism. Karen Till comments:

Even the marketing images that now adorn city billboards to promote the New Berlin as a cosmopolitan beauty queen, surrounded by corporate power and wealth and bejeweled by cultural icons, are haunted by former hopes for the future of Weimar, National Socialist, and Cold War Berlins. (Till 2005, 6)

Berlin thus offers a palimpsest of urban histories, layered upon each other in complex ways, while at the same time often disguised and distorted by a contemporary urban marketing programme which seeks to reinvent the city's modern identity at a distance from its past. As Eyse Erek and Eszter Gantner likewise reflect, this marketing 'illustrates a process of disappearing history: how history is disappearing from the present self-image and future vision of the city' (Erek and Gantner 2017, 194).

As referenced above in relation to Welsh's novel, urban theorists such as Benjamin, Michel de Certeau, and Pierre Nora have confronted this same critical anxiety in earlier eras, drawing attention to this space's uncanny and phantasmal aspects, and reflecting on how, in de Certeau's words, 'there is no place that is not haunted by many different spirits hidden there in silence, spirits one can "invoke" or not' (de Certeau 2002, 108). On a similar note, Benjamin embraces a project of 'profane illumination' (as also referenced in Chapter 2), which sees cultural artifacts as a ghostly insight on modern urban relations, affirming 'the valorization of the realm of a culture's ghosts and phantasms as a significant and rich field of social production' (Benjamin 1978, 179; Cohen 1995, 11).

Alongside these earlier writers, various contemporary Berlin artists, architects, and grassroots organizations have also responded to the city's 'hauntedness' (Ladd 2018, 1), creating new types of 'active' memorial, which rather than simply destroying signs of the past, or alternatively, commemorating them, instead invoke new, 'active' forms of reflection, urging viewers to interact with their presence and to relate their meaning personally. This can be seen, for example, in the Memorial to the Murdered Jews of Europe, which opened in 2005 and consists in 'an undulating field of 2711 concrete steles, which can be passed through from all sides' ('Holocaust Memorial' 2021, n.p.). 'While walking between the columns of different heights and the labyrinthine corridors,' the tourist site *berlin.de* explains, 'visitors may experience a brief moment of disorientation, which should open up space for discussion' (ibid.). On a similar note, Colomb explains how 'the proliferation of temporary uses of urban space in [twenty-first-century] Berlin' can be seen to demonstrate 'new forms of cultural and social expression' at odds with its previous 'commercial' agenda, instead eliciting renewed awareness of the significance of 'the ruins and ghosts of burdened, unwanted pasts' (Colomb 2012, 132–4). Rather than effacing the city's haunting dimensions, such projects place history at their centre, formally refocusing (or dis-focusing, as it were) unused 'wastelands' and 'dead' spaces for public contemplation (ibid., 135).

Chloe Aridjis' *Book of Clouds*, winner of the French Prix du Premier Roman Éstranger in 2009, offers an important contribution to this discussion, again reinforcing the value of historical engagement as a means to confronting the city's dark history and circumventing the undesired resurgence of buried violence. The novel tells the story of a Jewish Mexican woman in her early twenties, Tatiana, who having visited Berlin briefly as a child, returns to live there as an adult, embracing the city's layered and uncanny spaces as inspiration for her writing. A solitary and again *flâneurial* personality, prone to long walks and U-Bahn rides – enjoying the latter's mixture of 'old and new, logic and impulse, grit and glamour, all blurred into one long thread' (Aridjis 2009, 163) – Tatiana pointedly avoids interaction with others in order to probe her own surroundings and memories, again reinforcing a Baudelairian conception of the *flâneur* as a figure of urban estrangement – a 'passionate spectator' at once 'amid' and detached from 'the ebb and flow of movement' (Baudelaire 1863, 9). In this way, the novel begins with a vision from Tatiana's past, which returns to haunt her upon her return to Berlin: a seeming encounter with Hitler during a childhood trip on the U-Bahn. 'To my great surprise,' Tatiana reflects:

> not a single person seemed to notice the old woman in the head scarf. [...] But how could no one else notice the forehead and the eyes and the shaded patch between nose and mouth, when the combination of these features seemed so glaringly, so obscenely, real and factual and present? (Aridjis 2009, 7)

The tortured level of insistence in the narration of this passage, combined with such an unlikely event, recalls Tsvetan Todorov's seminal definition of the fantastic, wherein, as he describes, 'in a world which is indeed our world, the one we know [...] there occurs an event which cannot be explained by the laws of this same familiar world' (Todorov 1975, 25). Despite an initial lean towards an 'illusion of the senses', bolstered by the family's refusal of the narrator's vision, Tatiana pointedly insists on what she saw. When her employer raises the possibility that she has 'projected' the impression, perhaps due to what he terms 'Hitler syndrome' – the sick sense that 'Hitler is everywhere' (Aridjis 2009, 98) – Tatiana reiterates the truth of her experience: 'But it was him that day. [...] It wasn't a delusion' (Welsh 2002, 98). In this way, the novel moves between illusion and reality to invoke a Gothic experience of contemporary Berlin, where neither suspension of disbelief nor certainty seems entirely fitting. The attempt to negotiate this haunted and unpredictable space, and to give meaning to its equivocal reality, is what drives Tatiana's 'unselfconscious, uncompromising' reflections throughout (Jordon 2009): a relative stranger to Europe, she seeks to engage her own mythically imbued personal history to navigate Berlin's urban spectres and monsters.

This outlook is hinted at from the start, where the novel's opening is replete with *unheimlich* instances, both at the level of content and of style. There are witch-like spinsters, who watch Tatiana through the crack in their curtains; stormy weather, which 'shakes the dust of the past up from between her floorboards and closes with a freak fog that envelops the whole city' (Jordon 2009); a looming Brocken mountain, which calls forth a Faustian vision of Brocken spectres (visual illusions of ghosts caused by light on fog – also central to Niall Griffiths' *Broken Ghost*); and lastly, the insomniac electric lighting of the city, whose constant brightness converts sleep into a zombified consciousness, seeing 'night and day blurred into one' (Aridjis 2009, 26). In all these scenes, Berlin emerges as an updated Gotham, whose over-used technological capacity and unsleeping inhabitants make it familiarly unfamiliar.

Nevertheless, alongside its modern consumer façade, the city's dark, lingering history also contributes to its Gothic experience, where the war and the Stasi government's unspoken presence create a recurrent atmosphere of sinister ghostliness. This concern is highlighted most directly through Dr Weiss, whose spatial Berlin histories incorporate a Benjaminian 'digging' method in order to explore the way in which particular buildings – for example, those employed for Nazi persecutions – continue to exert their past meanings in overt ways. As Benjamin explains, 'Memory is not an instrument for surveying the past but its theater. It is the medium of past experience, just as the earth is the medium in which dead cities lie buried. He who seeks to approach his own buried past must conduct himself like a man digging' (2006, xii). This message is eloquently repeated in Tatiana's summation of one of Weiss' texts:

> Spaces cling to their pasts, he said, and sometimes the present finds a way of accommodating this past and sometimes it doesn't. At best, a peaceful coexistence is struck up between temporal planes but most of the time it is a constant struggle for dominion. Objects would also form part of the inquiry, [...] the reverberation of objects, the resonance of things long banished or displaced. (Aridjis 2009, 33)

The ghostly metaphors employed here, of spaces 'clinging' to their pasts and 'struggling' for domination, and of objects 'resonating' with history, give shape to a contemporary Gothic pointedly inspired by Benjamin's *Berlin Childhood around 1900*, working with a goal 'to identify the phantasmagorias of modern city life' and to engage with 'mobile networks of affect, meaning and power' in 'discarded' spaces and objects (Pile 2005, 48–9). For Weiss, as for Benjamin, the importance of history lies in its *embodied* and *felt* presence – as something which persists through time, and rather than simply progressing, carries suggestions of past meanings registering present historical change. 'That which is original never lets itself be known in the bare, public stock of the factual,' Benjamin writes, 'and its rhythm can be perceived only by a double insight' (Benjamin 2006, 30).

Indeed, for Benjamin, writing in the 1930s, this understanding brings to light the radical changes the city underwent from the turn of the century to the immediate pre-Second World War era, resulting in sense of ruined innocence and lost freedom. Remembering from his own childhood the 'serpentine paths', 'tender retreats' and 'lonely old men' of his now destroyed city, Benjamin sadly questions where these joys have gone and what lies to come (Benjamin 2006, 65). Similarly, for Weiss, a historical perspective informed by the interred Nazi and Stasi governments brings about clear anxiety, a Gothic uncertainty regarding the direction of contemporary neoliberal society and politics. Keeping in mind this contemporary governmental agenda, Weiss and Tatiana seek to excavate a consciously hidden past, whose horrors are entombed not only by time but also nationalist rhetoric: for example, the NPD's slogan 'We'll Let the Grass Grow Over' (Aridjis 2009, 55). In place of melancholy, then, Weiss' historical 'digging' brings to bear the pertinence of Gothic aesthetics, as these draws attention to eerie historical remnants and spectres, also offering the uncanny as a register of urban discomfort.

The novel foregrounds this awareness in two key ways: firstly, by juxtaposing Weiss' historical observations with Tatiana's travels around the city, and secondly, by registering explicit lived examples of the spatial uncanny. Respecting Tatiana's travels, these include, amongst various neighbourhood squares, the Reichstag, the Brandenburg Gate, the Berlin Wall, the new Holocaust Memorial, the Wasserturm, the Topography of Terror, and the underground 'ghost stations': the East Berlin train-stops which during the Cold War were left unused due to the unevenness of the city divide. For each of these structures, Aridjis reflects on a double meaning – a simultaneous past and present, or memorial and contemporary significance – which contributes to an underlying ghostliness.

The Reichstag is described, for example, as both a tourist destination and 'little more than a burnt skeletal silhouette of its former self' (Aridjis 2009, 1), at once attracting and repelling aesthetic attention. Likewise, the Brandenburg

Gate both 'grants' passage and 'obstructs' it, offering a gateway to the ancient city, as well as a reminder of Cold War division (ibid., 1). The Berlin Wall also surfaces as a structure intent on disturbing security, invoking the uncanny impression that 'no matter where you went – east, west, north, south – before long you [would] hit against [it]' (ibid., 2). Similarly, the 'ghost stations' retain a sense of subterranean presences: 'a world of dead silence and dead stillness, blitzed, every now and then, by trains from the West hurtling through their muffled realm' (ibid., 78). The city's underground Stasi bowling alley, which Tatiana connects in her mind to the Topography of Terror, is also pictured as a labyrinthine underworld: 'Everything, it seemed, was just the way it had been left decades ago. [...] I could almost feel the rustling of thick grey coats as the gruesome specters returned and tapped their feet, waiting impatiently for this foolish intruder to leave their bowling alley' (ibid., 113–18). Repeatedly across these scenes, Berlin appears as multi-layered and haunted, possessed by history's revenants, which continue to exist beyond everyday perception.

One other scene in which the Gothic elucidates memorial concerns is in Tatiana's visit, with Jonas, to the Memorial to the Murdered Jews of Europe, and it is here where the aesthetic of the uncanny most strongly resonates. Because this structure is dedicatory, rather than preservationist, offering a conscious tribute to Holocaust victims in the form described above, the character of its message is significant. Rather than dismissing history in an attempt to embrace the present, this structure plays upon a defamiliarizing tactic: immersing and confusing the viewer, it re-enacts uncanny trauma. Tatiana reflects, 'despite the hundreds of possible exits and entrances it was hard not to feel an immediate wave of claustrophobia and disorientation. [...] [A]nd before long everything was undulating and vertiginous and the only steady presence was the moon' (Aridjis 2009, 144).

In place of historical security, neat and digestible, the memorial presents disorder and alienation, its uneven topography mirroring ongoing disagreement regarding history's meaning. Indeed, the experience is presented not only as *intellectually* disorientating, but also *physically* and *affectively* so – it submerges the visitor, *and the reader*, in its labyrinths, making security and clear reflection impossible. As Tatiana reflects, 'I couldn't even fathom whether our movements were upward or downward since the ground robbed me of any surety' (Aridjis 2009, 144–5). In this way, this complex, alienating construction ensures an active audience participation in memory: the visitor must decide for herself (and not easily) how the past is interpreted.

At the close of the novel, this message's importance is given clear shape. In a twist of the plot, Tatiana and her teacher are assaulted, and Tatiana nearly raped by a pair of neo-Nazi skinheads. Fortunately, they manage to escape, and while Weiss is hospitalized, he has 'lived through the beating' (Aridjis 2009, 202). Nevertheless, the event reinforces for the narrator history's enduring relevance to the present, as events of anti-Semitic racism and violence continue to taint the twenty-first-century city, demanding confrontation with narratives of progress and supposed advancement. Within this context, *Book of Clouds* directly reminds the reader of Berlin's *ongoing* historical ghostliness, reasserting the need for reflection as a means to battling looming spectres.

## Conclusion

More generally, the representation of the twenty-first-century city in these novels is defined by a Gothic spatial aesthetic, underpinning a modernist, uncanny experience, which insists on disorientation and alienation, but also a monstrous neoliberal governance indifferent to xenophobic and patriarchal oppression. In Welsh's *The Cutting Room*, this comes through in a postmodern Glasgow saturated in tourist-friendly spectacle, even as it conceals a thriving pornography industry unabashedly enmeshed in transnational sex-trafficking. Likewise, in Aridjis' *The Book of Clouds*, a contemporary Berlin concerned to forget and *develop-over* its dark past again disguises persisting anti-Semitism and racist violence. In either case, the materialist feminist politics driving these narratives underline the urgency of urban re-examination, as the competitive and market-driven goal of contemporary planning initiatives threaten to prolong covert and buried horrors.

## Notes

1 Other prominent examples of twenty-first-century British Gothic fiction which directly navigate urban landscapes include Anna Burns' *No Bones* (2001), Jan Carson's *The Fire Starters* (2019), and Jenny McCartney's *The Ghost Factory* (2019), all of which reconnoitre a Gothic Belfast; Sarah Perry's *Melmoth* (2018), which explores both contemporary and Second World War Prague; Imogen Edwards-Jones' *The Witches of St Petersburg* (2018), a fictional inquiry into the Romanov dynasty within the titular city; Jessie Burton's *The Miniaturist* (2014), set in 1680s

Amsterdam; Sara Sheridan's *The Fair Botanists* (2021), set in 1820s Edinburgh; Catherine O'Flynn's *What Was Lost* (2007), focused on Birmingham in the 1980s; and Sarah Waters' *Fingersmith* (2002), Clare Evans' *The Graves of Whitechapel* (2020), Laura Purcell's *The Whispering Muse* (2023) and J. M. Varese's *The Company* (2023), all set in a Gothic Victorian London.

2  Germanà's account of the Scottish community is also central to her reading of *The Cutting Room*, which likewise focuses, as I do here, on an uncanny Gothic aesthetic. However, while Germanà is concerned principally with the representation of community secrets in the novel, considering at once how these create division and 'bind the community together' (2016, 240), I concentrate instead on the juxtaposition between Glasgow's globalized commercial surface and its criminal underground, considering both its heteronormative and queer extensions.

3  Bissett (2007) also makes note of several of these Glasgow-based novels, offering acute critical readings of Welsh's *The Cutting Room* itself, alongside Donovan's *Buddha Da* (2003), Saadi's *Psychoraag* (2004), and Miller's *Demo* (2006). His reading of Welsh's novel focuses, as I also do here, on her Marxist/Baudrillardian politics. However, whilst Bissett tends to align these politics to a postmodernist critical agenda, my concern is instead to explore how both modernist and postmodernist anxieties in the novel contribute to a larger queer Gothic aesthetic.

# 7

# Brexit Gothic

## Spectral Illusions and Affect Memories in Sarah Moss' *Ghost Wall* and Niall Griffiths' *Broken Ghost*

If the previous chapter explores European connections and urban topographies integral to the twenty-first-century British Gothic, this chapter highlights a notably different turn: prioritizing fictional explorations of Britain's 2016 decision to leave the European Union, especially as this is understood within local and rural contexts. As Youssef Ferdjani writes, '[t]oday, the labouring classes mainly live in small towns and in rural areas, culturally in the margins and geographically pushed away from the big cities. They are the losers of economic and social liberalism' as presently defined (2022, 48). In so far as this liberalism aligns to a Remainer vote, this helps to explain rural Leaver sentiment (especially in England and Wales), as does 'the emergence of a new English [and in some ways, British] identity' defined by a sense of lost tradition and cultural disinheritance. As Sally Brooks affirms, the centrality of Brexit within the 'politics of the rural' reflects a nostalgia for empire, but also for an 'agrarian-centred way of life' and a sense of displacement regarding 'once-familiar features of what had once been a "living and working countryside"' (2019, 11, 16). As I explore here, this surfaces culturally in a Gothic return to local superstition and folklore, both as right-wing tools of hatred and exclusion and as critical registers of defunct utopias defined by nationalist isolationism.

In fact, the importance of superstition and folklore, especially as this arises in local stories of supernatural apparitions and ecstatic moments, is central to Gothic as originally conceived, wherein encounters with the ghostly constitute key components of the Romantic sublime, a Gothic ideal (again) crucially associated with excessive emotions. As Fred Botting explains of early Gothic writing, '[t]hrough its presentations of supernatural sensational and terrifying incidents, imagined or not, Gothic produced emotional effects on its readers rather than developing a rational or properly cultivated response' (Botting 1996, 4). Inspired and impassioned by such emotive encounters, Gothic lectors of the Enlightenment period negotiated affects comparable to those produced by religious fervour, outside the commonly accepted boundaries of rational thought or social decency.

While on the one hand this reflected a sense of awe in the power of nature – engagements with sublime wilderness prompting 'spontaneous worship' alongside terror and dread (Kröger 2013, 18) – on the other hand, it also comprehended terror-inspiring political projects and manifestations, wherein 'sublime eruptions like the French Revolution' became known for invoking 'politically disruptive emotions,' challenging the rule of law through displays of spectacular anger and outrage (Eagleton 2005, 47). In this way, sublime displays of revolutionary passion within this period can be said to have depended crucially on aesthetic spectacle: extraordinary visions became, with just the right framing, a promise of freedom.

In Sarah Moss' *Ghost Wall* (2018) and Niall Griffiths' *Broken Ghost* (2019), this early Gothic understanding is brought to bear on the narratives and discourses of twenty-first-century Britain, in particular the 2016 Brexit referendum, an event whose political purchase again depends on both powerful shared emotions and popular collective histories. As Robert Eaglestone explains, 'Brexit is not only political, economic and administrative: perhaps most significantly it is an event in culture, too. Brexit grew from cultural beliefs, real and imaginary, about Europe and the UK' (2018, 1). Indeed, as Sara Upstone also reflects, such beliefs are by no means new to British cultural thinking, where texts such as Tom Nairn's *The Break-Up of Britain* (1981), Stephen Haseler's *The English Tribe* (1996), and Mark Perryman's *Imagined Nation: England After Britain* (2008) all underline familiar, often distinctly emotive appeals to a 'unique' English national belonging, often juxtaposed precisely to ideas of Europe as a space of 'otherness' (Upstone 2018, 45). As Upstone explains, such scholarship 'ask[s] us to consider how places and communities have been represented over time and [...] how attitudes to national and international identities and alliances exist as a long process of representation,' each 'individual cultural text' forming 'part of a complex cultural matrix [...] that produce[s] a dominant cultural discourse surrounding issues of identity' (ibid., 47). While on the one hand this includes canonical texts rhetorically set on grieving a lost empire, such as *Brideshead Revisited* (1945), *The Jewel in the Crown* (1966), and more recently, *Downton Abbey* (2010–15) (see also Haseler 1996, 92; Upstone 2018, 46–7), on the other hand, it also encompasses contemporary fictions intent to upset such melancholic imaginaries, looking towards the present and future, rather than the past, to readdress division.

The Gothic's relevance to this intention is again visible in the distinctly powerful emotions this genre negotiates, as these are used both to demonize and vilify 'Others' and, in more transgressive forms, to grant 'the Other' respect and power. As Neil McRobert writes, 'When Nigel Farage expresses concern about Romanian men moving in next door, it makes one wonder if he has read *Dracula* – the story of a Romanian man who literally moves in beside some stuffy British people' (McRobert 2019). In effect, Farage draws on canonical Gothic discourses to deprecate migrants. More largely, as Michael Gardiner notes, Brexit often draws on a hauntological 'aesthetics of anachronism' unmistakably familiar to the Gothic, revivifying a forgotten but haunting national past as a means of questioning Britain's ties to Europe, building on a legacy of nationalist struggle to justify political and economic independence. In perhaps surprisingly positive terms, Gardiner suggests that such anachronistic thinking might actually be read to defy the privatizing logic of neoliberalism, countering the 'developmental time' of corporate finance with an attention to post-war class consciousness: excavating the 'traces of lost collectivity' still holding out against encroaching global capitalist monetarization (Gardiner 2018, 108 and 112).

This spectral hauntology, he suggests, portends to offer a much needed 'politics of change' for twenty-first-century Britain, 'since it refuses the fixed progressive that keeps emptying out the present and making change impossible', rejecting the neoliberal promise of economic 'development' often joined to EU membership (Gardiner 2018, 113). As many other critics have noted, however, a reverse dimension to this cultural hauntology emerges in the xenophobic meanings widely attached to such anachronistic cultural histories, wherein uncritical nostalgia aligned to both empire and the Second World War patriotism revives and parades imperialist sentiments and exclusionary nationalism.[1] As Anshuman Mondal writes, 'We should remember that imperialism has long been the safety valve through which the political establishment of the United Kingdom has channelled working-class disaffection so as to disperse its energies elsewhere on distant shores' (Mondal 2018, 89). Thus, while Brexit's rhetoric in some ways speaks to disenfranchised communities left in the shadows of a Thatcherite market economy, it also problematically manipulates a nativist phantasmagoria to mobilize hatred.

Exploring *Ghost Wall* and *Broken Ghost* in this context, I hope to show how Gothic tropes in these texts, and especially the sublime and spectral, confront such Brexit-era imaginaries in transgressive ways.[2] In particular, drawing on Eaglestone's idea of 'affect memory' as defined by powerful emotions evoked through political cues and material culture, and often 'weaponised' for political purposes (2018, 97), both texts can be seen to register the emotional pull of nationalist collective mythologies inspired by engagement with the Gothic: in Moss' case, in relation to a supposedly authentic Iron Age nativism ripe with Gothic violence, and in Griffiths', a supernatural Marian vision seemingly prescinding revolutionary change. The radical energies these narratives garner in each case reflect ambiguous potential to incite both promise and brutality, a Gothic condition here made explicit in these texts' attention to spectral inspiration, with repeated references to politicized ghostly visions and sublime encounters. Alongside elation, however, horror also drives these novels' storylines, as shadows of encroaching violence accompany these characters on their respective trajectories, reshaping their everyday interactions to expose threat and vulnerability. In this respect, the cultural matrix aligned to Brexit in these texts is decidedly disturbing, a site of fear and repugnance much more than hope or collectivity.

## Atavistic Histories and Skull-laden Borders in Sarah Moss' *Ghost Wall*

Beginning with *Ghost Wall*, shortlisted for the 2019 Polari and Ondaatje Prizes, this is Sarah Moss' sixth novel out of eight, all with an eye towards the contemporary political landscape and its haunted facets. The text is set in the early 1990s, shortly following the fall of the Berlin Wall, an event explicitly discussed by the novel's cohort of university students near the start of the narrative. 'I've got a chunk of it,' one student brags, 'everyone's just nicking bits of it now, the wall, [...] you could kind of see the streets joint up again, fusing' (Moss 2018, 16). This positive description of cross-European connection and cosmopolitan freedom, so particular to the celebratory spirit of the post-Soviet 1990s, contrasts with the setting of the novel itself in the near vicinity of Hadrian's Wall, where the sense of still-persisting borders remains a constant within this dark landscape. As Moss reflects, 'Nowhere in England really feels like a border because it's an island, but that's the border with Scotland. It was also the border of the Roman Empire for a few hundred years. [...] So I had this sense of the edges of a place, in a country kind of grieving with the tide getting larger and smaller' (Carroll 2019). In this way, through her engagement with this Gothic Northumbrian setting, Moss offers a textual commentary on contemporary border debates, implicitly reminding the reader that 'progress is not inevitable' (Carroll 2019) and that fallen walls may yet be resurrected.[3]

It is worth noting that this borderland setting is pointedly rich with Gothic cultural significance, as ideas of ancient invasion and battle, established in relation to a seemingly invincible Roman intruder, balance prehistoric violence against contemporary politics and nativist sentiment. As Tobias Carroll affirms, this northern landscape 'abounds with sinister portents and ominous structures that seem designed to prevent escape and stifle dissent' (Carroll 2019): while beautiful and 'authentic' in its way – despite notable changes in the land since Iron Age 'England' (Moss 2018, 119, 53) – this site nevertheless encodes a space of danger and brutality that is expressly Gothic. As one passage describes it, recounting an incident in which the narrator accidentally falls in the marsh as a child:

> The bog seals around you, and it will of course go further than skin, or at least will fill the inner skins of every orifice, seeping and trickling through the curls of your ears, rising like a tide in your lungs, creeping into your vagina, it will embalm you from the inside out. (ibid., 98)

Here, the darkly preserving quality of the wetland topography reflects a 'liminal status between life and death' (Ryan 2020), as it at once conserves a younger Silvie's body and horrifically violates this. As Emily Toner likewise avers, the marshland can be seen to function as a 'national time capsule' filled with important artifacts, but also as a cemetery of 'preserved human remains' or 'bog bodies' associated with human sacrifice (Toner 2019). The novel's engagement with this dark museum or 'bone house', as Silvie's dad calls it, underpins its disquieting message on contemporary Brexit-era politics, which in fetishizing cultural heritage to glorify a savage national past, evades historical realities expressly ghoulish.

The students and their professor, alongside Silvie and her family, have come to this location to practice 'Experiential Archaeology,' a discipline seeking to re-enact a site-specific version of past life – in this case, the Iron Age – in order to better understand this. More precisely, Silvie, with her mother and brothers, has been dragged onto this expedition by her historically obsessed father, forced to wear a tunic and to sleep on a straw-stuffed sack for the sake of historical 'authenticity'. The idea is to live 'wild off the land, foraging and fishing and finding [their] way' (Moss 2018, 17) over several days, in order to attain 'the sort of physical contact with the world that our ancestors had, to "walk the land as they walked it two thousand years ago"' (Crown 2018). While the professor leading this group emphasizes this project's largely non-academic quality, seeing it as 'little more than a game' (Moss 2018, 91), with only minimal archaeological grounding, Silvie's father, Bill, instead invests it with a deep cultural significance, reading into it a means to connect with an 'original Britishness' of extreme conservative dimensions (ibid., 20). As Silvie puts it, 'He wanted his own ancestry, wanted a lineage, a claim on something. Not people from Ireland or Roman or Germania or Syria but some tribe sprung from English soil like mushrooms in the night' (ibid., 45). The novel's confrontation with this nativist imaginary thus proves central to its critique of Brexiteer politics, as it reinforces a dark connection between nationalist mythologies and authoritarian violence.

The dangerous and cynical implications of this nativist outlook buttress the novel's investment in the Gothic throughout, as the idea of an ancient English borderland fuels Bill's prejudice and sanctions his tyranny. From the very start of the excursion, Bill proclaims his nostalgically enabled racist and sexist viewpoint, as he negotiates an offensive language to regale Hadrian's Wall's slave-driven construction, and as he elegizes 'the old days [when] women weren't going round forever bleeding all over the place' (ibid., 24, 13). For him, as he eagerly emphasizes, the Wall represents 'a physical manifestation of Ancient British resistance,' a reaffirmation of nationalist and patriarchal pride in the face of cosmopolitan liberalism, even as the professor himself explains its merely symbolic importance, as a kind of tribal 'magic' (Moss 2018, 44). Likewise, Silvie's name, short for Sulevia, or '*of the woods* in Latin,' is intended to reinforce her local, land-bound identity, granting her 'a proper native British name,' even while the students explain that its origins are Latin, rather than English (Moss 2018, 26, 20, 19). Within this mindset, Bill takes pains to monitor his wife and daughter's behaviour in a dark performance of Iron Age patriarchy, negotiating overtly abusive practices to ensure conformity under the threat of violence. This includes beating Silvie with his belt when he finds her bathing naked in a nearby stream and leaving Alison nearly incapacitated through continual beatings. Throughout the novel, indeed, aggressive and controlling behaviours accompany Bill's increasingly morbid fascination with Iron Age rituals, as this supposedly light-hearted, academic re-enactment comes to mirror his pathological psychology.

The sociopolitical scaffolding upon which this depiction is based registers Moss' empathic understanding of a disenfranchised Northern English community, wherein the cruel nostalgia of this ancestral vision reflects an oft-ignored, if misdirected, working-class desire for a stronger voice and status within the national imaginary, particularly within the context of ongoing austerity. As Gardiner writes, invoking the collectivist focus of much working-class nationalism, 'a serious engagement' with this class' politics 'would [...] have to be able to actually hear those people whose lack of access to linguistic currency

[...] has been defined as a perverse kind of social good' (Gardiner 2018, 114–15). In other words, such communities are ignored by neoliberalism precisely on the back of their communal politics, which are understood as supposed redundant, a situation which disregards a widely felt desire to rebuild post-war collectivism (ibid., 109). Within this context, it seems no surprise that Silvie's memories of her childhood include regular visits to the Child Benefit office, nor that Bill sees ancient Britain as favouring communalism over privacy: as he expresses, 'privacy's a fancy modern idea, precisely what we are getting away from' (Moss 2018, 7–8).

Indeed, in what might be understood as a form of 'hauntological melancholia', a 'ghostly search for lost futures in the ruins of development' (Gardiner 2018, 110), not only Bill but also Silvie is concerned to reaffirm the North's now forgotten cultural importance, rejecting its 'status as a ghost' within the national imaginary (Moss 2018, 71). To defend this vision, Silvie openly chastises her companions' displays of cultural elitism, rejecting their jokes about her family's accent and interests, and calling for a greater respect regarding their background and heritage. As she puts it to Molly, 'It's not a different country, the north of England, [...] we're a tiny country to start off with, have you ever been past Birmingham before?' (Moss 2018, 95). In this reassertion of Northern pride, Silvie confronts problematic geographical divisions underpinning contemporary austerity politics, accentuating the fact that Brexit 'speaks to a desire to correct hermeneutical injustice through self-assertion' (Upstone 2018, 52). Even so, in her attempts to defend her education and cultural awareness against her new friends' prejudice, Silvie also often fails to distinguish real care from perceived snobbery, reducing Molly's valid critiques of her father's abuse to mere pretension: 'She didn't understand [...] couldn't see what it was like for us' (Moss 2018, 113). The text in this way emphasizes the dangers of elite dismissals of Eurosceptic politics, as Silvie's resentment morphs into a larger resistance to conversation. It reminds the reader of how easily snobbery and pretension, as well as close-mindedness, closes down constructive solutions, rather than opening these up.

For her part, Silvie does eventually become more receptive as the text continues, gradually admitting Molly's companionship, and also learning to ask questions and to challenge her father's viewpoint. As she expresses, she is desperate to learn how to 'leave home', how to 'get away' (Moss 2018, 21). By contrast, Bill represents an opposing perspective, a stubborn resistance to change and difference, and this is what ultimately decides the novel's anti-Brexit politics. This comes though perhaps most forcefully in the closing pages of the novel, wherein the Gothic aesthetic takes on its most extreme dimensions: first, in the macabre reconstruction of an Iron Age 'ghost wall', and second, in an act of ritual sacrifice, in this case involving Silvie herself as victim. In the first of these scenes, Bill and Jim together decide to re-erect an Iron Age border-wall, complete with decorative skulls strung along its ramparts to ward off intruders. As the professor explains, 'it's what one of the local tribes tried as a last-ditch defence against the Romans, they made a palisade and brought out their ancestral skulls and arrayed them along the top, dead faces gazing down, it was their strongest magic' (Moss 2018, 108). While Jim then admits that this idea was unsuccessful in obstructing attack, providing only talismanic protection against the invading Romans, it nevertheless gains popularity within the group for its symbolic purchase as a testament to ancient violence, invoking averred performative ceremonies of tribal self-assertion enacted through the reconstruction of rudimentary walls. The group's restaging of this Iron Age practice, combined with chanting and drumming, thus underlines the novel's condemnation of the deference so commonly granted to Brexit-era nativism, instead accentuating this outlook's underlying atavism and noxious pretence.

The final scene on the bog takes this one step further, bringing into view just how savage and Gothic the behaviour such mythologies can generate, encompassing liturgies of vestigial brutality on par with prehistoric murder ceremonies. This conclusion is prefaced at various points throughout the novel, both in the opening representation of Iron Age ritual sacrifice, and in Silvie's various interactions with her father betraying his desire to harm her. In one particularly ominous scene at a museum, Bill effectively maps out an Iron Age girl's death across Silvie's adolescent body, in this way reaffirming his belittling view of his daughter as an 'object of violence' (Moss 2018, 69). As Silvie recounts:

> He looked up at me, touched my forearm in its school uniform shirt and my shoulder. They'd be about there and there, see, not enough to kill, just done for the pain like, and this one on her face, there, for the shame of it maybe, folk watching. My forehead, along the hairline. Yes, I said. Her hands had been bound for two thousand years. (Moss 2018, 70)

The overtly threatening nature of this interaction, effectively shaming Silvie both through disturbing language and performative touch, offers a chilling testament to Bill's horrific parenting *and* his gruesome view of history, where the past becomes an increasingly grisly excavation site for imagined acts of barbarous violence. Unsurprisingly, this is then relived *en scene* as Silvie is tied up and led onto the bog in the final chapter, thus making clear her radical vulnerability within this murderous ecosystem. As Annalisa Quinn asserts, the novel 'shows what happens to the people around men who are obsessed with what is theirs, and whose idea of "freedom" is partly about the freedom to hurt others' (Quinn 2019). In effect, this closing reaffirms the text's damning view of Brexit as a nostalgically based authorization of backwardness and brutality, designed to legitimate a patriarchal traditionalism of extreme dimensions.

There is little to distract from this disturbing critical vision in the novel, hence its classification in this chapter as a work of Gothic horror: even as the police intervene on the bog to save Silvie, the reader anticipates future punishment: 'It was my fault when they arrested Dad,' she ruminates (Moss 2018, 144). Even so, it is worth stressing that the role of spectres in the novel is not limited to a singular morbid fetishization of the dead, but instead encompasses more overtly positive representations of ghosts, which pretend an alternative outlook. This becomes evident most overtly in Louise and Molly's contributions to the discussion, wherein the aim of experiential archaeology shifts from Bill's macabre contemplation of beloved 'dead things' to a more positive recognition that, in this transhistorical performance, 'we ourselves became the spectres,' mimicking and reviving the ways of the dead, in order to learn from them. As Molly affirms, 'I'd like to make things be alive again, [...] let visitors see that people's tools and jewellery and games are still here even when the people aren't' (Moss 2018, 40). From this recuperative perspective, being historically minded means recognising how the past lives on in its artifacts (its 'profane illumination' or 'vibrant matter', as explored in previous chapters), and also appreciating how the present may build on the past, to avoid its mistakes. Unlike nativism's call to dwell in lost grandeur, then, this outlook beseeches an embrace of a still unknown future, working with the tools of history to create a more democratic society.

## Ghostly Visions and Sublime Delusions in Niall Griffiths' *Broken Ghost*

Winner of the 2020 Wales Book of the Year Award and Griffiths' ninth novel since the millennium, *Broken Ghost* likewise negotiates the spectral, alongside the sublime, as a form of Brexit-era commentary, also registering the Gothic dimensions of austerity governance and its divisive implications. Set in the untamed wilderness of western Wales, in the region of the Pendam mountains near Aberystwyth, the novel incorporates a marginal British landscape to facilitate its political message, navigating both its visceral physical and supernatural dimensions to register violence. As in Moss' novel, both the landscape and the characters represent figures for the undervalued and disenfranchised, a forgotten underclass, overtly rejected by a neoliberal agenda. As one passage expresses, these characters possess 'a notion of the broken social contract' even from 'when they're very young, the rank unfairness of it', given that '*their* side of the contract was shattered long ago' (Griffiths 2019, 70). The cruelty of austerity government in this way surfaces even more explicitly here than in *Ghost Wall*, reaffirming stark socioeconomic tensions underpinning referendum voting and especially Wale's majority Leave vote. As Boyd Tonkin writes, 'The small-minded viciousness of post-austerity welfare policy, and the "bright new Brexit Britain" sarcastically hailed by its victims, have deepened the mood of alienation' in this text (Tonkin 2019), making it in some ways even more despairing than Griffiths' notably despondent previous novels. Nevertheless, there remains some hope in the text's always ambiguous engagement with spectral, wherein this functions both as a sign of Brexit's deception and, potentially, as a promise of meaningful social change, should this be admitted.

The principal form in which the ghost emerges in the text is as a Marian apparition: a glowing figure in the sky, in the shape of a woman. Witnessed by the three main characters, Emma, Adam, and Cowley, following a rave at Llyn Syfydrin on the top of Pendam mountain, news of the vision spreads quickly, via Emma's blog and twitter posts, across the whole of Wales, garnering attention as a site of national discussion. For Emma, a single mother facing sanctions on her unemployment benefit, the event promises a welcome release from pressing social and financial pressures, allowing her to briefly overcome depression and to regain a sense of affective balance. 'It was like everything went away, [...] like none of that mattered anymore' (Griffiths 2019, 3), she reflects, her life suddenly more manageable, less devoid of emotion. The other two characters, Adam and Cowley, are more reluctant to accredit this sighting, instead dismissing it as an effect of environmental factors and the 'slow release' of an MDMA tablet (ibid., 22). Adam sees it as 'something in the atmosphere', while Cowley insists, 'I saw nowt' (ibid., 6, 7). Even for these characters, however, the experience is life-altering in introducing a sense of hope more generally absent, a seeming delivery from everyday preoccupations connected to unemployment, poverty, addiction, and substance abuse. As the character Adam reflects, 'None of it matters. Just the memory of that glow. And the knowing that the complexity of it all is a thing to be celebrated' (ibid., 20). In this way, the sublime ecstasy attendant upon the politics of revelation is what stands at the heart of this novel's politicized Gothic, underpinning its transgressive response both to austerity and Brexit.

Justin D. Edwards reflects on how the supernatural within the contemporary emerges as intimately connected to the technological, as 'modern forms of technology project ghosts in the future and their power – a hauntology – increases its dominion' (Edwards 2015, 6). Such an apprehension clearly informs Griffiths' text, as Emma's online engagements act to transform this spectre's significance, stretching this from the local to the national and even beyond. As Emma reflects, 'The hits. The thousands of retweets. [...] [T]his is more viral than bubonic fucking plague. [...] What have I started? [...] What the fuck is going on?' (Griffiths 2019, 109). At first excited that her blog attracts new followers, Emma later shrinks in horror at the enormity of her popularity, pondering just how different it is to '[chuck] words out into cyberspace [...] alone in the house at the computer screen' than to 'have to answer questions and see the reactions in people's faces' (ibid., 96). Within this digital arena, the deception Emma identifies in her own blog's vision also speaks to the dubious quality of Brexit's online rhetoric, where here too, an ecstatic register functions not to inform but instead exaggerate, garnering followers precisely through strategic engagements with popular sentiment. As J. A. Smith writes, 'Both the populism that brought us to Brexit and the use to which digital technology is being put at the present time make precisely this claim to treat lives in "aggregate"', or in other words, to understand political truth as the product of popular feeling (2018, 128). Here, then, as with Emma's mythological apparition, Brexit emerges as the product of a widespread delusion: a grand 'event' ultimately fuelled by false emotion and digital hyperbole.

The media's distorting role in Brexit politics is indeed visible not only via the storyline but also the form of the novel itself, where overt changes in font and syntax running throughout the text indicate the unwanted encroachment of online voices, the monstrous incursion of internet preachers and twitter-mad politicians. As Kristian Shaw explains, 'the sudden intrusion of aggressive online message board conversations into the narrative indicate the increasingly disconnected national conversation taking shape around the vision and the means by which mediatized digital platforms often reduce citizens to shallow stereotypical caricatures' (Shaw 2021, 205). This becomes most apparent in the chapters entitled 'Messages', wherein radicalized voices battle it out across a range of social media platforms, issuing warnings ranging from repentance to '#takebackcontrol' (Griffiths 2019, 197). Moreover, in so far as, in Joseph Crawford's words, the internet's 'technological possibilities [...] find new ways of constructing and distributing Gothic narratives,' often questioning the extent to which 'online dissemination can be trusted' (ibid., 72–3), it is clear that this understanding is also directly applied by the novel to Brexit, where repeated reactionary postings reflective of anti-immigrant sentiment underline an express textual cynicism towards Eurosceptic politics, a self-conscious refusal of xenophobic thinking and online hatred.

This virtual online space is directly contrasted in the novel to the welcome 'reality' of an (almost) off-the-grid wilderness, which if also distinctly Gothic in various aspects, conjuring the sublime aesthetics of Romantic poetry, nevertheless retains a certain unmolested integrity connected to the planetary. As Adam reflects, 'sheep shit, bones, ragged severed wings, skulls. [...] Horrible, aye, but [...] the wildness of it all was in me and [...] I came from it. [...] All of this can be touched. It is all Real' (ibid., 77–8). The therapeutic authenticity attached to this landscape in the text is expressly what fuels Adam's distrust of the spectre, as he questions 'is this Reality? [...] Where does this fit in?' (ibid., 79). In this way, the novel openly challenges an idea of the immaterial as necessarily redemptive: to the contrary, it is nature that heals here. Despite this hesitation towards spectral thinking, however, the apparition does retain a clear critical appeal within the text, visibly enhanced by its connection to nature and the Romantic topography. As Griffiths himself reflects, despite rural Wales' contemporary financial status as 'a piggybank for many a rapacious entrepreneur', it remains a space of 'silence and ragged peaks and raptors and ancient traces of traffic of all and every kind [...]. There is value here, and magic, and much wonder' (Griffiths 2017, n.p.). This uneasy positioning of the spectre, then, between the natural and the technological, and between the illusive and sublime, is what makes this Gothic engagement so particular within the novel, as the text openly negotiates contrasting meanings thrown into focus within the present cultural-political landscape.

Adam's commentaries in particular help to elucidate this Gothic panorama, situating it further within a larger textual critique of austerity politics, challenging the lie that decreased public expenditure promises progress. As he affirms, 'out there people are killing themselves, in this isolated, inward-looking, mean country that its populace voted for it to become; [...] anyone who needs state support is now regarded as a scrounging parasite to be ostracised, and persecuted, to death if needs be' (Griffiths 2019, 74–5). This attention to austerity's violence, in the context of mass cultural despair, reinforces what Henry Giroux refers to as 'the terror of neoliberalism,' wherein 'citizenship has increasingly become a function of consumerism and politics has been restructured as "corporations have been increasingly freed from social control through deregulation, privatization, and other neoliberal measures"' (Giroux 2005, 2). Within this context, Brexit's promises to 'Take Back Control' through departure from Europe reflect a cynical exploitation of working-class distress, a distraction from the truth of neoliberalism's 'stinking hypocrisy' in favouring the rich (Griffiths 2019, 55). As George Monbiot likewise writes, 'the creation of emergency [in the context of Brexit] is the inevitable destination of an absolutist, failed system. But emergency also provides the last means by which the failed system can be defended and extended' (Monbiot 2019) – so much is clear here.

In the end, the narrative eventually reveals the characters' spectral sighting as illusory: a meteorological effect known as the 'Brocken Spectre', produced by 'an observer's shadow projected horizontally onto an opposing bank of fog or cloud' (Mitchell 2007, 168). The text takes its title from this reference, where 'Broken Ghost' is Cowley's pedestrian translation of the term, offered in outspoken frustration over the 'fuckin big words these twats use' (Griffiths 2019, 265). Despite this rejection of scientific language, however – reflective, as Shaw notes, of 'Govian resistance to expert analysis' (Shaw 2021, 206) – the novel nevertheless embraces Cowley's appellation as more critically appropriate to the current moment: speaking to the brokenness of austerity-driven society with an equally splintered solution (see also Shaw 2021, 206). As Adam puts it, '[Britain's] just refusing to lie down and be buried and Brexit is just fucking digging up the corpse. [...] It just can't let go of the fucking empire. That's what it is' (Griffiths 2019, 225). Indeed, the ghost identified here with Britain's brokenness is broken not only due to misplaced popular mythologies, but also (in connection with Griffiths' Romantic eco-politics), a contemporary social alienation from natural surroundings, where the mountain is described as 'so stuffed with history [...] that its matter is leaking out and has ruptured the seams' (ibid., 327). In this way, a Gothic engagement with sublime wilderness functions also as a figurative reminder of forgotten national histories: the 'broken ghost' reflecting a longer social and historical experience now forgotten.

In the context of austerity politics, this eco-historical vision is also critically significant, as it reminds the reader of Conservative governmental disregard for the environmental and local ecosystems, privatization increasingly impinging upon a publicly owned 'common land' now seen as profitable. As Jason Moore reflects, 'Finance capital in the neoliberal era has penetrated everyday life as never before, and in so doing, has sought to remake human and extra-human nature in its own image [...] – extending horrifically to the molecular relations of life itself' (Keefer 2017). Within this monstrous accumulative practice, global capitalism negotiates 'cyclical ecological crises,' repeatedly refusing to acknowledge its own destructive role in 'organizing nature' (ibid.). The novel's awareness of this eco-Gothic reality emerges especially in its attention to modernization's destruction, as increasingly even this untamed mountainside comes under the domain of media and police surveillance. Rejecting those now visiting the site as intruders – 'Bloody hippies spoiling it! Don't they have jobs!' (Griffiths 2019, 199) – the novel thus rejects the neoliberal idea of progress as pointedly illusive.

With the spectre's increasing popularity across internet networks, a commune nevertheless does begin to take form on the mountain, recalling 'a slumbering lacustrine tribe around smouldering firepits and crude crosses hammered into the earth' (ibid., 115). This prehistoric vision, so notably recollective of that of *Ghost Wall* – also invested with primitive rituals: 'offerings, here and there: [...] prayer words chalked onto stone' (Griffiths 2019, 115) – again invokes the radical significance granted to cultural mythology within contemporary politics, as a supposed basis for social restoration and nativist fortification. In Cowley's words, this is the space of 'forts n castles,' ancient battles with 'a Romans and the English, pair-a cunts' both eager to 'take over, turn us into slaves, like' (ibid., 134). Yet, while a scepticism towards anachronistic rhetoric remains clearly present throughout the novel – for example, fuelling the text's critique of Cowley's isolationist outlook – nevertheless, the focus of the novel's concern is not primarily historical, so much as political, where the law's arrival at the encampment, in the form of government sanctioned troops, turns this potential utopia into a site of brutal apocalypse. Indeed, implicit within this ending is a sharp reminder not only of neoliberalism's elitism, but also its biopolitics, such that, the state here continues to intervene through policing and punishment, even while denying the government's role in maintaining civic structures supposedly directed by an 'invisible hand'. As Richard Seymour reflects, 'attempts at circumventing or subverting the economic order [...] must be harshly punished [within neoliberalism]. The neoliberal state is a big, interventionist state, particularly in its penal mode' (Seymour 2014, 10). While ultimately this does not erase a hope of resistance in the novel, it does suggest that change will not be easy: a larger and more organized social movement is clearly lacking and urgently needed.

## Conclusion

In responding to contemporary politics, then, these texts offer a critical perspective both on austerity and Brexit, seeing these projects as intimately interwoven strategies of a larger neoliberal order. Their hauntological postures in particular invoke the oft-disguised violence of Conservative government, both as this calls on affect memory to manipulate an illusory past and as it reduces contemporary society to a profit-generating mechanism devoid of communal feeling. In the end, what emerges most clearly is a Gothic picture of contemporary Britain's underlying division at the start of this new millennium, and of the 'disjunction between the professed aims of neoliberal economics and the personal and social cost to the most disadvantaged members of society' (Blake and Soltysik Monnet 2017, 5). In effect, far from helping these characters in their search for empowerment, neoliberalism acts as the crucial obstacle blocking their way, conjuring morbid ghosts and spectral delusions that keep them looking backwards. While again this is not the only reading of the spectre these fictions offer, where more hopeful and revolutionary interpretations are also present, yet it is the dominant and guiding framework for both texts' visions.

## Notes

1. See, for example, Eaglestone (2018), 96; Mondal (2018), 86; Mukherjee (2018), 77–80.
2. I would note that Kristian Shaw also explores both these texts in *Brexlit* (see Shaw 2021, 202–8). While my focus is different from his in its attention to the Gothic, I remain inspired by his readings, which I draw on here.
3. Such marginalized settings are a central feature of many texts explored in this book, as emphasized in my introduction. It is also worth recognizing a handful of other recent Gothic fictions likewise concerned to explore Britain's geographical and socioeconomic peripheries, including John Burnside's *Glister* (2008), set in a fictional northern Scottish coastal town destroyed by a chemical factory; Graeme Macrae Burnet's *His Bloody Project* (2015), set in a deeply penurious nineteenth-century Scottish Highlands; Fiona Mozley's *Elmet* (2017), concerned with a likewise impoverished and exploited Yorkshire countryside; Daisy Johnson's *Sisters* (2020), also set in the North York Moors; Jon McGregor's *Reservoir 13* (2017), set in the rural Peak District; Andrew Michael Hurley's *The Loney* (2014), which navigates economic depression and folkloric ritual on the Lancashire coast; Wyl Menmuir's *The Many* (2016) and Lucy Wood's *The Sing of the Shore* (2018), both focused on socioeconomic hardship in coastal Cornwall; and Jenn Ashworth's *Fell* (2016), set in a deeply troubled Morecambe Bay. I continue to examine these (often littoral) settings in Chapter 9.

8

# Pandemic Gothic

## Childhood Terror and Monstrous Illness in the Fiction of Kazuo Ishiguro and M. R. Carey

On first sight, the fictions explored in this chapter, Kazuo Ishiguro's *Never Let Me Go* (2005) and *Klara and the Sun* (2021), and M. R. Carey's *The Girl with All the Gifts* (2014) and *The Boy on the Bridge* (2017), reflect notably different off-shoots of contemporary Gothic writing. The first two, by the 2017 Nobel Prize winning author, lauded for their simultaneous formal 'understatement' and thematic 'poignancy' (Clarke 2006; Capossere 2021; Battersby 2021), resemble what might be called literary appropriations or 'repurposings' of the aesthetic (Dancer 2021, 30), forays into genre scripted from a 'high cultural' standpoint (Leypoldt 2018). Ursula LeGuin, while responding to Ishiguro's fame with another novel, *The Buried Giant* (2015a), accuses him of 'despising' genre writing altogether, while other prominent critics, such as Michiko Kakutani and Susan Balée, either question his supposedly problematic reliance upon popular genre tropes (Kakutani 2015), or conversely praise his genre adaptations 'with literary flair' (Balée 2021). Such responses, while in some cases intended as charitable, nevertheless deny Ishiguro a visible place within mainstream genre writing, instead celebrating his achievements in the realm of 'literary fiction' and aesthetic experiment.

By contrast, Carey's *The Girl with All the Gifts* and *The Boy on the Bridge*, described in the first case by Waterstones (2014) as a 'million-copy bestseller that is also a BAFTA Award-nominated movie' and in both cases written by an author acclaimed for his popular DC and Marvel comic books, graphic novels, and scriptwriting, appear much more in line with popular readings of the genre as defined by conventional reference points: as zombie 'thrillers' that effectively capture 'the public imagination' (Smythe), or as two of 'the more imaginative and ingenious additions to the dystopian canon' (Kirkus). Despite these differences in audience and reception, however, all four texts overtly negotiate recognized sci fi Gothic tropes connected to the figure of the posthuman monster: in *Never Let Me Go*, the clone; in *Klara and the Sun*, the robot or 'Artificial Friend'; and in *The Girl with All the Gifts* and *The Boy on the Bridge*, the zombie or 'hungry'. All can also be read as simultaneously informed by and intervening in prominent Gothic narratives underpinning contemporary biomedical debates, in particular those connected to discourses of illness, pandemic, and contamination – discourses which both inform the popular representation of late twentieth and early-twenty-first-century viruses such as AIDS, SARS, and COVID-19 *and* complicate this representation by showcasing their connection to minority cultures conceived under a rhetoric of infection and contagion. As Ruth Mayer notes, 'the trope of the infection is an integral part of the discourse of cultural contact' in the contemporary era, though one which has shifted in recent years, 'since the idea of a clear-cut boundary between "us" and "them," "self" and "other," "here" and "there" is becoming increasingly difficult to maintain' (2007, 1). Within this fluid and border-crossing framework, the prevalence of the virus or 'outbreak' narrative raises questions regarding 'the power and danger of bodies in contact, and the fragility and tenacity of social bonds' within a transnational era (Wald 2021, xv), emerging as representative of biopolitical fears presently circulating.

In this chapter, I develop these concerns to read these four novels in light of their 'viropolitical' meaning, where this is defined in terms 'metaphors of disease and methods for its containment within a sociopolitical discourse of otherness and consumption' (de Bruin-Molé 2021, 161). More broadly, in an era of supposedly 'monstrous' intrusions, read both as metaphorical and factual/ scientific, and wherein Frankensteinian references and posthuman allusions proliferate (Alliheibi, Omar and Horais 2021; Reis Filho 2020),[1] these texts anticipate and prophetically respond to contemporary pandemic-related discourses, offering reference to strategies of immunization unmistakeably Gothic in character. Indeed, if as Megen de Bruin-Molé and Sara Polak reflect, 'each [new] outbreak has contributed to a larger contemporary obsession with metaphors and modalities of contagion' (2021, 2), often in ways which overlap with right-wing narratives of hate and exclusion, these fictions' Gothic aesthetics work precisely to dismantle this cultural fascination, questioning the implicitly violent and anti-communal ideology upon which it is structured. Exposing the vindictiveness of medical and legal discourses seeking to cordon and militarize health and security, and underlining the need to look beyond established biopolitical systems, these fictions situate contemporary immunity as a site of terror much more than promise, entreating a re-examination of current institutions and practices.

One central aspect of this depiction, connected to these novels' shared Gothic emphasis on monstrous embodiment, involves a concern with minority precarity and abjection seen as *a result of* rather than *a defence for* immunological thinking. As Catherine Bernard notes, 'Covid-19 produces a hermeneutic short-cut in which the body is shown from the start to be collective and, symmetrically, the body politic experienced as always already individual in its corporeality' (2022, 14). In other words, Covid-19 makes evident how fundamentally dependent the human body is on collective experience, while at the same time underlining the corporeal manifestation of the health crisis in the conditions of disease-ridden bodies and pervasive contagions, especially where pre-existing conditions or inadequate healthcare make this inevitable. As Judith Butler likewise explains, the pandemic results in an awareness not only of innate human vulnerability in the face of illness, but also of certain minority populations' 'greater likelihood of dying, understood as the fatal consequence of a pervasive social inequality' (Yancy 2020, 2). Put differently, the pandemic accentuates the underlying socio-political conditions facilitating unequal precarity – hence these critics' repeated call for collective awareness and social responsibility.

In the fictions examined in this chapter, this viropolitical landscape is investigated and critically challenged, brought into question through Gothic narratives which expressly upend immunity's authority, highlighting the inequality confronting certain minority demographics. Indeed, for the fictional societies imagined in these novels, the cost of health care is outrageously excessive, involving practices of systematic child abuse excused on the back of biomedical 'progress', where a neoliberal, individualist rhetoric repeatedly invokes immunity as *necessarily* violent. The logic by which these horrific institutions are systemically permitted, then, is at once both (pseudo)medical and ideological in nature, citing on the one hand the urgency of the medical crisis which would make such drastic measures permissible, and on the other hand, the monstrous posthuman status of these child subjects as clones, robots, and zombies.[2]

In Ishiguro's *Never Let Me Go*, this takes places in a fictional 1990s England systematically breeding and harvesting clone children: 'students' whose organs are extracted to replace those of infirm humans. By contrast, in Carey's novels, a sci-fi Gothic landscape introduces a speculative England of post-apocalyptic dimensions, wherein surviving militants look to capture and dissect zombie children, a process again authorized on the back of a quest for a vaccine. And in *Klara and the Sun*, robot 'Artificial Friends' (or 'AFs') are created to 'continue' the lives of dying human children, normalizing the latter's deaths, even as they themselves endure systemic abuse (2021, 210). These structural infringements of child welfare thus emerge via discourses of immunity and well-being, but also through collective labels of monstrosity and threat tied to mere children. By making this violence explicit, connecting it to viropolitical 'treatments' and 'break throughs' invoked without concern for the well-being of minority populations, these novels reinterpret twenty-first-century medicine as a space of Gothic extermination, wherein anything is permitted given the premise of individual advancement.

Nevertheless, there is some hope here, especially where inter-species 'monstrous' relationships become textually prominent. Thus, in their Gothic investments with posthuman monstrosity, these novels go further than to merely question immunology, also intervening in debates regarding how this might be reconceived and critically rectified, emphasizing, in Kari Nixon's words, 'the value of human [and, I would add, non-human] connection, however contagious' (2020, 9). More specifically, following Ed Cohen and Margrit Shildrick's conjoint understandings of contemporary immunology as better understood in terms of entanglement and/or 'chimerism', wherein 'cellular nomadism [...] challenges immunity at all its levels' (Shildrick 2015, 10), these novels can be seen to set in place a tentative posthuman conception of inter-species and cross-organism dependency which directly complicates this viropolitical outlook and its neoliberal coordinates, instead reaffirming an eco-critical vision of interconnectivity and relationality. This understanding by no means undercuts these novels' Gothic representation of contemporary state brutality and minority aggression. Nevertheless, it does suggest that such altered viewpoints are not beyond imagination, only requiring a rethinking of the body politic and its planetary make-up.

## Viropolitics and Immunology

Given the importance of both medicine and law to these novels, in each case informed by curative and legal/military discourses, one way of approaching these Gothic landscapes critically is by turning to the figure of Robert Esposito, a theorist well known for his legal-medical reading of '*immunitas*'. As Esposito explains, the dominant logic of viropolitical immunity currently circulating in the twenty-first-century emerges primarily from Latin roots, where its meaning is specifically legal. Here, *immunitas* functions centrally as a way of indicating how social policies or behaviours might work to obstruct improved collectivity, replacing this instead with a logic of self-defence and self-protection. The viropolitical anxiety introduced by contemporary pandemics can in this way be traced back to socio-political anxieties, its significance derived negatively via recognition of that which it excludes: that is, the *munus*. Esposito elucidates:

> The meaning of *immunitas* can be arrived at by examining the predominant meaning of its opposite: where *munus* refers to an office – a task, obligation, duty (also in the sense of a gift to be repaid) – by contrast, *immunis* refers to someone who performs no office [...]. Whoever is [...] disencumbered, exonerated, exempted [...] from the *pensum* of paying tributes or performing services for others, is defined as immune. (2019, 5)

Moreover, it is not simply that *immunis* represents an exception or exemption from dictates of the common rule: as Esposito clarifies, 'it is also a privilege', and it is the intersection of these overlapping meanings which explains its contemporary relevance: 'immunity is perceived as such when it occurs as an exception to a rule that everybody else must follow [...]: its semantic focus is more on difference from the conditions of others than on the notion of exemption itself' (2019, 6). In this way, rather than *munus*, immunity's most fitting antonym is, for Esposito, the Latin *communitas* or community: it is its 'anti-social, or more precisely, anti-communal character' that defines its meaning (2019, 6).

For the fictions explored in this chapter, this immunological privilege is foregrounded via reference to distinct social classes, in each case connected to modalities of exemption and privilege, or alternatively, sacrifice. For example, in *Never Let Me Go*, the human community is allowed to live without disease or suffering, depending for this privilege on clone populations raised to be harvested for their organs. Likewise, in *Klara and the Sun*, even while humans remain subject to disease and serious illness – notably as part of a larger neoliberal project of 'lifting' or genetic restructuring – nevertheless, AI communities are designed to care for humans and (in Klara's case) to technologically 'continue' them following their passing, serving as replacements who must imitate their identities to console bereaved relatives. In either case, *munus* (or duty, or sacrifice) is a condition solely applied to non- or post-humans, the monstrous Others whose sacrifices themselves ensure human *immunitas*. Indeed, the labels of 'monster' and 'Other' predicate the normalization of this unequal system, as however human these characters appear, their societies deny them this status, instead confining them to the realm of abject difference. As Kathy H. writes of the supposedly pro-clone advocate Madame in *Never Let Me Go*, '[she] was afraid of us. She was afraid of us in the way someone might be afraid of spiders'

(Ishiguro 2005, 35). Thus, trepidation of the monstrous serves as a justification for ongoing violence.

In *The Girl with All the Gifts* and *The Boy on the Bridge*, this system likewise underwrites these narratives' graphic and state-authorized brutalities, wherein human survivors of a zombie pandemic hunt down and imprison child 'hungries' to be dissected and examined, this generation showing signs of continued cognitive functioning despite infection. The goal of this (pseudo)scientific project – to discover a vaccine for the *Ophiocordyceps unilateralis* fungus – begins from a premise of refused responsibility for the hungry community placed under human jurisdiction. Thus, as Dr Caldwell, the chief scientist in *The Girl with All the Gifts*, reflects upon initiating a dissection, 'the subject presents as a child but is actually a fungal colony animating a child's body. There's no place for sentiment here' (Carey 2014, 112). In this refusal of empathetic connection – also visible in the militant outlook espoused by human survivors in *The Boy on the Bridge* – all measures are justified: human life alone becomes sacrosanct in the search for immunity.

What ties these narratives together, then, in their respective Gothic and posthuman sci-fi landscapes, is a shared critical scepticism towards the notion of *immunitas*, echoing Esposito's reading of this concept as anti-communal and self-serving: 'something that interrupts the social circuit of reciprocal gift-giving, [...] plac[ing] him- or herself outside the community' (2019, 6). Indeed, for Esposito, what connects this historically *legal* terminology to its contemporary *biopolitical* and *biomedical* usage is its paradigmatic reliance not only on exclusion, but on a (circular) strategy of 'exclusionary inclusion': pro-actively including the foreign Other within the self in order to ultimately exclude it (ibid., 8). Thus, 'the living being begins to enter onto the horizon of visibility of modern knowledge' precisely in 'the moment its constitutive relationship with what continually threatens to extinguish it emerges', as bodily sickness becomes at once a fear and at the same time 'the internal fold which dialectically brings [life] back to itself' (ibid., 9, 14–15). Likewise, in the fictions explored in this chapter, this circular understanding directly informs the narratives' Gothic premises, wherein in all cases, these 'monster' children are taught to recognize humanity's privileges, even while being made *a biopolitical means to furthering these*: 'posthuman' vehicles employed for human advancement. In this manner, the novels underline immunity's cruelty in viewing Otherness as an ethical dispensation, questioning the designation of viropolitical 'monstrosity' as more properly human (or Capitalocene) than posthuman.

## Biomedicine as Violence in Ishiguro's *Never Let Me Go*

It is worth outlining in further detail how this aggression plays out within each narrative, as these novels map out diverse and contrasting critical responses to pandemic-related governance. One way of approaching this textual anxiety is by identifying immunity's predominantly militarized and reactionary rhetoric: its formulation, in Ed Cohen's words, of medicine as a 'weapon in the body's necessary struggle to defend itself from its life-threatening context' (2009, 6). Within this outlook, again as under Esposito's reading, the healthy organism is seen as inherently agonistic, the body (or body politic) organized *in response to* perceive aggression, in this way legitimizing 'a defense based on killing the nonself' as a means of self-protection (Martin 1990, 421). As Emily Martin likewise describes, bodies here become 'imperilled nations continuously at war to quell alien invaders', as they seek to throw out the supposedly predatory enemy that lurks within (ibid., 421).

Indeed, for Martin, immunology entails not only the militarized expulsion of perceived intruders, but also the regulated *policing* of biological relations and bodily functions, as the cellular identification of foreign antigens is conceived as the detection of 'illegal aliens [...] inside a feeding cell' or as the body is said to provide '"technical colleges," [or] "training sites" located in lymph nodes, the thymus gland, and elsewhere' – a 'highly trained administrative apparatus' for the exposure of unwanted cells, fungus, or bacterium (1990, 412–13). Within this oppositional rhetoric, as Cohen notes, 'bioscience affirms that living [itself] entails a ceaseless problem of boundary maintenance', as human beings are understood to rely upon 'a perpetual engagement against the world to maintain our integrity', inoculating all that cannot be perceived as 'essentially "natural"' (2009, 8).

This understanding motivates the biopolitical regimens of both Ishiguro's and Carey's novels, as these fictions Gothically investigate immunological indoctrination and brutality within contemporary society. In Ishiguro's *Never Let Me Go*, this encompasses a narrative set in a speculative version of 1990s England, where the clone narrator, Kathy H., is made to rehearse and interpellate her monstrous status and that of her friends, interiorizing the immunological reading society imposes upon them. As her teacher or 'guardian', Miss Lucy, comments,

> None of you will go to America, none of you will be film stars. And none of you will be working in supermarkets as I heard some of you planning the other day. Your lives are set out for you. You'll become adults, then before you're old, before you are even middle-aged, you'll start to donate your vital organs. (2005, 73)

In a notably neoliberal register (clashing with the directness of this above confrontation), Kathy's society systematically masks this inferior social standing through a discourse of agency and professionalism, as the clones are classed as 'donors' or 'carers', and as their death itself is celebrated as 'completion' (ibid., 3, 4, 189, 193, 255). As Kathy herself reflects, 'I'm not trying to boast. But then I do know for a fact that they've been pleased with my work, and by and large, I have too' (ibid., 3). Within this aspirational rhetoric, exploitation becomes an accepted facet of market-driven individualism; Kathy herself assimilates the state's 'performance of liberal empathy' and congratulates herself for her unquestioning compliance as a clone 'carer' (Black 2009, 790–1). More generally, the students are indoctrinated into a discourse of servitude comparable to that of a range of marginalized populations – as Shameem Black reflects:

> homogenized, deprived of cultural specificity, and raised to serve the needs of others, the condition of the students [...] offers a frightening parable for the assimilative energies of First World metropoles that absorb the embodied labor and cultural identity of people from diverse parts of the world. (2009, 797)

In other words, the clones become posthuman figures for global Northern privilege and ethical accommodation, even as they themselves are excluded from this privilege and made to 'give'. Equally centrally, this community stands in for the affective and material implications of immunology's reactionary outlook, as they interiorize their despised Otherness and learn to see themselves as '"excessive" and "redundant"' (Bauman 2004, 5). As Ruth comments, 'We all know it. We're modelled from trash. Junkies, prostitutes, winos, tramps. Convicts, maybe, just so long as they aren't psychos. That's where we come from' (Ishiguro 2005, 152). Indeed, the violence enacted on the 'students' through biomedical institutions is here understood in distinctly Gothic tones, as they prepare themselves for and then endure ongoing bodily extractions. As Kathy explains, even after so-called 'completion', 'there are more donations, plenty of them, on the other side of that line; [...] there are no more recovery centres, no carers, no friends; [...] there's nothing to do except watch your remaining donations until they switch you off. It's horror movie stuff' (ibid., 255–6). In this saga of continuous dismemberment, cynically juxtaposed with an institutional performance of gratitude and 'special respect' – the 'whitecoats smiling and shaking [the donor's] hand', seeing the 'fourth donation' in particular as 'worthy of congratulations' (ibid., 255) – the alter-side of immunity is identified in terms of body horror, as the clones become living repositories for organ breeding and harvesting (see also Wasson 2015b, 115).

Various descriptions and phrasings throughout the novel, seemingly inconsequential at first, further contribute to this Gothic depiction. The students joke about how their bodies 'can all unzip like a bag opening up' (Ishiguro 2005, 77), and about how their 'guardians' seem to be able to 'see right inside you' (ibid., 67), this latter description affecting Kathy with 'a little chill' (ibid.) as she reflects on it. Kathy also portrays Hailsham as corralled by a surrounding fence, a knowledge which inspires student performances of mock-electrocution (ibid., 70–1); while her friends also worry over the search for their own 'lost property' (ibid., 60) and establish a 'secret guard' (ibid., 45) amongst themselves. Indeed, at one point, while discussing the stuffiness of a classroom, Kathy describes how 'students literally had to pile on top of each other' (ibid., 51), thus recalling scenes of mass graveyards reminiscent of holocaustic violence. These Gothic descriptions reinforce the students' abject status as disposable posthuman technologies, whose parts are used or 'lost' and whose bodies are dispensed with as the state sees fit.

Indeed, as Sara Wasson reflects, this Gothic biomedical scenario need not be read as merely metaphorical, as its horror-intoned representation of 'state sanctioned' organ procurement has real-life parallels (2015b, 110). She explains, 'while in no way "realist" fiction, [these] fantasies of predation are not entirely unfounded: there is evidence that certain groups are more likely to be organ sources [...] and given the realities of economic incentives, living donation correlates with particularly striking economic and gender divisions' (Wasson 2015b, 107). The novel's emphasis on clones as a minority 'monster' population, represented by a female narrator, whose exploitation emerges *in conjunction with* larger biomedical procedures, and whose involvement is defined by a euphemistic rhetoric of 'exchanges', 'sales', and 'token' payments (Ishiguro 2005, 14, 35, 38, 54), reiterates this correspondence, where a minority-based organ-transplant economy is directly implicit in the novel's immuno-discourse. While the characters thus learn to see themselves as worthless, their value is carefully quantified by the state, as they become the mechanism by which neoliberal governance promotes and advances itself. As Henry Giroux likewise writes, 'corruption, commodification, and repressive state apparatuses have become the central features of a predatory state', in which market-driven politics make violence 'acceptable, valued, and eroticized' (2013, 258, 259).

This unmistakably Gothic representation, moreover, speaks directly to contemporary viropolitics, as this (child) community is killed so that human society does 'not die from cancer, motor neurone disease, heart disease' (Ishiguro 2005, 240). As Miss Emily elucidates, 'How can you ask a world that has come to regard cancer as curable [...] to put away that cure, to go back to the dark days? There was no going back. [...] People did their best not to think about you' (Ishiguro 2005, 240). In this way, a language of *inevitability* and *denial* legitimates murder at a systematic level, positioning violence as the necessary condition for wider well-being. As Titus Levy likewise writes, the novel 'imagines the realization of [...] individuals and societies numbed to atrocity and unwilling or unable to shake themselves out of the empathetic stupor that masks the daily horrors that occur barely out of sight' (2011, 13). In other words, immunity's *normalization* keeps minority oppression concealed and critically unquestioned, as, in Colleen Walsh's words, the novel witnesses 'an increasingly "hyper-individualistic society," where many people often choose to focus on the well-being of their small circle of family and friends' (2021, n.p.).

### Monster-Human Hybridity in Carey's *The Girl with All the Gifts* and *The Boy on the Bridge*

In Carey's *The Girl with All the Gifts* and *The Boy on the Bridge*, a similar contemporary immuno-politics becomes visible, again drawing on Gothic-Horror tropes of child exploitation and bodily dismemberment. While the militarized postapocalyptic setting of these novels seemingly sets them apart from Ishiguro's Hailsham, the latter's pastoral facade contrasting the mobilized violence of Carey's speculative battlefield, in all three texts an explicit authoritarianism cuts through this opposition, prioritizing a Gothic (British) landscape of unease and oppression. In Carey's novels, this encompasses a zombie 'school' on a military barracks, wherein hybrid 'hungry'-human children are captured and detained to be later dissected, in the meantime offered an education as a means of testing their reasoning capacities. As Dr Caldwell, the chief scientist, explains, 'When you walk into that classroom, you think you're talking to children. But you're not [...]. You're talking to the thing that killed the children. [...] I am interested in what's going on inside their heads' (Carey 2014, 60–2). Thus, a programme of rationalistic bioscience places examination above cross-species empathy, looking to analyse and dissect these zombie children for immunological objectives.

Under this pretence of biomedical investigation, positioning the children as disposable test-subjects in the search for a vaccine, the novel's Gothic understanding of immunology is made explicit. As Miss Justineau responds, 'You're dissecting kids! [...] My God, you're the wicked witch in a fairy tale'

(Carey 2014, 56), thus pinpointing the rapacious nature of this scientific programme. However, more centrally, what comes through in this passage is the presumptive callousness of immunological thinking, where Anthropocene survival overshadows and dismisses all other concerns. As Caldwell again reflects, '*The class* is a maze you've built for them to run through. Don't reify it into something that merits consideration on its own account' (ibid., 62–63). In other words, empathy and compassion for these 'hungry' children is denied on the back of biomedical 'progress': the children are introduced *into* human society (or the *munus*), only to be excluded.

The horror-inspiring scenes portrayed in conjunction with this project, including accounts of children caged in cells at gunpoint, and graphically detailed panoramas of unanesthetized cranial dissections (ibid., 5, 41–5), further reiterate the Gothic implications of this viropolitical outlook, describing, for example, how one child's eyes continue 'tracking [Caldwell's] movements' even after the top of his skull has been plied open with a screwdriver, his spinal cord removed and his brain sliced into pieces (ibid., 44–5). What is critical here, alongside the gore, is the way in which these stylized Gothic passages also bring to attention the fungus' complex ecosystem, registering how this hungry-human hybrid biome eludes the immuno-oriented viewpoint of contemporary bioscience. Take, for example, the following passage, focalized by Caldwell:

> With a pleasant tingle of anticipation, she puts her eyes to the output rig. The central nervous system of the Wainwright House hungry is instantly there, laid out before her avid gaze. Having chosen green as the key colour, she finds herself strolling under a canopy of neuronal dendrites, a tropical brainforest. [...] She sees exactly how the cuckoo *Ophiocordyceps* builds its nests in the thickets of the brain – how its mycelia wrap themselves, thread-thin, around neuronal dendrites, like ivy around an oak. Except that ivy doesn't whisper siren songs to the oak and steal it from itself. (Ibid., 387)

In this passage, on the one hand, Caldwell begins to appreciate the symbiotic nature of the *Ophiocordyceps* fungus, which refuses to feed on the neurons to which it attaches, in this way explaining how these 'hungry' children continue to resist zombification. As she puts it later on in the narrative, 'it doesn't feed on the brain. It gets nourishment only when the host eats. It's become a true symbiote rather than a parasite' (ibid., 432). In other words, this fungus evidences a different, non-traditional and second-generation order of human-zombie relations, one which functions in terms of symbiosis, rather than parasitism. Nevertheless, even as this awareness comes to her while looking through her microscope, Caldwell finds herself confused by her metaphorical thinking, this appraisal of the fungus *as forest* testing her received, immunological hermeneutic. As she tells herself, 'Cuckoos? Ivy? Sirens? Focus, Caroline [...]. *Look at what's in front of you, and draw appropriate inferences where the evidence exists to support them*' (ibid., 387). In other words, she struggles to accommodate an incipient awareness that biomedicine is not what she assumes and that, to the contrary, it encompasses cooperation and cross-species interaction.³

Moreover, while Caldwell herself resists and denies this cooperative viewpoint, the protagonist, Melanie, readily embraces it, quickly recognizing how her own hungry identity favours a symbiotic outlook, and more largely, a planetary-oriented critique of immunology. As she reflects,

> There's no cure for the hungry plague, but in the end the plague becomes its own cure. It's terribly, terribly sad for the people who get it first, but their children will be okay and they'll be the ones who live and grow up and have more children of their own and make a new world. (Carey 2014, 456)

In other words, Melanie recognizes how the brutalities enacted on the hungry populations do not ultimately contribute to saving the planet: humans will continue to die, and 'in the end the world will be empty' (ibid., 456). The advantage of allowing the fungus to spread, then – and indeed, in catalysing its advancement, as Melanie does – is to permit the continuation of a new, more ecocritical and outward-looking community: one whose hybrid status contests immunological violence in favour of cohabitation. Borrowing Neel Ahuja's words, this gesture transforms 'the dominant military' paradigm into an 'ecological balance and a problem of reproducing the self by managing the complexity of its interspecies relation' (2016, 13). It favours networked inter-connection and movement over individualist 'essentialism' (Ahuja 2016, 15–16).

As Johan Högland remarks, this ecocritical reading introduces a Gothic petition on behalf of the planet: 'a request to form emotional attachments across the species barriers erected by Enlightenment anthropocentrism' (2022, 266). In other words, it negotiates a classic sci-fi horror trope, the zombie plague, only to turn this on its head, challenging the 'typical resolution [of...] machine gun fire and the antidote produced by the scientists sheltered by this fire' (Högland 2022, 264–5), in favour of the successful survival of the 'hungry'-human population. Indeed, as Högland reflects, the publication of *The Boy on the Bridge* not as a sequel, but rather a *prequel* to this novel is significant in that it upsets the dominant biomedical presumption regarding the supposedly 'natural' origins of the fungus, making explicit 'that anthropogenic manipulation of the fungus was the probable cause' (2022, 261). This message comes through in a revelatory scene in the latter novel in which the protagonist, Stephen Greaves, considers how an earlier version of the fungus, *Cordyceps*, was prized in Chinese folk legends 'as a treatment for heart disease and impotence', and how 'later generations found that the fungus could grow through damaged nerve tissue and partially repair it' (Carey 2017, 199). In this way, scientists came to theorize that 'these medicinal uses of the fungus were the precursors to the hungry plague – the doorway through which *Cordyceps* infected human populations' (ibid., 199).

Put differently, *The Boy on the Bridge* further clarifies how current widespread illnesses find their cause largely in *human* attitudes and behaviours, as an 'overuse of antibiotics both in human health care and in animal farming' and 'the release of chemicals and microplastics into the environment' contribute to what is otherwise perceived as unpredictable pandemics (Högland 2022, 256–7). The corresponding dispatch granted through this prequel text, again coherent with the other-centred politics of Carey's earlier novel, is thus that immunology erroneously blames the fungus/virus/bacteria, seeing this as an environmental predator or parasite, rather than critically considering its contextual relationship to Capitalocene institutions. In ignoring ethically dubious medical and farming practices, environmental pollutants and unhealthy diets, which might otherwise explain both viral pandemics and 'non-communicable diseases' (Högland 2022, 256), this outlook contributes to an overly simplistic view of medicine and illness, seeing these ahistorically and without attention to contextual factors. In other words, it reiterates an immunological architype of self *vs* Other or human *vs* monster, without attention to relevant social, cultural, and economic practices.

## Frankenstein for the Pandemic: Ishiguro's *Klara and the Sun*

This reading thus offers a damning take on contemporary biomedicine, especially as this ignores the human body's complex and multi-species eco-system, but also as it extends this exclusionary politics to encompass both minorities and the planet. As Nixon comments, immunology 'revealed the physicality of humanity's connections to itself', but 'also simultaneously mutated this concept of connection into that which did not support the whole, but rather deeply threated individual existence within the social body' (2020, 4). In other words, it transformed the human body into a (much rehearsed) metaphor for a militarized body politic battling against foreign invasion, even where no threat was visible or where cohabitation might result as more productive.

Ishiguro's *Klara and the Sun* offers yet another pandemic-era response to this biomedical anxiety, reaffirming global capitalism's central role in spreading and maintaining human illnesses, even as it also considers the normalized function of posthuman 'monsters' as immunological scapegoats.[4] In this framework, the central premise of a futuristic society in which serious maladies produced by genetic 'lifting' confine children to ongoing bedrest and online schooling, effectively prophesies the soon-to-be-real onslaught of the COVID-19 era – this, despite the fact that the novel itself only arrived on bookshelves in early 2021. The central conceit implicit within this premise – that genetic enhancement authorizes child-endangering technologies, thus endorsing a deeply ethically compromised viewpoint on social 'progress' – effectively reinforces immunology's implicit violence as a form of biomedical thinking, seeing humanity waiving its children's health in a frantic effort to 'get ahead'. In other words, the novel confronts the Capitalocene's problematic reliance on science as an authorized form of competition, bringing into relief what Aspasia Stephanou identifies as 'displaced anxieties about the monstrosity of the neoliberal system itself' (2017, 29).

One implicit takeaway from this viropolitical reading is that the 'monster' most visibly present in the novel – the AI robot, or 'Artificial Friend' – is *not* in fact the only, or perhaps even the primary focus of the text's Gothic narrative. Klara, the narrator, is of course a recognizable Gothic figure, her story incorporating an overt Frankensteinian subtext, wherein a 'mad-scientist', Mr Capaldi, offers to remodel her identity so as to 'continue' the infirm Josie. As Capaldi explains, 'The new Josie won't be an imitation. She *really will be Josie. A continuation* of Josie. [...] I'll use everything I've learned to train the new Josie up there to be as much like the former one as possible' (Ishiguro 2021, 208). The sci fi horror conceit implicit in this passage – invoking 'an unnamed "Creature" composed of [in this case, technological, rather than] human and animal parts, brought to life by the scientist's ambition' (O'Loughlin 2021, 85) – fuels the fiction's Gothic critique of a (neo)colonial and patriarchal Capitalocene science, especially as Klara emerges, like Shelley's 'Creature', as systematically exploited. In Franco Moretti's terms, she is the quintessential 'worker', 'denied [...] an individuality' and belonging finally to her owner, just as the 'Creature' himself 'belongs wholly to his creator' (Moretti 2005, 85). It is no surprise then, that she is compared to a vacuum cleaner and made to ride in the trunk of the family car (Ishiguro 2021, 145, 174).

This narrative thus presents one facet of how the novel's Gothicism functions to critique Capitalocene institutions, chronicling their *ongoing* and technologically invested capacity for humanist violence. As Amit Katwala comments, 'AFs occupy one of the lower rungs of the ladder – they follow their owners around like loyal puppies until they're no longer wanted' (2021, n.p.): in other words, they facilitate majoritarian privilege similarly to the way the clones do in Ishiguro's earlier novel, even as they also confront social hatred and blame for their supposed parasitism – for example, when a woman harasses Klara for 'tak[ing] the jobs' and then 'the seats at the theatre' (Ishiguro 2021, 242). Even so, at the other end of this materialist analysis is the knowledge that widespread illness itself *predicates* these social interactions, describing the very condition upon which 'AFs' are invited to enter into this community. Within this framework, what might be conceived as ultimately *most* monstrous for this *polis* are the Capitalocene institutions underpinning its social ties, introducing immuno-oriented technologies to 'lift' children's genomes and in this way maintain a competitive and market-driven individualism. Put differently, Frankenstein is here, as in Shelley's novel, more properly the scientist (or scientists and politicians) leading biotechnology itself, rather than their supposedly monstrous creation.

Indeed, this materialist understanding of contemporary science and medicine, like that of Carey's novels above, can be seen to encompass not only sci fi Gothic concerns regarding the ethically slippery direction of contemporary technology, but also and more principally, a Gothic revisionist reading of biomedicine enfocusing interspecies cohabitation and exchange. What is initially seen as 'invading' or 'parasitic' is subsequently repositioned as relationary and participant, inviting re-reading of the robot/AI character in relation to her unique ability to interconnect worlds. This comes through in Klara's critical importance as a figure of *posthuman* affirmation, where this is understood not as transcendence or otherworldliness, but rather, connection: reframing human/non-human interaction in such a way as to challenge 'any notion of the bounded self or of individuality while, at the same time, *reinforcing* the trope of uniqueness by multiplying its specific markers' (Shildrick 2015, 9). In this way, Klara emerges as a model for exemplary cross-species behaviour, pioneering a new, posthuman take on critical environmentalism: where what is celebrated is not human empathy for the planet, but rather embodied vitality, understood as a relational outlook on one's surroundings. In this qualification on Klara's significance, the novel seems to draw on recent posthumanist theory, most visibly in the work of Rosi Braidotti and N. Katherine Hayles.

Thus, for Braidotti, humanism is not the empathetic or beneficious sociopolitical philosophy that many believe it to be, but rather encodes a history of strategic oppression against various minorities, including 'sexualized, racialized and naturalized others, who are reduced to the less than human status of disposable bodies' (2013, 15). 'We are all humans,' Braidotti writes, 'but some of us are just more mortal than others' (ibid., 15). More generally, decades of feminist, postcolonial, Marxist, and eco-critical theory have sought to expose exploitation and disenfranchisement, making evident how these so-called '"others" raise issues of power and exclusion' (ibid., 15). Set against the novel's framework of immunological bioscience, which sees humans as the rightful arbitrators of the planet, this perception underlines one central concern for contemporary viropolitics, where precisely due to humanism's implicit biases, some populations are consciously *left outside* biomedical jurisdiction; some (like Rick and his friends) positioned as exceptions to the socio-political norm. As Cohen likewise writes, 'modern presumptions about personhood and collectivity saturate both immunity and defense. [...] Both [...] play central roles in framing what we now understand as liberal or democratic governance' (2009, 3), including biomedical governance as seen in Ishiguro's novel.

Responding to this history of discrimination, posthumanism offers itself as a model for a more *grounded* understanding, reinforcing the subject's 'embedded[ness] in a material world of great complexity' (Hayles 1997, 266): in other words, foregrounding the individual's inevitable materiality and entanglement with non-human matter. As Hayles writes, 'From the get-go, the posthuman subject is an amalgam, a collection of heterogeneous components, a material-informational entity whose boundaries undergo continuous construction and reconstruction' (1997, 243). Human embodiment thus becomes critical to posthumanism, providing a notion of life beyond mere 'inscription' or articulation – inserting 'back into the picture the flesh that continues to be erased in contemporary discussions about cybernetic subjects' (Hayles 1997, 246, 266), including that of figures like Josie, who may soon merge with Klara into another entity.

Similarly, Braidotti defends the figure of the posthuman robot precisely for its rejection of 'humanistic arrogance' and of 'the "exceptionalism" of the Human as a transcendental category' (2013, 28, 66). Put differently, she sees posthumanism as disavowing humanism and the Anthropocene's exceptionalist presumptions, instead favouring materialist thinking as a means to positioning the subject both contextually and relationally, as part of a wider '"assemblage" of human and non-human actors' (ibid., 45). As Peter Vermeulen likewise writes, 'posthumanism displaces humanist sensibilities by suggesting that they have never been more than an illusion' – it proclaims, 'the end of humanism by insisting that the discrete, disembodied entity of the human never existed' (2014, 123). In brief, it registers the *failure* of humanism precisely in its refusal of human relationality.

Returning to the novel, this understanding predicates this fiction's innovative championing of posthuman monstrosity, both as a metaphor for sympathetic 'Otherness' and as a model for a more planetary-oriented and anti-immunological thinking. More specifically, implicit in this text's Gothic framework is a critical recognition of humanity's *own* abject materiality, and with this also a need to engage with shared and cohabitational biosystems for the sake of mutual survival. This comes through, on the one hand, in the reader's dawning awareness that Josie is *not* in fact so different from Klara or other AI technology, and that moreover, the notion that Klara might 'continue' Josie not so unbelievable. As Josie's father reflects, 'science has now proved beyond a doubt there's nothing so unique about my daughter, nothing there our modern tools can't excavate, copy, transfer' (Ishiguro 2021, 224); there is something 'true' to Capaldi's idea that Klara can indeed 'be' Josie – indeed, this replaceability is central to the novel's posthuman viewpoint (ibid., 208, 224).

Moreover, even as Klara is shown to be able to 'continue' Josie, Josie herself is pictured as more *embodied* than she would like to admit, as repeated references throughout to her physical condition underline her materiality. For example, textual depictions of her illness, prominent in the second section of the novel, repeatedly emphasize its toll on her energy and mobility, just as, in contrast, her father's favoured nickname of 'animal' relates her perceived vitality (ibid., 187, 188, 198, 205). More generally, implicit within these passages is an awareness regarding Josie's underlying *corporeal* connections to the world, as well as her *affective* connections in her feelings of vulnerability, confusion, and pain. As Klara comments at one point, responding to a picture that Rick has drawn of Josie as a 'Water Blob': here, Josie resembles something entirely 'lack[ing] the usual human features', as she tries 'to protect herself' from the surrounding world – she reflects a kind of shapeless Otherness that does not 'represent a person at all' (ibid., 126–7). This non- or extra-human depiction thus reaffirms Josie's posthuman ties to her material surroundings: even as she tries to encase herself in a shielding bubble, her sensitivity comes through.

Indeed, repeatedly throughout the novel, humans are likened to monstrous or non-human figures, for example, when two strangers coming together appear as 'a large creature with numerous limbs and eyes' (Ishiguro 2021, 217), or when Josie herself is said to become 'part of a shape the five girls [in a room] made together' (ibid., 74). More largely, what Klara's pixilated and off-kilter perception makes clear is another, more complex order of human life, wherein regular divisions and oppositions between individuals are no longer relevant. Under this monstrous, posthuman perspective, discrete individualism falls apart, replaced instead by a critical consciousness of underlying relationality and interconnection. To borrow Margrit Shildrick's words, these images reveal the 'science of self/non-self-discrimination' to be 'illusory' (2015, 95). Klara's posthuman viewpoint offers a clue to planetary entanglement, the 'chimerism' of interpersonal or inter-species connectedness and exchange.

Klara's titular reverence for a 'kind' and 'nourishing' 'Sun' can also be seen as an aspect of this posthuman perspective, as her technological dependence upon the sun makes her especially aware of its critical necessity (Ishiguro 2021, 6, 29, 37, 166, 276). Confined to the 'AF' store at the start of the novel, and later to Josie's house after she is purchased, Klara feels strongly the need for regular sunlight, which allows her to re-charge her batteries and to see the world more clearly. On the one hand, this dependence is visibly misunderstood by Klara in her relationship with Josie, conceived under a messianic fervour which sees her praying for it to 'save' the latter: asking it to 'show his great compassion to Josie' to make her well (ibid. 2021, 273). Nevertheless, in another sense, Klara is indeed right to revere the sun as part of a larger extra-planetary eco-system, which, as the barn next to Josie's house makes clear, does indeed 'feed' both human and non-human life, allowing for its sustenance, growth, and development. In this sense, the anger Klara harbours towards 'Pollution' is in fact a critical facet of the novel's posthumanism (ibid. 29, 220, 272), urging greater reverence for the planetary eco-system as a means to joint survival. More generally, what comes through in this titular focus on the sun is again the interconnectivity of human and extra-human life, again reinforcing a 'monstrous' critique of immuno-political thinking.

## Conclusion

Looking back on all four novels, then, what becomes evident throughout these texts is a conjoint focus on Gothic Otherness, understood not as form of violence or threat, but rather, symbiotic thinking. In each case, these texts situate this in a dystopic contemporary setting, wherein biopolitics have become the socio-political and medical norm, and wherein immuno-centric procedures see children sacrificed for the 'greater good'. Nevertheless, through a Gothic introduction to the 'sympathetic monster', and contrastingly, to the unsympathetic monstrousness of neoliberalism, these narratives allow their readers to question Capitalocene arrogance and to envision posthuman entanglement and humility.

# Notes

1. It is worth highlighting the recent popularity of the female monster or witch in connection with themes of illness, poisoning, and contagion, especially in works navigating the porous boundary between fantasy and the Gothic, as well as in historical Gothic fiction. Notable examples include Stacey Halls' *The Familiars* (2019), Bethany Clift's *Last One at the Party* (2021), C. J. Cooke's *The Lighthouse Witches* (2021), Angharad Walker's *Once Upon a Fever* (2022), Kat Dunn's *Bitterthorn* (2023), and Kirsty Logan's *Now She is Witch* (2023).
2. Writing on the twentieth-century Gothic, Lucie Armitt notes how 'we reinvent Gothic horror most absolutely and "feel" it most acutely in relation to the threats we believe face our children' (2011, 3). This seems to me also relevant to the twenty-first-century Gothic, as evidenced by the child-centred narratives of Ishiguro and Carey's novels, as also by the film adaptations of these.
3. The symbolic violence of the scalpel is also critical to this scene, reaffirming the role of the scientist as aggressor. Indeed, while Dr Caldwell is a woman, what J. Andrew Brown writes of this instrument is clearly true here, namely that it 'functions as a phallic object, metallic and penetrating and in whose function we see the application of the mechanical to the organic as it acts as the prosthetic extension of the desiring male gaze' (2010, 13).
4. I also discuss these posthuman politics in a longer reading of the novel and its view on twenty-first-century community – see Horton (2022). A brief section of that chapter appears here, though with a slightly different phrasing and orientation.

# 9

# Wet Gothic

## Ecofeminism and Horror in Julia Armfield's *Our Wives Under the Sea*, Daisy Johnson's *Fen*, and Zoe Gilbert's *Folk*

Chapter 8 ends with a celebration of 'chimerism', understood in terms of inter-species coexistence within an individual organism – functioning to overthrow the exclusionary (bio)logic that the body and immunity so often represent within contemporary culture (see Shildrick 2015). By contrast, this chapter begins with this same notion as a basis for approaching recent Gothic engagements with water: or more specifically, the supposedly fixed and unmoving (but ultimately hybrid and dynamic) coastlines, wetlands, rivers, and oceans included under the banner of 'Wet Gothic'. As Emily Alder notes, this watery interest – what she herself refers to as 'Nautical Gothic', in this way favouring the sea and maritime passages – is a critical element of the genre's long and topographically amorphous cultural history, which has nevertheless only recently come to attention as a legitimate focus of scholarly interest:

> General discussions of the sea, oceanic, nautical, maritime, or any other kind of watery Gothic are not to be found in the recent companion volumes of *Encyclopedia of the Gothic* or *The Gothic World*, while the introductions to *Dark Cartographies* and *EcoGothic* are silent on the subject of the sea despite attention to it in contributing chapters. (Alder 2017, 3)

On a similar note, Marek Błaszak comments on how 'owing to the incorporation of the sea, Gothic fiction as such seems to have acquired an extra dimension', wherein new readings of 'Gothic novels with a view to the sea, such as *Melmoth the Wanderer* or *Dracula*, together with scholarly focus on the Gothicized rendering of the sea in later nautical fiction' offer a new angle on this already much-read modality (2021, 41). More generally, recent critical conversations between the Gothic and oceanic studies register a shared interest in expanding this field, acknowledging how 'there is already a decidedly Gothic dimension to a critical framework championing "nonhuman scale and depth" and "multi-dimensional flux"' – both decidedly Gothic attributes (Packham and Punter 2017, 17).

For scholars interested in the Gothic's material dimensions more specifically, this is inviting. Alder notes how water's long-lived and multisided role within the genre need not be read under conventional Enlightenment principles of Gothic sublimity but can instead be celebrated as 'a critical position in itself' (Alder 2017, 6). She elaborates, 'nautical Gothic [is] a project that recognises the sea's distinctive material, conceptual, and social characteristics and the intersections between those and its metaphorical and narrative uses', rather than simply being seen as 'timeless, inhuman, impervious, trackless, and empty of history' (ibid.). On a similar note, Jimmy Packham and David Punter also underline a need 'to foreground the lived experience of the sea' and to refuse a tendency to read this in 'fundamentally anthropocentric' terms (2017, 16–17). Accordingly, while these critics recognize classic sublime Gothic settings in the watery landscapes of (for example) Ann Radcliffe's *A Sicilian Romance* (1790), Samuel Coleridge's *The Rime of the Ancient Mariner* (1798), and Herman Melville's *Moby Dick* (1851), their readings prioritize generic engagements that reaffirm human and nonhuman interactions *beyond* the sea's surface, in ways that '"investigate questions of affiliation, citizenship, economic exchange, mobility, rights, and sovereignty"' (Alder 2017, 6; Blum 2013, 152). Put differently, Wet Gothic scholars highlight socioeconomic and political difficulties raised by watery immersions and trespasses, while also registering key Gothic interventions and challenges to these often ecophobic histories.

In the context of contemporary Britain, the importance of this project resounds against recent right-wing calls to exploit and expand national oceanic and wetland spaces in search of economic profit (Lynch 2023; Bowcott 2007) and to tighten and securitize Britain's coastal borders to expel sea-faring migrants (Adu and Syal 2023). Thus, Mark Bould notes how 'the monsters lurking in the great midden of the [Horror] genre' can also be connected to sea-faring passages and coastal encounters, in particular, those navigated by displaced climate refugees, often refused entry or 'labelled illegal immigrants, undocumented workers and economic migrants' (2021, 32, 31). Similarly, Jimmy Packham writes of how 'the coast – the space that illuminates Britain's relation to the wider world – [functions] as a potent site to explore a current crisis of national identity', especially as evidenced in 'the virulent and xenophobic language of Britain's 2016 EU membership referendum' (2019, 206). Arguably, this rhetoric has only worsened since that event, where, speaking on UK coastal borders in April 2023, Home

Secretary Suella Braverman warned of 'heightened levels of criminality when related to the people who've come on boats', while Immigration Minister Robert Jenrick suggested that 'people who cross the Channel [...] threatened to "cannibalise" the UK's compassion' (Adu and Syal 2023). Within this far right discourse, Wet Gothic emerges as a politicized and topical contemporary modality, often concerned to disrupt antagonistic watery readings, and to open up national waters and wetlands to more fluid passages and cohabitations.

Such sea-oriented concerns already inform several previous texts examined in this study, including Tash Aw's *The Harmony Silk Factory* (with its spectral vision of colonial ventures into the South China Sea); Helen Oyeymi's *White is for Witching* (with its monstrous take on coastal Dover); Mohsin Hamid's *Exit West* (with its fantastic sea-facing doors and oceanic crossings); and Sarah Moss' *Ghost Wall* (with its dark, folklore-inspired reading of the Northumberland boglands). Despite this (often implicit, rather than explicit) attention to water's importance within the genre, however, critical scholarship in this field remains incipient, especially when it comes to new fiction only recently published. Accordingly, this chapter draws attention to new British women's writing in this modality, specifically tied to an ecofeminist agenda, and to a view of water as not only uncanny, but also eerie, weird, and monstrous – radically Other, but intimately intertwined within humanity's own weird history. Texts comprised here, alongside those which I examine, include: Michelle Paver's *Dark Matter* (2010), Lane Ashfeldt's *Saltwater* (2014), Sarah Perry's *The Essex Serpent* (2016), Jenn Ashworth's *Fell* (2016), Lucy Wood's *The Sing of the Shore* (2018), Daisy Johnson's *Everything Under* (2018), Chloe Aridjis' *Sea Monsters* (2019), Kirsty Logan's *The Gloaming* (2019), Jan Carson's *The Fire Starters* (2019), Sarah Moss' *Summerwater* (2020), Susanna Clarke's *Piranesi* (2020), Molly Aitken's *The Island Child* (2020), Sarah Hall's *Burntcoat* (2021), and Chloe Timm's *The Seawomen* (2022), all of which identify Wet Gothic anxieties regarding dark and uncanny waters connected both to ecophobic patriarchal systems and capitalist institutions. In Guilia Champion's words, they reflect 'fear *with* the ocean', rather than fear *of* or even *for* this (2022, 290). Their squelchy depths and fluid and leaky movements affirm a Wet Gothic ecofeminist engagement with new immersive 'becomings' and chimeric belongings.

In this chapter, I examine Julia Armfield's *Our Wives Under the Sea* (2022), Daisy Johnson's *Fen* (2016), and Zoe Gilbert's *Folk* (2018) with a view to reinforcing this critical reading, highlighting watery transformation and dependencies which exemplify Wet Gothic ecofeminism. As Astrida Neimanis comments, one shared problem for humanist and 'phallologocentric' thinking alike, especially in the context of contemporary neoliberalism, is an insistence on overlooking humanity's connectedness to other organisms, including those found in water (2019, 3). 'With a drop of cliché,' Neimanis argues, 'I could remind you that our human bodies are at least two-thirds water, but more interesting [...] is what this water does – where it comes from, where it goes, and what it means along the way' (ibid., 2):

> Our wet matters are in constant process of intake, transformation, and exchange – drinking, peeing, sweating, sponging, weeping. [...] For us humans, the flow and flush of waters sustain our own bodies, but also connect them to other bodies, to other worlds beyond our human selves. Indeed, bodies of water undo the idea that bodies are necessarily or only human. (Neimanis 2019, 2)

Margrit Shildrick, writing on contemporary biomedicine, also underlines this watery connection, highlighting the 'leakiness' of human bodies and emphasizing how research in this field contests Anthropocentric exceptionalism and a 'highly damaging historical elision between women and their bodies' (1997, 10). She explains, 'neither the feminine nor the body itself are valorised as lived presences', each instead being seen as 'both absent and excessive' – too disruptively disproportionate to be admitted under the Capitalocene's rationalistic categories (ibid.). Accordingly, the strength of ecofeminism is its confirmation that *all* bodies are in fact fluid, but also that specific historical denials of this reality obstruct feminist, decolonial, and planetary advances in key ways. As Donna Haraway writes, an attention to our own 'Chthulucene' weirdness *in* and *through* new ecological engagements, allows us to take seriously other 'organism's practices, their interventions and experiments crafting interspecies lives and worlds' in ways that might, if viewed receptively, inform our own (2017, M32). The more we can do this, she suggests, the more successfully we will learn to take care of each other: 'No one acts alone', she writes: 'connections and corridors are material [...]. Stories for the Anthropocene must learn with these complex histories' (ibid., M44).

Developing this outlook in the following pages, I connect it to the Wet Gothic politics of Armfield's novel and Johnson and Gilbert's short stories, reaffirming how these fictions at once denounce Capitalocene practices and explore chimeric, ecofeminist cohabitation. I would stress that this writing is not without hesitancies regarding how possible it is to 'stay with the trouble' (in Haraway's diction), or in other words, to successfully engage inter-species modes of connection in pursuit of change (2017, M44). Repeatedly indeed, these fictions contemplate Capitalocene and patriarchal appropriations of water in dark and disturbing forms, as well as parochial readings of folkloric legends in pursuit of reactionary purposes. Even so, by chronicling Gothic transformations aligned to ecofeminism, and more largely, registering shared (often institutionally unrecognized) dependencies on water – common between human *and* nonhuman bodies – these fictions proffer significant modes of thinking *outside* the dominant terrestrialism, and likewise *beyond* established global capitalist and patriarchal world systems.

## Weird Transformation and the Deep in Julia Armfield's *Our Wives Under the Sea*

Shortlisted for the *Sunday Times* Writer of the Year in 2019 and winner of both the White Review Short Story Prize in 2018 and the Pushcart Prize in 2020, Julia Armfield is a salient new writer in the Gothic-Horror milieu. The two intertexts referenced in her first novel's epigraph, *Moby-Dick* (1851) and *Jaws* (1974), immediately establish the Wet Gothic modality navigated by *Our Wives Under the Sea*. In the first of these, the juxtaposition between 'subtleness' and 'dreaded creatures [. . .] treacherously hidden beneath the loveliest tints of azure', immediately institutes an uncanny aesthetic characterized by concealed turbulence and unknown dangers. That this is attributed both to the sea and the human psyche is further reinforced by this opening passage, wherein Melville questions: 'and do you not find a strange analogy to something in yourself?' (Armfield 2022, epigraph). By contrast, the second excerpt, taken from *Jaws*, more bluntly underscores this landscape's brute materiality, indicating how the science explaining the incidents witnessed in the film indicates nothing more complex or multipart than 'Drowning'. In this way, the intricacy of uncanny depths and surfaces, seen as facets both of the psyche and the sea, is contrasted with the brutal violence of oceanic suffocation in the event of being attacked by a giant shark: what starts as a statement about subjective multidimensionality ends as a reflection on bodily agony and torture. The uncanny is juxtaposed to horror and monstrous megalodon feeding.[1]

This contrast between *unheimlich* dream-depths and material horror informs the central structure of the novel itself, which in one sense concerns a reflection on the pain of separation and abandonment propelled by the protagonists' estrangement, and on the other, navigates a horror-laden realm of watery Otherness. What Sarah Waters describes as a 'wonderful novel, deeply romantic and fabulously strange' could in this way be read to indicate bittersweet sentiments emerging from the fracturing of a touching love story. That this response is bluntly quoted in yellow on the novel's cover further indicates its centrality to the text's marketing: not as a tale of sea-bound horror or promise, so much as a deliberation on human loss and disaffection accompanying a break-up. As the inside cover reflects, 'It's a story of falling in love, loss, grief, and what life there is in the deep, deep sea' (Armfield 2022, cover).

Nevertheless, drawing attention to the second epigraph and to its Horror-genre message and inception, there is something important to what Waters refers to here as 'fabulously strange', and indeed to what the inside cover articulates as the 'deep, deep sea': in short, the text is entranced by weird and unknown creatures found at the very bottom of the ocean, and by how the sea's depths escape and confound human preconceptions. Likewise, it also underlines a post- or extra-human Gothic awareness of our own interconnection to the sea and other waters, even as we perceive the ocean (and indeed, experience it) as threatening. That the central narrative is structured not only as a bi-part reflection split between the viewpoints of estranged lovers, but also as a descent into the deep – characterized by carefully demarcated zones of degree and succession, ever downward – further reinforces this interest, gradually immersing the reader, alongside Leah, into the ocean's dark gravities. Leah herself transforms in this encounter into the scaly and flippered body of a sea creature, in this way highlighting a human connection to the ocean's radical difference. Through this metamorphosis, what Packham and Punter explain as a Poean 'displacement of the human by the nonhuman in the ocean depths', and as a 'Shakespearean "sea-change" through which the mutable human body is transfigured' (2017, 20) is clearly paramount, shaping the novel's ecofeminist politics and its posthuman engagement with 'weird' transmutation.

Indeed, throughout the novel the uncanny and horror are aesthetically juxtaposed, as when Miri registers the painful, dreamlike experience of being accompanied but still 'alone', while Leah retrospectively navigates her memories of a strange, unknown, and never 'empty' sea (Armfield 2022, 4). It is worth revisiting, in order to better understand this opposition, the critical writing of China Mieville and Mark Fisher, both writers key touchpoints on the speculative categories of the 'weird', 'haunted', and 'eerie'. Notably, each of these critics sees these notions expressly in relation to their readings of M. R. James, but also in connection with their views on late capitalism and Britain's neoliberal politics. For Mieville, James is misunderstood as the writer of haunting ghost stories, as his fiction more aptly reflects the anxieties of the weird: 'the touchability of his "ghosts" is not a return to that of their 18th-century cousins: this is a new (Weird) haptos, with little to do with human somaticism, and everything to do with the horror of matter' (Mieville 2011b). He reflects, 'James's repeated insistence that he is an "antiquary" is not convincing. He is acutely conscious of capitalist modernity, and a surprising number of his "ghosts" manifest through it' (ibid.). Put differently, Mieville suggests that James be reread under the guise of the Weird – including an attention to folkloric monsters 'more than once, *tentacled*' – but also that he be conceptualized as a Marxist, whose writing offers a critique of impinging capitalist systems: commenting on 'mass commodification' within 'the age of mechanical reproduction' (ibid.). A rejection of modern market relations is in this way conceptually implicit throughout Mieville's rereading, as well as in his understanding of the Weird more broadly as an anti-capitalist genre.

Mark Fisher responds to this analysis by further finessing Mieville's categories and suggesting a subtle differentiation between the 'weird' and the 'eerie', both of which he positions directly in opposition to the uncanny (or, as he puts it, the *unheimlich*). As he explains, while the *unheimlich* 'is commensurate with a compulsion towards a certain kind of critique, which operates by always processing the outside through the gaps and impasses of the inside', by contrast, 'the weird and the eerie make the opposite move: they allow us to see the inside from the perspective of the outside' (Fisher 2016, 10). The weird operates through a direct engagement with the Other: it is 'that *which does not belong*' – it 'cannot be reconciled with the "homely"' or the domestic, and therefore privileges incongruity and juxtaposition (ibid.). Contrastingly, the eerie is connected to anxieties regarding nonhuman responsibility and/or agency: it favours 'landscapes partially emptied of the human' and asks: 'What happened to produce these ruins, this disappearance? What kind of entity was involved? What kind of thing was it that emitted such an eerie cry?' (ibid., 11).

Again here, this differentiation propels a critique of late capitalism and of the violence of neoliberal politics, where these aesthetics speak to particular cultural anxieties and fears witnessed within a commodified and market-driven contemporary global society. Where the uncanny is psychological – concerned with an inside ('gap'-ridden) view of the outside – the weird and eerie are material and historically specific: disturbed by monstrous entities and abandoned landscapes, which fail to *fit in* within the present moment, or which *upset* this precisely on account of their (seemingly) unexplained or inexplicable occurrence. Such tropes, while potentially reflective of conservative viewpoints – James himself, of course, is well known for his reactionary politics – nevertheless *can* also denote an awareness of Otherness beyond the realm of 'capitalist realism' (Fisher 2014). They catalogue significant alternate experiences and perspectives

– as well as 'creeping authoritarianism and looming ecological catastrophe' – *outside* the remit of neoliberal claims that '*there [is] no alternative* to globalised capitalism' (Fisher 2014, xviii). Put differently, they speak to ecoGothic registers of Capitalocene violence.

Returning to Armfield's novel, what is immediately visible is just how directly these categories reflect the text's Wet Gothic aesthetics, where uncanny descriptions of Miri's distraught psychology are repeatedly juxtaposed with Leah's oceanic weirdness, and with a critical acknowledgement of eerie corporate/governmental experiments connected to the 'Centre for Marine Inquiry' (Armfield 2022, 37). The institutionalized language surrounding Leah's dive, together with Miri's inability to communicate with the centre, reflect an experience of knowledge concealed and events secretly managed, such that Leah's loss of power on the submarine is revealed as probably intended, rather than incidental. As Leah reflects, '[t]en minutes later, when the craft's whole system went offline, it would occur to me that the comms hadn't faded like a wavering signal so much as been switched off' (ibid., 11). There seems to be an organizational presence here covertly managing this catastrophe, reflecting what Robert MacFarlane describes as the eerie 'military and security infrastructure that occupies much of England's land and air space, from Salisbury Plain to Otterburn to Foulness' (2015), and in this case, also incorporating England's seas.

These weird and eerie relations are connected both to systems of power and to mundane interactions, affects, and sensations, as the routine contemporary world is revealed as a place of strangeness and distortion. The opening sentence describes the deep sea as 'a haunted house', where 'things that ought not to exist move about in the darkness' (ibid., 3), in this way immediately recalling Fisher's definition of the weird as 'that *which does not belong*' (2015, 10). In the following sentence, when Leah then tilts 'her head to the side as if in answer to some sound' (Armfield 2022, 3), the eerie is expressly present: this is Fisher question of 'What kind of thing was it that emitted such an eerie cry?' (Fisher 2016, 11). We are not given a response to this question until the end of the novel, wherein it emerges in the form of a giant watching eye (Armfield 2022, 217). Similarly, evoking Mieville's reading of James as offering something more disturbing than the traditional ghost story, one character reflects, 'Most of the time, if you hear something speaking, it's not a ghost – it's something worse' (Armfield 2022, 156). Clearly, this is also the case here.

Perhaps equally significant to these modal reference points is that way the novel interweaves eerie and weird textual episodes disconnected from the main narrative, which, despite (or precisely on account of) their horror, say something meaningful about inter-species coexistence. For example, a newspaper article recounts a 'woman who ate improperly prepared seafood' and subsequently 'found the bodies of twelve tiny organisms, squirming with suckers' living in her mouth – a photograph presenting the woman holding these 'specimens' in a 'jam jar': 'ossified little bodies in their greenish liquid', while the caption reads '*Ms Moon presents her offspring*' (Armfield 2022, 28). While Miri responds to this article with disgust and expressly immunological violence, wanting 'to tell her it should all come out, every piece of it – bad cells extracted from her body' (ibid., 29), the novel itself encodes a different logic, noting how Leah resists this abjection, instead questioning Miri and embracing inter-species cohabitation. As she reflects, 'I remember only the vastness of the creature rising up before us and a sudden certainty that it had been here all along. [...] I wrote my name on the first page of the log book and pressed it to the window, so that the creature could see' (ibid., 217). This gesture of self-introduction sets the scene for Leah's gradual metamorphosis into a fish or sea creature, where her own body slowly adapts to the contours of the ocean.

These Wet Gothic tropes are overtly interlinked to women's bodies and lives throughout the novel: in the eerie and weird landscape of the deep, but also in the fluid and leaky delineations of female anatomy, where repeatedly, attention is drawn to 'slipping', 'spilling', 'floating', 'pooling', 'seething', 'bleeding', 'squelching', 'foaming', 'swelling', 'oozing', 'soaking' and 'sinking' bodily and oceanic fluids (ibid., 3, 8, 12, 15, 21, 29, 41, 71), including 'tide pools', salt water, bath water, 'buccal mucosa', blood and vaginal liquids (ibid., 42, 71, 28, 21, 26). As one passage would have it, 'I thought about my lungs being wrenched through my back and still swelling, contracting, thought of water spilling into the space where my ribcage had been and my lungs going on regardless' (ibid., 18–19). Here, the horror-laden description of forced drowning, taken from 'a practice in Norse mythology' (ibid., 18), underlines the materiality of watery immersion, even as it conjures the pain of separation. Indeed, the novel's jointly uncanny and weird registers are intertwined in what can be read as both intimately personal and distinctly political: as indexes of individual pain and trauma, but also of 'monstrous' Otherness otherwise unrecognized from a terrestrial viewpoint, and relatedly, as ecofeminist insights on environmental protest against neoliberal destruction. Borrowing from Neimanis, these watery bodies offer a challenge to 'the masculinist logic of sharp-edged self-sufficiency', while at the same time underlining 'our ethical responsibility towards the many other bodies of water we are becoming all the time' (Neimanis 2019, 4). 'Becoming', in this way, lies at the heart of the novel's deep-sea politics.

## Wetland Sacrifice and Superstition in Daisy Johnson's *Fen*

Daisy Johnson is another salient young voice within contemporary literature, having won the 2014 AM Heath Prize, the 2016 Harper's Bazaar short story prize, the 2017 Edge Hill Short Story Prize, and been shortlisted in 2018 for her debut novel *Everything Under* (2018). 'Starver', the first story of her 2016 short story collection, *Fen*, could easily be read as a direct intertext for *Our Wives Under the Sea*. While set in the Norfolk fens, rather than the ocean, it is also a story of a young woman's transformation into a fish, and likewise, it overtly ties this metamorphosis both to Gothic Horror and ecofeminist politics. In this case, negotiating a weird representation of female anorexia also comparable to Oyeyemi's *White is for Witching* – representing this *not* (or not only) as an eating disorder, but also as a stepping-stone for monstrous transmutation – this story responds to patriarchy by making clear its radical violence directed both at women and the planet, using this strategically to embrace watery Otherness and promote ecocritical thinking. If *Our Wives Under the Sea* starts with 'drowning' as its focal point for Wet Gothic horror, 'Starver' instead begins with 'starving' (Johnson 2016, 6) – connecting this to Gothic anxieties represented by fenland draining, as well as by the violence women enact on their own bodies with a view to phallogocentric approval. In this ostensibly self-destructive engagement, the narrator's sister at first seems to reject and destroy her own form, only later to reveal this as an act of self-conscious change, playing on patriarchal expectations to subvert and oppose the norm.

It is significant that, as in *Our Wives Under the Sea*, this story also negotiates weird watery imagery to reinforce its ecocritical politics, tying its Horror aesthetics to post- or extra-human visions of mud monsters, sea-faring vampires and women transformed into fish.[2] While Miri describes Leah in terms of 'a semi-porous membrane in place of what was once a solid scaffolding of muscle and skin' (Armfield 2022, 204), 'Starver' outlines how the narrator's sisters hands 'were not fingered now, only heavy unwieldy paddles she used', and how 'the flapping of gills shuttering on the side of her neck' (Johnson 2016, 13) betrays her excitement. Throughout the text, the sister requires increasing subaquatic immersion to stay alive, 'drinking gallons of water so her stomach swelled, mountain-like, out of her ribs' (ibid., 12), and inhabiting the bathtub to avoid 'drowning in air' (ibid.). Water in this way affords a nurturing, rather than threatening environment: it remains uncanny – even eerie – in its Otherness, but also promises freedom beyond that available on land. In entering the canal's dark realms at the close of the story, the sister escapes patriarchal violence in favour of movement and autonomy. As the narrator notes, her sister does not 'roll her white belly to message me goodbye' as she enters the water, but rather, '[o]nly ducked deep and was gone' (ibid., 14) in an embrace of difference.

This transgression and its celebration of wet Otherness is tied, with the story's first paragraph, to a critique of Capitalocene systems, where practices of land drainage see subaquatic life reduced either to foodstuffs or waste. 'There were too many eels', the narrator reflects, 'and not enough men. [...] They burnt the eels they could not eat in piles, stood watching' (ibid., 3). The sacrifice enacted here on these creatures can (in part) be understood in terms of what Jennifer Wenzel calls a '*resource logic*', whereby 'nature is understood as natural resource, disposed for human use and subject to human control' (Wenzel 2017, 169). When the eels do not cooperate in their predicted behaviours, and instead over-reproduce, they are culled, burned 'in piles' for being inedible. This violence is then juxtaposed in the story to a similar logic enacted on young women: in either case, bodies refusing consumption or expected performances of compliance are read as excessive, even monstrous, and then attacked and disposed. Notably, the narrator jumps to see her sister carried naked from a house-party bedroom: what disturbs her is not simply what this body looks like (partially transformed into a fish), but more significantly, what is left implicit about what has been done to her. 'Where are her clothes?' the narrator repeats twice over. Borrowing Justin D. Edward's words, 'it is not only nonhuman animals who are consumed' in this narrative. Rather, 'meat consumption and violence against animals are structurally related to other forms of violence, specifically against women' (Edwards 2022, 155).

Indeed, the problem goes beyond this crucial ecofeminist anxiety, where from the start it is clear that these workers *themselves* are being exploited under this system, and the explanations they propose for these events speak to their lurking unease regarding capitalist economic structures. As the narrator explains, not only do they burn the eels and 'stand watching', in a kind of ritual designed to expel a curse, they use this occasion to comment on 'a calling down of something upon the draining', even claiming to hear 'words coming from the ground' that explain how the pumping 'was what made the eels do it, starve themselves in that way' (Johnson 2016, 3–4). A further layer is thus added to the narrative (in retrospect), connecting the eels' starving to that of the sister, and reinforcing how this strategic disobedience, on both parts, manifests as a water-born protest against Capitalocene destruction – in this case, in what Timothy Morton describes as an 'agrilogistic space' (ibid., 76). As he reflects, 'Since agrilogistics requires human vectors, something in the structure of the inner logic of agrilogistics must mesh with the human desire to eliminate anxiety' (Morton

2016, 76). Accordingly, the aim in drainage is to make the land more amenable to farming, but also, when this fails, it requires other compensatory mechanisms as reparation. The men, alongside the ecosystem, are disadvantaged by their role in the draining economy, and their superstitious outlook reflects a troubled response to this awareness.

It is worth recalling that this is a *flat* landscape – indeed, the fens are also known as the Norfolk Broads, coming from the Old English brād, meaning 'flat, open, extended' (etymonline.com). Within this context, there is a sense (redoubled by popular folklore) in which not only *space*, but also *time* is extended, opened up to encompass *longer* and *deeper* planetary histories connected to the earth itself and *as the folklore would have it*, primordial (watery) rhythms. Within this viewpoint, as Rob Coley explains, 'natural or geopolitical resources become chthonic entities, manifestations of an occulted Planet that does not threaten the human antagonistically but in its utter neutrality to human life' (2017, 140). Arguably, this is what a later story in the collection – 'Birthing Stones' – references when it describes its mud-formed protagonist as 'limbed to the ground. To that place, this town. Like a root. Planted in' (Johnson 2016, 157). Her extra-human, chthonic state sees her rooted to the fens, and if not exactly indifferent to humanity, at least immersed in her own distinct, water-born preoccupations. Even so, the reference in 'Starver' to a 'calling down of something upon the draining' suggests a more sinister (or at least, aggrieved) force *acting* in these events: an agential entity protesting human violence. In other words, the earth is seen *not* as merely indifferent, but as angry and demanding retribution, in connection with what is presented as a long and local British folk tradition.

I would emphasize that this outlook is proffered by the (male) workers themselves in this story, who feel aggrieved in being denied food and ease in their exertions – who are not given *what they bargained for* in agreeing to work on this draining project. As Alan Dundes reflects, 'folk' logic is 'predicated upon a two-tier system whereby folklore and folk communities were seen as the subjugated element of a classist society' (1980, 2): the classic folk horror landscape reflects institutional divisions between the elite and the masses, connected both to pre-industrial communities and present-day agrarian society. As David Punter and Glynnis Byron explain, this isolated, rural backdrop often institutes a reactionary textual ideology even in more mainstream Gothic texts, wherein 'the Gothic is [...] associated with the primitive but this primitive has now become identified with the true, but lost, foundations of a culture' (2004, 5). Within this antiquated, farming context, 'the Gothic past is [...] seen as retaining [...] more power and vigour than the present' (ibid.), even as its traditions and rituals themselves reveal its datedness. Likewise, in folk horror, this sanctioning of the primitive becomes even more conspicuous: as Paul Cowdell explains, '[t]he superstitious peasantry, in all their muddy reality, move from background to centerstage in folk horror. They become less plot adjuncts than the defining milieu' (2019, 301). In this way, 'agrilogistic space' and its 'folk' values are established as textually central.

The problem, of course, is that this 'folk' outlook contributes in the text to further oppressive practices and institutions connected to the Capitalocene: its commitment to 'the land' often also endorses a commitment to parochial conservatism and patriarchal values. As Adam Scovell explains, the accent in this genre is on a landscape which 'isolates its communities and individuals, skewing the dominant moral and theological system enough to cause violence, human sacrifices, torture and even demonic and supernatural summonings' (Scovell 2016). The ceremonial burning the men enact on the eels in 'Starver' thus parallels the sacrificial brutality imposed on women throughout this collection: for example, in 'The Cull', wherein the offering the text describes finally encompasses a paganistic murder of both horse and female protagonist; or in 'The Scattering', where impregnation is repeatedly read in terms of animalistic patriarchal aggression. In both cases, the explicit gendering of practices 'tied to the land', and of local community relations understood as 'timeless' and 'universal', is revealed to authorize phallogocentric exploitation and destruction, with repercussions for women, minorities (or 'outsiders'), and the planet. The collection thus navigates this aggrieved and distorted folk perspective both to underline its overwhelming threat to human and non-human populations, and to register a critical need to take seriously a challenge to this politics, precisely in defence of ecofeminism.

The final story in the collection, 'The Lighthouse Keeper', reaffirms this anxiety explicitly, in this case foregrounding metamorphosis as a metaphor for 'staying with the trouble'. Here, the female lighthouse keeper whose perspective focalizes the story is bluntly aware of her gendered difference, concerned at once to admit and defend this. Recalling the condescension with which she is greeted by local fishermen, she reflects, 'They could say what they wanted about a woman lighthouse keeper. They could say anything they liked, and they would' (Johnson 2016, 180). Despite her critical consciousness of her oppressed position, the protagonist initially emulates a deferral to patriarchy, endeavouring to *prove* her professional adequacy by means of a series of carefully enacted tasks:

> She womanned the radio all night without feeling tired at all, sluiced and scrubbed the walkway up top in the early light shift, mopped the lens on her tiptoes so the water ran down and onto her face. Later she tidied the book piles

into alphabetical perfection, rearranging the cushions, put the shelves into system. (Johnson 2016, 180)

These sundry exertions – notably both domestic and linguistic, tied to practices of house-keeping and phallogocentric systems – underline her eagerness to meet patriarchal expectations. Rather than questioning this heteronormative and sexist matrix, she diligently acknowledges its dominance, and struggles to maintain her status within it, reinforcing what Claire Colebrook describes as the *taken-for granted* 'masculinity of reason' (2004, 40). As Colebrook explains, 'Traditionally, reason has been associated with qualities that have also been used to define men and male bodies', while 'not-yet-original, unthinkable and formless ground is feminine' (ibid., 52). Correspondingly, when the lighthouse keeper spots a fish whose size and power recalls the monstrous 'Other' of local folkloric legends – 'Fish like that could breathe air and travel on land – of that she was relatively certain' (Johnson 2016, 178) – her first instinct is to catch it, in this way confirming both her questioned authority and the fish's subordination: 'Nothing got rid of a fish curse as well as a feast', she reflects (ibid., 179).

Moreover, her will to eat the fish, and to feed it so as to catch it, again mimics a larger 'resource logic', reinstituting the Darwinian food chain as a symbol of Anthropocene dominance and control. As Simone Dennis and Alison Witchard reflect,

> Our access to flesh is made on the basis that it is significantly different from human flesh: we do not, by and large, consume our own flesh, but instead that of the animal other. This hierarchically arrayed difference is the basis upon which humans can enact culturally acceptable violence upon the body of the animal, to produce the fleshy commodification of its parts. (2015, 151)

By viewing the fish as an object of consumption, in other words, the lighthouse keeper exerts her own evolutionary ascendency over the animal 'Other', authorizing ingestion as a form of control and a violence legitimized by 'nature'. Forming strategies of preparation and capture, she imagines herself 'hunting to bring it head down onto the rock' and sees her efforts as a 'heroic endeavour', which consolidate her status as a local authority (Johnson 2016, 181–2).

Against this project, the protagonist's dawning awareness of this creature's 'almost human intelligence' and of the possibility that it may *not* be 'a food source or a pretty thing to watch but, maybe, a friend' (ibid., 184), grants her new perspective on her encounter, illuminating a possible companionship, as opposed to predation, which leads her to read her own life differently. Indeed, the protagonist's intuition that 'maybe everything that she'd guessed about the fish was wrong; that it was, rather, a sort of metamorphosis', hints at the possibility that this fish is in fact 'Starver's' sister character: a post- or extra-human lifeform come to elucidate to her the sea's nonconformity and freedom. Her subsequent decision to 'protect' the fish, and later, to join it, register a dawning consciousness around this awareness, allowing her to leave the land and physically embrace the unknown deep (Johnson 2016, 185). This immersive enactment sees her feeling 'something brushing at her leg', suggesting that she is not alone in this watery underworld, but has achieved a successful comradery (ibid., 192). The formless and 'Chthulucene' strangeness of the ocean thus registers a possibility of watery chimerism, a realization that circles back and critically informs the collection's first pages. This cyclical structure reflects and confirms the text's simultaneous Gothic and ecofeminist message, reasserting a critical commitment to posthuman becoming.

## Island Folklore, Monstrous Women, and Watery Desire in Zoe Gilbert's *Folk*

The fictions explored thus far involve watery submersions understood as willed, rather than forced, reflecting 'monstrous' female (and indeed 'monstrous-feminine') acts of protest and resistance in line with contemporary ecofeminist theory, and in line with a longer tradition of feminist critical Horror studies. To quote Barbara Creed in her seminal 1993 work *The Monstrous-Feminine*, these narratives see 'the *difference* of female sexuality as a difference which is grounded in monstrousness' (1993, 2) – they negotiate patriarchal fears and anxieties about women as a form of feminist empowerment, rather than shame, and they contest conventional active/passive gender binaries in order to enable the female reader, rather than confine her to masochism (ibid., 3). Indeed, what Creed more recently writes of Feminist New Wave Cinema can also be seen as relevant to these texts, not in terms of camera's eye or 'gaze', but rather, the narrative focalization and imagery of these fictions:

> The feminist gaze is not a reversed male gaze, nor is it a disembodied look. The feminist gaze invokes all the senses. It is compassionate and empathic; it invites the spectator to situate herself in the place of the protagonist on the screen, to experience what the other is experiencing through affect. It is an all-embracing sensory gaze, one that understands the protagonist's daily life, emotions, relationships, bodily states, and desires. (Creed 2022, 17)

The attention to affect in this passage, and to embodied emotions and relationships registered through a feminist lens, speaks to the materialist values encouraged by these fictions. Indeed, the onus in these texts on water, and on monstrous feminine encounters with watery spaces, buttresses this bodily emphasis throughout, where textual descriptions of fluidity, wetness, and water-bound liminality and immersion speak to materialist invocations of sensory difference, invocations here associated with both women and the planet. In *Our Wives Under the Sea*, this encompasses Miri's uncanny pain in confronting Leah's changing mind and body, but also Leah's own horror-induced shock in navigating the eerie depths of the ocean. Images of Leah 'silvered over, oystered at her elbow creases and around the neck', contrast abject descriptions of a giant 'eye rearing toward the ship' (Armfield 2022, 21, 216), revealing both uncanny and monstrous associations linked to Wet Gothic encounters. Similarly, in *Fen*, stories such as 'Starver' and 'The Lighthouse Keeper' accentuate sensual movements associated with weird and eerie geographies, where descriptions of 'thrash[ing]', 'flapping of gills', 'coming topside', and 'back-flipping' (Johnson 2016, 13, 184), in the context of dark unknown waterways, articulate monstrous aquatic and amphibian energies here connected to the liquidity of water. In both cases, the monstrous feminine behaviours of the protagonists harbour both feminist desire and ecological critique, overtly upending established Capitalocene modalities in favour of liberatory female, queer, and extra-human movements.

In Zoe Gilbert's *Folk*, set on the fantastical island of 'Neverness', based loosely on Gilbert's memories of the Isle of Man,[3] this female 'monstrosity' is also textually central, again scaffolding this collection's Wet Gothic critique of contemporary patriarchal institutions. The winner of the 2014 Costa Short Story Award (for 'Fishskin, Hareskin') and shortlisted for the International Dylan Thomas Prize, Gilbert's investment in folk horror aesthetics is visible from the start, the ceremonial and deeply traditional practices of Neverness situating this island as a site of male violence connected both to littoral and provincial spaces.[4] The opening story, 'Prick Song', recounts the horrific events of a yearly 'gorse running', in which young girls shoot monographed arrows into gorse bushes, and boys are required to find them to initiate the courting season. While at first this tradition seems relatively innocent, involving exhibitions of young love and chivalry on the part of boys seeking to impress their favoured partners, ultimately its brutality becomes evident, as the boys' flesh is torn apart by the brambles; girls are expected to reward the boys sexually; and unsuccessful boys may be shamed or even murdered. Angry at his lack of virility, the protagonist's father aggressively 'dunks him in the sea', urging him to be 'less like a girlie' and to prove his manliness

(Gilbert 2018, 10). This watery Neverland, then, is far from the fairy-tale paradise of Peter Pan and other island fables, instead exchanging innocence for ritualistic courtship in a way that is both vicious and institutionally mandated.

Like *Fen*, this short story collection is thus replete with patriarchal brutality, including a rape culture which meets communal approval, rather than being hidden or disguised. In 'Fishskin, Hareskin' and 'Water Bull Bride' this violence emerges at centre stage within the texts, where in the first case, a woman's marriage to a fisherman, who effectively buys her from her father for forty-two herrings, involves an unwanted pregnancy and domestic confinement under her stepmother's watch. As the protagonist, Ervet, reflects, 'When she scolds Ervet her voice is like a seal's bark' (Gilbert 2018, 16), chastising her for her domestic failures. In 'Water Bull Bride', a woman's efforts to express herself sexually likewise see her confined to her house and later, brutally raped by a local man while being asked, 'You like that, girlie?' (Gilbert 2018, 82). Here, *Folk* refuses to shy away from island horrors, instead overtly connecting these to local folklore, and to parochial 'watery' culture which manipulates local mythology in pursuit of phallogocentric power. As Dawn Keetley writes, the key aspect of folk horror is 'the monstrous "tribe"' community, which is 'bound together by shared (folkloristic) beliefs, traditions and practices' (2020, 9). This clan mentality is clearly apparent in these stories.

Nevertheless, these fictions also overtly contest this tribalism and undermine its authority, primarily via monstrous-feminine engagements with water: drawing attention to sea-oriented descriptions of bodily rage, desire, and love, which reinforce female characters' maternal confidence and open sexual expression. In 'Fishskin, Hareskin', this encompasses the pregnant protagonist's changing attitude towards her baby, whom she first imagines in the form of a fish, swimming and flipping in her body. As she reflects, 'Turpin planted inside her the gleaming herring that swelled her belly, all winter and into spring, slithering and flicking its awful tail' (Gilbert 2018, 15). This description registers the narrator's aversion to her child; she does not desire motherhood, just as she does not embrace her new life as a fisherman's wife: Turpin is preferable to her father, but also unchosen. Moreover, her move from her father's house to Turpin's is especially traumatic in requiring the death of her beloved hares, who are deemed 'the worst bad luck for a fisherman' but are her 'mawkins' (ibid., 15, 20). Thinking of Turpin, Ervet thus imagines him in distinctly abject terms: 'dragging up fish from their hidden swarms, dragging them up and bringing them home on his skin' (ibid., 21). Likewise, her baby is described as having 'fishskin' and a 'mouth that pops open and sucks at air' (ibid., 17). This focus on fleshly feeling and slippery contact – the abject touch of fish scales on human skin – articulates her revulsion towards her life as she now lives it and her indifference to her child. While her stepmother chides her for failing to manage her daily 'fishwife tasks' (ibid.) – for finding activities 'more pressing that making spick and span for [her] husband' (ibid., 16) – her underlying attitude is one of numbness and disgust.

This haptic tactility, in this way, sets the stage for the story's embodied affects, as it also plays with the reader's own unease around these fishy contacts and sensations. Borrowing Tarja Laine's words, this intimate experience 'move[s] outward' from text to reader 'as touch' (2006, 101), prompting a similar felt discomfort concerning Ervet's new life and fishwife identity. We see that Turpin treats her aggressively, 'gripp[ing] her by the shoulders' as she vomits due to morning sickness, and berating her as his mother does for her failures in housework and caring for the baby (Gilbert 2018, 22). Nevertheless, rather than allowing violence and abjection to continue as the dominant aesthetic in the text, the story makes room for contrasting emotions, granting Ervet *and the reader* hope via means of another haptic gesture. Returning to her father's house, where the hares' skins hang in the corner of the leanshed, Ervet takes one down and wraps it around the baby: 'The feel of the fur warmed from within is soothing sweet' (ibid., 26). In this way, this monstrous-feminine enrapture – swapping baby skin for leveret fur; exchanging human touch for animal softness – allows the child to become her 'mawkin' itself, a creature she can love despite her trauma and despite its ties to her fisherman husband. The story thus ends endearingly, with Ervet 'fold[ing]' herself around the baby on the floor (ibid.), adding yet another layer of skin to the swaddling.[5]

In 'Water Bull Bride', the story again moves from horror to female empowerment, however, more ambiguously, with obstacles along the way. The monster (or supposed monster) in this story is male, rather than female, though he stands in for the monstrous-feminine in so far as his animal lure relates the 'monstrous' power of female sexual desire. This is the titular 'water bull', who comes to the narrator on a stormy night, as strong winds 'beat for the devil to dance to, leaving the prints of hooves around the house' (ibid., 67). Following her grandmother's folklore-inspired stories, the water bull is the biggest threat to unmarried young women on the island: coming 'inland with the sea surf on wild nights' and disposing 'his bull-hide', he 'hunts himself a maiden' (ibid., 69). In this oceanic context, water negotiates double meanings: both as a source and cure for danger. 'The only way she can save herself is to cross water' (ibid.), her grandmother tells her.

Touch is again central to this narrative, especially the touch of waterborn Otherness. Running her fingers through the water bull's hair as he rests his head on her lap, the narrator discovers 'tiny shells [...] hundreds of them, pinky white or crusted green, some trailing a ghost of hair behind them' (ibid., 68–9). These littoral artifacts alert the grandmother to the man's danger, but the girl fails to escape and is submerged in the river, where the water bull 'turns [her] easily in the currents and kisses [her]' (ibid., 71). While the grandmother's story foretells brutality, however, the scene which ensues is distinctly tender: the narrator relates how her movements loosen and soften, 'not as a struggling lump of a girl tangled in muddy clothes, but as waterweeds move in the eddies of a stream' (ibid.). Rather than pain, she recounts 'the sweetest ache I have ever felt' (ibid.), in this way contesting the older women's provincialism with an embrace of pleasure. The water bull becomes her liberator, setting her free to exercise female touch and sexuality.

Yet this is not the end. The rape scene mentioned above emerges as the supposed 'punishment' the young narrator receives for exercising her desires in this island setting, and for endeavouring to satiate her 'monstrous-femininity' with other men in the community. 'Trucks of sheets and frill-edged gowns are for daft-headed maidens', she reflects. 'Love is a dance with a water bull, it is the pleasure that poured from his fingers into me' (ibid., 76). Her embrace of touch in this way, in place of marriage, sets her against the local community, infringing provincial values as she moves from lover to lover, declaring, 'I shall have a bull of a man' (ibid., 80–1). The important message here is one of sexual assertion, in that even despite her subsequent failure in this project – even despite her horrific, murderous rape – she does not denounce her memories of the water bull, but rather returns to these as a site of consolation. 'It is his gentle beast strength that carries me to the pool's edge,' she reflects, 'and his dive that saves me', as she imagines 'plunging into deep water [...], his arms about me' (ibid., 82). The violence enacted upon the narrator in the name of patriarchal control and discipline is in this way shown as inoperable and fruitless – the girl retains her recollections of pleasure and this releases her emotionally, even while what finally happens to her is left ambiguous. While the ending thus sees her grandmother mourning her absence from the island – sewing a dress of water weeds for the 'water bull bride' (ibid., 84) – the reader appreciates her desire not as her enemy, but rather, her strength.

## Conclusion

In summary, the fictions explored in this chapter navigate a range of Gothic sentiments and emotions connected to female sexuality and desire, but also to extra-human waters and planetary relationships opened up by Wet Gothic encounters. These depictions participate in ecofeminist politics by celebrating weird transformations and inter-species chimerism, as well as by recognizing 'monstrous-feminine' perspectives that disturb and upend the terrestrial norm. In the end, the most monstrous figures in these texts are the patriarchal and Capitalocene institutions represented within them, together with folkloric communities that discipline and punish women in the name of phallogocentric power. By exposing and challenging these horrific structures and pointing instead to alternatives of cohabitation, empathy, and contact, these texts make evident the importance, as well as the possibility, of 'staying with the trouble'.

## Notes

1 For a fascinating discussion of the more conservative dimensions of the Gothic megalodon, see Schell (2022).
2 I would note that Paul March-Russell also negotiates this speculative vocabulary in his reading of Johnson's collection, likewise tying it to the text's eco-feminist politics – see March-Russell (2020). While I have sought a different focus here in my attention to Wet Gothic transformations and chimerism in these stories, I remain indebted to his insights, which are plentiful.
3 See 'Folk, Folklore' (2021), wherein Gilbert describes the Isle of Man's central importance to the collection.
4 Sophie Parkes-Nield offers a fascinating discussion of Gilbert's representation of traditional folkloric practices, and especially 'summonings' (2022).
5 Sherilyn MacGregor's concept of 'ecomaternalism' seems especially relevant here, drawing on a perceived 'connection between women's caring for people and their environmental concern' and recognizing how ecofeminists often 'regard women's private identities as the bases for public engagement and political empowerment.' See MacGregor (2006), 4, 8.

# Bibliography

Abbas, S. (2014), *At Freedom's Limit: Islam and the Postcolonial Predicament*, New York: Fordham University Press.

Ackroyd, P. (1985), *Hawksmoor*, London: Penguin.

Adams, L. (2008), 'Torch Song for Afghanistan', *The New York Times*, Sunday Book Review, 11 October.

Addario, L. (2015), *It's What I Do: A Photographer's Life of Love and War*, New York: Penguin.

Adu, A. and R. Syal (2023), 'Suella Braverman: Small Boat Arrivals Have "values at odds with our country"', *The Guardian*, 26 April. Available at: https://www.theguardian.com/uk-news/2023/apr/26/suella-braverman-small-boat-arrivals-have-values-at-odds-with-our-country (accessed 16 June 2023).

Ahmed, A. (1997), 'Postcolonial Theory and the "Post-" Condition', *Socialist Register*, 18 March. Available at: https://socialistregister.com/index.php/srv/article/view/5695 (accessed 26 August 2023).

Ahmed, S. (2007), 'A Phenomenology of Whiteness', *Feminist Theory*, 8 (2): 149–68.

Aldana Reyes, X. (2015), 'Gothic Affect: An Alternative Approach to Critical Models of the Contemporary Gothic', in L. Piatti-Farnell and D. L. Brian (eds), *New Directions in 21st Century Gothic: The Gothic Compass*, 1st edn, 11–23, London: Routledge.

Aldana Reyes, X. (2018), *Horror Film and Affect: Towards a Corporeal Model of Viewership*, London: Routledge.

Alder, E. (2017), 'Through Oceans Darkly: Sea Literature and the Nautical Gothic', *Gothic Studies*, 19 (2): 1–15.

Alexandrescu, L. (2020), 'Streets of the "Spice Zombies": Dependence and Poverty Stigma in Times of Austerity', *Crime Media Culture*, 16 (1): 97–113.

Allardice, L. (2018), 'Sarah Waters: "Some of My Readers Really Did Hate Me. They Felt Let Down"', *The Guardian*, 15 September.

Allen, J. (2004), *Homelessness in American Literature: Romanticism, Realism, and Testimony*, London: Routledge.

Agamben, G. (1998), *Sovereign Power and Bare Life*, 1st edn, Redwood City, CA: Stanford University Press.

Ahmad, A. (1995), 'The Politics of Literary Postcoloniality', *Race and Class*, 36 (3): 1–20.

Ahuja, N. (2016), *Biosecurities: Disease Interventions, Empire, and the Government of Species*, Durham, NC: Duke University Press.

Aitken, M. (2020), *The Island Child*, Edinburgh: Canongate Books.

Alliheibi, F. M., A. Omar, and N. Al Horais (2021), 'The Reproduction of the Gothic Motifs of Frankenstein in the COVID-19 Journalistic Discourse: A Corpus-Based Critical Discourse Analysis Approach', *Journal of Language and Linguistic Studies*, 17 (3): 1129–40.

Anatol, G. L. (2004), 'A Feminist Reading of Soucouyants in Nalo Hopkinso's "Brown Girl in the Ring" and "Skin Folk"', *Mosaic: An Interdisciplinary Critical Journal*, 37 (3): 3–50.

Anderson, B. (2013), *Us and Them?: The Dangerous Politics of Immigration* Control, Oxford: Oxford University Press.

Anderton, J. (2020), 'The Postmillennial Rise of British Homeless Literature', *Alluvium*, 7 December. Available at: https://www.alluvium-journal.org/2020/12/07/the-post-millennial-rise-of-british-homelessness-literature/ (accessed 24 April 2022).

Arata, S. D. (1990), 'The Occidental Tourist: "Dracula" and the Anxiety of Reverse Colonization', *Victorian Studies*, 33 (4): 621–45.

Arias, R. and P. Pulham (2009), *Haunting and Spectrality in Neo-Victorian Fiction: Possessing the Past*, London: Palgrave Macmillan.

Aridjis, C. (2009), *Book of Clouds*, London: Grove Press.

Aridjis, C. (2019), *Sea Monsters*, London: Penguin.

Armfield, J. (2022), *Our Wives Under the Sea*, London: Picador.

Armitt, L. (2011), *Twentieth-Century Gothic*, Cardiff: University of Wales Press.

Ashfeldt, L. (2014), *Saltwater*, Dublin: Liberties Press.

Ashworth, J. (2016), *Fell*, London: Spectre.

Ashworth, J. (2021), *Ghosted: A Love Story*, London: Sceptre.

Aslam, N. (2004), *Maps for Lost Lovers*, London: Faber and Faber.

Aslam, N. (2008), *The Wasted Vigil*, London: Faber and Faber.

Augé, M. (1995), *Non-Spaces: Introduction to an Anthropology of Supermodernity*, London: Verso.

Aw, T. ([2005] 2006), *The Harmony Silk Factory*, London: Harper Perennial.

Azzopardi, T. (2004), *Remember Me*, London: Picador.

Baer, U. (2002), *Spectral Evidence*, Cambridge, MA: The MIT Press.

Baldick, C. (1992), *The Oxford Book of Gothic Tales*, Oxford: Oxford University Press.

Balée, S. (2021), 'Portals Between Worlds: Recent Sci-Fi and Fantasy and Vintage Octavia Butler', *The Hudson Review*, July. Available at: https://hudsonreview.com/2021/07/portals-between-worlds-recent-sci-fi-and-fantasy-and-vintage-octavia-butler/#.Y-ZsgOzP1-U (10 February 2023).

Ballard, J. G. (1973), *Crash*, London: Jonathan Cape.

Ballard, J. G. (1975), 'Some Words About Crash', *Foundation*, 9 (November): 45–54.

Ballard, J. G. (2003), *Millennium People*, London: Flamingo.

Banks, I. (2002), *Dead Air*, London: Hachette.

Barbrook, R. and A. Cameron (1995), 'The Californian Ideology', *Mute*, 1 September. Available at: https://www.metamute.org/editorial/articles/californian-ideology (accessed 25 August 2023).

Barker, P. (1982), *Union Street*, London: Virago.

Barker, P. (1984), *Blow Your House Down*, London: Virago.

Barker, P. (1986), *Liza's England*, London: Virago.

Barker, P. ([1991, 1993, 1995] 2014), *Regeneration Trilogy*, London: Penguin.

Barker, P. (1998), *Another World*, London: Penguin.
Barker, P. (2001), *Border Crossing*, London: Penguin.
Barker, P. ([2003] 2005), *Double Vision*, London: Penguin.
Battersby, D. (2021), 'Reading Ishiguro Today: Suspicion and Form', *MFS: Modern Fiction Studies*, 67 (1): 6–88.
Baudelaire, C. ([1863] 1995), *The Painter of Modern Life and Other Essays*, trans. and ed. J. Maine, New Edn. London: Phaidon Press.
Bauman, Z. (2000), *Liquid Modernity*, London: Polity.
Bauman, Z. (2004), *Wasted Lives: Modernity and Its Outcasts*, Oxford: Polity.
Baym, N. (2010), *Personal Connections in the Digital Age*, Cambridge: Polity Press.
BBC News (2013), 'Glasgow Ranked UK's Most Violent Area', 24 April. Available at: http://www.bbc.co.uk/news/uk-scotland-glasgow-west-22276018 (accessed 30 May 2023).
Beck, U. (1999), *World Risk Society*, Cambridge: Polity.
Becker, S., M. de Bruin-Molé and S. Polak, eds (2021), *Embodying Contagion: The Viropolitics of Horror and Desire in Contemporary Discourse*, Cardiff: University of Wales Press.
Beer, G. ([1983] 2000), *Darwin's Plots: Evolutionary Narrative in Darwin, George Eliot and Nineteenth-Century Fiction*, Cambridge: Cambridge University Press.
Bekers, E. and H. Cousins (2021), 'At the Vanguard of Innovation in Contemporary Black British Women's Literature', in K. Aughterson and D. Phillips (eds), *Women Writers and Experimental Narratives: Early Modern to Contemporary*, 205–26, London: Palgrave Macmillan.
Bell, D. (2001), *An Introduction to Cybercultures*, London: Routledge.
Benchley, P. (1974), *Jaws*, New York: Doubleday.
Benjamin, W. ([1968] 1969), *Illuminations*, ed. H. Arendt, trans. H. Zohn. New York: Schocken Books.
Benjamin, W. ([1974] 2006), *Berlin Childhood around 1900*, trans. H. Eiland, Cambridge, MA: Belknap Press.
Benjamin, W. ([1978] 1986), *Reflections: Essays, Aphorisms, Autobiographical Writings*, ed. P. Demetz, trans. E. Jephcott, New York: Harcourt Brace Jovanovich.
Bennett, J. (2010), *Vibrant Matter: A Political Ecology of Things*, Durham, NC: Duke University Press.
Berger, J. (2003), 'There's No Backhand to This', in J. Greenberg (ed.), *Trauma at Home: After 9/11*, 52–9, Lincoln, NE: University of Nebraska Press.
Berlant, L. (2011), *Cruel Optimism*, Durham, NC: Duke University Press.
Beville, M. (2009), *Gothic-Postmodernism: Voicing the Terrors of Postmodernity*, Boston, MA: Brill.
Bernard, C. (2022), 'Vibrant Allegories: Questioning Immunity with Ali Smith's *Seasonal Quartet* (2016–2020)', *Études anglaises*, 75 (1): 13–29. Available at: https://www.cairn.info/revue-etudes-anglaises-2022-1-page-13.htm (accessed 30 May 2023).
Bissett, A. (2007), 'The "New Weegies": The Glasgow Novel in the 21st Century', in B. Schoene (ed.), *The Edinburgh Companion to Contemporary Scottish Literature*, 59–67, Edinburgh: Edinburgh University Press.

Black, S. (2009), 'Ishiguro's Inhuman Aesthetics', *MFS Modern Fiction Studies*, 55 (4), 785–807.

Blake, L. and A. Soltysik Monnet (2017), 'Introduction: Neoliberal Gothic', in L. Blake and A. Soltysik Monnet (eds), *Neoliberal Gothic: International Gothic in the Neoliberal Age*, 1–18, Manchester: Manchester University Press.

Blanco, M. del Pilar (2010), 'Haunting of the Everyday in the Thoughtographs of Ted Serios', in M. del Pilar Blanco and E. Peeren (eds), *Popular Ghosts: The Haunted Spaces of Everyday Culture*, 253–67, London: Continuum.

Blanco, M. del Pilar and E. Peeren, (2010), 'Introduction', in M. del Pilar Blanco and E. Peeren (eds), *Popular Ghosts: The Haunted Spaces of Everyday Culture*, ix–xxiv, London: Continuum.

Błaszak, M. (2021), 'Ann Radcliffe's Gothic Romances and the Sea', *Explorations: A Journal of Language and Literature*, 9: 30–42.

Blum, H. (2013), 'Introduction: Oceanic Studies', *Atlantic Studies*, 10: 151–5.

Boehmer, E. and S. Morton, eds ([2010] 2015), *Terror and the Postcolonial*, Oxford: Wiley Blackwell.

Boehm, K. (2011), 'Historiography and the Material Imagination in the Novels of Sarah Waters', *Studies in the Novel* 43 (2): 237–257.

Botting, F. (1996), *Gothic*, London: Routledge.

Botting, F. ([2008] 2011), *Limits of Horror: Technology, Bodies, Gothic*, Manchester: Manchester University Press.

Botting, F. (2022), 'Monstrocene', in J. D. Edwards, R. Graulund and J. Höglund (eds), *Dark Scenes from Damaged Earth: The Gothic Anthropocene*, 314–37, Minneapolis, MN: University of Minnesota Press.

Botting, F. and J. D. Edwards (2013), 'Theorising Globalgothic', in G. Byron (ed.), *Globalgothic*, 11–24, Manchester: Manchester University Press.

Botting, F. and C. Spooner (2015), *Monstrous Media/Spectral Subjects: Imaging Gothic from the Nineteenth-Century to the Present*, Manchester: Manchester University Press.

Bould, M. (2021), *The Anthropocene Unconscious: Climate Catastrophe Culture*, London: Verso.

Bowcott, O. (2007), 'The New British Empire? UK Plans to Annex South Atlantic', *The Guardian*, 22 September. Available at: https://www.theguardian.com/uk/2007/sep/22/oil.politics (accessed 18 June 2023).

Braddon, M. E. ([1862] 2003), *Lady Audley's Secret*, Peterborough, ON: Broadview.

Braidotti, R. (2013), *The Posthuman*, Cambridge: Polity Press.

Brannigan, J. (2005), *Pat Barker*, Manchester: Manchester University Press.

Brantlinger, P. (1988), *Rule of Darkness: British Literature and Imperialism, 1830–1914*. Ithaca, NY: Cornell University Press.

Brock, R. (2008), 'An "Onerous Citizenship": Globalization, CulturalFlows and the HIV/AIDS Pandemic in Hari Kunzru's *Transmission*', *Journal of Postcolonial Writing*, 44 (4): 379–90.

Brontë, C. ([1847] 2001), *Jane Eyre*, New York: Norton.

Brontë, E. ([1847] 2003), *Wuthering Heights*, New York: Norton.
Brookes, L. (2009), *Gay Male Fiction Since Stonewall: Ideology, Conflict, and Aesthetics*, London: Routledge.
Brooks, M. (2014), *The Extinction Parade*, Rantoul, IL: Avatar Press.
Brooks, P. (2003), 'If You Have Tears', in J. Greenberg (ed.), *Trauma at Home: After 9/11*, 48–51, Lincoln, NE: University of Nebraska Press.
Brooks, S. (2019), 'Brexit and the Politics of the Rural', *Sociologia Ruralis*, 60 (4): 790–809.
Brothers, C. (1997), *War and Photography: A Cultural History*, London: Routledge.
Brouillette, S. (2017), 'On Some Recent Worrying over World Literature's Commodity Status', *Multilingual Locals and Significant Geographies*, School of Oriental and African Studies, University of London. Available at: http://mulosige.soas.ac.uk/world-literature-recent-worrying/ (accessed 1 February 2023).
Brown, J. A. (2010), *Cyborgs in Latin America*, London: Palgrave Macmillan.
Buckley, C. G. (2019), *Twenty-First-Century Children's Gothic*, Edinburgh: Edinburgh University Press.
Bulman, M. (2019), 'Austerity and Privitisation by Consecutive Governments Led to Grenfell Tragedy, Says Fire Union', *The Independent*, 23 September. Available at: https://www.independent.co.uk/news/uk/home-news/grenfell-fire-austerity-privatisation-cuts-deregulation-labour-conservatives-fire-union-a9115396.html (accessed 23 June 2023).
Burnet, G. M. (2015), *His Bloody Project*, Glasgow: Contraband.
Burns, A. (2001), *No Bones*, London: Flamingo.
Burnside, J. (2008), *Glister*, London: Vintage.
Burton, J. (2014), *The Miniaturist*, London: Picador.
Bush, G. W. (2001), 'Transcript of Present Bush's Address', CNN.com, 21 September. Available at: http://edition.cnn.com/2001/US/09/20/gen.bush.transcript/ (accessed 23 February 2022).
Butler, J. (2004), *Precarious Life: The Powers of Mourning and Violence*, London: Verso.
Butler, J. (2009), *Frames of War: When is Life Grievable?* London: Verso.
Butler, J. and G. Chakravorty Spivak (2010), *Who Sings the Nation State?* Chicago, IL: University of Chicago Press.
Byron, G. (2013), 'Introduction', in G. Byron (ed.), *Globalgothic*, 1–10, Manchester: Manchester University Press.
Byron, G. (2015a), 'Global Gothic', in D. Punter (ed.), *A New Companion to the Gothic*, 369–78, Oxford: Wiley Blackwell.
Byron, G. (2015b), 'Gothic in the 1890s', in D. Punter (ed.), *A New Companion to the Gothic*, 186–96, Oxford: Wiley Blackwell.
Calvert, B. (2014), '"This Means Bodies": Body Horror and the Influence of David Cronenberg', in T. R. Cochran, S. Ginn, and P. Zinder (eds), *The Multiple Worlds of Fringe: Essays on J.J. Abrams Science Fiction Series*, 186–200, Jefferson, NC: MacFarland and Company.
Cameron, D. and E. Frazer (1987), *The Lust to Kill*, Cambridge: Polity.

Campbell, K. (2008), *The Twilight Time*, London: Hodder Paperbacks.
Capossere, B. (2021), '*Klara and the Sun*: An Understated Masterpiece', *Fantasy Literature*, March. Available at: https://fantasyliterature.com/reviews/klara-and-the-sun/ (accessed 10 February 2023).
Carey, M. R. (2014), *The Girl with All the Gifts*, London: Orbit Books.
Carey, M. R. (2017), *The Boy on the Bridge*, London: Orbit Books.
Carlo, C. (2018), '9 Steps to Disconnect from Social Media and Connect with Life Again', *Lifehack*, 18 September. Available at: https://www.lifehack.org/280613/9-steps-disconnect-from-social-media-and-connect-with-life-again (accessed 21 September 2018).
Carroll, T. (2019), 'Sarah Moss on Brexit, Borders, Bog Bodies, and "The Foundation Myths of a Really Damaged Country"', *Longreads*, January. Available at: https://longreads.com/2019/01/09/interview-with-sarah-moss/ (accessed 30 May 2023).
Carson, J. (2019), *The Fire Starters*, Dublin: Black Swan Ireland.
Carson, J. (2022), *The Raptures*, New York: Doubleday.
Carter, P. (2002), *Repressed Spaces: The Poetics of Agoraphobia*, London: Reaktion Books.
Caruth, C. (1995a), 'Introduction', in C. Caruth (ed.), *Trauma: Explorations in Memory*, 3–12, Baltimore, MD: Johns Hopkins University Press.
Caruth, C., ed. (1995b), *Trauma: Explorations in Memory*, Baltimore, MD: Johns Hopkins University Press.
Castells, M. (1996), *The Rise of the Network Society*, Oxford: Wiley-Blackwell.
Castells, M. (2001), *The Internet Galaxy: Reflections on the Internet, Business and Society*, Oxford: Oxford University Press.
Cavallaro, D. (2002), *The Gothic Vision: Three Centuries of Horror, Terror, and Fear*, London: Continuum.
Champion, G. (2022), 'Decolonising Deep-Sea Gothic: Perspectives from the Americas', *Gothic Studies*, 24 (3): 275–94.
Chakrabarty, D. (2009), 'The Climate of History: Four Theses', *Critical Inquiry*, 35 (2): 197–222.
Chaudhuri, A. (2009), 'Qatrina and the Books', *London Review of Books*, 31 (16), 27 August. Available at: https://www.lrb.co.uk/the-paper/v31/n16/amit-chaudhuri/qatrina-and-the-books (accessed 11 February 2022).
Cheah, P. (2016), *What is a World?: On Postcolonial Literature as World Literature*, Durham, NC: Duke University Press.
Chikwava, B. (2009), *Harare North*, London: Cape.
Clarke, A. (2006), '*Never Let Me Go*', *The Observer*, 19 February. Available at: https://www.theguardian.com/books/2006/feb/19/features.review (accessed 30 May 2023).
Clarke, S. (2020), *Piranesi*, London: Bloomsbury.
Cleave, C. (2005), *Incendiary*, London: Sceptre.
Clements, M. (2016), *Writing Islam from a South Asian Muslim Perspective*, London: Palgrave Macmillan.
Clift, B. (2021), *Last One at the Party*, London: Hodder and Stoughton.

Coddington, K. (2015), 'Feminist Geographies "Beyond" Gender: De-Coupling Feminist Research and the Gendered Subject', *Geography Compass*, 9 (4): 214–24.
Cohen, E. (2009), *A Body Worth Defending: Immunity, Biopolitics, and the Apotheosis of the Modern Body*, Durham, NC: Duke University Press.
Cohen, J. (1996), *Monster Theory: Reading Culture*, Minneapolis, MN: University of Minnesota Press.
Cohen, M. (1995), *Profane Illumination: Walter Benjamin and the Paris of Surrealist Revolution*, Oakland, CA: University of California Press.
Colebrook, C. (2004), *Gender*, London: Palgrave Macmillan.
Coleridge, S. T. (1798), *The Rime of the Ancient Mariner*, in *Lyrical Ballads, with a Few Other Poems*, London: J. & A. Arch.
Coley, Rob (2017), '"A World Where Nothing is Solved": Investigating the Anthropocene in True Detective', *Journal of Popular Television*, 5 (2): 135–57.
Collins, J. and J. Jervis, eds (2008), *Uncanny Modernity: Cultural Theories, Modern Anxieties*, London: Palgrave Macmillan.
Collins, W. ([1860] 2006), *The Woman in White*, Peterborough, ON: Broadview.
Colomb, C. (2011), *Staging the New Berlin: Place Marketing and the Politics of Urban Re-invention Post-1989*, London: Routledge.
Colomb, C. (2012), 'Pushing the Urban Frontier: Temporary Uses of Space, City Marketing, and the Creative City Discourse in 2000S Berlin', *Journal of Urban Affairs*, 34 (2): 131–52.
Connell, L. (2010), 'E-terror: Computer Viruses, Class and Transnationalism in Transmission and One Night @ the Call Centre', *Journal of Postcolonial Writing*, 46 (3–4): 279–90.
Cook, D. (2005), *Contemporary Muslim Apocalyptic Literature*, Syracuse, NY: Syracuse University Press.
Cooke, C. J. (2021), *The Lighthouse Witches*, London: HarperCollins.
Cooke, C. J. (2022), *The Ghost Woods*, London: HarperCollins.
Coulter, C. (2021), 'Learning to Live with Ghosts: Spectres of "The Troubles" in Contemporary Northern Irish Cinema', *Irish Studies Review*, 29 (3): 287–310.
Cousins, H. (2012), 'Helen Oyeyemi and the Yoruba Gothic', *Journal of Commonwealth Literature*, 47 (1): 47–58.
Cowdell, P. (2019), '"Practicing Witchcraft Myself during the Filming": Folk Horror, Folklore and the Folkloresque', *Western Folklore*, 78 (4): 295–326.
Cox, J. (2019), *Neo-Victorianism and Sensation Fiction*, London: Palgrave Macmillan.
Coyne, R. (1995), *Designing Information Technology in the Postmodern Age*, Cambridge, MA: MIT Press.
Crawford, J. (2019), 'Gothic Digital Technologies', in M. Wester and X. Aldana Reyes (eds), *Twenty-First-Century Gothic: An Edinburgh Companion*, 72–86, Edinburgh: Edinburgh University Press.
Creed, B. (1993), *The Monstrous-Feminine: Film, Feminism, Psychoanalysis*, London: Routledge.

Creed, B. (2022), *Return of the Monstrous-Feminine: Feminist New Wave Cinema*, London: Routledge.
Crown, S. (2018), 'Ghost Wall by Sarah Moss Review: Back to the Iron Age', *The Guardian*, 28 September. Available at: https://www.theguardian.com/books/2018/sep/28/ghost-wall-sarah-moss-review (accessed 30 May 2023).
'Folk, Folklore and the Isle of Man: An Interview with Zoe Gilbert' (2018), *Culture Vannin*, Isle of Man, 1 October. Available at: https://culturevannin.im/news/folk-folklore--the-isle-of-man-an-interview-with-zoe-gilbert-548125/ (accessed 21 June 2023).
Dagognet, F. (1982), *Faces, Surfaces, Interfaces*, Paris: Librairie Philosophique J. Vrin.
Dalby, S. (2003), 'Calling 911: Geopolitics, Security and America's New War', *Geopolitics*, 8 (3): 61–86.
Daly, S. (2014), 'Imperial Gothic', *The British Library*, 15 May. Available at: https://www.bl.uk/romantics-and-victorians/articles/the-imperial-gothic (accessed 24 February 2023).
Dancer, T. (2021), *Critical Modesty in Contemporary Fiction*, Oxford: Oxford University Press.
Darwin, C. (1859), *On the Origin of the Species by Means of Natural Selection or the Preservation of Favoured Race in the Struggle for Life*, London: John Murray.
Davey, M. (2008), '"The Strange Heart Beating": Bird Imagery, Masculinities and the Northern Irish Postcolonial Gothic in the Novels of Sean O'Reilly and Peter Hollywood', *Irish Journal of Gothic and Horror Studies*, 5: 18–29.
Davidson, E., B. Nugent and S. Johnsen (2021), 'Charting the Rough Journey to "Home": The Contribution of Qualitative Longitudinal Research to Understandings of Homelessness in Austerity', *Social Policy and Society*, 20 (4): 684–700.
Davis, E. S. (2013), *Rethinking the Romance Genre: Global Intimacies in Contemporary Literary and Visual Culture*, London: Palgrave Macmillan.
Davison, C. M. (2017), *The Gothic and Death*, Manchester: Manchester University Press.
Dayal, S. (1998), 'The Liminalities of Nation and Gender: Salman Rushdie's "Shame"', *Journal of the Midwest Modern Language Association*, 31 (2): 39–62.
de Bruin-Molé, M. (2021), 'Killable Hordes, Chronic Others, and "Mindful" Consumers: Rehabilitating the Zombie in Twenty-First-Century Popular Culture', in S. Becker, M. de Bruin-Molé, and S. Polak (eds), *Embodying Contagion: The Viropolitics of Horror and Desire in Contemporary Discourse*, 159–78, Cardiff: University of Wales Press.
de Bruin-Molé, M. and S. Polak (2021), 'Embodying the Fantasies and Realities of Contagion', in S. Becker, M. de Bruin-Molé, and S. Polak (eds), *Embodying Contagion: The Viropolitics of Horror and Desire in Contemporary Discourse*, 1–12, Cardiff: University of Wales Press.
deCaires Narain, D. (2010), 'Affiliating Edward Said Closer to Home: Reading Postcolonial Women's Texts', in A. Iskandar and H. Rustom (eds), *Edward Said: A Legacy of Emancipation and Representation*, 121–41, Berkeley, CA: University of California Press.

de Certeau, M. ([1980] 2002), *The Practice of Everyday Life*, Berkeley, CA: University of California Press.

de Groot, J. (2016), *Consuming History: Historians and Heritage in Contemporary Popular Culture*, 2nd edn, London: Routledge.

De Lint, C. (2001), *The Onion Girl*, New York: Tor Books.

Deane, S. (1996), *Reading in the Dark*, London: Vintage.

del Pilar Blanco, M. and Esther Peeren (eds) (2013), *The Spectralities Reader: Ghosts and Haunting in Contemporary Cultural Theory*, New York and London: Bloosmbury.

Deleuze, G. and F. Guattari ([1987] 2014), *A Thousand Plateaus*, London: Bloomsbury.

Dennis, S. and A. Witchard (2015), 'We Have Never Been Meat (But We Could Be)', in Human Animal Research Network Editorial Collective (Ed.), *Animals in the Anthropocene: Critical Perspectives on Nonhuman Futures*, Series: *Animal Publics*, 4, 151–64, Sydney: Sydney University Press.

Derrida, J. (1994), *Spectres of Marx: The State of the Debt, the Work of Mourning, and the New International*, trans. P. Kamuf, New York: Routledge.

Derrida, J. and C. Malabou (2004), *Counterpath: Travelling with Jacques Derrida*, Palo Alto, CA: Stanford University Press.

Dimock, W. C. (2007), 'Introduction: Genres as Fields of Knowledge', *Remapping Genre*, PMLA, Special Issue, W. C. Dimock and B. Robbins (eds), 122 (5): 1377–88.

Dinnen, Z. (2018), *The Digital Banal: New Media and American Literature and Culture*, New York: Columbia University Press.

Doherty, J., V. Busch-Geertsema, V. Karpuskiene, J. Korhonen, E. O'Sullivan, I. Sahlin, A. Petrillo and J. Wygnanska (2008), 'Homelessness and Exclusion: Regulating Public Space in European Cities', *Surveillance & Society*, 5 (3): 290–314.

Donovan, A. (2003), *Buddha Da*, Edinburgh: Canongate.

*Downton Abbey* (2010–15), TV series, ITV.

du Maurier, D. (1938), *Rebecca*, London: Victor Gollancz Ltd.

Duncan, R. (2017), 'Gothic Vulnerability', in L. Blake and A. Soltysik Monnet (eds), *Neoliberal Gothic: International Gothic in the Neoliberal Age*, 122–41, Manchester: Manchester University Press.

Duncan, R. (2022), 'Decolonial Gothic: Beyond the Colonial in Gothic Studies', *Gothic Studies*, 24 (3): 304–22.

Duncan, R. and M. Foley (2020), 'Introduction: McGrath in the World: Madness, Gothic, and Transnational Consciousness', in M. Foley and R. Duncan (eds), *Patrick McGrath and His Worlds: Madness and the Transnational Gothic*, 1–18, London: Routledge.

Dundes, A. (1980), *Interpreting Folklore*, Bloomington, IN: Indiana University Press.

Durán-Almarza, E. M. and E. Álverez López, eds (2013), *Diasporic Women's Writing of the Black Atlantic: (En)Gendering Literature and Performance*, London: Routledge.

During, S. (2015), 'Choosing Precarity', *South Asia: Journal of South Asian Studies*, 38 (1): 19–38.

Dryden, L. (2003), *The Modern Gothic and Literary Doubles: Stevenson, Wilde and Wells*, London: Palgrave Macmillan.

Dunn, K. (2023), *Bitterthorn*, London: Anderson Press.
Dylan, K. (2022), *Mindwalker*, London: Hodder and Stoughton.
Eaglestone, R. (2018), 'Cruel Nostalgia and the Memory of the Second World War', in R. Eaglestone (ed.), *Brexit and Literature: Critical and Cultural Responses*, 92–104, London: Routledge.
Eagleton, T. (2005), *Holy Terror*, Oxford: Oxford University Press.
Edkins, J. (2003), *Trauma and the Memory of Politics*, Cambridge: Cambridge University Press.
Edkins, J. (2014), 'Time, Personhood, Politics', in G. Buelens, S. Durrant, and R. Eaglestone (eds), *The Future of Trauma Theory: Contemporary Literary and Cultural Criticism*, 127–39, London: Routledge.
Edwards, J. D. (2015a), 'Introduction: Technogothics', in J. D. Edwards (ed.), *Technologies of the Gothic in Literature and Culture: Technogothics*, 1–16, New York: Routledge.
Edwards, J. D. (2022), 'Beyond the Slaughterhouse', in J. D. Edwards, R. Graulund, and J. Höglund (eds), *Dark Scenes from Damaged Earth: The Gothic Anthropocene*, 314–37, Minneapolis, MN: University of Minnesota Press.
Edwards, J. D., ed. (2015b), *Technologies of the Gothic in Literature and Culture: Technogothics*, New York: Routledge.
Edwards, J. D. and S. Guardini Vasconcelos (2016), 'Introduction: Tropicalizing Gothic', in J. D. Edwards and S. Guardinin (eds), *Tropical Gothic in Literature and Culture: The Americas*, 1–10, London: Routledge.
Edwards, J. D., R. Graulund and J. Höglund (2022), 'Introduction', in J. D. Edwards, R. Graulund, and J. Höglund (eds), *Dark Scenes from Damaged Earth: The Gothic Anthropocene*, ix–xxvi, Minneapolis, MN: University of Minnesota Press.
Edwards-Jones, I. (2018), *The Witches of St Petersburg*, New York: Harper.
Elliott, L. (2016), 'Spread of Internet Hs Not Conquered Divide between Rich and Poor – Report', *The Guardian*, 13 January. Available at: https://www.theguardian.com/technology/2016/jan/13/internet-not-conquered-digital-divide-rich-poor-world-bank-report (accessed 21 September 2018).
Erek, A. N. and E. Gantner (2017), 'Disappearing History: Challenges of Imagining Berlin after 1989', in K. Bauer and J. R. Hosek (eds), *Cultural Topographies of the New Berlin*, 181–202, New York, NY: Berghan Books.
Erman, I. M. (2021), 'Sympathetic Vampires and Zombies with Brains: The Modern Monster as a Figure of Self-Control', *Journal of Popular Culture*, 54 (1): 1–19.
Esposito, R. ([2011] 2019), *Immunitas: The Protection and Negation of Life*, trans. Zakiya Hanafi, Cambridge: Polity.
Evans, C. (2020), *The Graves of Whitechapel*, London: Sphere.
Farrell, K. (1998), *Post-Traumatic Culture: Injury and Interpretation in the Nineties*, Baltimore, MD: John Hopkins University Press.
Felman, S. (1977), 'Turning the Screw of Interpretation', *Yale French Studies*, 55/56: 94–207.
Felman, S. and D. Laub, eds (1992), *Testimony: Crises of Witnessing in Literature, Psychoanalysis, and History*, New York: Routledge.

Ferdjani, Y. (2022), 'Brexit and the Emergence of a New English Identity', *Observatoire de la société britannique*, 28: 47–65.
Fisher, M. ([2014] 2022), *Capitalist Realism? Is there No Alternative?*, Winchester: John Hunt Publishing.
Fisher, M. (2016), *The Weird and the Eerie*, London: Repeater.
Flannery, E. (2013), 'Internationalizing 9/11: Home and Redemption in Nadeem Aslam's *The Wasted Vigil* (2008) and Colum McCann's *Let the Great World Spin* (2009)', *English*, 62 (238): 294–315.
Fletcher, J. (2013), *Freud and the Scene of Trauma*, NY: Fordham University Press.
Forbes, M. (2013), *Ghost Moth*, London: Weidenfeld and Nicolson.
Foster, H. (1996), *The Return of the Real: The Avant-garde at the End of the Century*, Cambridge, MA: MIT Press.
Foucault, M. (1986), 'Of Other Spaces', trans. J. Miskowiec, *Diacritics* 16 (1): 22–7.
Fountain, J. (2001), *Building the Virtual State: Information Technology and Institutional Change*, Washington, DC: Brooklings Institution Press.
Fraiman, S. (2017), *Extreme Domesticity: A View from the Margins*, New York: Columbia University Press.
France, L. (2004), 'A Bag Lady with Plenty of Baggage', *The Guardian*, 22 February. Available at: https://www.theguardian.com/books/2004/feb/22/fiction.features1 (accessed 5 May 2022).
Frawley, O. (2013), 'Global Civil War and Post-9/11 Discourse in *The Wasted Vigil*', *Textual Practice*, 27 (3): 438–57.
Freud, S. ([1919] 2001), 'The Uncanny', in J. Strachey, A. Freud, A Strachey, and A. Tyson (eds), *The Standard Edition of the Complete Psychological Works of Sigmund Freud*, 17: 217–56, London: Vintage.
Gagiano, A. (2013), 'African Library: *Harare North* by Brian Chikwava', *Litnet*, 18 December. Available at: https://www.litnet.co.za/african-library-harare-north-by-brian-chikwava/ (accessed 18 October 2021).
Gaiman, N. (1996), *Neverwhere*, London: BBC Books.
Galloway, A. (2012), *The Interface Effect*, Cambridge: Polity Press.
Gamer, M. (2000), *Romanticism and the Gothic: Genre, Reception and Canon Formation*, Cambridge: Cambridge University Press.
García Agustín, E. (2014), 'Louise Welsh, Then and There', *Journal of the Spanish Association of Anglo-American Studies*, 36 (2): 205–18.
Gardiner, M. (2018), 'Brexit and the Aesthetics of Anachronism', in R. Eaglestone (ed.), *Brexit and Literature: Critical and Cultural Responses*, 105–17, London: Routledge.
Germanà, M. (2010a), 'Death and the City', Blog post on *The Gothic Imagination*, University of Stirling, 27 April. Available at: http://www.gothic.stir.ac.uk/ guestblog/death-and-the-city-2/ (accessed 30 May 2023).
Germanà, M. (2010b), *Scottish Women's Gothic and Fantastic Writing: Fiction Since 1978*, Edinburgh: Edinburgh University Press.

Germanà, M. (2014), 'The Awakening of Caledonias? Scottish Literature in the 1980s', in Emily Horton, Philip Tew, and Leigh Wilson (eds), *The 1980s: A Decade of Contemporary British Fiction*, 51–74, London: Bloomsbury.

Germanà, M. (2016), 'Community Spirit? Haunting Secrets and Displaced Selves in Contemporary Scottish Fiction', in S. Lyall (ed.), *Community in Modern Scottish Literature*, 235–53, Boston: Brill Rodopi.

Ghosh, A. (2016), *The Great Derangement: Climate Change and the Unthinkable*, Chicago, IL: University of Chicago Press.

Giddens, A. (2002), *Runaway World: How Globalisation Is Shaping Our Lives*, 2nd edn, London: Profile.

Gilbert, Z. (2018), *Folk*, London: Bloomsbury.

Gilman, C. Perkins ([1892] 2010), 'The Yellow Wall-Paper', in *The Yellow Wall-Paper, Herland, and Selected Writings*, 179–96, London: Penguin.

Gilmartin, S. (1998), *Ancestry and Narrative in Nineteenth-Century British Literature: Blood Relations from Edgeworth to Hardy*, Cambridge: Cambridge University Press.

Gilroy, P. (2005), *Postcolonial Melancholia*, New York: Columbia University Press.

Giroux, H. A. (2005), 'The Terror of Neoliberalism: Rethinking the Significance of Cultural Politics', *College Literature*, 32 (1): 1–19.

Giroux, H. A. (2013), 'The Disimagination Machine and the Pathologies of Power', *symploke* 21 (1–2): 257–69.

Gluck, M. (2003), 'The Flaneur and the Aesthetic Appropriation of Urban Culture in Mid-19th-Century Paris', *Theory, Culture & Society*, 20 (5): 53–80.

Gold, T. (2009), 'Nazi Cows, Nazi Cats, Actors Playing Depressed Nazis. It's All Just Hitler Porn and It Disgusts Me', *The Guardian*, 23 April. Available at: http://www.guardian.co.uk/commentisfree/2009/apr/23/nazi-culture-film-hitler (accessed 30 May 2023).

Goodfellow, M. (2019), *Hostile Environment: How Immigrants Became Scapegoats*, London: Verso.

Gordon, A. (2008), *Ghostly Matters: Haunting and the Sociological Imagination*, Minneapolis, MN: University of Minnesota Press.

Graham, S. (2004), 'Beyond the "Dazzling Light": From Dreams of Transcendence to the "Remediation" of Urban Life', *New Media & Society*, 6 (1): 16–25.

Graham-Harrison, E. (2014), 'Afghanistan: Land of Beauty and Brutality', *The Guardian*, 4 May. Available at: https://www.theguardian.com/artanddesign/2014/may/04/afghanistan-land-beauty-brutality (accessed 11 February 2022).

Gray, A. ([1981] 1994), *Lanark: A Life in Four Books*, London: Picador.

Gray, R. (2009), 'Open Doors, Closed Minds: American Prose Writing at the Time of Crisis', *American Literary History*, 21: 128–51.

Greenberg, J. (2003), 'Wounded New York', in J. Greenberg (ed.), *Trauma at Home: After 9/11*, 21–38, Lincoln, NE: University of Nebraska Press.

Gregory, D. ([2010] 2015), 'Vanishing Points: Law, Violence, and Exception in the Global War Prison', in E. Boehmer and S. Morton (eds), *Terror and the Postcolonial*, 55–98, Chichester: Wiley Blackwell.

Griffiths, N. (2017), 'How I Wrote . . .: Niall Griffiths on *Broken Ghost*', *Wales Art Review*, 21 July. Available at: https://www.walesartsreview.org/how-i-wrote-niall-griffiths-on/ (accessed 30 May 2023).

Griffiths, N. (2019), *Broken Ghost*, London: Vintage.

Gronlund, M. (2014), 'Return of the Gothic: Digital Anxiety in the Domestic Sphere', *e-flux Journal*, 51 (January). Available at: https://www.e-flux.com/journal/51/59962/return-of-the-gothic-digital-anxiety-in-the-domestic-sphere/ (accessed 13 June 2023).

Grossman, L. (2013), *We Gotta Get Out of This Place: Popular Conservatism and Popular Culture*, London: Routledge.

Gunning, D. (2015), 'Dissociation, Spirit Possession, and the Languages of Trauma in Some Recent African-British Novels', *Research in African Literatures*, 46 (4): 119–32.

Hadley, L. (2010), *Neo-Victorian Fiction and Historical Narrative: The Victorians and Us*, London: Palgrave Macmillan.

Haggard, R. ([1886] 2008), *She*, Oxford: Oxford University Press.

Hall, S. (1998a), 'Cultural Identity and Diaspora', in J. Rutherford (ed.), *Identity: Community, Culture, Difference*, 222–37, London: Lawrence and Wishart.

Hall, S. (1998b), 'The Great Moving Nowhere Show', *Marxism Today*, November/December.

Hall, S. (2021), *Burntcoat*, London: Faber and Faber.

Halls, S. (2019), *The Familiars*, London: Zaffre.

Hamid, M. (2017), *Exit West*, London: Hamish Hamilton.

Hammad, I. (2023), *Enter Ghost*, London: Penguin.

Haraway, D. (1992), 'The Promises of Monsters: A Regenerative Politics for Inappropriate/d Others', in L. Grossberg, C. Nelson, and P. A. Treichler (eds), *Cultural Studies*, 295–96, New York: Routledge.

Haraway, D. (2017), 'Symbogenesis, Sympoiesis, and Art Science Activisms For Staying with the Trouble,' in A. Lowenhaupt Tsing, H. A. Swanson, E. Gan, and N. Bubandt (eds), *Arts of Living on a Damaged Planet: Ghosts and Monsters of the Anthropocene*, M25–M50, Minneapolis, MN: University of Minnesota Press.

Haraway, D. (2020), 'The Promise of Monsters: Regenerative Politics for Inappropriate/d Others', in J. A. Weinstock (ed.), *The Monster Theory Reader*, 459–521, Minneapolis, MN: University of Minnesota Press.

Hardt, M. and A. Negri (2000), *Empire*, Cambridge, MA: Harvard University Press.

Harkaway, N. (2008), *The Gone Away World*, London: Heinemann.

Harper, D. (n.d.), 'Broad', *Online Etymology Dictionary*. Available at: https://www.etymonline.com/word/broad (accessed 16 June 2023).

Harris, R. (2007), *The Ghost*, London: Arrow.

Hartman, G. (1995), 'On Traumatic Knowledge and Literary Studies', *New Literary History*, 26 (3): 537–63.

Hartman, G. (2003), 'On that Day', in J. Greenberg (ed.), *Trauma at Home: After 9/11*, 5–10, Lincoln, NE: University of Nebraska Press.

Harwood, J. (2004), *The Ghost Writer*, Boston, MA: Houghton Mifflin.
Haseler, S. (1996), *The English Tribe: Identity Crisis in the New Europe*, London: Palgrave Macmillan.
Hawthorne, N. (1851), *The House of the Seven Gables*, Boston, MA: Ticknor, Reed, and Fields.
Hayles, N. Katherine (1997), 'The Posthuman Body: Inscription and Incorporation in *Galatea 2.2* and *Snow Crash*', *Configurations*, 5 (2): 241–66.
Haythornthwaite, C. and B. Wellman (2002), *The Internet in Everyday Life*, Oxford: Wiley-Blackwell.
Heilmann, A. (2012), 'Specters of the Victorian in the Neo-Forties Novel: Sarah Waters's *The Little Stranger* (2009) and Its Intertexts', *Contemporary Women's Writing*, 6 (1): 38–55.
Heilmann, A. and M. Llewellyn (2010), *Neo-Victorianism: The Victorians in the Twenty-First-Century, 1999–2009*, London: Palgrave.
Heise-von der Lippe, A. (2017), 'Introduction: Post/human/Gothic', in A. Heise-von der Lippe (ed.), *Posthuman Gothic*, 1–16, Cardiff: University of Wales Press.
Hennessy, R. (2017), *Profit and Pleasure: Sexual Identities in Late Capitalism*, 2nd edn, London: Routledge.
Hitchcock, A. (1960), *Psycho*, Hollywood, CA: Paramount Pictures Studios.
Hitchcock, P. (2010), 'Uncanny Marxism: Or, Do Androids Dream of Electric Lenin', in M. del Pilar Blanco and E. Peeren (eds), *Popular Ghosts: The Haunted Spaces of Everyday Culture*, 35–49, London: Continuum.
Hogle, J. E. (1997), 'The Ghost of the Counterfeit – and the Closet – in the Monk', *Romanticism on the Net*, 8. Available at: https://ronjournal.org/articles/n8/the-ghost-of-the-counterfeit-and-the-closet-in-the-monk/↑per-fulltext (accessed 1 February 2023).
Hogle, J. E. (2010), 'Hyper-Reality and the Gothic Affect: The Sublimation of Fear from Burke and Walpole to *The Ring*', *English Language Notes*, 48 (1): 163–76.
Hogle, J. E. (2014a), 'Introduction: Modernity and the Proliferation of the Gothic', in J. E. Hogle (ed.), *The Cambridge Companion to the Modern Gothic*, 3–19, Cambridge: Cambridge University Press.
Hogle, J. E., ed. (2014b), *The Cambridge Companion to the Modern Gothic*, Cambridge: Cambridge University Press.
Höglund, J. (2020), 'Challenging Ecoprecarity in Paolo Bacigalupi's Ship Breaker Trilogy', *Journal of Postcolonial Writing*, 56 (4): 447–59.
Höglund, J. (2022), 'The Anthropocene Within: Love and Extinction in M. R. Carey's *The Girl with All the Gifts* and *The Boy on the Bridge*', in J. D. Edwards, R. Graulund, and J. Höglund (eds), *Dark Scenes from Damaged Earth*, 253–69, Minneapolis, MN: University of Minnesota Press.
Holmes, D. (2002), 'Virtual Globalization – An Introduction', in D. Holmes (ed.), *Virtual Globalization: Virtual Spaces/Tourist Spaces*, 1–52, London: Routledge.
Holmes, D., ed. (2002), *Virtual Globalization: Virtual Spaces/Tourist Spaces*, London: Routledge.

'Holocaust Memorial' (2021), *Berlin.de: The Official Website of Berlin*. Available at: https://www.berlin.de/en/attractions-and-sights/3560249-3104052-holocaust-memorial.en.html (accessed 26 April 2022).

Homeless Link (2021a), '2020 Rough Sleeping Snapshot Statistics', *homelessness.org.uk*. Available at: https://www.homeless.org.uk/sites/default/files/site-attachments/Analysis%20of%20rough%20sleeping%20statistics%20for%20England%202020.pdf (accessed 24 April 2022).

Homeless Link (2021b), 'Rough Sleeping – Our Analysis', *homelessness.org.uk*. Available at: https://www.homeless.org.uk/facts/homelessness-in-numbers/rough-sleeping/rough-sleeping-our-analysis (accessed 24 April 2022).

hooks, b. (1990), *Yearning: Race, Gender, and Cultural Politics*, Boston, MA: South End Press.

hooks, b. (1992), *Black Looks: Race and Representation*, Boston, MA: South End Press.

Horton, E. (2009), 'Gothic, Global Berlin: Urban Gothic in Chloe Aridjis' *Book of Clouds*', University of Nottingham Landscape, Space, Place Research Group Website, 9 June. Available at: https://www.nottingham.ac.uk/cas/documents/landscapes/emilyhortonfinal.pdf.

Horton, E. (2018a), 'A Voice without a Name: Gothic Homelessness in Ali Smith's *Hotel World* and Trezza Azzopardi's *Remember Me*', in S. Adieseshiah and R. Hildyard (eds), *Twenty-First-Century Fiction: What Happens Now*, 132–46, London: Palgrave Macmillan.

Horton, E. (2018b), 'The Queer Gothic Spaces of Contemporary Glasgow: Louise Welsh's *The Cutting Room*', in M. C. Michael (ed.), *Twenty-First-Century British Fiction and the City*, 181–204, London: Palgrave Macmillan.

Horton, E. (2019), '21st Century Trauma and the Uncanny: A Gothic Reading of Trauma in Pat Barker's *Double Vision*', *C21 Literature: A Journal of 21st-Century Writings*, 7 (1): 1–22.

Horton, E. (2022), '"Why Would You Play a Game Like That?": Community and the Pandemic in Kazuo Ishiguro's *Klara and the Sun*', in S. Upstone and P. Ely (eds), *Community in Contemporary British Fiction*, 177–97, London: Bloomsbury.

Hu, A., S. Chancellor and M. De Choudhury (2019), 'Characterizing Homeless Discourse on Social Media', *CHI*, 4–9 May. Available at: http://library.usc.edu.ph/ACM/CHI2019/2exabs/LBW1213.pdf (accessed 5 May 2022).

Hughes, W. (2018), 'The Uncanny Space of Regionality: Gothic Beyond the Metropolis', in W. Hughes and R. Heholt (eds), *Gothic Britain: Dark Places in the Provinces and Margins of the British Isles*, 1–24, Cardiff: University of Wales Press.

Hugo, E. (2022), 'A Violence "Just below the Skin": Atmospheric Terror and Racial Ecologies from the African Anthropocene', in J. D. Edwards, R. Graulund, and J. Höglund (eds), *Dark Scenes from Damaged Earth: The Gothic Anthropocene*, 81–103, Minneapolis, MN: University of Minnesota Press.

Humphreys, L. (2005), 'Cell Phone is Public: Social Interactions in a Wireless Age', *New Media & Society*, 7 (6): 810–33.

Hurley, A. M. (2014), *The Loney*, London: John Murray.

Hurley, K. (2002), 'British Gothic Fiction, 1885–1930', in J. E. Hogle (ed.), *The Cambridge Companion to Gothic Fiction*, 189–207, Cambridge: Cambridge University Press.

Huskinson, L., ed. (2016), *The Urban Uncanny*, London: Routledge.

Ilott, S. ([2019] 2021), 'Postcolonial Gothic', in M. Wester and X. Aldana Reyes (eds), *Twenty-First-Century Gothic*, 19–32, Edinburgh: Edinburgh University Press.

Irr, C. (2014), *Toward the Geopolitical Novel: U.S. Fiction in the Twenty-First-Century*, New York: Columbia University Press.

Ishiguro, K. (2005), *Never Let Me Go*, London: Faber and Faber.

Ishiguro, K. (2015a), *The Buried Giant*, London: Faber and Faber

Ishiguro, K. (2015b), 'Writer's Indignation: Kazuo Ishiguro Rejects Claims of Genre Snobbery', *The Guardian*, 8 March. Available at: https://www.theguardian.com/books/2015/mar/08/kazuo-ishiguro-rebuffs-genre-snobbery (accessed 30 May 2023).

Ishiguro, K. (2021), *Klara and the Sun*, London: Faber and Faber.

Ivanchikova, A. (2019), *Imagining Afghanistan: Global Fiction and Film of the 9/11 Wars*, West Lafayette, IN: Purdue University Press.

Jacobson, H. (2017), 'Howard Jacobson: Manchester, United in Grief and Kindness', *The New York Times*, 23 May. Available at: https://www.nytimes.com/2017/05/23/opinion/manchester-arena-bombing-ariana-grande-howard-jacobson.html (accessed 21 February 2022).

Jaggi, M. (2013), 'Nadeem Aslam: A Life in Writing', *The Guardian*, 26 January. Available at: https://www.theguardian.com/culture/2013/jan/26/nadeem-aslam-life-in-writing (accessed 25 August 2023).

James, H. ([1898] 1986), *The Aspern Papers and The Turn of the Screw*, London: Penguin.

Jameson, F. ([1997] 2000), 'Culture and Finance Capital', in M. Hardt and K. Weeks (eds), *The Jameson Reader*, 255–74, Oxford: Blackwell.

Jess-Cooke, C. (2012), *The Boy Who Could See Demons*, London: Piatkus.

Johansen, E. (2013), 'Becoming the Virus: Responsibility and Cosmopolitan Labor in Hari Kunzru's *Transmission*', *Journal of Postcolonial Writing*, 49 (4): 419–31.

Johnson, D. (2016), *Fen*, London: Vintage.

Johnson, D. (2018), *Everything Under*, London: Jonathan Cape.

Johnson, D. (2020), *Sisters*, London: Vintage.

Johnstone, D. (2005), 'Louise Welsh—*The Cutting Room* (2002)', *The List*, 1 January. Available at: https://www.list.co.uk/article/2749louise-welsh-the-cutting-room-2002/ (accessed 30 May 2023).

Jordon, J. (2009), '*Book of Clouds* by Chloe Aridjis', *The Guardian*, 29 August. Available at: https://www.theguardian.com/culture/2009/aug/29/books-of-clouds-chloe-aridjis (accessed 30 May 2023).

Kahane, C. (2003), 'Uncanny Sights: The Anticipation of the Abomination', in J. Greenberg (ed.), *Trauma at Home: After 9/11*, 107–16, Lincoln, NE: University of Nebraska Press.

Kakutani, M. (2015), 'Review: In *The Buried Giant*, Ishiguro Revisits Memory and Denial', *The New York Times*, 23 February. Available at: https://www.nytimes.com/2015/02/24/books/review-in-the-buried-giant-ishiguro-revisits-memory-and-denial.html (accessed 10 February 2023).

Kapoor, N. (2015), 'Removing the Right to Have Rights', *Studies in Ethnicity and Nationalism*, 15 (1): 105–10.

Katwala, A. (2021), '*Klara and the Sun* Imagines a Social Schism Driven by AI', *Wired*, 8 March.

Keefer, T. (2017), 'Wall Street is a Way of Organizing Nature: An Interview with Jason Moore', *Upping the Anti: A Journal of Theory and Action*, 12, 16 August. Available at: https://uppingtheanti.org/journal/article/12-wall-street-is-a-way-of-organizing-nature (accessed 30 May 2023).

Keetley, D. (2020), 'Introduction: Defining Folk Horror', *Revenant*, 5: 1–32. Available at: www.revenantjournal.com/issues/folk- horror-guest-editor-dawn-keetley (accessed 21 June 2023).

Kerr, P. (1995), *Gridiron*, London: Chatto and Windus.

Keuhnelian, R. (2017), 'The Internet and Social Media: How to Disconnect', *Huffington Post*, 1 August. Available at: https://www.huffingtonpost.com/entry/the-internet-and-social-media-how-to-disconnect_us_597b73c1e4b06b305561d031?guccounter=1 (accessed 21 September 2018).

Khair, T. ([2009] 2015), *The Gothic, Postcolonialism and Otherness: Ghosts from Elsewhere*, London: Palgrave Macmillan.

Kirkus (2014), '*The Girl with All the Gifts*', *Kirkus Reviews*, 10 June. Available at: https://www.kirkusreviews.com/book-reviews/mr-carey/girl-with-all-the-gifts/ (accessed 10 February 2023).

Kirschenbaum, M. G. (2012), *Mechanisms*, Cambridge, MA: MIT Press.

Kociejowski, M. (2011), 'A Tree Grows in Brixton', *Wasafiri*, 26 (3): 55–60.

Kohlke, M. and C. Gutleben (2012), 'The (Mis)Shapes of Neo-Victorian Gothic: Continuations, Adaptations, Transformations', in M. Kohlke and C. Gutleben (eds), *Neo-Victorian Gothic: Horror, Violence and Degeneration in the Re-imagined Nineteenth-Century*, 1–48, Boston, MA: Brill.

Kristeva, J. (1982), *The Powers of Horror*, trans. L. S. Roudiez, New York: Columbia University Press.

Kristeva, J. (1989), *Black Sun: Depression and Melancholia*, trans. L. S. Roudiez, New York: Columbia University Press.

Kröger, L. (2013), 'Panic, Paranoia and Pathos: Ecocriticism in the Eighteenth-Century Gothic Novel', in A. Smith and W. Hughes (eds), *Ecogothic*, 15–27, Manchester: Manchester University Press.

Kubrick, S. (1980), *The Shining*, Burbank, CA: Warner Bros. Pictures.

Kucała, B. (2022), 'A Metafictional Reflection on Historiography: The Inclusiveness of Truth in Graeme Macrae Burnet's *His Bloody Project*', *UWM Olsztyn Acta Neophilologica*, 24 (2): 151–63.

Kummer, D. (2019), 'Author Interview: Sarah Waters', *David Kummer*, 24 May. Available at: https://davidkummer.com/2019/05/24/author-interview-sarah-waters/ (accessed 20 April 2023).

Kunzru, H. (2004), *Transmission*, London: Hamish Hamilton.

Kuo, J. S. (2007), '9/11 as American Gothic: Terror and Historical Darkness in Patrick McGrath's *Ghost Town*', *Concentric: Literary and Cultural Studies*, 33 (1): 53–73.

Kyprianides, A., C. Stott, and B. Bradford (2021), '"Playing the Game": Power, Authority and Procedural Justice in Interactions between Police and Homeless People in London', *British Journal of Criminology*, 61 (3): 670–89.

Ladd, B. (2018), *The Ghosts of Berlin: Confronting German History in the Urban Landscape*, Chicago, IL: University of Chicago Press.

Lagji, A. (2019), 'Waiting in Motion: Mapping Postcolonial Fiction, New Mobilities, and Migration through Mohsin Hamid's *Exit West*', *Mobilities*, 14 (2): 218–32.

Laine, T. (2006), 'Cinema as Skin: Under the Membrane of Horror Film', *New Review of Film and Television Studies*, 4 (2): 9–106.

Lampert-Weissig, L. (2022), 'Sarah Perry's *Melmoth* and the Implications of Gothic Form', *Critique: Studies in Contemporary Fiction*, 64 (4): 659–71.

Langhamer, C. (2005), 'The Meanings of Home in Postwar Britain', *Journal of Contemporary History*, 40 (2): 341–62.

Lanigan, D. (2022), *The Ghost Variations*, New York: Weatherglass Books.

Laub, D. (1992), 'An Event without Witness: Truth, Testimony and Survival', in S. Felman and D. Laub (eds), *Testimony: Crises of Witnessing in Literature, Psychoanalysis, and History*, 75–92, New York: Routledge.

Laub, D. (2003), 'September 11, 2003 – An Event without a Voice', in J. Greenberg (ed.), *Trauma at Home: After 9/11*, 204–15, Lincoln, NE: University of Nebraska Press.

Lazarus, N. (2011), *The Postcolonial Unconscious*, Cambridge: Cambridge University Press.

Lee, C. (2017), 'Introduction: Locating Spectres', in C. Lee (ed.), *Spectral Spaces and Hauntings: The Affects of Absence*, 1–15, London: Routledge.

Leetsch, Jennifer (2021), 'Longing Elsewhere: Helen Oyeyemi', in J. Leetsch (ed.), *Love and Space in Contemporary African Diasporic Women's Writing*, 137–98, London: Palgrave Macmillan.

Lehan, R. (1998), *The City in Literature: An Intellectual and Cultural History*, Berkeley, CA: University of California Press.

Leonard, P. (2014), '"A Revolution in Code"? Hari Kunzru's *Transmission* and the Cultural Politics of Hacking', *Textual Practice*, 28 (2): 267–87.

Levy, T. (2011), 'Human Rights Storytelling and Trauma Narrative in Kazuo Ishiguro's *Never Let Me Go*', *Journal of Human Rights*, 10 (1): 1–16.

Lewis, T. and D. Cho (2006), 'Home is Where the Neurosis Is: A Topography of the Spatial Unconscious', *Cultural Critique*, 64: 69–91.

Leypoldt, G. (2018), 'Social Dimensions of the Turn to Genre: Junot Díaz's *Oscar Wao* and Kazuo Ishiguro's *The Buried Giant*', *Post45*, 31 March. Available at: https://post45.

org/2018/03/social-dimensions-of-the-turn-to-genre-junot-diazs-oscar-wao-and-kazuo-ishiguros-the-buried-giant/ (accessed 10 February 2023).

Leys, R. (2000), *Trauma: A Genealogy*. Chicago, IL: University of Chicago Press.

Liao, P. (2013), *'Post'-9/11 South Asian Diasporic Fiction: Uncanny Terror*, London: Palgrave Macmillan.

Lindholm, M. (1986), *Wizard of Pigeons*, New York: Ace Books.

Ling, R. (2004), *The Mobile Connection: The Cell Phone's Impact on Society*, San Francisco, CA: Elsevier.

Logan, K. (2019), *The Gloaming*, London: Harvill Secker.

Logan, K. (2023), *Now She is Witch*, London: Harvill Secker.

Long, D. (2017), *Ghost-Haunted Land: Contemporary Art and Post-Troubles Northern Ireland*, Manchester: Manchester University Press.

Luckhurst, R. (2003), 'Cultural Governance, New Labour, and the British SF Boom', *Science Fiction Studies*, 30 (3): 417–35.

Luckhurst, R. (2008), *The Trauma Question*, London: Routledge.

Lundberg, A., K. Ancuta, and A. Stasiewicz-Bieńkowska (2019), 'Tropical Gothic: Arts, Humanities and Social Sciences', *eTropic*, 18 (1): 1–11.

Lynch, D. (2023), 'Ministers "Brave or Foolish" to Refuse Attenborough Call for Deep-Sea Mining Ban', *Evening Standard*, 13 June. Available at: https://www.standard.co.uk/news/politics/uk-government-david-attenborough-annemarie-trevelyan-david-lynch-kerry-mccarthy-b1087501.html (accessed 18 June 2023).

MacFarlane, R. (2015), 'The Eeriness of the English Countryside', *The Guardian*, 10 April. Available at: https://www.theguardian.com/books/2015/apr/10/eeriness-english-countryside-robert-macfarlane (accessed 12 June 2023).

MacGregor, S. (2006), *Beyond Mothering Earth: Ecological Citizenship and the Politics of Care*, Vancouver: UBC Press.

Machell, B. (2009), 'Helen Oyeyemi: *The Times* Interview', *The Times*, 23 May. Available at: https://www.thetimes.co.uk/article/helen-oyeyemi-the-times-interview-x7wv7f5hqqm (accessed 18 October 2021).

MacLeod, G. and K. Ward (2002), 'Spaces of Utopia and Dystopia: Landscaping the Contemporary City', *Geografiska Annaler, Series B, Human Geography*, 84 (3/4): 153–70.

Magennis, C. (2021), *Northern Irish Writing after the Troubles*, London: Bloomsbury.

Magrs, P. (2002), 'More Tease, Less Strip', 'Review of *The Cutting Room* by Louise Welsh', *The Guardian*, 31 August. Available at: https://www.theguardian.com/books/2002/aug/31/featuresreviews.guardianreview18 (accessed 30 May 2023).

Maitland, C. (2018a), 'Introduction', in C. Maitland (ed.), *Digital Lifeline? ICTs for Refugees and Displaced Persons*, Information Policy, 1–14, Cambridge, MA: MIT Press.

Maitland, C. (2018b), 'The ICTs and Displacement Research Agenda and Practical Matters', *Digital Lifeline? ICTs for Refugees and Displaced Persons*, Information Policy, 239–58, Cambridge, MA: MIT Press.

Malm, A. and A. Hornborg (2014), 'The Geology of Mankind? A Critique of the Anthropocene Narrative', *Anthropocene Review*, 1 (1): 62–9.

Malzahn, M. (2011), 'Hells, Havens, Hulls: Literary Reflections of Scottish Cities', *International Journal of Scottish Literature*, 8: 1–15.

Mamdani, M. (2005), 'Whither Political Islam?', *Foreign Affairs*, January/February. Available at: http://www1.udel.edu/globalagenda/2005/student/readings/FA-Mamdani-Islam.html (accessed 30 May 2023).

Mangena, F. (2015), 'Restorative Justice's Deep Roots in Africa', *South African Journal of Philosophy*, 34 (1): 1–12.

Mantel, H. (2009), 'Haunted by Shame', *The Guardian*, 23 May. Available at: https://www.theguardian.com/books/2009/may/23/little-stranger-sarah-waters (accessed 25 August 2023).

March-Russell, P. (2020), 'Re-Gendering the Eerie: Border Crossings in Daisy Johnson's Fen', *Journal of the Short Story in English*, 75: 27–43.

Marler, W. (2022), 'You Can Connect with Like, the World!' Social Platforms, Survival Support, and Digital Inequalities for People Experiencing Homelessness', *Journal of Computer-Mediated Communication*, 27 (1): 1–19.

Martin, E. (1990). 'Toward an Anthropology of Immunology: The Body as Nation State', *Medical Anthropology Quarterly*, 4 (4): 410–26. Available at: https://www-jstor-org.ezproxy.brunel.ac.uk/stable/649224?seq=1#metadata_info_tab_contents (accessed 30 May 2023).

Marx, K. ([1867] 1990), *Capital, Volume I*, trans. B. Fowkes. London: Penguin.

Mason, P. (2017), 'Overcoming the Fear of Freedom', Heinrich Geiselberger (ed.), *The Great Regression*, 88–103, Cambridge: Polity Press, 2017.

Massumi, B. (2002), *Parables for the Virtual: Movement, Affect, Sensation*, Durham, NC: Duke University Press.

Maughan, T. (2019), *Infinite Detail*, New York: Farrar, Straus and Giroux.

Mayblin, L., M. Wake and M. Kazemi (2020), 'Necropolitics and the Slow Violence of the Everyday: Asylum Seeker Welfare in the Postcolonial Present', *Sociology*, 54 (1): 107–23.

Mayer, R. (2007), 'Virus Discourse: The Rhetoric of Threat and Terrorism in the Biothriller', *Cultural Critique*, 66: 1–20.

Mbembe, A. ([2011] 2019), *Necropolitics*, Durham, NC: Duke University Press.

Mbiba, B. (2012), 'Zimbabwe's Global Citizens in Harare North: Livelihood Strategies of Zimbabweans in the United Kingdom', in S. Chiumbu and M. Musemwa (eds), *Crisis! What Crisis? The Multiple Dimensions of the Zimbabwean Crisis*, 81–99, Cape Town: Human Sciences Research Council Press.

McCartney, J. (2019), *The Ghost Factory*, London: Forth Estate.

McCleery, A. (2004), 'So Many Glasgows: From "Personality of Place" to "Positionality in Space and Time"', *Scottish Geographical Journal*, 120 (1–2): 3–18.

McCue, K. (2003), 'A Survey of Work on Scottish Women's Writing from 1995', *Women's Writing*, 10 (3): 527–33.

McDonald, I. (1994), *Necroville*, London: Orion.

McDonald, I. (2007), *Brasyl*, Buffalo, New York: Prometheus Books.

McDowell, L. (2002), 'The Cutting Room by Louise Welsh: The Literary Beauty of a Glaswegian Beast', The Independent, 8 August. Available at: http://www. independent.co.uk/arts-entertainment/books/reviews/the-cutting-room-bylouisewelsh-5360182.html (accessed 30 May 2023).

McEvoy, E. (2016), Gothic Tourism, London: Palgrave Macmillan.

McEwan, I. (2005), 'How Could We Have Forgotten that this was Always Going to Happen?', The Guardian, 8 July. Available at: https://www.theguardian.com/world/2005/jul/08/terrorism.july74 (accessed 21 February 2022).

McEwen, T. (2005), 'The City that Ate the World', The Guardian, 16 October. Available at: https://www.theguardian.com/books/2005/sep/24/featuresreviews.guardianreview18 (accessed 24 February 2022).

McFarlane, A. (2024, forthcoming), 'Speculative Fiction of the 2010s', in N. Bentley, E. Horton, N. Hubble and P. Tew (eds), The 2010s: A Decade of Contemporary British Fiction, London: Bloomsbury.

McGill, B. (2011), The Butterfly Cabinet, London: Headline Review.

McGrath, P. ([1990] 1992), Spider, London: Penguin.

McGrath, P. ([1993] 1994), Dr Haggard's Disease, London: Vintage.

McGrath, P. ([1996] 2015), Asylum, London: Penguin.

McGrath, P. (2004), Port Mungo, New York: Alfred A. Knopf.

McGrath, P. (2005), Ghost Town: Tales of Manhattan Then and Now, London: Bloomsbury.

McGrath, P. ([2008] 2009), Trauma, London: Bloomsbury.

McGrath, P. (2013), Constance, London: Bloomsbury.

McGrath, P. and L. Welsh (2006), 'We All Have Dreaming Minds, and We are Capable of Being Terrified: Gothic Nightmares', Tate Etc., 6, Spring. Available at: https://www.tate.org.uk/tate-etc/issue-6-spring-2006/we-all-have-dreaming-minds-and-we-are-all-capable-being-terrified (accessed 25 February 2022).

McGregor, J. (2010), Even the Dogs, London: Bloomsbury.

McGregor, J. (2017), Reservoir 13, London: Fourth Estate.

McNally, D. (2012), Monsters of the Market: Zombies, Vampires and Global Capitalism, Chicago, IL: Haymarket Books.

McRobert, N. (2019), 'Project Fear: What Will Brexit Gothic Fiction Look Like?' The Guardian, 11 February. Available at: https://www.theguardian.com/books/booksblog/2019/feb/11/project-fear-what-will-brexit-gothic-fiction-look-like (accessed 30 May 2023).

Meaker, M. (2018), 'Europe is Using Smartphone Data as a Weapon to Deport efugees', Wired, 2 July. Available at: https://www.wired.co.uk/article/europe-immigration-refugees-smartphone-metadata-deportations (accessed 21 September 2018).

Melville, H. (1851), Moby-Dick, New York: Harper & Brothers, Publishers; and London: Richard Bentley.

Menadue, C. (2017), 'Trysts Tropiques: The Torrid Jungles of Science Fiction', eTropic, 16 (1): 125–40.

Mendoza, K. (2015), *Austerity: The Demolition of the Welfare State and the Rise of the Zombie-Economy*, Oxford: New Internationalist.

Menmuir, W. (2016), *The Many*, Cromer: Salt Publishing.

Metzidakis, S. (1995), 'Reviewed Work(s): Profane Illumination: Walter Benjamin and the Paris of Surrealist Revolution by Margaret Cohen', *French Review*, 69 (1): 172–4.

Michel, L. (2015), 'The Last Holdouts of the Genre Wars: on Kazuo Ishiguro, Ursula K. Le Guin, and the Misuse of Labels', *Electric Lit*, 9 March. Available at: https://electricliterature.com/the-last-holdouts-of-the-genre-wars-on-kazuo-ishiguro-ursula-k-le-guin-and-the-misuse-of-labels/ (accessed 30 May 2023).

Michlin, M. (2012), 'The Haunted House in Contemporary Filmic and Literary Gothic Narratives of Trauma', *Transatlantica*, 1: 1–24.

Mieville, C. (2000), *Perdido Street Station*, London: Pan Macmillan.

Mieville, C. (2011a), *Embassytown*, London: Pan Macmillan.

Mieville, C. (2011b), 'M. R. James and the Quantum Vampire', *Weird Fiction Review*, 29 November. Available at: https://weirdfictionreview.com/2011/11/m-r-james-and-the-quantum-vampire-by-china-mieville/ (accessed 12 June 2023).

'Migrants with Mobiles: Phones are Now Indispensible for Refugees' (2017), *The Economist*, 11 February. Available at: https://www.economist.com/international/2017/02/11/phones-are-now-indispensable-for-refugees (accessed 21 September 2018).

Miles, R. and Cleary, E., eds (2000), *Gothic Documents: A Sourcebook 1700–1820*, Manchester: Manchester University Press.

Miller, A. (2006), *Demo*, London: Penguin.

Miller, G. (2006), 'Aesthetic Depersonalization in Louise Welsh's *The Cutting Room*', *Journal of Narrative Theory*, 36 (1): 72–89.

Mitchell, D. (1995), 'The End of Public Space? People's Park, Definitions of the Public, and Democracy', *Annals of the Association of American Geographers*, 85 (1): 108–33.

Mitchell, D. (2001), 'Postmodern Geographical Praxis? Postmodern Impulse and the War against Homeless People in the "Post-Justice City"', in C. Minca (ed.), *Postmodern Geography: Theory and Praxis*, 57–92, Oxford: Blackwell.

Mitchell, S. (2007), 'Dark Interpreter: Literary Uses of the Brocken Spectre from Coleridge to Pynchon', *Dalhousie Review*, 87 (2): 167–88.

Monbiot, G. (2019), 'The Insidious Ideology Pushing Us towards a Brexit Cliff-Edge', *The Guardian*, 11 September. Available at: https://www.theguardian.com/commentisfree/2019/sep/11/brexit-ultras-triumph-neoliberalism (accessed 30 May 2023).

Mondal, A. (2018), 'Scratching the Post-Imperial Itch', in R. Eaglestone (ed.), *Brexit and Literature: Critical and Cultural Responses*, 82–91, London: Routledge.

Moore, J. (2022), 'Global Capitalism in the Great Implosion From Planetary Superexploitation to Planetary Socialism?', Foreword to W. I. Robinson, *Can Global Capitalism Endure?*, Binghamton, NY: PM Press. Available at: https://jasonwmoore.

com/wp-content/uploads/2022/03/Moore-The-Great-Implosion-for-Robinson-book-FOR-website-March-2022.pdf (accessed 1 February 2023).

Moore, J. (2017), 'The Capitalocene, Part I: On the Nture and Origins of Our Ecological Crisis', *Journal of Peasant Studies*, 44 (3): 594–630.

Moore, J., ed. (2016), *Anthropocene or Capitalocene? Nature, History, and the Crisis of Capitalism*, Binghamton, NY: PM Press.

Moretti, F. ([1983] 2005), *Signs Taken for Wonders: On the Sociology of Literary Forms*, London: Verso.

Morey, P. (2018), *Islamophobia and the Novel*, New York: Columbia University Press.

Morgan, P. (2017), *The Spice Boys*, London: Austin Macauley Publishers.

Morton, T. (2013), *Hyperobjects: Philosophy and Ecology after the End of the World*, Minneapolis, MN: University of Minnesota Press.

Morton, T. (2016), *Dark Ecology*, New York: Columbia University Press.

Moss, S. (2018), *Ghost Wall*, London: Granta.

Moss, S. (2019), 'Sarah Moss: Brexit and Heaney's Bog Bodies', *Irish Times*, 8 June. Available at: https://www.irishtimes.com/culture/books/sarah-moss-brexit-and-heaney-s-bog-bodies-1.3909594 (accessed 30 May 2023).

Moss, S. (2020), *Summerwater*, London: Picador.

Mousoutzanis, A. (2016), 'Network Fictions and the Global Unhomely', *C21 Literature: Journal of 21st-Century Writings*, 4 (1): 7: 1–19.

Mozley, F. (2017), *Elmet*, Chapel Hill, NC: Algonquin Books.

Mukherjee, A. (2018), 'Migrant Britain', in R. Eaglestone (ed.), *Brexit and Literature: Critical and Cultural Responses*, 92–104, London: Routledge.

Mulvey, L. ([1975] 1998), 'Visual Pleasure and the Narrative Cinema', in J. Rivkin and M. Ryan (eds), *Literary Theory: An Anthology*, 585–95, Oxford: Blackwell.

Murnane, B. (2017), 'Staging Spectrality: Capitalising (on) Ghosts in German Postdramatic Theatre', in L. Blake and A. Soltysik Monnet (eds), *Neoliberal Gothic: International Gothic in the Neoliberal Age*, 56–79, Manchester: Manchester University Press.

Musanga, T. (2017), '"Ngozi" (Avenging Spirit), Zimbabwean Transnational Migration, and Restorative Justice in Brian Chikwava's *Harare North* (2009)', *Journal of Black Studies*, 48 (8): 775–90.

Musharbash, Y. (2014), 'Introduction: Monsters, Anthropology, and Monster Studies', in Y. Musharbash and G. Henning Presterudstuen (eds), *Monster Anthropology in Australasia and Beyond*, 1–24, London: Palgrave Macmillan.

Mutis, A. M. (2020), 'Monsters and Agritoxins: The Environmental Gothic in Samanta Schweblin's *Distancia de Rescate*', in I. Kressner, A. M. Mutis, and E. M. Pettinaroli (eds), *Ecofictions, Ecorealities, and Slow Violence in Latin America and the Latinx World*, 39–54, London: Routledge.

Nadler, L. and Z. Thompson (2017), *The Dregs*, Los Angeles, CA: Black Mask Studios.

Nairn, T. (1981), *The Break-Up of Britain: Crisis and Neo-Nationalism*, London: Verso.

Naughton, J. (2018), 'Anti-Social Media: How Facebook Disconnects Us and Undermines Democracy by Siva Vaidhyanathan – Review', *The Guardian*, 25 June. Available at: https://www.theguardian.com/books/2018/jun/25/anti-social-media-how-facebook-disconnects-us-undermines-democracy-siva-vaidhyanathan-review (accessed 21 September 2018).

Nayar, P. (2019), *Ecoprecarity: Vulnerable Lives in Literature and Culture*, London: Routledge.

Neal, E. (2020), *Obeah, Race and Racism: Caribbean Witchcraft in the English Imagination*, Mona: University of West Indies Press.

Neimanis, A. ([2017] 2019), *Bodies of Water: Posthuman Feminist Phenomenology*, London: Bloomsbury.

Nelson, L. (2002), 'Protecting the Common Good: Technology, Objectivity, and Privacy', *Public Administration Review*, 62: 69–73.

Nevins, A. Shaw (2019), *Working Juju: Representations of the Caribbean Fantastic*, Athens, GA: University of Georgia Press.

Newton, P. (2008), 'From Chempaka, the Muslim Tree of Death, to Scarf-Wrapped Banana Plants: Postcolonial Representations of Gardening Images in Tash Aw's *The Harmony Silk Factory*', *Kunapipi*, 30 (1): 170–82.

Ngai, S. ([2005] 2007), *Ugly Feelings*, Cambridge, MA: Harvard University Press.

Nixon, K. (2020), *Kept from All Contagion: Germ Theory, Disease, and the Dilemma of Human Contact in Late Nineteenth-Century Literature*, New York: State University of New York Press.

Nixon, R. (2011), *Slow Violence and the Environmentalism of the Poor*, Cambridge, MA: Harvard University Press.

Novy, J. (2016), 'The Selling Out of Berlin and the De- and Re-politicization of Urban Tourism in Europe's "Capital of Cool"', in C. Colomb and J. Novy (eds), *Protest and Resistance in the Tourist City*, 52–72, London: Routledge.

Noxolo, P. (2014), 'Towards an Embodied Securityscape: Brian Chikwava's *Harare North* and the Asylum Seeking Body as Site of Articulation', *Social & Cultural Geography*, 15 (3): 291–312.

O'Flynn, C. (2007), *What was Lost*, Birmingham: Tindal Street Press.

O'Loughlin, K. (2021), 'The Pathless Seas: Configuring Displacement in British Romanticism', *Ler História*, 78: 85–107.

O'Neal, E. (2020), *Obeah, Race and Racism: Caribbean Witchcraft in the English Imagination*, Kingston: University of West Indies Press.

Orwell, G. ([1933] 2021), *Down and Out in Paris and London*, London: William Collins.

Oyeyemi, H. (2009), *White is for Witching*, London: Picador.

Packham, J. (2019), 'The Gothic Coast: Boundaries, Belonging, and Coastal Community in Contemporary British Fiction', *Critique: Studies in Contemporary Fiction*, 60 (2): 205–21.

Packham, J. and D. Punter (2017), 'Oceanic Studies and the Gothic Deep', *Gothic Studies*, 19 (2): 17–29.

Parekh, B. (2000), *The Future of Multi-Ethnic Britain: The Parekh Report*, London: Profile Books.stephan
Parikka, J. (2007), *Digital Contagions: A Media Archaeology of Computer Viruses*, Oxford: Peter Lang Publishing.
Parker, E. (2013), 'The Country House Revisited: Sarah Waters' *The Little Stranger*', in K. Mitchell (ed.), *Sarah Waters*, 99–113, London: Bloomsbury.
Parkes-Nield, S. (2022), 'The Summoning: Folk Horror and the Calendar Custom in Molly Aitken's *The Island Child* (2020) and Zoe Gilbert's *Folk* (2019)', *Critique: Studies in Contemporary Fiction*. Doi: 10.1080/001116192022.2143256.
Partners for Berlin (2000), 'Perfect Place to Live', postcard, n.d. Available at: http://www.berlin.de/partner-fuer-berlin/english/newberlin/leben.html (accessed 30 May 2023).
Passey, J. (2020), 'The Subterranean Gothic', *Joan Passey Wordpress*, Call for Papers, Special edn of *Revenant*: Obscene Surfacings and the Subterranean Gothic. Available at: https://joanpassey.wordpress.com/the-subterranean-gothic/ (accessed 11 February 2022).
Paton, D. (2015), *The Cultural Politics of Obeah: Religion, Colonialism and Modernity in the Caribbean World*, New York: Cambridge University Press.
Paul, C. (2004), *Whoever You Choose to Love*, London: Weidenfeld and Nicolson.
Paver, M. (2010), *Dark Matter: A Ghost Story*, London: Orion.
Peeren, E. (2010), 'Everyday Ghosts and the Ghostly Everyday in Amos Tutuola, Ben Okri, and Achille Mbembe', in M. del Pilar Blanco and E. Peeren (eds), *Popular Ghosts: The Haunted Spaces of Everyday Culture*, 106–17, London: Continuum.
Perry, S. (2016), *The Essex Serpent*, London: Serpent's Tail.
Perry, S. (2018), *Melmoth*, London: Serpent's Tail.
Perryman, M., ed. (2008), *Imagined Nation: England After Britain*, London: Lawrence and Wishart.
Piatti-Farnell, L. and D. L. Brien (2015), *New Directions in 21st Century Gothic: The Gothic Compass*, 1st edn, London: Routledge.
Pile, S. (2005), *Real Cities*, London: Sage.
Poe, E. A. ([1839] 2003), 'The Fall of the House of Usher', in *The Fall of the House of Usher and Other Writings*, 90–109, London: Penguin.
Pollitt, C. (2012), *New Perspectives on Public Services: Place and Technology*, Oxford: Oxford University Press.
Porter, J. (2013), '[Im]Migrating Witchcraft: Transatlantic Gothic Hybridity in White is for Witching', *Monsters and the Monstrous*, 3 (1): 23–38.
Priest, C. (2011), *The Islanders*, London: Gollancz.
Procter, J. (2003), *Dwelling Places: Postwar Black British Writing*, Manchester: Manchester University Press.
Pun, R. (2013), 'Digital Images and Visions of Jihad: Virtual Orientalism and the Distorted Lens of Technology', *CyberOrient*, 7 (1): 94–115.
Punter, D. ([1980] 1996), *A Literature of Terror: A History of Gothic Fictions from 1765 to the Present Day*, 2nd edn, London: Routledge.

Punter, D. and Byron, G. (2004), *The Gothic*, Oxford: Blackwell Publishing.
Purcell, L. (2017), *The Silent Companions*, London: Raven Books.
Purcell, L. (2023), *The Whispering Muse*, London: Raven Books.
Quinn, A. (2019), '*Ghost Wall* Explores the Human Cost of Nativist Nostalgia', *The Atlantic*, 25 January. Available at: https://www.theatlantic.com/entertainment/archive/2019/01/ghost-wall-more-brexit-parable-review/581068/ (accessed 26 August 2023).
Radcliffe, A. (1790), *A Sicilian Romance*, London: Hookham and Carpenter.
Radcliffe, A. ([1794] 2008), *The Mysteries of Udolpho*, Oxford: Oxford University Press.
Radstone, S. (2003), 'The War of the Fathers: Trauma, Fantasy, and September 11', in J. Greenberg (ed.), *Trauma at Home: After 9/11*, 117–23, Lincoln, NE: University of Nebraska Press.
Radstone, S. (2007), 'Trauma Theory: Contexts, Politics, Ethics', *Paragraph*, 30 (1): 9–29.
Ratmoko, D. (2005), *On Spectrality: Fantasies of Redemption in the Western Canon*, Oxford: Peter Lang.
Ravenhill, M. (2008), *The Culture of Homelessness*, London: Routledge.
Rawlinson, M. (2010), *Pat Barker*, London: Palgrave Macmillan.
Reis Filho, L. (2020), 'No Safe Space: Zombie Film Tropes during the COVID-19 Pandemic', *Space and Culture*, 23 (3): 253–8.
Rilke, R. M. ([1910] 1949), *The Notebooks of Malte Laurids Brigge*, trans. M. D. Herter Norton, New York: W. W. Norton.
Roberts, A. (2010), *New Model Army*, London: Gollancz.
Rodríguez González, C. (2016), 'The Rhythms of the City: The Performance of Time and Space in Suhayl Saadi's *Psychoraag*', *Journal of Commonwealth Literature*, 51 (1): 1–18.
Rothberg, M. (2003), '"There is No Poetry in This": Writing, Trauma, and Home', in J. Greenberg (ed.), *Trauma at Home: After 9/11*, 147–57, Lincoln, NE: University of Nebraska Press.
Rothberg, M. (2019), *The Implicated Subject: Beyond Victims and Perpetrators*, Stanford, CA: Stanford University Press.
Rotter, R. (2016), 'Waiting in the Asylum Determination Process: Just an Empty Interlude?', *Time & Society*, 25 (1): 80–101.
Royle, N. (2003), *The Uncanny*, Manchester: Manchester University Press.
Ryan, R. (2020), 'Resurrecting the Bog Queen: Exploring the Gender Politics of Ireland's Bogs in Postcolonial and Nationalist Literature', *Inquiries*, 12 (10): 1. Available at: http://www.inquiriesjournal.com/articles/1826/resurrecting-the-bog-queen-exploring-the-gender-politics-of-irelands-bogs-in-postcolonial-and-nationalist-literature (accessed 30 May 2023).
Saadi, S. (2004), *Psychoraag*, Edinburgh: Black and White Publishing.
Sachikonye, L. (2012), *Zimbabwe's Lost Decade: Politics, Development and Society*, Harare: Weaver Press.
Sage, V. (2011), '"The Grail, or the Holy Bloodshed . . .": Cruelty, Darkness and the Body in Janice Galloway, Alison Kennedy and Louise Welsh', *Gothic Studies*, 13 (2): 63–77.

Sage, V. and A. L. Smith, eds (1996), *Modern Gothic: A Reader*, Manchester: Manchester University Press.

Said, E. (1979), 'Zionism from the Standpoint of Its Victims', *Social Text*, 1: 7–58.

Said, E. (2006), 'The Essential Terrorist', *The Nation*, 15 August. Available at: https://www.thenation.com/article/archive/essential-terrorist/ (accessed 15 February 2022).

Sandhu, S. (2017), '*Exit West* by Mohsin Hamid – Magical Vision of Refugee Crisis', *The Guardian*, 12 March. Available at: https://www.theguardian.com/books/2017/mar/12/exit-west-mohsin-hamid-review-refugee-crisis (accessed 21 September 2018).

Saxena, V. (2020), 'Carnivalesque Memoryscapes in Multiculturism: History, Memory, Storytelling in Tash Aw's *Harmony Silk Factory*', *Critique: Studies in Contemporary Fiction*, 63 (1): 1–14.

Schell, J. (2022), 'Monstrous Megalodons of the Anthropocene: Extinction and Adaptation in Prehistoric Shark Fiction, 1974–2018', in J. D. Edwards, R. Graulund, and J. Höglund (eds), *Dark Scenes from Damaged Earth: The Gothic Anthropocene*, 64–80, Minneapolis, MN: University of Minnesota Press.

Schultz, M. (2014), *Haunted Historiographies: The Rhetoric of Ideologies in Postcolonial Irish Fiction*, Manchester: Manchester University Press.

Scott, P. ([1966] 1996), *The Jewel in the Crown*, London: Arrow.

Scovell, A. (2016), 'Where to begin with Folk Horror', British Film Institute (BFI), 8 June. Available at: https://www.bfi.org.uk/features/where-begin-with-folk-horror (accessed 18 June 2023).

Scully, B. (2016), 'Precarity North and South: A Southern Critique of Guy Standing', *Global Labour Journal*, 7 (2): 160–73.

Sedgwick, E. (1980), *The Coherence of Gothic Conventions*, rev. edn, New York: Arno.

Sedgwick, E. (1990), *Epistemology of the Closet*, Berkeley, CA: University of California Press.

Seltzer, M. (1997), 'Wound Culture: Trauma in the Pathological Public Sphere', *October*, 80: 3–26.

Setterfield, D. (2006), *The Thirteenth Tale*, London: Orion.

Seymour, R. (2014), *Against Austerity: How We Can Fix the Crisis They Made*, London: Pluto Press.

Shaw, K. (2021), *Brexlit: British Literature and the European Project*, London: Bloomsbury.

Shelley, M. (1818), *Frankenstein*, London: Lackington, Hughes, Harding, Mavorr, & Jones.

Sheridan, S. (2021), *The Fair Botanists*, London: Hodder and Stoughton.

Shildrick, M. (1997), *Leaky Bodies and Boundaries: Feminism, postmodernism and (Bio) ethics*, London: Routledge.

Shildrick, M. (2015), 'Chimerism and *Immunitas*: The Emergence of a Posthumanist Biophilosophy', in S. E. Wilmer and A. Žukauskaitė (eds), *Resisting Biopolitics: Philosophical, Political, and Performative Strategies*, 95–109, London: Routledge.

Sim, W. (2011), 'History and Narrative: The Use of the Sublime in Tash Aw's Fiction'. *Journal of Commonwealth Literature*, 46 (2): 293–310.

Simmel, G. ([1903] 2002), 'The Metropolis and Mental Life', in G. Bridge and S. Watson (eds), *The Blackwell City Reader*, 11–19, Oxford: Blackwell.

Simpson, D. (2006), *9/11: The Culture of Commemoration*, Chicago, IL: University of Chicago Press.

Smith, A. (2001), *Hotel World*, London: Penguin.

Smith, A. (2004), 'Migrancy, Hybridity, and Postcolonial Literary Studies', in N. Lazarus (ed.), *The Cambridge Companion to Postcolonial Literary Studies*, 241–61, Cambridge: Cambridge University Press.

Smith, A. (2005), *The Accidental*, London: Hamish Hamilton.

Smith, A. (2012), 'The Limits of Neo-Victorian History: Elizabeth Kosova's *The Historian* and *The Swan Thieves*', in M. Kohlke and C. Gutleben (eds), *Neo-Victorian Gothic: Horror, Violence and Degeneration in the Re-imagined Nineteenth-Century*, 51–74, Boston, MA: Brill.

Smith, J. A. (2018), 'Fake News Literary Criticism', in R. Eaglestone (ed.), *Brexit and Literature: Critical and Cultural Responses*, 118–30, London: Routledge.

Smythe, J. (2014), '*The Girl with All the Gifts* by MR Carey – Review', *The Guardian*, 15 January. Available at: https://www.theguardian.com/books/2014/jan/15/girl-with-gifts-mr-carey-review (accessed 10 February 2023).

Sparke, M. B. (2006), 'A Neoliberal Nexus: Economy, Security and the Biopolitics of Citizenship on the Border', *Political Geography*, 25 (2): 151–80.

Spivak, G. C. (2006), *In Other Worlds: Essays in Cultural Politics*, London: Routledge.

Spooner, C. (2004), *Fashioning Gothic Bodies*, Manchester: Manchester University Press.

Spooner, C. (2006), *Contemporary Gothic*, London: Reaktion Books.

Spooner, C. (2007), 'Gothic in the Twentieth-Century', in C. Spooner and E. McEvoy (eds), *The Routledge Companion to Gothic*, 38–47, New York: Routledge.

Spooner, C. (2010), 'Preface', in B. Cherry, P. Howell, and C. Ruddell (eds), *Twenty-First-Century Gothic*, ix–xii, Newcastle upon Tyne: Cambridge Scholars Publishing.

Spooner, C. (2017), *Post-Millennial Gothic*, London: Bloomsbury.

Spring, I. (2001), *Phantom Village: Myth of the New Glasgow*, Edinburgh: Polygon.

Starr, M. (2014), 'Whedon's Great Glass Elevator: Space, Liminality, and Intertext in *The Cabin in the Woods*', *Slayage: The Journal of the Whedon Studies Association*. Available at: http://nectar.northampton.ac.uk/14441/1/Starr_Michael_Slayage_2014_Whedons_Great_Glass_Elevator_Space_Liminality_and_Intertext_in_Cabin_in_the_Woods.pdf (accessed 6 May 2022).

Stephanou, A. (2014), 'Helen Oyeyemi's "White is for Witching" and the Discourse of Consumption', *Callaloo*, 37 (5): 1245–59.

Stephanou, A. (2017), 'Game of Fangs: The Vampire and Neoliberal Subjectivity', in L. Blake and A. Soltysik Monnet (eds), *Neoliberal Gothic: International Gothic in the Neoliberal Age*, 21–37, Manchester: Manchester University Press.

Stephanou, A. (2019), *Inhuman Materiality in Gothic Media*, London: Routledge.

Stevenson, R. L. ([1886] 2020), *The Strange Case of Dr Jekyll and Mr Hyde*, 2nd Norton Critical edn, New York: Norton.
Stoker, B. ([1897] 2021), *Dracula*, 2nd Norton Critical edn, New York: Norton.
Strachan, Z. (2004), *Spin Cycle*, London: Picador.
Suliza Hashim, R. and N. Md Yusof (2014), 'Counter-Discourses in Post-9/11 Muslim Women's Narratives', in P. Childs, C. Colebrook, and S. Groes (eds), *Women's Fiction and Post-9/11 Contexts*, 125–39, London: Lexington Books.
Summerfield, P. (1994), 'Women in Britain Since 1945: Companionate Carriage and the Double Burden', in P. Obelkevich and J. Catterall (eds), *Understanding Postwar British Society*, 58–72, London: Routledge.
Tay, E. (2011), *Colony, Nation, and Globalisation: Not at Home in Singaporean and Malaysian Literature*, Hong Kong: Hong Kong University Press.
Taylor, C. (2003), '*The Cutting Room* by Louise Welsh', *Salon*, April 9. Available on: http://www.salon.com/2003/04/08/cutting_2/ (accessed 26 April 2022).
Taylor, D. J. (2004), 'In Search of the Invisible Woman', *The Independent*, 12 March. Available at: http://www.independent.co.uk/arts-entertainment/books/reviews/remember-me-by-trezza-azzopardi-565970.html (accessed 20 April 2010).
Tey, J. (1948), *The Franchise Affair*, London: Peter Davies.
The Bookseller Editorial Team (2014), 'Mike Carey's New Direction', *The Bookseller*, 8 January. Available at: https://www.thebookseller.com/features/features/mike-careys-new-direction-338473 (accessed 10 February 2023).
Thomas, S. (2006), *The End of Mr Y*, London: Canongate.
Thrift, N. (2004), 'Intensities of Feeling: Towards a Spatial Politics of Affect', *Geografiska Annaler, Series B, Human Geography*, 86 (1): 57–78.
Till, K. (2005), *The New Berlin: Memory, Politics, Place*, Minneapolis, MN: University of Minnesota Press.
Timm, C. (2022), *The Seawomen*, London: Hodder Studio.
Toase, S. (2020), 'Confronting the Default: Portraying Homeless in Science Fiction and Fantasy', Tor.com, 15 April. Available at: https://www.tor.com/2020/04/15/confronting-the-default-portraying-homelessness-in-science-fiction-and-fantasy/ (accessed 6 May 2022).
Todorov, T. (1975), *The Fantastic: A Structural Approach to A Literary Genre*, trans. R. Howard, Ithaca, NY: Cornell.
Tondeur, L. (2003), *The Water's Edge*, London: Headline Review.
Toner, E. (2019), 'The Secret World of Life (and Death) in Ireland's Peat Bogs', *The New York Times*, 19 October. Available at: https://www.nytimes.com/interactive/2019/10/19/multimedia/ireland-peat-bogs.html (accessed 30 May 2023).
Tonkin, B. (2019), 'Niall Griffiths: *Broken Ghost* Review: Welsh Visions of Hope and Loss', *Theartsdesk.com*, 18 August. Available at: https://theartsdesk.com/books/niall-griffiths-broken-ghost-review-welsh-visions-hope-and-loss (accessed 30 May 2023).
Trexler, A. (2015), *Anthropocene Fictions: The Novel in a Time of Climate Change*, Charlottesville, VA: University of Virginia Press.

United Nations Children's Fund (UNICEF) (2020), 'Ending Preventable Child Deaths: How Britain Can Lead the Way'. Available at: https://www.unicef.org.uk/campaign-with-us/child-health-report/ (accessed 23 June 2023).

Upstone, S. (2010), *British Asian Fiction: Twenty-First-Century Voices*, Manchester: Manchester University Press, 2010.

Upstone, S. (2018), 'Do Novels Tell Us How to Vote?', in R. Eaglestone (ed.), *Brexit and Literature: Critical and Cultural Responses*, 44–58, London: Routledge.

Valencia, S. (2018), *Gore Capitalism. Semiotex(e)* Intervention Series, 24, South Pasadena, CA: Semiotext(e).

van Elferen, I. (2014), 'Techno-Gothics of the Early-Twenty-First-Century', in J. E. Hogle (ed.), *The Cambridge Companion to Modern Gothic*, 138–54, Cambridge: Cambridge University Press.

van Schipstal, Inge L. M. and W. J. Nicholls (2014), 'Rights to the Neoliberal City: The Case of Urban Land Squatting in "Creative" Berlin', *Territory, Politics, Governance*, 2 (2): 173–93.

Varese, J. M. (2023), *The Company*, Salisbury: Baskerville Press.

Vermeulen, P. (2014), 'Posthuman Affect', *EJES: European Journal of English Studies*, 18 (2): 121–34.

Vidler, A. (1992), *The Architectural Uncanny: Essays in the Modern Unhomely*, Cambridge, MA: The MIT Press.

Vidler, A. (2000), *Warped Space: Art, Architecture, and Anxiety in Modern Culture*, Cambridge, MA: The MIT Press.

Wacquant, L. (2009), *Punishing the Poor: The Neoliberal Government of Social Insecurity*, Durham, NC: Duke University Press.

Walawalkar, A., E. Rose and M. Townsend (2023), 'UK Coastguard "Left Channel Migrants Adrift" in Lead-Up to Mass Drowning', *The Guardian*, 29 April. Available at: https://www.theguardian.com/world/2023/apr/29/uk-coastguard-left-channel-migrants-adrift-in-lead-up-to-mass-drowning (accessed 30 May 2023).

Wald, P. (2021), 'Preface', in S. Becker, M. de Bruin-Molé and S. Polak (eds), *Embodying Contagion: The Viropolitics of Horror and Desire in Contemporary Discourse*, xiii–xviii, Cardiff: University of Wales Press.

Walker, A. (2022), *Once Upon a Fever*, Frome: Chicken House Books.

Walker, P. (2017), 'Grenfell Tower Tragedy Shows Effects of Austerity, Corbyn Tells May', *The Guardian*, 28 June. Available at: https://www.theguardian.com/politics/2017/jun/28/grenfell-tower-effects-austerity-corbyn-may-pmqs (accessed 23 June 2023).

Wallace, G. and R. Stevenson, eds (1993), *The Scottish Novel Since the Seventies*, Edinburgh: Edinburgh University Press.

Walpole, H. (1765), *The Castle of Otranto*, London: Tho. Lownds.

Walsh, C. (2021), 'Young Adults Hit Hardest by Loneliness During Pandemic', *Harvard Gazette*, 17 February. Available at: https://news.harvard.edu/gazette/story/2021/02/young-adults-teens-loneliness-mental-health-coronavirus-covid-pandemic/ (accessed 15 February 2023).

Ward, J. (2011), 'Re-Capitalizing Berlin', in Mark Silberman (ed.), *The German Wall*, 79–97, London: Palgrave Macmillan.
Warwick, A. (2007), 'Feeling Gothicky?', *Gothic Studies*, 9 (1): 5–15.
Wasson, S. (2015a), 'Useful Darkness: Intersections between Medical Humanities and Gothic Studies', *Gothic Studies*, 17 (1): 1–12.
Wasson, S. (2015b), 'Scalpel and Metaphor: The Ceremony of Organ Harvest in Gothic Science Fiction', *Gothic Studies*, 17 (1): 104–23.
Wasson, S. (2020), *Transplantation Gothic*, Manchester: Manchester University Press.
Waters, S. (2002), *Fingersmith*, London: Virago
Waters, S. (2009), *The Little Stranger*, London: Virago.
Waterstones (2004), '*The Girl with All the Gifts* by M. R. Carey', Waterstones.com. Available at: https://www.waterstones.com/book/the-girl-with-all-the-gifts/m-r-carey/9780356500157 (accessed 26 August 2023).
Watkin, W. (2021), *Bioviolence: How the Powers that Be Make Us Do What They Want*, London: Routledge.
Watson, M. (2009), 'Planning for a Future of Asset-Based Welfare? New Labour, Financialized Economic Agency and the Housing Market', *Planning, Practice & Research*, 24 (1): 41–56.
Watts, J. (1999), *Contesting the Gothic: Fiction, Genre and Cultural Conflict, 1764–1832*, Cambridge: University of Cambridge Press.
Waugh, E. ([1945] 1989), *Brideshead Revisited*, London: Penguin.
Weinstock, J. A. (2020), 'Introduction: A Genealogy of Monster Theory', in J. A. Weinstock (ed), *The Monster Theory Reader*, 1–36, Minneapolis, MN: University of Minnesota Press.
Weinstock, J. A. (2023), *Gothic Things: Dark Enchantment and Anthropocene Anxiety*, New York: Fordham Press.
Wells, H. G. (1896), *The Island of Dr Moreau*, London: Heinemann.
Wells, H. G. ([1898] 2005), *The War of the Worlds*, London: Penguin.
Welsh, L. (2002), *The Cutting Room*, Edinburgh: Canongate.
Wenzel, J. (2017), 'Turning Over a New Leaf: Fanonian Humanism and Environmental Justice', in U. K. Heise, J. Christensen and M. Nieman (eds), *The Routledge Compassion to the Environmental Humanities*, 165–73, London: Routledge.
Wester, M. L. (2014), 'The Gothic and the Politics of Race', in J. E. Hogle (ed), *The Cambridge Companion to the Modern Gothic*, 157–73, Cambridge: Cambridge University Press.
Wester, M. L. ([2019] 2021), 'Black Diasporic Gothic', in M. Wester and X. Aldana Reyes (eds), *Twenty-First-Century Gothic: An Edinburgh Companion*, 289–303, Edinburgh: Edinburgh University Press.
Wester, M. and X. Aldana Reyes ([2019] 2021), 'Introduction: The Gothic in the Twenty-First-Century', in M. Wester and X. Aldana Reyes (eds), *Twenty-First-Century Gothic: An Edinburgh Companion*, 1–16, Edinburgh: Edinburgh University Press.

Whittle, M. (2020), 'Gill Plain (ed.), *British Literature in Transition, 1940–1960*, Cambridge: Cambridge University Press, 2018', Book Review, *Journal of British Studies*, 59 (3): 701–2. Available at: https://www.cambridge.org/core/journals/journal-of-british-studies/article/abs/gill-plain-ed-british-literature-in-transition-19401960-postwar-british-literature-in-transition-cambridge-cambridge-university-press-2018-pp-438-11000-cloth/4D21AB5C790756DC30044B07BB872C29 (accessed 13 March 2023).

Wigley, M. (2002), 'Insecurity by Design', in M. Sorkin and S. Zukin (eds), *After the World Trade Center: Rethinking New York City*, 69–85, New York: Routledge.

Wilde, O. ([novella 1890, novel 1891] 2019), *The Picture of Dorian Gray*, 3rd Norton Critical edn, New York: Norton.

Williams, C. (2021), 'Glasgow Named among Most Dangerous Cities in Europe in a New Poll', *Glasgow Live*, 30 September. Available at: https://www.glasgowlive.co.uk/news/glasgow-news/glasgow-named-among-most-dangerous-21716710 (accessed 26 April 2022).

Willis, C. (2018), *Lovers and Strangers: An Immigrant History of Postwar Britain*, London: Penguin.

Wilson, A. N. (2005), *A Jealous Ghost*, London: Arrow.

Wilson, J. (2001), *The Dark Clue*, London: Faber and Faber.

Winslow, R. G. (2004), 'Troping Trauma: Conceiving (of) Experiences of Speechless Terror', *Journal of Advanced Composition*, 24 (3): 607–33.

Wisker, G. (2007), *Key Concepts in Postcolonial Literature*, London: Palgrave Macmillan.

Wisker, G. (2016), 'Hauntings, Liminal Spaces, Silences, Echoes and Misreadings in Sarah Waters's Feminist Gothic *The Little Stranger*: Toubling Narratives of Romance and Class, Continuity and Change', in A. Waters and C. O'Callaghan (eds), *Sarah Waters and Contemporary Feminism*, 97–113, London: Palgrave Macmillan.

Wood, L. (2018), *The Sing of the Shore*, London: Fourth Estate.

Yancy, G. (2020), 'Judith Butler: Mourning is a Political Act Amid the Pandemic and Its Disparities', *Truthout*, 30 April. Available at: https://truthout.org/articles/judith-butler-mourning-is-a-political-act-amid-the-pandemic-and-its-disparities/ (accessed 24 August 2023).

Yeo, Colin (2020), *Welcome to Britain: Fixing our Broken Immigration System*, Croydon: Biteback Publishing.

Yost, M. (2012), 'The Invisible Become Visible: An Analysis of How People Experiencing Homelessness Use Social Media', *Elon Journal of Undergraduate Research in Communications*, 3 (2). Available at: http://www.inquiriesjournal.com/articles/830/the-invisible-become-visible-an-analysis-of-how-people-experiencing-homelessness-use-social-media (accessed 5 May 2022).

Yuval-Davis, N. (2011), *The Politics of Belonging: Intersectional Contestations*, London: Sage.

Zanger, J. (1997), 'Metaphor into Metonymy: The Vampire Next Door', in Joan Gordon and Veronica Hollinger (eds), *Blood Read: The Vampire as Metaphor in Contemporary Culture*, 17–26, Philadelphia, PA: University of Pennsylvania Press.

Zapata, B. Pérez (2021), 'Transience and Waiting in Mohsin Hamid's *Exit West*', *The European Legacy*, 26 (7-8): 764–74.
Žižek, S. (2002), *Welcome to the Desert of the Real*, New York: Verso.
Zlosnik, S. (2011), *Patrick McGrath*, Cardiff: University of Wales Press.
Zlosnik, S. (2020), 'Foreward', in M. Foley and R. Duncan (eds), *Patrick McGrath and his Worlds: Madness and the Transnational Gothic*, ix–xiii, London: Routledge.

# Index

abject (*see also* Kristeva, Julia), 1, 15, 39, 40, 44, 45, 61, 117, 120, 123, 181, 185, 193, 212, 213, 214
    abjection, 3, 25, 39, 44, 56, 70, 85, 125, 137, 179, 205, 214
Abbas, Sadia, 61
affect(s) (*see also affect memory*), vii, 10, 11, 21, 22, 27, 74, 88, 90, 95, 97, 128, 149, 156, 161, 162, 163, 175, 204, 211, 212, 214
    affective, 10, 11, 12, 15, 22, 41, 44, 70, 81, 95, 101, 103, 108, 109, 111, 113, 120, 144, 157, 170, 184, 193
Afghanistan, 6, 12, 21, 40, 49n3, 52, 53, 59–62, 64, 66n3
Africa, 75, 78, 133, 136, 236,
    African, 26, 69, 74, 78, 79, 80, 81, 115, 122, 132
Afro-Caribbean, 78, 80
Agamben, Giorgio, 20
Ahmed, Aijaz, 121
Ahmed, Sara, 25, 74, 75, 82, 121
Aitken, Molly, 199
    *The Island Child,* 199
Alder, Emily, 197, 198
Aldana Reyes, Xavier, 5, 7, 8, 10, 15, 30n3
American Horror Story (tv series), 18
ancestor(s), 72, 75, 76, 78, 79, 80, 82, 165
Ancuta, Katarzyna, 54, 55
animal(s), 17, 57, 58, 76, 189, 190, 193, 207, 209, 210, 214
Anthropocene, 15, 19, 23, 187, 192, 200, 210
anti-Semitism, 158
Arata, Stephen, 76
Arias, Rosario, 73
Aridjis, Chloe, vii, x, 6, 26, 139, 140, 141, 152, 154, 155, 156, 157, 158, 199
    *Book of Clouds,* vii, x, 26, 139, 140, 152, 154
    *Sea Monsters,* 199

Armfield, Julia, vii, 16, 28, 201
    *Our Wives Under the Sea,* vii, 16, 28, 201
Armitt, Lucie, 3, 195n2
Ashfeldt, Lane, 199
    *Saltwater,* 199
Ashworth, Jenn, 17, 175
    *Fell, The,* 175, 199
    *Ghosted: A Love Story,* 17
Aslam, Nadeem, vii, 6, 21, 25, 26, 38, 51, 52, 53, 59–65, 66n5, 67
    *Maps for Lost Lovers,* 67n8
    *Wasted Vigil, The,* vii, 6, 25, 26, 38, 51, 52, 53, 59–65, 66n5
Asia, 12, 55
    Asian, 47, 51, 102, 103, 115
Augé, Marc, 124, 149
austerity, 2, 20, 27, 83, 86, 116, 117, 123, 126, 166, 167, 169, 170, 172, 173, 174
Aw, Tash, vii, 6, 21, 25, 26, 51, 52, 53, 54–9, 62, 63, 73, 199
    *Harmony Silk Factory, The,* vii, 6, 25, 26, 51, 52, 53, 54–9, 62, 63, 73, 199
Alexandrescu, Liviu, 30n1, 117, 137
Azzopardi, Trezza, vii, x, 7, 20, 26, 115, 121, 122, 127–31
    *Remember Me,* vii, x, 20, 26, 115, 121, 122, 127–31

Baldick, Chris, 10
Ballard, J. G., 38, 40
    *Crash,* 40
    *Millennium People,* 38
Barker, Pat, vii, x, 7, 22, 24, 33, 34, 35, 39–43, 44, 48, 49
    *Another World,* 35
    *Blow Your House Down,* 35
    *Border Crossing,* 35
    *Double Vision,* vii, x, 22, 24, 33, 34, 35, 39–43
    *Liza's England,* 35
    *Regeneration Trilogy,* 35
    *Union Street,* 35

Bauman, Zygmunt, 29, 137, 150, 184
Beer, Gillian, 71, 72
*Being Human* (tv series), 18, 29
Belfast, 158n1
Berlin, 10, 27, 140, 141, 152–8, 164
Benjamin, Walter, 21, 27, 61, 153, 155, 156
Bennett, Jane, 21, 88, 89
Berlant, Lauren, 22
Berlin, x, 27, 140, 141, 152–8, 164
Birmingham, 158n1, 167,
Black British, 69, 74, 132
Blake, Linnie, 2, 34, 118, 175
Blanco, Maria del Pilar, 17, 18, 19, 30n5, 90
blood, 29, 39, 40, 45, 56, 76, 79, 103, 134, 138, 146, 151, 205
   bloodied corpse, 151
   bloodline, 76
   bloodlust, 76
   bloodshed, 109
   bloody, 73, 174, 175n3
biomedicine, 183, 188, 189, 191, 200
biotechnology, 93, 191
bioviolence, 20
body, 14, 18, 25, 39, 40, 60, 61, 74, 78, 104, 106, 123, 132, 137, 147, 148, 151, 165, 168, 179, 180, 182, 183, 184, 189, 197, 200, 202, 205, 207, 210, 212, 213
   bodily, 10, 13, 17, 29, 30n6, 74, 88, 91, 97, 107, 134, 182, 183, 184, 186, 201, 205, 211, 212, 213
   body horror, 18, 184
Boehmer, Elleke, 69
bog(s), 165, 168, 169, 199
border(s), 1, 6, 12, 28, 29, 35, 52, 53, 74, 79, 82, 98, 101, 102, 103, 105, 121, 164, 165, 166, 168, 178, 198
   border control, 79
   border policing, 12, 74, 102
Botting, Fred, 3, 9, 10, 14, 29, 30n5, 51, 93, 134, 135, 139, 140, 161
Bould, Mark, 23, 198
   *Anthropocene Unconscious, The*, 23, 198
Braddon, Mary Elizabeth, 71
   *Lady Audley's Secret*, 71
Bradford, 7
Braidotti, Rosi, 191, 192
Brantlinger, Patrick, 76

Brexit, 102, 161–74
Brien, Donna Lee, 8, 31n8
Britain, 1, 2, 3, 5, 6, 7, 14, 26, 27, 30n2, 34, 35, 75, 76, 77, 82, 86, 102, 116, 122, 161, 162, 163, 167, 170, 173, 175n3, 198, 202
Brixton, 26, 122, 132
Brocken spectre, 155, 173
Brönte, Charlotte, 71
   *Jane Eyre*, 71
Brönte, Emily, 71
   *Wuthering Heights*, 71
Brooks, Max, 117
   *Extinction Parade, The*, 117
Brooks, Peter, 37, 48
Brouillette, Sarah, 5
*Buffy the Vampire Slayer* (tv series), 29
Burnet, Graeme Macrae, 83, 175n3
   *His Bloody Project*, 83, 175n3
Burns, Anna, 30n4, 158n1
   *No Bones*, 30n4, 158n1
Burnside, John, 175n3
Burton, Jessie, 158n1
   *The Miniaturist*, 158n1
Butler, Judith, 19, 20, 121, 179
Byron, Glennis, 5, 140, 208
   *Globalgothic*, 5

Campbell, Karen, 142
   *The Twilight Time*, 142
Candy Gothic, 29
capitalism (*see also* global capitalism), 2, 13, 14, 15, 18, 19, 21, 22, 23, 29, 86, 95, 103, 119, 120, 121, 127, 142, 146, 150, 173, 190, 202, 203, 204
Capitalocene, 11, 15, 16, 17, 19, 21, 23, 25, 28, 29, 69, 182, 189, 190, 191, 194, 200, 204, 207, 209, 212, 216
Carey, M. R., vii, 14, 16, 21, 27, 177, 179, 182, 183, 186–9, 191, 195n2
   *Boy on the Bridge, The*, 16, 27, 189
   *Girl with All the Gifts, The*, 14, 16, 21, 27, 182, 186–9
*Carnivore* (software), 114n5
Carson, Jan, 30n4, 158n1, 199
   *Fire Starters, The*, 158n1, 199
   *Raptures, The*, 30n4
Castells, Miguel, 99, 101, 113n3
Cavallaro, Dani, 115

Champion, Guilia, 199
Cheah, Pheng, 11, 61
Chikwava, Brian, vii, 6, 16, 26, 115, 121, 122, 131–7
   *Harare North*, vii, 16, 26, 115, 121, 122, 131–7
child(ren)/childhood, vii, 12, 35, 45, 75, 83, 128, 130, 133, 138n3, 146, 154, 156, 165, 167, 177, 179, 180, 182, 185, 186, 187, 188, 190, 191, 194, 195n2, 199, 213, 214
chimerism, 28, 180, 194, 197, 211, 216
   chimeric 199, 200
Chthulucene (*see also* Haraway, Donna), 200, 211
Clarke, Susanna, 199
   *Piranesi*, 199
class(es), 2, 4, 14, 17, 35, 45, 71, 73, 83–90, 99, 118, 123, 135, 142, 143, 145, 146, 149, 150, 161, 163, 166, 170, 173, 181
Cleary, Emma, 3
Clift, Bethany, 195n1
   *Last One at the Party*, 195n1
clone(s), 6, 94, 178, 179, 181, 183, 184, 185, 191
city, vii, x, 7, 26, 27, 44, 99, 100, 101, 106, 107, 108, 125, 126, 128, 131, 139–59
   cities, 2, 4, 33, 116, 132, 140, 149, 155, 161
coast (*see also* shore(s)), 175n3
   coastal (*see also* littoral), 28, 74, 175n3, 198, 199
   coastlines, 197
Cohen, Ed, 180, 183, 192
Cohen, Jeffrey, 16
Cohen, Margaret, 61, 153
Colebrook, Claire, 210
Coleridge, Samuel, 198
   *Rime of the Ancient Mariner, The*, 198
Coley, Rob, 208
Collins, Wilkie, 4, 71
   *Women in White, The* 71
colonial(ism), (*see also* decolonial, neocolonial, and postcolonial) 3, 5, 10, 12, 13, 25, 30n4, 53, 54, 56, 57, 58, 59, 64, 65, 71, 74, 76, 77, 199

consume, 210
   consumed, 207
   consumer(s), 5, 78, 98, 99, 101, 102, 104, 124, 126, 139, 142, 148, 149, 150, 151, 155
   consumerism, 85, 149, 172
   consumerist, 124
contaminate(d), 104, 119, 126
   contamination, 5, 71, 104, 134, 178
Cooke, C. J., 195n1
   *The Lighthouse Witches*, 195n1
Cornwall, 173n1
COVID-19 (*see also* pandemic), 1, 27, 116, 178, 179, 190
Cox, Jessica, ix, 70, 71
Cowdell, Paul, 209
Crawford, Joseph, 171
creature(s), 6, 16, 28, 190, 193, 201, 202, 205, 207, 210, 214
Creed, Barbara, 211
   *Monstrous-Feminine, The*, 211, 213, 214, 216
   *Feminist New Wave Cinema*, 211
cruel optimism (*see also* Berlant, Lauren), 22
cybergothic, 93
cyber jihad, 102
cyberspace, 99, 171
cyborg(s), 17, 94

Davison, Carol Margaret, 23
Deane, Seamus, 30n4
   *Reading in the Dark*, 30n4
de Bruin-Molé, Megan, 30n3, 178
death(s), 1, 23, 26, 38, 40, 42, 44, 47, 59, 60, 61, 75, 81, 82, 85, 96, 106, 109, 110, 111, 112, 121, 123, 124, 128, 129, 136, 151, 165, 168, 172, 179, 184, 213
decolonial, vii, 3, 5, 6, 10, 11, 18, 21, 25, 28, 51, 53, 54, 55, 56, 57, 58, 59, 61, 63, 65, 67, 73, 75, 77, 81, 135, 200
   decolonized, 69
deep time, 6, 62
De Lint, Charles, 117
   *Onion Girl, The*, 117
demon(s), 119, 30n4
   demonic, 46, 80, 91, 209
   demonization, 102

demonize(d), 1, 48, 51, 120, 163
demonizing, 56, 66n7, 102
deportation(s), 12, 79, 96, 97
Derrida, Jacques, 19, 146
*Dexter* (tv series), 18
digital, vii, 6, 25, 93, 94, 95, 96, 98, 99, 100, 101, 102, 103, 105, 106, 107, 108, 109, 110, 111, 112, 113, 148, 171
    digital banal, the (*see also* Dinnen, Zara), 97, 107, 110, 148
    digital Gothic, 93, 94
    digital media, 95, 109
    digital monsters, 94
    digital technology, 93, 94, 95, 97, 98, 102, 111, 112, 171
    digitalized, 104
    digitally, 26, 110
Dimock, Wai Chee, 5
Dinnen, Zara, 95, 97, 148
disease(s) (*see also* illness), 12, 35, 46, 178, 179, 181, 185, 189
    diseased, 1
Donovan, Anne, 142, 159
    *Buddha Da*, 142, 159
Dover, 7, 74, 75, 199
Dryden, Linda, 140
du Maurier, Daphne, 119
    *Rebecca*, 119
Duncan, Rebecca, x, 9, 10, 11, 18, 19, 35, 53
Dunn, Kat, 195n1
    *Bitterthorn*, 195n1
During, Simon, 11, 13, 22
Dylan, Kate, 93
    *Mindwalker*, 93
dystopian, 11, 177,
    dystopic, 194

Eaglestone, Robert, 27, 162, 163, 175n1
Eagleton, Terry, 162
ecofeminism, vii, 197, 199, 200, 201, 209, 211
    ecofeminist(s), 16, 28, 199, 200, 202, 205, 206, 207, 211, 216
ecoGothic, 197, 204
Edinburgh, 7, 158n1
Edkins, Jenny, 33, 34, 51
Edwards, Justin D., 3, 11, 14, 51, 52, 54, 93, 171, 207

Edwards-Jones, Imogen, 158n1
    *The Witches of St Petersburg*, 158n1
eerie, 22, 64, 94, 156, 199, 202, 203, 204, 205, 206, 212
Empire, 6, 44, 54, 55, 57, 66n5, 83, 143, 161, 162, 163, 164, 173
England, 35, 161, 162, 164, 165, 167, 179, 183, 204
Enlightenment, 3, 6, 25, 74, 81, 88, 162, 188, 198
entanglement(s), 28, 63, 95, 180, 192, 194
Esposito, Roberto, 27, 180-3
Evans, Claire, 159
    *The Graves of Whitechapel*, 159
extra-human, 11, 13, 15, 20, 21, 28, 173, 193, 194, 202, 206, 208, 211, 212, 216

*FaceIt* (software), 114n5
fear(s), 1, 4, 7, 11, 14, 15, 24, 29, 38, 43, 49, 70, 71, 72, 75, 76, 81, 84, 90, 93, 94, 96, 97, 109, 113, 139, 144, 164, 178, 182, 199, 203, 211
Felman, Shoshana, 36, 49n1, 87
feminism (*see also* ecofeminism), 151
    feminist (*see also* ecofeminist), 3, 6, 16, 21, 27, 28, 77, 148, 150, 151, 158, 192, 200, 211, 212
Fisher, Mark, 22, 94, 202, 203, 204
flâneur, 144, 148, 154
    flâneurie, 152
    flâneurial, 144, 146, 154
flesh, 56, 85, 192, 210, 212
    fleshly, 213
Fletcher, John, 10
Foley, Matt, 35
folk, vii, 7, 16, 21, 22, 28, 168, 189, 197, 199, 208, 209, 211, 212, 213, 216n3
    folk horror, 7, 22, 28, 208, 209
folklore, 25, 78, 81, 122, 135, 161, 199, 208, 211, 213, 214, 216n3
folkloric, 28, 29, 74, 175, 201, 203, 210, 216, 216n4
folktales, 56, 122
Forbes, Michele, 17
    *Ghost Moth*, 17, 30n4
Foucault, Michel, 123, 127
*Fringe* (tv series), 18
fungal, 182
    fungus, 182, 183, 187-9

Gamer, Michael, x, 3, 4
Gailman, Neil, 117
   *Neverwhere*, 117
Gardiner, Michael, 27, 163, 166, 167
genetic, 93, 94, 181, 190
   genetic engineering, 93
   genetic enhancement, 190
Germaná, Monica, ix, 123, 127, 139, 142, 145, 149n2
Ghosh, Amitav, 23
ghost(s), vii, 6, 14, 17, 18, 19, 20, 22, 24, 25, 27, 30n4, 30n5, 30n6, 33, 34, 35, 36, 39, 43, 44, 46, 47, 48, 51, 56, 59, 61, 73, 83, 84, 87, 88, 90, 93, 119, 121, 122, 123, 128, 136, 140, 144, 153, 155, 156, 157, 158, 161, 162, 163, 164, 168, 169, 170, 171, 173, 174, 175, 199, 202, 203, 204, 215
   ghostly, 8, 17, 18, 19, 20, 21, 38, 53, 55, 57, 59, 60, 61, 62, 64, 73, 94, 103, 111, 122, 124, 135, 137, 149, 153, 155, 161, 164, 167, 169
Gilbert, Zoe, vii, 7, 16, 21, 28, 197, 199, 200, 211, 212, 213, 214, 216n3, 216n4
   *Folk*, vii, 7, 16, 21, 28, 197, 199, 200, 211, 212, 213, 214, 216n3, 216n4
Gilman, Charlotte Perkins, 25, 73, 84, 85
   'Yellow Wallpaper, The', 73, 84
Gilmartin, Sophie, 70, 72
Gilroy, Paul, 75
Glasgow, x, 7, 27, 140–7, 149–52, 158, 159n2, 159n3
global capitalism, 14, 15, 29, 121, 127, 146, 150, 173, 190
Gordon, Avery, 18, 20, 61
gore capitalism (*see also* Valencia, Sayak), 13, 15
Graulund, Rune, x, 11, 14
Gray, Alasdair, 141–2
   *Lanark*, 141–2
Grenfell Tower, 2
Griffiths, Niall, 27, 123, 162, 154, 169–74
   *Broken Ghost*, 27, 162, 169–74
Gutleben, Christian, 70, 72

Hadley, Louise, 70, 74
Haggard, Rider, 76
   *She*, 76
Hall, Sarah, 199

*Burntcoat*, 199
Halls, Stacey, 195n1
   *The Familiars*, 195n1
Hamid, Mohsin, vii, 6, 13, 26, 93, 94, 97, 106–12, 199
   *Exit West*, vii, 13, 26, 93, 94, 97, 106–12, 199
Happy Gothic, 29
Haraway, Donna, 17, 200
Hardt, Michael, 104
Harkaway, Nick, 93
   *Gone Away World, The*, 93
hauntology (*see also*, Derrida, Jacques), 19, 163, 171
   hauntological, 30n6, 163, 167, 175
haunted, vii, 7, 9, 30n4, 35, 44, 59, 60, 69, 73, 75, 78, 82, 83, 84, 91, 119, 123, 129, 131, 137, 144, 153, 155, 157, 164, 202, 204
   haunted house(s), vii, 59, 69, 73, 78, 84, 91, 119, 137, 204
Hawthorne, Nathaniel, 119, 123
   *House of Seven Gables, The*, 119
Hayles, N Katherine, 191, 192
Heilmann, Ann, 70, 73, 82, 85, 88
heritage, 57, 60, 72, 74, 75, 76, 80, 83, 85, 86, 103, 143, 150, 165, 167
   heritage industry, 74, 85
Hitchcock, Alfred, 123
   *Psycho*, 123
Hitchcock, Peter, 20
Hogg, James, 143, 145
Hogle, Jerrold E., 10, 11, 33
Höglund, Johan, 10, 11, 14
Holocaust, 36, 49n1, 153, 156, 157
   holocaustic, 185
homeless, 2, 20, 30n1, 115–28, 130, 131, 133, 137, 138n1, 138n2,
   homelessness, vii, x, 20, 26, 115–29, 131, 134, 135, 137, 138n3, 139
homeplace (*see also* hooks, bell), 79, 80
hooks, bell, 25, 77, 79, 80
horror(s) (*see also* folk horror), vii, 7, 10, 11, 15, 16, 18, 22–4, 28, 29, 30n6, 33, 34, 36–9, 41, 54, 56, 59, 62, 70, 73, 75, 76, 81, 91, 93, 94, 96, 97, 113, 117, 123, 134, 139, 156, 158, 164, 169, 171, 184, 185–88, 190, 195n2, 197, 198, 201–6, 208, 209, 211–14

Hughes, William, 7, 131
humanism, 191, 192
Hurley, Andrew Michael, 175n3
  *The Loney*, 175n3
hybrid(s), 9, 28, 53, 120, 186, 187, 188, 197
  hybridised, 29
  hybridity, 16, 186

illness(es), vii, 1, 56, 75, 79, 121, 123, 126, 127, 128, 131, 134, 137, 177, 178, 179, 181, 189, 190, 191, 193, 195n1
Ilott, Sarah, 53, 75
immigrant(s) (*see also* migrant(s)), 45, 74, 76, 78, 79, 133, 172, 198
  immigration (*see also*, migration), 1, 70, 75, 77, 79, 83, 97, 102, 103, 132, 199
immunity (*see also* Esposito, Robert), 178–84, 186, 192, 197
  *immunitas*, 27, 28, 180, 181, 182
  immunological, 178–84, 186, 192, 197
  immuno-oriented, 187, 191
imperial, vii, 3, 18, 24, 25, 51–8, 62, 64, 69, 70, 71–8, 82–6, 131, 135, 142, 143
  imperial Gothic, 76, 77, 134
  imperialism, 11, 52, 53, 54, 58, 64, 78, 163
  imperialist, 77, 90, 163
  neoimperial(ism), 46, 118
infect(ed), 23, 104, 189
  infection, 178, 182
  infectious, 12
inheritance, vii, 4, 25, 45, 69, 70, 71, 72, 73, 74, 75, 78, 82, 83, 86, 90
  disinheritance, 17, 73, 161
interface(s), 100, 103, 110, 111, 112,
intraface, 111
invade(s), 79, 104
  invader(s), 106, 183,
  invading, 2, 90, 117, 168, 191
  invasion, 37, 52, 104, 165, 189
Ishiguro, Kazuo, vii, 6, 14, 16, 21, 27, 94, 177, 179, 182, 183–6, 189–94, 195n2
  *Klara and the Sun*, 6, 14, 21, 27, 177–9, 181, 189–94
  *Never Let Me Go*, 6, 16, 27, 177–9, 181, 183–6
Isle of Man, 7, 212, 216n3
Ivanchikova, Alla, 61, 62

James, Henry, 25, 73, 87
  *Turn of the Screw, The*, 73, 87
James, M. R., 30n6, 94, 202
Jameson, Fredric, 101
*Jaws*, 201
Jess-Cooke, Carolyn, 30n4
  *The Boy Who Could See Demons*, 30n4
Johnson, Daisy, vii, 7, 16, 21, 28, 175n3, 197, 199, 200, 206–12, 216n2
  *Fen*, vii, 16, 21, 28, 197, 199, 206–12, 216n2
  *Sisters*, 175n3, 199
  *Everything Under*, 199
*juju*, 74, 79, 80, 81, 82

Keetley, Dawn, 213
Kerr, Philip, 124
  *Gridiron*, 124
Khair, Tabish, 52, 65n1
Kohlke, Marie-Louise, 70, 72
Kristeva, Julia, 85, 123, 129
Kubrick, Stanley, 124
  *Shining, The*, 124
Kunzru, Hari, vii, 6, 13, 16, 26, 93, 94, 97–106, 113n4
  *Transmission*, vii, 13, 16, 26, 93, 94, 97–106, 113n4

Leeds, 7
Liao, Pei-chen, 66n6, 102
littoral, 175n3, 212, 215
Llewellyn, Mark, 73
Logan, Kristy, 195n1, 199
  *Now She is Witch*, 195n1
  *The Gloaming*, 199
London, 7, 34, 131, 132, 134, 136, 137, 140, 141, 152, 159n1
Long, Declan, 30n4
  *Ghost-Haunted Land*, 30n4
Luckhurst, Roger, 39, 86
Lundberg, Anita, 54, 55

MacFarlane, Robert, 94, 204
Maitland, Carleen, 96, 97, 108
Malaysia, 6, 21, 52, 53, 54
  Malaysian, 55, 57
male gaze, 148, 151, 195n3, 211
Mamdani, Mahmood, 64, 66n5
Manchester, 7, 34, 137n1

Mantel, Hillary, 87
material, 2, 4, 9–13, 15, 18, 19, 22, 25, 31n7, 33, 48, 52, 65, 69, 74, 77, 79, 81, 82, 88, 89, 90, 95, 98, 99, 106, 120, 121, 125, 134, 141, 144, 163, 184, 192, 193, 198, 200, 201, 203
   immaterial, 98, 172
   materially, 71
   materialism, 61
   materialist, 3, 10, 15, 19, 20, 22, 25, 29, 61, 70, 88, 89, 91n1, 121, 147–51, 158, 191, 192, 212
   materiality, 88, 192, 193, 201, 205
   re-materialize, 18, 127
Maughan, Tim, 93
   *Infinite Detail*, 93
Mbembe, Achille, 79, 82
McCartney, Jenny, 17, 30n4, 158n1
   *The Ghost Factory*, 158n1
McDonald, Ian, 93
   *Necroville*, 93
   *Brasyl*, 93
McEvoy, Emma, x, 30n2
McEwan, Ian, 34
McGill, Bernie, 30n4
   *The Butterfly Cabinet*, 30n4
McGrath, Patrick, vii, 17, 22, 24, 33–5, 39, 43–9, 73
   *Asylum*, 35
   *Constance*, 35
   *Dr Haggard's Disease*, 35
   *Ghost Town*, vii, 17, 22, 24, 33–5, 39, 43–9, 73
   *Port Mungo*, 35
   *Spider*, 35
   *Trauma*, 35
McGregor, Jon, 117, 123, 138n1, 175
   *Even the Dogs*, 117, 138n1
   *Reservoir 13*, 175
McNally, David, 146, 147
meat, 76, 207
Melville, Herman, 198, 201
   *Moby Dick*, 198, 201
memory, 27, 39, 40–2, 49n1, 88, 129, 155, 157, 163, 170, 175
   affect memory, 27, 163, 175
Menmuir, Wyl, 175n3
   *The Many*, 175n3
metamorphosis, 28, 202, 205, 206, 209, 211

metropolitan, 3, 26, 99, 131, 140, 144, 145, 149
Mieville, China, 30n6, 93, 94, 202–4
   *Perdido Street Station*, 93
   *Embassytown*, 93
migrant(s), 1, 2, 6, 12, 14, 25, 26, 75, 79, 82, 94, 96–98, 101–4, 106–9, 111–13, 115, 118, 121, 122, 132, 135, 137, 146, 163, 198
migration, vii, 5, 93, 94, 97, 106, 108, 109, 113, 118, 131, 133–5
Miles, Rob, 3, 70
military, 19, 21, 24, 25, 27, 33, 34, 44, 51, 54, 133, 180, 186, 188, 204
   militarized, 1, 12, 34, 66n5, 183, 186, 189
Miller, Alison, 142, 159n3
   *Demo*, 142, 159n3
Monnett, Agnieszka Soltysik, 2, 34, 118, 175
monster(s), 2, 4 6, 15–18, 24, 25, 27, 30n3, 30n5, 55, 57, 64, 93, 94, 125, 137, 155, 178, 181, 182, 186, 189, 190, 194, 195n1, 198, 199, 203, 206, 214,
monster-human, 186
monstrous, vii, 1, 3, 6, 14–17, 26–8, 30n5, 53, 56, 66n5, 71, 73, 74, 75, 76, 78, 87, 91, 94, 103, 117, 137, 138n2, 139, 140, 146, 158, 171, 173, 177–83, 191, 193, 194, 199, 201, 203, 205–7, 210–16
Moore, Jason, 11–15, 173
Morecambe Bay, 175n3
Morey, Peter, 62
Morgan, Peter, 117, 137n1
   *Spice Boys, The*, 117, 137n1
Morton, Timothy, 11, 19, 21, 30–1n7, 54, 207
Morton, Stephen, 59
Moss, Sarah, vii, 7, 14, 17, 20, 27, 161, 162, 164–9, 199
   *Ghost Wall*, vii, 14, 17, 20, 27, 161, 162, 164–9, 199
   *Summer Water*, 199
Mousoutzanis, Aris, 22
Mozley, Fiona, 175n3
   *Elmet*, 175n3
*Mr Robot* (tv series), 18

multicultural, 143
  multiculturalism, 77
Murnane, Barry, 20
mutants, 18

Nadler, Lonnie and Thomson, Zac, 117
  *Dregs, The*, 117
nation(s), 5, 12, 41, 44, 45, 46, 48, 58, 62, 72, 75, 76, 83, 152, 162, 183
  national, 1–4, 6, 7, 25, 28, 30n2, 34, 41, 42, 43, 44, 46, 52, 61, 62, 63, 65, 66n5, 70, 71, 74, 76, 79, 97, 98, 102, 116, 125, 126, 132, 142, 143, 153, 162–7, 170, 171, 173, 198, 199
  nationalist(ic), 5, 6, 14, 16, 20, 28, 75, 120, 156, 161, 163
  international, x, 6, 7, 17, 37, 54, 65, 66n5, 98, 102, 132, 143, 162, 212
  transnational(ism), 3, 5, 6, 7, 8, 11, 13, 14, 16, 21, 24, 26, 29, 35, 41, 54, 60, 65, 67n9, 72, 94, 99, 102, 104, 110, 111, 112, 122, 131, 132, 135, 136, 140, 146, 148, 150, 158, 178
Negri, Antonio, 104
neoliberal, 2, 3, 12, 13, 14, 17, 22, 27, 34, 39, 46, 47, 100, 116, 117, 123, 125, 139, 140, 141, 152, 152, 156, 158, 163, 170–5, 179–85, 190, 202–5
  neoliberalism, 13, 34, 100, 105, 115, 116, 118, 123, 137, 163, 167, 172, 173, 174, 175, 194, 200
*Neoliberal Gothic* (*See also* Blake, Linnie and Monnet, Agnieszka Soltysik), 2
neocolonial, 3, 5, 11, 12, 13, 14, 15, 16, 17, 22, 24, 25, 33, 36, 41, 51, 53, 54, 61, 65, 77, 78, 91, 115, 190
  neocolonialism, 6, 69, 73
Nevins, Andrea Shaw, 80
New York, 35, 44, 46, 47, 49n3, 152
Ngai, Sianne, 22, 90
*ngozi*, 135–7
Nixon, Rob, 15, 21
nonhuman, 88, 192, 198, 201–3, 207
non-space (*see also* Augé, Marc), 131
Norfolk, 7, 26, 28, 131, 206, 208
Northern Ireland, 1, 30n4
  Northern Irish, 30n4

object(s), 8, 17, 19, 21, 37, 38, 61, 88–90, 90n1, 131, 151, 155–6, 168, 195n3, 210
  objectifying, 120
  objectification, 151
  object-oriented, 19
  hyperobjects, 19, 21, 30–1n7
  preobject, 129
ocean(s), 28, 197, 199, 202, 205, 206, 211, 212
  oceanic, 12, 28, 55, 197, 198, 199, 201, 204, 205, 214
O'Flynn, Katherine, 158n1
  *What Was Lost*, 158n1
O'Loughlin, Katrina, ix, 190
ominous, 165, 168
organ donation, 12
  organ procurement, 185
Oyeyemi, Helen, vii, 6, 7, 16, 25, 26, 69, 73, 74–82, 83, 88, 90, 102, 122, 206
  *White is for Witching*, vii, 16, 25, 69, 73, 74–82, 88, 102, 122, 206

Packham, Jimmy, 198, 202
pandemic(s), vii, 1, 14, 27, 116, 177, 178, 179, 181, 182, 183, 185, 187, 189, 190, 191, 193, 195
panic, 4, 93, 94, 103, 108
paranormal, 74, 89, 90
parasite(s), 102, 126, 139, 172, 187, 189
  parasitic, 191
  parasitism, 87, 187, 191
Parikka, Jussi, 105
Paris, 142, 145, 152
Parker, Emma, 69, 86
patriarchal, 3, 15, 16, 17, 24, 45, 47, 67n8, 84, 119, 151, 158, 166, 169, 190, 199, 200, 201, 206, 209, 210, 211, 212, 213, 215, 216
  patriarchy, 73, 77, 78, 86, 124, 166, 206, 209
Paul, Colette, 142
  *Whoever You Choose to Love*, 142
Paver, Michelle, 199
  *Dark Matter*, 199
Peeren, Esther, 17–19, 30n5
Perry, Sarah, 66n4, 158n1, 199
  *Essex Serpent, The*, 199
  *Melmoth*, 66n4, 158n1

phantom(s), 6, 17, 56, 142
   phantasmagoria(s), 132, 156, 163
   phantasmal, 127, 129, 153
   phantasm(s), 61, 153
phenomenology of whiteness (*see also* Ahmed, Sara), 74
Piatti-Farnell, Lorna, 8, 31n8
planet, 14–16, 18, 23, 24, 54, 101, 149, 188, 189, 191, 192, 206, 208, 209, 212
   planetary, 3, 5, 11–15, 17, 19, 21, 23, 28, 29, 53, 172, 180, 188, 193, 194, 200, 208, 216
Poe, Edgar Allan, 25, 73, 78, 81, 83, 84, 119, 145
   Poean, 82, 202
   'Fall of the House of Usher, The', 73, 78, 83, 84, 119
Polak, Sara, 178
pollute, 126
   pollutants, 189
   pollution, 12, 19, 21, 194
poltergeist(s), 74, 83, 88, 91
portal(s), 26, 94, 106, 108, 109, 110, 111, 114, 138
postcolonial, 5, 6, 9, 18, 52, 55, 65n1, 69, 120, 121, 192
   postcolonialism, 9
posthuman, 27, 94, 178, 179, 180, 180, 184, 185, 190, 191, 192, 193, 194, 195n4, 202, 211
   posthumanism, 192, 194
   posthumanist, 191
Priest, Christopher, 93
   *Islanders, The*, 93
precarity, 13, 14, 15, 17, 22, 29, 107, 123, 128, 132, 137, 179
   precarious, 13, 24, 97, 109, 111, 113
   precariously, 45, 145
   precariousness, 20
profane illumination (*see also* Benjamin, Walter and Cohen, Margaret), 16, 21, 61, 153
provincial, 20, 26, 122, 127, 131, 137, 212, 215
   provincialism, 215
psychoanalysis, 19, 87, 129, 135
psychokinesis, 74, 87, 91n1
psychology, 22, 39, 59, 90, 122, 139, 144, 166, 204

psychological(ly), 21, 24, 29, 33, 35, 36, 37, 46, 49, 51, 81, 88, 89, 120, 128, 130, 131, 137, 203
Pulham, Patricia, 73
Punter, David, 4, 10, 71, 134, 135, 198, 202, 208
Purcell, Laura, 73, 159n1
   *Silent Companions, The*, 73
   *Whispering Muse, The*, 159n1

queer, x, 3, 6, 21, 28, 78, 89, 90, 144, 159n2, 159n3, 212

Radcliffe, Ann, 2, 4, 84, 119, 122, 198
   *A Sicilian Romance*, 198
   *The Mysteries of Udolpho*, 84, 119, 122
Radstone, Susannah, 41–2, 47
refugee(s), 2, 23, 75, 78, 96, 97, 107, 108, 110, 111, 113, 115, 133, 136, 149, 198
revenant(s), 17, 45, 73, 157
reverse colonization, 75, 76
ritual(s), 20, 28, 81, 166, 168, 174, 175n3, 207, 209
   reritualizing, 77
   ritualistic, 213
Roberts, Adam, 93
   *New Model Army*, 93
robot, 6, 18, 178, 179, 190, 191, 192
Romantic, 4, 72, 83, 145, 161, 172, 173

Saadi, Suhayl, 141, 142
   *Psychoraag*, 142
sacrifice(s), 40, 165, 168, 181, 206, 207, 209
   sacrificed, 194
Sage, Victor, 144
Saxena, Vandana, 57
science(s), 15, 81, 94, 101, 113, 190, 191, 193, 194, 201
   bioscience, 183, 186, 187, 192
   scientist, 140, 182, 186, 188, 189, 190, 191, 195n3
   mad-scientist, 190
sci-fi, 26, 93, 94, 109, 110, 118, 138n2, 178, 179, 182, 188, 190, 191
Scotland, 141, 164
   Scottish, 141–3, 159n2, 175n3
Scovell, Adam, 209

sea(s), 16, 28, 55, 151, 197, 198, 199, 201, 202, 204, 205, 206, 211, 212, 213, 214
  sea creature, 16, 202, 205
  sea-faring vampires, 206
security, 15, 28, 48, 51, 63, 73, 90, 94, 97, 102, 103, 105, 112, 114n5, 116, 125, 157, 178, 204
  insecurity (insecurities), 3, 4, 13, 15, 33, 43, 52, 107, 129
  securitize, 196
  securitization, 34
Sedgwick, Eve Kosofsky, 8, 96
Setterfield, Diane, 73
  *Thirteenth Tale, The*, 73
September 11, 33, 36, 40, 114n5,
  9/11, vii, 1, 24, 25, 33–49, 49n2, 51, 102, 103, 114n5, 115, 125
sex trade, 151, 152
sex-trafficking, 27, 146, 158
Shaw, Katy, ix
Shaw, Kristian, 171, 173, 175n1
Shelley, Mary, 190, 191
  *Frankenstein*, 93, 189, 190, 191
  Frankensteinian, 178, 190
Sheridan, Sara, 158n1
  *The Fair Botanists*, 158n1
Shildrick, Margrit, 180, 191, 194, 197, 200
shore(s), 163, 175, 199
  shorelines, 28
Simmel, George, 27, 148
sinister, 75, 89, 90, 155, 165, 208
slow violence (*see also* Nixon, Rob), 1, 15, 21
Smith, Ali, vii, x, 13, 20, 26, 115, 121, 122, 123–7, 131, 149
  *Hotel World*, 13, 20, 26, 115, 121, 122, 123–7, 131, 149
Smith, Andrew (gothic critic), 10, 70
Smith, Andrew (postcolonial theorist), 9, 11
strange, 6, 38, 57, 75, 76, 93, 131, 134, 135, 140, 201, 202
  strangely, 21
  strangeness, 30, 90, 204, 211
  stranger(s), vii, 2, 20, 25, 69, 70, 73, 75, 82, 83, 87, 89, 146, 147, 149, 155, 193
Stasiewicz-Bieńkowska, Agnieszka, 54, 55
Stephanou, Aspasia, 78, 138, 190

spectre(s), vii, 17–19, 24, 27, 30n4, 30n5, 35, 59, 61, 83, 90, 123, 129, 137, 139, 155, 156, 158, 169, 171–5
spectral, vii, 1, 3, 8, 13, 15, 17, 18, 19, 20, 21, 26, 27, 30n4, 43, 44, 53, 54, 60, 61, 87, 93, 103, 106, 110, 115, 122, 123, 128, 131, 138n1, 138n2, 139, 140, 142, 146, 161, 163, 164, 169, 170, 172, 173, 175, 199
spectrality, 19, 20, 26, 39, 60, 74, 127
spectrally, 20, 101, 103
speculative, 23, 93, 94, 113, 113n1, 179, 183, 186, 202, 216n2
spirit(s), 46, 48, 56, 57, 61, 89, 90, 119, 131, 132, 135, 137, 142, 153, 164
  spiritual, 74, 78, 80, 81, 99, 135, 136
  spirituality, 80, 81,
  spiritualism, 25, 79, 80, 88
  spiritualist, 74, 78, 81, 135
Spivak, Gayatri Chakravorty, 19, 20
Spooner, Catherine, 2, 4, 29, 30n2, 30n5, 43, 70
Spring, Ian, 142
  *Phantom Village*, 142
Strachan, Zoe, 141, 142
  *Spin Cycle*, 142
Stevenson, Robert Louis, 76, 131, 134–136, 140, 143, 145
  *Strange Case of Dr Jekyll and Mr Hyde, The*, 76, 131, 134, 135, 136, 140
Stoker, Bram, 4, 25, 73, 75, 76, 77, 78, 140
  *Dracula*, 73, 75, 76, 77, 140
*soucouyant(s)*, 74–6, 78–82, 91
sublime, the, 4, 139, 161–4, 169, 170, 172, 173, 198
  subliminal, 89
subterranean, vii, 21, 25, 51, 59, 62, 65, 144, 150, 157
summoning(s), 39, 62, 64, 110, 209, 216n4
supernatural, 35, 39, 74, 84, 88, 89, 161, 164, 169, 171, 209
  supernaturalized, 4
  supernaturally, 123
superstition, 161, 206
surveillance, 2, 26, 48, 93, 94, 101, 102, 105, 107, 112, 114n5, 115, 124, 174
Swansea, 7

symbiote, 187
  symbiosis, 187
  symbiotic, 139, 187, 188, 194

technology (*see also* digital technology and surveillance technology), vii, 25, 26, 93–106, 109–13, 114n5, 143, 147, 171, 191, 193
  biotechnology, 191
  technological(ly), 13, 21, 27, 40, 52, 94, 99, 100, 103, 155, 171, 172, 181, 190, 194
terror(s), vii, 1, 4, 7, 24, 25, 31n8, 34, 42, 44, 47, 51–6, 58, 59, 61, 62, 65n1, 72, 102, 103, 118, 119, 156, 157, 162, 172, 177, 178
  cyberterrorist, 105
  terrorism, 37, 44, 52, 55, 65, 102
  terrorist(ic), 24, 34, 37, 44, 52, 53, 55, 56, 58, 59, 64, 66n1, 66n7, 102, 103
  'War on Terror', 1, 34, 36, 52, 62, 64, 102, 103, 118
Tey, Josephine, 69
  *Franchise Affair, The*, 69
Timms, Chloe, 199, 245
  *Sea Women, The*, 199, 245
Tondeur, Louise, 124
  *Water's Edge, The*, 124
torture, 12, 24, 56, 143, 145, 151, 201, 209
  tortured, 154
transform(ed), 42, 76, 80, 123, 150, 171, 188, 189, 202, 206, 207
  transformation(s), 41, 93, 94, 111, 140, 152, 199, 200, 201, 206, 216, 216n2
  transformative, 17
transgression, 9, 94, 130, 131, 207
  transgressive, 4, 5, 16, 74, 83, 93, 94, 137, 163, 170
trauma(s), vii, x, 24, 33–49, 49n1, 51, 59–61, 108, 118–21, 123, 127, 129, 130, 132, 133, 135, 157, 205
  traumatic, 24, 35–7, 39–45, 49n1, 49n2, 120, 128, 129, 132, 134, 135, 213, 214
  traumatological, 35, 37, 44, 48, 121, 123
tropical, vii, 21, 25, 51, 54, 55, 56, 58, 59, 65, 187
  tropical Gothic, vii, 54, 55, 58
*True Blood* (tv series), 29

ugly feelings (*see also* Ngai, Sianne), 90
uncanny, vii, x, 1, 3, 4, 6, 14, 15, 19, 21–7, 33–6, 38, 39, 41, 43, 44, 49, 53–5, 62–64, 66n6, 73, 75, 94, 115, 118, 119, 122, 123, 131, 132, 134, 137, 138n2, 139, 140, 145–9, 153, 154, 156, 157, 158, 159n2, 199, 201–6, 212
  *unheimlich*, 38, 63, 118, 155, 201, 203
unconscious, 11, 23, 26, 33, 37, 38, 42, 43, 44, 87, 89, 133, 144
Upstone, Sara, ix, 67n8, 162, 167
urban, x, 13, 22, 27, 45, 56, 62, 84, 99, 121–3, 125, 131, 139, 140, 141, 143–56, 158, 158n1, 161
  suburban, 99
  urbanity, 26, 139, 151
*umbuyiso*, 133–4

vampire(s), 16, 29, 75–78, 87, 93, 146, 148, 206
  vampiric, 27, 75, 77, 78, 100, 144, 146–9
  vampirism, 28, 76, 78, 86, 140
Varese, J. M., 159n1
  *The Company*, 159n1
Vermeulen, Pieter, 192
vibrant matter (*see also* Bennett, Jane), 21, 88, 89, 169
Victorian, 4, 70–4, 76, 77, 88, 90, 135, 139, 140, 145, 159n1
  neo-Victorian, 20, 25, 69, 70, 72–4, 83, 88, 90
Vidler, Anthony, 21, 22, 119
virtual, 8, 13, 25, 98, 99, 103, 106, 107, 172
virus(es), 6, 16, 26, 94, 97, 102–6, 178, 189,
  viropolitical, 28, 178–82, 187, 190
  viropolitics, 180, 185, 192

Wald, Patricia, 178
Wales, 161, 169, 170, 172
  Welsh, 7
Walker, Angharad, 195n1
  *Once Upon a Fever*, 195n1
*Walking Dead, The* (tv series), 144
Warwick, Alexandra, 8, 9
Wasson, Sara, 113n1, 184, 185

waste, 85, 126, 137, 207
   wasted, vii, 6, 25, 26, 29, 38, 51–3, 59, 64, 65, 66n3, 66n6
   wasteland(s), 44, 154
Waters, Sarah, vii, 20, 25, 26, 69, 73, 74, 78, 82–90, 91n1, 159n1, 201, 202
   *Fingersmith*, 159n1
   *Little Stranger, The*, vii, 20, 25, 69, 73, 82–90
Watkin, William, 20
Watts, Jim, 3, 4
Waugh, Evelyn, 69
   *Brideshead Revisited*, 69
Wells, H.G., 76, 93, 140,
   *The War of the Worlds*, 76
   *The Island of Dr Moreau*, 93, 140
Welsh, Louise, vii, 7, 13, 45, 139–41, 143–52, 153–4, 159n3
   *Cutting Room, The* vii, 13, 26, 139–52, 153–4, 159n2, 159n3
Wenzel, Jennifer, 207
Wester, Maisha, 5, 7, 8, 15, 30n3, 69, 75, 76, 77
wet, vii, 28, 134, 197–201, 204, 205, 207, 212, 216, 216n2
   wetland(s), 28, 165, 197, 198, 199, 206
   wetness, 212
Weinstock, Jeffrey, 16, 19, 114
weird, 17, 19, 23, 30n6, 94, 199, 201–6, 212, 216
   weirdness, 200, 204

Whitby, 7
Whitechapel, 140, 159n1
white supremacy, 63, 82
   white supremacism, 77
   white supremacist, 6, 77, 78, 80
Wilde, Oscar, 4, 140
   *The Picture of Dorian Gray*, 140
wilderness, 45, 46, 56, 162, 169, 172, 173
Wilson, A. N., 17
   *Jealous Ghost, A*, 17
Wilson, James, 73
   *Dark Clue, The* 73
Wisker, Gina, x, 55, 85
witch(es), 80, 91, 155, 158, 186, 195n1
   witchcraft, vii, 69
   witching, vii, 16, 25, 69, 70, 73, 74, 77–81, 102, 199, 206
Wood, Lucy, 175n3, 199
   *Sing of the Shore, The*, 175n3, 199
world literature, 5, 11, 29
   world literary, 5

York Moors, 175n3
Yuval-Davis, Nira, 6

Zanger, Jules, 77
Zimbabwe, 132, 134
   Zimbabwean(s), 131, 133–6
zombie, 2, 23, 117, 177, 179, 182, 186, 187, 188
   'hungry', 178, 182, 186–9

www.ingramcontent.com/pod-product-compliance
Lightning Source LLC
Chambersburg PA
CBHW071814300426
44116CB00009B/1314